# The Romance of Sir Degrevant

EARLY ENGLISH TEXT SOCIETY

Original Series No. 221

1949 (for 1944), reprinted 1970

MS. Lincoln Cathedral A. 5. 2 (Thornton), folio 133
(ll. 606–704).

# The Romance of Sir Degrevant

A PARALLEL-TEXT EDITION

FROM MSS. LINCOLN CATHEDRAL A.5.2 AND

CAMBRIDGE UNIVERSITY Ff.1:6

EDITED BY

L. F. CASSON

*Published for*

THE EARLY ENGLISH TEXT SOCIETY

*by*

OXFORD UNIVERSITY PRESS
LONDON   NEW YORK   TORONTO

First Published 1949 (for 1944)
Reprinted 1970

To
M. E. K.
AND
IN MEMORY OF
A. E. M. K.

*Reprinted Lithographically in Great Britain by*
*Fletcher & Son Ltd, Norwich*

# PREFACE

One of the more pleasant duties of an editor is to acknowledge his indebtedness to those who have helped him. In the nature of things, only he can fully realize the extent to which he has availed himself of others' time, encouragement, or erudition, for which a brief mention in the Preface seems an all too inadequate return.

I thank Dr. O. K. Schram, my official supervisor for the degree of Ph.D., for his unfailing interest and encouragement throughout the progress of the work, and also for his help in technical matters, all ungrudgingly bestowed.

I must also thank the Dean and Chapter of Lincoln Cathedral, and especially the Librarian, Canon W. H. Kynaston, for permission to publish the Thornton text, for allowing me to consult the manuscript in Lincoln, and later for placing it on deposit in the Edinburgh University Library; Dr. L. W. Sharp, the University Librarian, for receiving it and for help in palæographical matters; the Syndics of the Cambridge University Library for permission to publish the text of the poem in MS. Ff. i. 6, the Librarian for granting me access to this MS., and the staff (especially Mr. H. L. Pink) for their courtesy and assistance under difficult conditions; the former Lord Lyon, King of Arms (Sir Francis Grant) and the Lyon Clerk (Lt.-Col. H. A. B. Lawson) for heraldic information; Professor R. L. G. Ritchie and Miss C. Gooderson, of the University of Birmingham, for information about *Les Vœux du Paon*; Miss L. W. Stone, of King's College, London, and Professor H. A. Cronne, of the University of Birmingham, for help in matters relating to Old French; Miss C. van Heyningen and Mrs. N. J. Marquard, of the University of Stellenbosch, South Africa, for reading and commenting upon the earlier sections of the Introduction; and especially Dr. C. T. Onions, Sir William Craigie, and Dr. Mabel Day for much help in preparing the edition for the press.

*King's College, London,* October, 1948                                    L.F.C.

# CONTENTS

| | | PAGE |
|---|---|---|
| INTRODUCTION | | |
| I The Manuscripts | . . . . . . . | ix |
| II Editions | . . . . . . . . | xv |
| III The Text; The Present Edition | . . . . . | xvi |
| IV Metre | . . . . . . . . . | xxxi |
| V Alliteration | . . . . . . . . | xlii |
| VI Vocabulary | . . . . . . . . | xlv |
| VII Language | . . . . . . . . . | li |
| VIII Analysis and Sources | . . . . . . | lxii |
| IX Author; Date | . . . . . . . . | lxxii |
| X Literary Estimate | . . . . . . . | lxxiii |
| SELECT BIBLIOGRAPHY | . . . . . . | lxxvi |
| TEXT | . . . . . . . . . . | 2 |
| NOTES | . . . . . . . . . . | 116 |
| GLOSSARY | . . . . . . . . . | 150 |
| INDEX OF PROPER NAMES | . . . . . | 166 |

# INTRODUCTION

## I. THE MANUSCRIPTS

There are two manuscripts of *Sir Degrevant*, both imperfect:—
1. Lincoln Cathedral A. 5. 2 (here denoted by L), ff.130r–138v, one leaf missing between f.133 and f.134. This is the well-known Thornton MS., and dates from *c*. 1430. It is written on paper, partly at least by Robert Thornton, whose name appears in several places (e.g., ff.98v, 176r). The size of the page is 290×215 mm. As its contents and its general condition have several times been described before, the reader may be referred to Mr. R. M. Woolley's *Catalogue of the Manuscripts of Lincoln Cathedral Chapter Library* (London 1927), p. 51, where an account of them is given, based on a thorough examination of the MS. The editor of a more recent work, *The 'Liber de Diversis Medicinis'* (M.S. Ogden, EETS. 1938), regards the MS. as the work of a single scribe, who also wrote MS. BM. Add. 31042.[1] Dr. Ogden identifies this scribe with a Robert Thornton of East Newton in the wapentake of Ryedale, North Riding of Yorkshire. From internal evidence (for which see Dr. Ogden's *Introduction*) the Thornton MS. of Lincoln must have been compiled between 1422 and 1453.

The pages of *Sir Degrevant* are ruled horizontally top and bottom, and are vertically divided into two columns, each containing about 48 lines. The text is not punctuated, but each group of three triplet lines is bracketed together, and the tail-rime line written to the right of the bracket. Occasionally (e.g., ff.131v, 132, 134) there is space for only two triplet rimes at the end of a column, the third is carried over to the next, and the tail-rime line is written opposite the two triplet lines. This results in the virtual displacement of a line. In these cases, the bracket is halved to show what has happened. There are three large red capitals at lines 1, 1073, 1617.

*Marginalia*

In so far as these relate to the Thornton family, see Dr. Ogden's *Introduction*. The rest are *probationes pennæ*:—

(i) f.131a, foot of the column, in a contemporary hand: vt dicunt multi Cito transit lancea stulti.[2]

---

[1] On this point, I suggest that the conclusions be received with caution, pending a more thorough palæographical examination of the MSS. (if possible side by side) than Dr. Ogden has apparently given them. In answer to my query whether MS. BM. Add. 31042 was the work of one scribe or of more, Dr. Eric G. Millar wrote, 'It is of course extremely difficult to say definitely that a given MS. is the work of one or of several scribes, especially at this period, when the scribes working together were trained to write a more or less uniform hand, while apparent variations in size and general appearance of the writing may be due only to a change of pen or a different quality in the ink. With this proviso, however, we are inclined to agree . . . that f. 66vo is probably by another scribe; there is in particular a marked use of the thorn from f. 66vo onwards, which does not seem to occur in the previous portion; the et symbol is also rather different.' The whole question needs to be gone into again, especially in view of the considerable variation in the writing of the Lincoln MS. I hasten to add that Dr. Ogden notices this variation, without fully explaining it.

[2] This leonine hexameter is found also in the miscellaneous collection of proverbs, poems, songs, etc., contained in MS. Harl. 3362 (f.4) (see also Skeat's ed. of the *Proverbs of Alfred*, l. 421 and note).

(ii) f.135ᵛa, foot of the column, in a later hand: Waged.

The text of *Sir Degrevant* is written in a somewhat larger and less tidy hand than the poems to which Robert Thornton's name is appended, though it is contemporary. Various other points of difference are noticeable: the downstrokes are appreciably thicker, the upper bow of the ʒ is narrower, and the lower bow swings in ampler curve. The downstroke through the middle of the capital *C* often overlaps the lower part of the bow in the *Sir Degrevant* hand, never in the other. The text has been corrected in the same hand. The ink varies in colour from medium brown to black.

The usual abbreviations are found for *þat, þou, with, and, þis*. Superscript ᵃ is frequent: it is the common abbreviation for *ra* (e.g., *grace, minstrals, graunte*; and redundantly above the *u* of *recreaunt* 595), and is sometimes used for *a* only (e.g., *þai* 1284, *ham* 1603). Other abbreviations involving *r* are the final curl (e.g., *euer, þer, oþer, letter* 181) used except after *p*, when crossed *p* is used for *per* and *par* (e.g., *perceuelle, par amours*); *p* with loop crossing the down-stroke for *pro* (e.g., *profird*); and the superscript forms ᵘ for *ru*, ⁱ for *ri*, ᵉ for *re*, and ʳ for *ur*.

The usual suspension mark — is used for *m, n*; and *n* is also represented by a curved stroke resembling a pause mark in music, sometimes with dot beneath it, sometimes without (e.g., *launde* 306, *resouns* 1239). In preparing the text and glossary, I have ignored this stroke in words already ending in *n* where it appears to have no historical or other significance (e.g., *in* 413, *in* 512), and also in *wirchip* 1888, where the stroke has been written over the *p*. Final -*p*, the contraction for *es, is*, is not common: as the rime shows, it is redundant in *wedis* 236. *m, n*, with final curl are frequent (e.g., *þam, when, heuen, herken*). As the scribe can have meant nothing by these signs, which are occasionally found even when an -*e* follows in the MS. (e.g., *sone* 133), they have been ignored; ƚƚ has usually been treated in the same way, and for the same reason (cf. the forms *wiƚƚ, saƚƚ* [*passim*], with *aƚƚe* [*passim*], *beraƚƚe* 531, *cristaƚƚe* 532; though crossed ƚ has significance in *ƚre* 121, 126, etc. for *lettre*). h̄ (e.g., *both̄, thorgh̄*) has likewise not been extended, except where it has obvious significance (e.g., h̄t for *hert* 1308, 1312; *Jh̄u* for *Jhesu* 1, 1917).

The handwriting is big and bold, and is usually very legible; though as with the abbreviations, the scribe shows little sign of consistency in letter forms: *u, n*, are frequently indistinguishable (this is almost inevitable in MSS. of this period), and sometimes also *þ, y*. This last-named carelessness sometimes makes it doubtful whether the scribe intended the singular or the plural form of the second personal pronoun (1230, 1342, 1396). A badly made *e* sometimes resembles *o*, and *vice versa*. The combinations -*af-, -as-* are often difficult, owing to the scribe's habit of joining succeeding letters to his *a* with the horizontal stroke that runs through the middle. Sometimes this stroke passes through the middle of a following long -*s*, and makes it resemble *f* (e.g., *hase* 1366).

The first letter of a line is usually a capital, but frequently it is not. Capital *H* is not often found either at the beginning or in the middle of a line; and *ff* is the usual form for *F*. When the difference between the majuscule and the minuscule forms of the same letter is merely one of size (as with *a*) it is frequently impossible to be sure whether the scribe intends a capital or not. Capital letters are often found for words in the middle of the line, and minuscules are often found for proper names in any position; in neither case is any guiding principle apparent. The hero's name, for example, is written throughout with a small *d*.

For a variety of causes, the text is incomplete. A whole folio is missing between f.133 and f.134, entailing the loss of 802–1008. Small holes in ff.133, 134, 135 have each involved one or more letters. There is a brown stain also on f.134.

Other losses must be ascribed to the copyist, or to the defects of his original. Lines omitted are 221–224; 651–654; 1189–1193, i.e., always a quatrain of three triplet-rimes and a tail-rime. In no case does he indicate that he was aware of an omission.

2. Cambridge University Library MS. Ff.i. 6, ff. $96^r$–$109^v$ (here denoted by C). This MS. was originally catalogued as No. 90 in the library of John Moore, Bishop of Norwich and Ely (1646–1714). This library was bought by George I and given to the University Library of Cambridge. The MS. appears as No. 9246 in Bernard's *Catalogi Librorum Manuscriptorum Angliæ et Hiberniæ* (Oxford 1697) and is inaccurately described as 'Poema historicum lingua Anglica vetere 8vo'. As the description in the *Catalogue of the Manuscripts preserved in the Library of the University of Cambridge* (Cambridge 1857), Vol. II, pp. 286–90, is also inadequate, the MS. has been re-examined by courtesy of the University Librarian.

It is written on paper, in various hands of the mid-fifteenth century, usually one column to the page (*Sir Degrevant* is the only exception, and is written in double columns). There are two systems of foliation, both modern, the second being the work of Henry Bradshaw, who has also added pencilled comments. The chain-lines are horizontal. The size of the pages varies between 220×153 mm. and 212×143 mm.; there are at present 190 ff., but some were added (especially at the beginnings and ends of gatherings) when the MS. was rebound in half morocco in 1896, in order to mark the place where leaves had been lost. The edges of the leaves are much frayed, especially at the corners. The colour of the ink varies from black to light brown.

There are 15 gatherings, signed A to P in Bradshaw's hand, the number of leaves in each varying from 6 to 24. Three of them (B. E, N) are composite. The watermarks, so far as C. M. Briquet (*Les Filigranes*, Paris, 1907, 4v.) can provide indication, point to the mid-fifteenth century as the date of manufacture.

The MS. consists of several (probably nine) originally distinct parts bound together: apart from the difference in character of the hands, the paper is not uniform either in quality or size, the outer sheets of the present gatherings show signs of being rubbed, and the individual items of the contents are usually complete within the gathering. When the MS. was first bound together in its present form cannot be determined; all the gatherings may not have been assembled at the same time, since there are marginal scribblings in the same fifteenth-century hand on ff.$63^v$ (E), $89^r$ (G), and $95^v$ (G).

The contents are almost entirely in verse: excerpts from Gower's *Confessio Amantis*, Chaucer's *Anelida and Arcite, Legend of Good Women*, Occleve's *Letter of Cupid*, minor poems of Lydgate, De Burgh's *Cato*, a translation of Jacques de Longueyon's *Les Vœux du Paon*, together with complete texts of Chaucer's *Parlement of Foules*, the *Compleyntes of Venus*, *unto Pitee, to his Purse,* the apocryphal *Cuckoo and Nightingale, La Belle Dame Sans Mercy,* and a number of unidentified love poems and complaints, many of which have been printed in *Reliquiæ Antiquæ,* Furnivall's *Political, Religious, and Love Poems* (EETS. 1866, 1903) and C. Brown, *Religious Lyrics of the XV Century* (Oxford, 1939).

*Sir Degrevant* is included in the last few leaves of sig. G and the first part of sig. H. The work of the first scribe ends in the middle of a stanza at 1. 564; it is followed by a blank leaf (G 12). The work of the second scribe begins the new gathering.

The text is followed in this gathering (H) by a list of the principal events in the history of England, beginning with Brutus and ending with Henry VI. It is headed (110r):—

The cronekelys of seyntes & kynges of yngelond.

The length of each previous reign is recorded, but no figure is given for Henry VI. He was therefore still reigning.

On the next page appears the following:—

And fro þe incarnacion of Jhesu crist til þe xx [blank space] of kyng henre vj m iiijc xlvj yere.

This part of the MS., including *Sir Degrevant,* was almost certainly written in or immediately before 1446, and could not have been written after 1461, when the reign ended. Thus the evidence from handwriting, from the watermarks, and from the subject matter are all consistent.

The text is written continuously on unruled pages in double columns, 29–40 lines to the column, the usual number being about 36. Holes in the MS. on ff.106–9 have caused the loss of a number of words, which have been conjecturally restored in my text. There are no rubricated capitals.

Three hands are used in the text, which has been corrected later by two more. Hand A writes on ff.96r–99v (11. 1–564), also the title at the head of the first column, and the running title across the top of each page. Large capitals are commonly used to begin a line on the top of a page, but are found also elsewhere, without apparent reason. Paragraph signs mark the beginning of each of stanzas I–VI, VIII–X, XII–XVIII, XXI–XXIX, XXXI and XXXV. There is an unnecessary sign at the head of f.98v, col. 1, before the second quatrain of stanza XXII. The text is unpunctuated except for a slanting stroke followed by a curly line in the middle of stanza XIV (1. 216).

The character of the hand changes somewhat in the middle of f.96vb, (i.e., after stanza VII), as though the scribe had taken a thicker pen. This thicker hand persists for three stanzas (VIII–X), and the remainder of this scribe's contribution to the text is written in his more normal hand.

The punctuation mark, the unnecessary paragraph sign, and the lack of uniformity in the hand lead to the possible conclusion that this part of the text was not written all at one sitting, and this suggestion is further borne out by the fact that stanza XI is omitted, as though after discarding the thick pen the scribe resumed work at the wrong place.

The hand itself is cursive, untidy, and irregular, though usually quite legible, even in the photostatic copies from which my text has been chiefly prepared. The scribe has taken no pains with the general appearance of his page: in many places the ink has run, and has smudged the letter, which has then usually been cancelled and re-written. Crossings out are frequent, both of words and sometimes of whole lines. At one point, between stanzas VI and VII, three lines have been cancelled. As these and all other lines cancelled are to be found correctly written in other parts of the poem, the general impression conveyed is that the scribe was in a hurry, and was not always careful to look closely at his original.

This portion of the text has been corrected, partly in hand A, and partly also in hand D, which has corrected words in 11. 4, 383; inserted a word into 7, and single letters in 155, 264 (possibly also into 181); altered a single letter in 361; and added a line on f.98ᵛa. after stanza XXIII, capping scribe A's:—

Her endyth þe first fit

with:—

How say ye ? will ye any more of hit.

Hand D is neat, fine writing, and the letters are carefully made. It is also a cursive. The rather widely separated individual minims of *m*s and *n*s, together with the thin lines of the joining strokes give a general appearance of pointedness to the hand. It is considerably later than Hand A.

Hand A employs the same abbreviated forms as the scribe of L for *and*, *with*, *that*. Superscript ᵃ is invariably *ra* (e.g., *grace*, *fram*). Other abbreviations involving *r* are the final curled stroke for *er*, *re* (e.g., *degreuant*, *oþer* [*passim*], *geterne* 36), and the *p*-signs: representing *per*, *par* in *soper* 369, *sper* 330, *parkes* 143; *pur* in *purveyede* 245; and *pre* in *precious* 537. *ri* is sometimes represented by a curled tick after and above the preceding letter (e.g., *gentriese* 497), while a straight stroke resembling *i* in the same position usually requires the insertion of *r* only (e.g., *maystries* 112, *tenantrie* 141). *ur* is represented by superscript ʳ (e.g., *oþur* 246, *chartur* 266);[1] *er* by a curved stroke above the preceding letter (*reueres* 113), and also by a loop above it (*euer* 383).

The suspension stroke for *m*, *n* is frequent (e.g., *him*, *hem*, *non* [*passim*], *wentten* 683, *wexen* 311), but since it is usually indistinguishable in this part of the MS. from the fine horizontal stroke mentioned below, the question of whether or not to extend is difficult. The following principles have been adopted, not only in the part written by scribe A, but throughout:—

1. It has been extended to *n*, *m* when these letters are unambiguously required, as in the examples above.
2. It has been ignored after final *n* (e.g., *on* 580, *non* 988), and retained after medial *n* (e.g., *menne* 1476, *rybanne* 655, *spanne* 653).

The same rules have been adapted to govern the extension of *r* with final tick to -*re*.

The scribe of this part of the MS. also uses a long thin horizontal stroke extending over four or more letters, e.g., *Englond* 14, *Gawayne* 23, *houndered* 69, *heygh* 73). These strokes seem to be merely flourishes, and have also been ignored.

The contractions for plural endings are -⁹, extended to -*us* (e.g., *cheualerous* 422), and -ρ, extended to -*es* (e.g., *bokes* 43).

*m*, *n* with final curl are very common (e.g., *gamen* 3, *known* 19, *bryttayne* 22, *sone* 282, *vncouplede* 249, *schom* 127, *hem* 51); *u* with final curl (e.g., *you* 116, *thou* 186) much less so. These curls have not been extended. It

---

[1] *er* may possibly be intended by this sign, as the scribe occasionally employs *e* in unstressed syllables when written in full.

clear that he aimed at providing material for metrical research rather than preparing a critical text. His transcripts were made in 1889, and were not revised before publication. Neither the Glossary nor the Index of Proper Names is complete. None the less, this is the most important edition published to date.

## III. THE TEXT; THE PRESENT EDITION

In this section I propose to discuss the relation between the MSS., the types of variant reading that occur, scribal error and omission, and what can fairly be deduced from this evidence regarding the transmission of the texts. At the end of the section will be found a statement of the editorial principles adopted in preparing this edition. The following conclusions may be stated briefly.

1. Neither MS. is an immediate copy of the other.
2. Both MSS. are derived from a common archetype that was not the original text of the poem.
3. A period of non-scribal transmission intervenes between this archetype and the copying of the texts; both MSS. show signs of dependence (direct or indirect) upon versions transmitted orally and written out from memory.
4. Neither MS. provides a wholly satisfactory text, and each of them can be corrected by reference to the other.
5. The readings of C are on the whole to be preferred, even though its dialect is further removed from the original than that of L.

1. The mutual independence of the two MSS. may be demonstrated by an inspection of the omissions. L omits 221–4, 297–300, 652–5, and 1189–92. In addition, the third and fourth tail-rime lines in stanzas III, XV, XXII, XXV, XXX, XXXVI, XXXVII, LXXX, LXXXIX, C, and CXVII do not rime with the first and second, but form a pair of rimes by themselves. The effect of this is to split a long stanza of sixteen lines into two half-stanzas of eight. By omitting whole quatrains, L reduces the length of the stanza to twelve lines. As the corresponding text of C nearly always correctly continues and completes the rime-scheme of the stanza, and as C preserves the lines that L omits, then C cannot be derived from L unless one is to suppose a drastic revision of the text in C or in one of C's ancestors, and this is most improbable. On the contrary, one is entitled to assume that the poem was probably first written in stanzas of equal length, and that the lines corresponding to the lacunæ in L represent a version of the original.

Conversely, L cannot derive from C, because C omits stanza XI, which L preserves. Moreover, unless one is to assume that the scribe of L was more incompetent than anyone will believe him to be, his dislocations of rime are far too numerous for them to have been taken over from C by a series of scribal errors.

2. Blunders of the same kind found in both texts in the same place point to their having been derived from a common archetype, which was derived from, and not identical with, the author's MS. Since these readings are common to both texts, they probably go back to the archetype; since they are errors, the archetype could not have been the author's autograph MS. Thus in 340 both verbs have a singular ending in -*s*, while

both of words and sometimes of whole lines. At one point, between stanzas VI and VII, three lines have been cancelled. As these and all other lines cancelled are to be found correctly written in other parts of the poem, the general impression conveyed is that the scribe was in a hurry, and was not always careful to look closely at his original.

This portion of the text has been corrected, partly in hand A, and partly also in hand D, which has corrected words in 11. 4, 383; inserted a word into 7, and single letters in 155, 264 (possibly also into 181); altered a single letter in 361; and added a line on f.98ᵛa. after stanza XXIII, capping scribe A's:—

Her endyth þe first fit

with:—

How say ye ? will ye any more of hit.

Hand D is neat, fine writing, and the letters are carefully made. It is also a cursive. The rather widely separated individual minims of *m*s and *n*s, together with the thin lines of the joining strokes give a general appearance of pointedness to the hand. It is considerably later than Hand A.

Hand A employs the same abbreviated forms as the scribe of L for *and*, *with*, *that*. Superscript ᵃ is invariably *ra* (e.g., *grace*, *fram*). Other abbreviations involving *r* are the final curled stroke for *er*, *re* (e.g., *degreuant*, *oper* [*passim*], *geterne* 36), and the *p*-signs: representing *per*, *par* in *soper* 369, *sper* 330, *parkes* 143; *pur* in *purveyede* 245; and *pre* in *precious* 537. *ri* is sometimes represented by a curled tick after and above the preceding letter (e.g., *gentriese* 497), while a straight stroke resembling *i* in the same position usually requires the insertion of *r* only (e.g., *maystries* 112, *tenantrie* 141). *ur* is represented by superscript ʳ (e.g., *opur* 246, *chartur* 266);[1] *er* by a curved stroke above the preceding letter (*reueres* 113), and also by a loop above it (*euer* 383).

The suspension stroke for *m*, *n* is frequent (e.g., *him*, *hem*, *non* [*passim*], *wentten* 683, *wexen* 311), but since it is usually indistinguishable in this part of the MS. from the fine horizontal stroke mentioned below, the question of whether or not to extend is difficult. The following principles have been adopted, not only in the part written by scribe A, but throughout:—

1. It has been extended to *n*, *m* when these letters are unambiguously required, as in the examples above.
2. It has been ignored after final *n* (e.g., *on* 580, *non* 988), and retained after medial *n* (e.g., *menne* 1476, *rybanne* 655, *spanne* 653).

The same rules have been adapted to govern the extension of *r* with final tick to -*re*.

The scribe of this part of the MS. also uses a long thin horizontal stroke extending over four or more letters, e.g., *Englond* 14, *Gawayne* 23, *houndered* 69, *heygh* 73). These strokes seem to be merely flourishes, and have also been ignored.

The contractions for plural endings are -⁹, extended to -*us* (e.g., *cheualerous* 422), and -ρ, extended to -*es* (e.g., *bokes* 43).

*m*, *n* with final curl are very common (e.g., *gamen* 3, *known* 19, *bryttayne* 22, *sone* 282, *vncouplede* 249, *schom* 127, *hem* 51); *u* with final curl (e.g., *you* 116, *thou* 186) much less so. These curls have not been extended. It

---

[1] *er* may possibly be intended by this sign, as the scribe occasionally employs *e* in unstressed syllables when written in full.

would be impossible to extend consistently, and the value of extending at all is doubtful. *ll* and final *d* with tail have been treated in the same way (though *l* in *lre* 121, 153, etc., has obvious significance). A horizontal stroke above the -*ute* of *quite* 443 has been extended to *i*.

In the work of hand A, it is sometimes easy to confuse *e* and *o*, *u* and *n*. *þ*, *y* are usually kept distinct: the long stroke of the *þ* curves to the left, that of *y* to the right, with a hook at the end, often slightly thickened. *ff* is invariably used for *F*. These characteristics apply also to hands B and C in this MS.

Hand A comes abruptly to an end after four lines of stanza XXXVI on f. 99$^v$. A whole leaf (unfoliated) separates the text of hand A from that of hand B, which begins on f.100, and carries on the poem to the end of f.108. Except on f.100, there is no running title. The text is not punctuated, but the triplet-rimes are bracketed together on ff.100a, 100b (first three only), 100$^v$a. There are no paragraph signs or spaces between stanzas. Owing to holes in the MS. on ff.106–8, words, letters, and portion of letters have been lost.

Hand B is a uniform book-hand: the letters are bold and square, and the component lines are thick. Each letter is made separately, and in general is not joined by a line to the next, but the letters of a word are very close together. The scribe has made many corrections at the time of writing: the greater number of these are words or parts of words cancelled and re-written because the ink has run into the texture of the paper, or, owing to the thickness of his lines, because it has blotted the enclosed spaces of such letters as *a*, *o*, *þ*. Lines written in the wrong order are corrected (whether or no by the scribe is impossible to say) by means of marginal letters *b*, *a*. There are no clear signs of correction by another hand in this part of the text. Rather more ornate letters are found on the top line of each column: some *f*s and long *s*s are given a preliminary ornamental tick, which curls over as many as four letters of the rest of the word; the first two vertical strokes of the *w* extend well into the margin; the uprights of *h*, *k*, *l* are considerably lengthened, and are followed by an ornamental hook, detached from the letter. The scribe sometimes employs an *h* of approximately this type in other parts of the text (e.g., the second *h* of *why3th* 642, *hur* 649, *hom* 684, *worþelych* 692) but nowhere is it of any significance, though Luick sometimes extends the hook to -*e*.

The care expended upon the appearance of the earlier pages in hand B (and especially the first page) is not maintained. After f. 106 especially, the hand gradually deteriorates, and though its general character is preserved, it approaches the cursive type. In particular, one may notice a tendency to join letters together, and there is some loss of regularity.

Hand C begins on f.108$^v$ (1. 1717) and carries the poem to the end. It is a running hand of the same general type as A, but neater, more regular, and with better formed letters. Even more nearly, it resembles the deteriorated hand B. In particular, there are in both hands distinctive forms of capital 3 (the lower bow of which is almost vertical), *T* (with flat top, the lower part resembling *S* with curtailed upper bow), and *R* (without final tail, the following letter being joined to it by a stroke beginning in the middle of the upright,[1] which resembles a pot-hook). It may well be that hands

---

[1] For examples of this type of *R*, without distinctive pot-hook, see R. B. McKerrow, *The Capital Letters in Elizabethan Handwriting*, R.E.S., Jan. 1927, p. 33, examples 1 and 2.

B and C, though distinct, represent the formal and the cursive writing of the same scribe.

Since the same abbreviations and contractions are used by both B and C, they may be taken together. As before, we find the usual abbreviations for *and, with, þat,* and in addition þ$^u$, h$^t$ (extended to þou, hyt). Superscript [a] is commonly used for *ra*; final curl for *er* (though the same stroke is without significance in *kyng* 986, and *ryng* 993); small curved tick above the word also for *er* (e.g., *þer* 643, *euer* 659) or *ri* (e.g., *prikes* 1279). A straight superscript stroke also represents *ri* in *prime* 1225 and *degriuaunt* (*passim*). Hands B and C frequently employ a superscript sign, extended as *ur* (e.g., *chaumbur* 777, *ʒondur* 744, *murþes* 1438). The usual symbols are used for *ser* (e.g., *seruaunt* 695, *seruyd* 1404), *per, par,* and *pro,* and have been thus extended, except in *preferrys* 855. This word begins with a *pro*-symbol. *p* with curved stroke over the top has been extended to *per* in *peres* 1903 (once only). ƚƚ, ꝯ, the *m/n* suspensions, and *n* and *r* with final curls have been treated as before. The usual contraction is used for *Ihesu* in 694.

Suspensions and contractions have been extended in roman.

## II. EDITIONS

(i) J. O. Halliwell: *The Thornton Romances* (Camden Society, London, 1844). Halliwell prints the Cambridge MS., but some variant readings from the Lincoln MS. are included in the notes. The Introduction contains a detailed description of the contents of the MSS.; there is also an Essay on terminal contractions. The text is usually sound; slightly modernized spelling.

(ii) G. Schleich: *Collationen zu ME. Dichtungen* (Englische Studien Bd. XII, pp. 139–42). Contains a collation of Halliwell's text (ll. 1–256), and prints ll. 1–97 of Thornton MS., not always quite accurately, even on his own principles (e.g., l. 65 cessid] MS. sessid; l. 81 almonsdede] MS. almous dede).

His comments on Halliwell's text are favourable, though he points out that Halliwell has not always been consistent in extending the abbreviations of C.

(iii) F. S. Ellis: *The Romance of Sir Degrevant* [Colophon]: 'Edited by F. S. Ellis after the edition printed by J. O. Halliwell from the Cambridge MS., with some additions and variations from that in the Library of Lincoln Cathedral. Printed by William Morris at the Kelmscott Press . . . Hammersmith . . . 1896.' A pleasant book to read, but useless for textual study. Contains one illustration (Degrevant and Melidor in her bower) by Burne-Jones.

(iv) E. Rickert: *Romances of Love* (London, 1908). A translation, not always accurate, but occasionally brilliant. The introduction and notes are stimulating.

(v) K. Luick: *Sir Degrevant* (Wiener Beiträge zur Englischen Philologie, Bd. 48, 1917). Both MSS. in parallel, with Glossary, Index of Proper Names, short Preface, and Introduction. The text is complete, though it contains a large number of small errors: misreadings of words, substitutions of *u* for *v*, *th* for *þ*, and *vice versa*. His Preface makes it clear that he aimed at providing material for metrical research rather than preparing a critical text. His transcripts were made in 1889, and were not revised before publication. Neither the Glossary nor the Index of Proper Names is complete. None the less, this is the most important edition published to date.

## III. THE TEXT; THE PRESENT EDITION

In this section I propose to discuss the relation between the MSS., the types of variant reading that occur, scribal error and omission, and what can fairly be deduced from this evidence regarding the transmission of the texts. At the end of the section will be found a statement of the editorial principles adopted in preparing this edition. The following conclusions may be stated briefly.

1. Neither MS. is an immediate copy of the other.
2. Both MSS. are derived from a common archetype that was not the original text of the poem.
3. A period of non-scribal transmission intervenes between this archetype and the copying of the texts; both MSS. show signs of dependence (direct or indirect) upon versions transmitted orally and written out from memory.
4. Neither MS. provides a wholly satisfactory text, and each of them can be corrected by reference to the other.
5. The readings of C are on the whole to be preferred, even though its dialect is further removed from the original than that of L.

1. The mutual independence of the two MSS. may be demonstrated by an inspection of the omissions. L omits 221–4, 297–300, 652–5, and 1189–92. In addition, the third and fourth tail-rime lines in stanzas III, XV, XXII, XXV, XXX, XXXVI, XXXVII, LXXX, LXXXIX, C, and CXVII do not rime with the first and second, but form a pair of rimes by themselves. The effect of this is to split a long stanza of sixteen lines into two half-stanzas of eight. By omitting whole quatrains, L reduces the length of the stanza to twelve lines. As the corresponding text of C nearly always correctly continues and completes the rime-scheme of the stanza, and as C preserves the lines that L omits, then C cannot be derived from L unless one is to suppose a drastic revision of the text in C or in one of C's ancestors, and this is most improbable. On the contrary, one is entitled to assume that the poem was probably first written in stanzas of equal length, and that the lines corresponding to the lacunæ in L represent a version of the original.

Conversely, L cannot derive from C, because C omits stanza XI, which L preserves. Moreover, unless one is to assume that the scribe of L was more incompetent than anyone will believe him to be, his dislocations of rime are far too numerous for them to have been taken over from C by a series of scribal errors.

2. Blunders of the same kind found in both texts in the same place point to their having been derived from a common archetype, which was derived from, and not identical with, the author's MS. Since these readings are common to both texts, they probably go back to the archetype; since they are errors, the archetype could not have been the author's autograph MS. Thus in 340 both verbs have a singular ending in -*s*, while

the rime demands a word without -*s*; 392 provides an example of the opposite kind of error: the rime requiring an -*s* that neither text provides. In 336 the readings are *wondide, y-wounded*, r.w. *stownde*, etc., i.e., a past participle with full inflexional ending instead of the contracted form *wounde* (see note). In 657 both texts read *on hold(e)* which makes very inferior sense, even though the line is alliterating on *h*. Indeed, it was probably the impulse to continue the alliteration that prompted the error. The true reading, suggested by Holthausen, may well be *on mold(e)*, on the top of the head (cf. 1055). Again, 1041:—
   The duk ansuerd on hight (C answerus on hy3th)
is suspicious, because the Duke's answer to the Earl's complaint of Sir Degrevant's conduct has already been given in the last quatrain of the previous stanza, and the first line of this quatrain makes clear that it is the Duke speaking. That a poet would waste a line in repeating the formula is unlikely, especially as the 'answer' comes in the form of a question, and consists only of one line.[1]
 The C-version of 651-2 is—
   With topyes and trechoure
   Overtrasyd þat tyde;
where *and* is almost certainly a scribal error for *hir*. L has—
   With terepys and with tredoure,
followed by a lacuna. That is, *and* is a common error, going back to the archetype, the *with* an editorial intrusion. Further examples of L's meddling with the text are given in § 3 below.

 There may also be some significance in the arrangement of 1030-1. In both MSS. the lines are in the same order, but marginal letters, *b, a* indicate that the order is to be reversed in C. As the MS. order is inferior, and identical, it may go back to a lost archetype of L and C, and the present state of the texts may be explained by supposing that C saw the error only after he had written it, and that L perpetuated it. The only editing necessary by C would have been to transfer *and* from one line to the other. Lastly, the pointless repetition in both versions of 692 eight lines later, and *liked, lyked* 1468 (with consequential alteration in L) probably derive from the archetype.

 3. The divergences between the readings of the MSS. are very numerous; and the disparity between a line and the corresponding one in the other MS. can be so great as to preclude altogether the possibility of accounting for them by the ordinary processes of scribal transmission. It will be convenient to begin with examples of variation showing generally that one or other text has been written out from memory or transmitted orally, without committing oneself as to which text has been so transmitted. The version in L is given first; that in C is put in brackets.
 The following is a representative list:—
  40 He *wane* þe pryse aye (bare).
  69 Many ploughes in þe maynes (An houndered plows in demaynus).
  194 Sir, þat es euyll done (is nat well).
  220 What *mendis* he hym sent (answer).

[1] The present state of the lines 1037, 1041 in both MSS. is most satisfactorily accounted for on the supposition that 1041 is an error found already in the archetype, and that the exact form of C 1037 (*on hy3th*) is a memorial anticipation of it (see below p. xx). L 1037 may well be original.

1035-6 Þat did me þat velany
 And wroght me this woghe.
 (He wroȝthe me þis vylany
 And dud me þis wouȝh).
1347 Sythyn hamward he ȝede (And to forest þei spede).
1458 Standand on þe pelers (Syttyng).
1537-40 Wete ȝe weile, with-owttyn lett,
 Þe firste tym þat I ȝow mett,
 Myn hert was hally on ȝow sett.
 (Leff þou well withouten lette,
 Þe ferste tyme Y þe mette
 Myn hert on þe was sette).
1652 He cuttid awaye (kerues).
1681 By þat it drewe nere daye (hyt dawed ney).
1710 Thus oure clothis were torne (gownus).

These lines, together with scores of others that might have been chosen, show textual variation at its simplest: one ordinary word or phrase of commonplace meaning replaces another, and all of them point to a series of lapses of memory rather than to mistakes in copying. Mental lapses of this kind are not surprising in a minstrel poem[1] written for recitation. Each version makes good sense; it is usually impossible to determine, even to hazard a guess, which is the author's version. Indeed, there is no guarantee that either of them exactly reproduces his words.

The next five lists contain examples designed to show where L either has or points to the better reading. The first includes those wherein L may preserve the original, while the variant contained in C will show that failure of memory has occurred, probably on the part of the copyist of some text from which C is derived. As before, the L-version is given first.

(i) 7 Of beryns þat by-fore were (Off gode).

Here C[2] has replaced one of the synonyms for 'man' traditional in alliterative poetry by a weaker word, and has upset the alliteration. The possible argument that C was using a familiar word in place of one that he did not know is much weakened by the fact that he uses it later in the poem (317, 516, 563).

(ii) 129 Þe knyghte no langare habade
 (Wyth þe knytht was non abad).

C, having forgotten the true version, changes the verb to a noun, and fills out the line with weak expletives.

(iii) 225-6 Than Sir Degreuant hase hight
 To Hym þat maste es of myghte

 (Þan Syr Degreuuaunt syght,
 And by-held the heven vp-an hyght).

---

[1] For a discussion of the evidence, see below, Section IX.

[2] In these discussions 'C' and 'L' must be taken to mean the scribes responsible for copying these texts, and any earlier scribes from whose texts these MSS. were derived, including the reciters who first committed their versions to paper; the terms are not exclusively applied to the actual scribes whose work we are studying. 'C' and 'L' are sometimes applied to the MSS. in certain contexts.

The reading of L is stronger and more direct, and provides a more fitting introduction to the invocation in the following lines. C's version is sanctimonious by comparison, and there is no particular occasion for sighing.

(iv) 261–3  Þan spake þe Erle on þat launde:
'Where es now þis geaunte?
Why will noghte Sir Degreuant', etc.

(Þane seys þe dukes on þe land:
'Wher ys now Sir Degreuuaund?
Why wol not com þis gyant', etc.).

C is obviously wrong in the first line: no dukes have so far been mentioned. In the second and third lines he offers a possible but rhetorically less effective version of what is to be found in L.

(v) 288  And freschely þay fyghte (ferysly).

A commonplace word is substituted for one that is comparatively rare, and hence more easily forgotten. C is given to substituting *ferys(ly)* for a more vigorous, less trite word, either because the true reading had been forgotten, or because it was unfamiliar. See 248 (L *kant*), 301 (L *frekly*), 323 (L *freschely*). In 290, however, he is probably right. See *Morte Arthure*, 1897–8.

(vi) 341  He bristis bacenettis fele
(He playtede her basnetus well, C 342).

The stanza of which this is the fifth line is strongly alliterated throughout: L continues the chain of alliterating sounds, but C breaks it. The phrase *brist bacenettis* is in the alliterative tradition of phrase-making, while *playtede ... basnetus* is an odd and somewhat forced expression.

(vii) 352  Lyand in lynge
(Ded in the lyng).

In its context *ded* is unnecessary, for we have already been told (349) that the Earl's retinue has been slain.

(viii) 625  Sir Degreuant tuk gud hede (tok non hede).

L preserves the better of these contradictory readings: the squire has just advised the hero to enter the Earl's castle by the gate and suggests their secreting themselves until the lady appears. Sir Degrevant falls in with the plan in 633–6.

(ix) 679  Bothe þe smale and þe grete
(So duden all þe grete).

C's version is weak even as it stands, but in its context it is grammatically awkward in addition:—

Trompers tromped to þe mete,
Þey weshen and went to sette,
So duden all þe grete, etc.

*þey* cannot refer to *trompers*, its natural antecedent; it can only refer to *grete* in the following line. L offers a much better articulated reading, where *þay* is impersonal throughout, and *smale and grete* are in apposition with it. The phrase *so did* is a mannerism

(x) 1765-7 with C¹ when his memory fails: cf. the variants in 1581, 1861. C 1581 in its context implies that the wait was in two places at once; C 1861 is grammatically defensible, but rhetorically loose.

(x) 1765-7  I dare hardyly say
Þat he went hym to playe,
Þay withsett hym þe waye.

(I dar sauely say
Þe kny3th went on his way,
Owre men bysett hym þe way).

C's version is suspicious because it repeats the rime-word *way*. C has apparently combined into an alliterative cliché a confused memory of *way* (1767) and *went* (1766). He then makes a passable shot at 1767 without realising how awkward is the effect of the sentence as a whole.

(xi) 1849  Of Almayne þe Emperour
(And þe ryche Emperour).
L preserves the fuller meaning.

The most convincing evidence of memorial transmission is in general to be found in examples of anticipation, and to a lesser degree, of recollection. A scribe writing out an imperfectly remembered poem may be expected to replace the correct phrase or line by one taken from further on, or may repeat one already used. Anticipation, if it can be proved, usually carries more weight; a scribe, attempting to carry in his head more than he can accurately remember, may unconsciously substitute for the correct reading a line that comes from earlier in the poem. This could conceivably happen, even if he were transcribing from a written copy in the ordinary way, and especially in such a poem as this, wherein romance clichés are so frequent. On the other hand, a scribe with a written copy in front of him could scarcely anticipate a reading unless it was itself a cliché, in which case he might reproduce it in the wrong place, with no detriment to the sense, during a moment of inattention. If we suppose that the substituted phrase were to occur later in the poem, the text would manifest symptoms pointing to memorial transmission that would in effect be quite misleading, the source of the phrase being not this poem but the scribe's memory of some other.

Traces of both recollection and, less clearly, of anticipation are found in C, and are here offered for what they are worth. There are not many of them in comparison with those found in L, presumably because the reporter in the C-tradition had a better memory.

(i) C 1793-5  Bylyue a lettur ho sent
Þorw þe 3orlus comandment,
A messenger has hyt hent.

For 1795, L has:—
And talde hym alle hir atent,

which, summarising what was in Melidor's mind, fits more easily into the context. The C-reading is probably an echo from much earlier in the poem (122), where also it is associated with the

¹ The *so did* formula seems to be the natural refuge of the slovenly reciter: one is reminded of E. A. G. Lamborn's story of the schoolboy repeating *The Ancient Mariner* (*Expression in Speech and Writing*, p. 10).

sending of a letter; i.e., on the theory of memorial transmission, the recurrence of a similar incident has prompted the recurrence of the phrase narrating it. This example points towards the conclusion more surely than the next, partly because the line in question is not a formula, and partly because an interval of nearly 1700 lines separates the two appearances of it. A transcriber straying from a written copy would hardly remember a line from so far back.

(ii) C 1523–4 'When wolt þou, þe worþely wyȝt
Lysten me tyll?'
L 1523 'When will ȝe, swete wyghte', etc.

The variants might be regarded as indifferent, were it not that the phrase 'worthy wight' has already been used in C 530, 680, and the present example may be a recollection of these. On the other hand, the fact that the phrase is exceedingly common in other poems diminishes the value of the evidence.

For the same reason, not much more weight can be given to the best examples of possible anticipation that I have observed:—

(iii) C 575 'And we frendes for euermar,
What doel þat I drye.'
L 575 'What-so-euer I drey.'

The reading in C may anticipate 1752, where the alliteration is continued from the previous line. In C 576 it is not, and this is some evidence in favour of rejecting it as unoriginal, and accounting for the error by supposing anticipation.

(iv) C 1863 Bryȝth burdys and schene
Was joye to be-holde.
L 1864 And frely to folde (cf. C 1872)

The error in C may be reporter's anticipation of C 1872, or C 1872 may be a reporter's recollection of 1864; but as the interval is so small, it may be simply that the scribe's eye picked up the wrong tail-rime. Reconstruction of the text is here made more difficult by the fact that the readings vary in 1872, and there is no sure means of deciding between them.

These examples show how apparently correct readings may have been corrupted if they were imperfectly remembered. An ineffective phrase may displace a vigorous one, to the detriment of sense and consistency; syntax may become disjointed; alliteration may be impaired, or even unnecessarily imposed upon a line, especially if a ready-made and already well-worn phrase is to hand.

The examples in the next list are more doubtful: they are possibly memorial errors in C of the kind already considered, possibly scribal substitutions such as are found in other ME. poems of which later transcripts have been made in dialects other than the original, e.g., Laȝamon's *Brut*, *The Cursor Mundi*, *The Wars of Alexander*.

(i) 113 He drew his veuers of fysche (reueres with).

*Veuers*, fish-ponds, is not a common word, and C has substituted the much more usual *reueres*, also to be associated with *fyshe*. He has done the same in 434. Similarly *wyght horse* for *aueres* 150; *kene* C 314 for *kynde*, well-born L 315.

- (ii) 302 Þare wiste nane witterly (non so myghty).
  
  C abandons the alliteration.
- (iii) 1276 This worthily vndir wedis (Þes douȝty on dedus).
  
  C substitutes one alliterative formula for another, the hint being supplied by 1273.
- (iv) 1578 Alle þe gatis þat þay ȝode (weyes).
- (v) 1655 Þe stede strak ouer þe force (fosse).
  
  *Gatis* and *force* are words with a strongly marked dialectal colouring, even at the period when the poem was written.

There are also in C a number of scribal errors in the narrower sense, usually quite easily distinguishable for what they are, and set right by reference to L. The following is a representative list, in which the L-reading is given in brackets:—

- (i) 681 When þe lordys were drawin (borde).
  
  The mistake has occurred through confusion of *l* and *b*. Confusion between *c* and *t* has misled C into writing *conn* for *ton*, (=*tane*) in 1030.
- (ii) 1152 And þat hym seyen (And all þat hym see).
- (iii) 1857 Þan þe semelede þe sale (Sone þay sembled in sale).
- (iv) 1885 And on þe fyfteþe day (i.e., of the wedding feast).
  
  L has *fyftened*, and this is the only possible version as we have already been told that the tournament has been continued for a fortnight (1881). C's error is due to an omitted *n*-suspension rather than to a mere desire to exaggerate. Other *n*-suspensions have been omitted in C 345, C 353.

In spite of the conclusions already established, it is clear that the immediate original of C was a MS.: it was not written out from memory. The fact that two scribes were at work upon it is itself almost sufficient proof, for it can hardly be supposed that both of them, speaking what is substantially the same dialect, had it off by heart, and wrote it down turn and turn about, the second taking it up where his colleague left off, in the middle of a stanza. Since the textual evidence points in the same direction, it will be well to consider it, if only to show how the two kinds of testimony are consistent.

- (i) C 391 At þe barnekynch he abad.
  
  The unusual and possibly unique form *barnekynch* for *barnekyn* or *barmkyn* may owe its final *-ch* to assimilation with *lordelych* in the following line (see note). If so, then the error is scribal rather than memorial.
- (ii) C 765 'And here my trouȝth: er I leton.'
  
  This is the probable MS. reading (see note). The correct version is certainly *be ton*, be taken. The *l/b* confusion points to an ill-written copy.
- (iii) C 1187 And callyd to hym tolly knyȝthus.
  
  I take the correct reading to be *two*, spelt *tow* in the original, the *w* being misread as *lli* and transcribed as *lly* (see note). If this emendation is accepted, then it points quite clearly to a mistranscription; a reciter who had forgotten the right word would

not put down nonsense. Emendation to *tow* is supported by the L-reading 'a knyghte'.

(iv) C 1343　　y haþe nat y my lyff.
The true reading is *y hope nat y may lyff*, i.e., 'I do not expect to live'. This line is almost certainly the result of a series of transcriptional errors (*o/a* confusion, *p/þ* confusion, accidental omission of a letter through oversight).

The foregoing lists have been compiled to show how now and again L offers a better text than C, and in particular how the deficiencies of C are partly due to the failure of a reporter's memory. Final judgement upon this text in a general sense may be deferred for the present.

We now pass to a discussion of some special peculiarities of L. The following lists make no claim to exhaust the subject; fuller information and additional items are given in the notes. One of its most noticeable textual characteristics is its tendency to replace a perfectly satisfactory line, or pair of lines, by a weak paraphrase; if only one word is affected, it is often commonplace in comparison with what C offers, and sometimes degenerates into a mere tag. Insertion of one or more unnecessary words produces the same effect. Such dilution of the literary flavour is pretty sure evidence of memorial transmission.

The C-reading is given first; L follows in brackets.

(i) 147–9　　He lent he[m] oxon and wayn
　　　　　　　Of his own store;
　　　　　　　And also sede for [to] sowe.
　　　　　　　(He lent þam oxen a-gayne
　　　　　　　Of his awen store;
　　　　　　　Alsua, þe sothe for to schewe).

(ii) 287　　*Wyghtly* wepenes þey weld (Worthy).

(iii) 374–5　　He was wonded to scham,
　　　　　　　Þe lady ses he was lam.
　　　　　　　(He was wondid all to schame
　　　　　　　Þe lady sawe þat he was lame.)

(iv) 1617　　Syre Degriuaunt *at euene-ly3th* (þat hend knyght).

(v) 1799–1800　　As he was gode and dou3ty
　　　　　　　And holden for trewe.
　　　　　　　(Trow it righte trewely,
　　　　　　　And trow it for trewe.)

(vi) 1913　　*At Port Gaff* was he slon (Sertanly).

Compare also the versions in 332, 1465, 1793, 1822–3 (loosening of syntax), 1839, 1877–9 (awkward inversion).

Another characteristic of L is to avoid a rare word or expression, replacing it by something more usual. This may be regarded as a special form of the paraphrasing tendency already described, but nevertheless there is a distinction to be drawn between them. In most of the examples given below, the variant consists of a single word, with a minimum of consequential alteration. It is therefore arguable that some of them at least may be the work of an editor deliberately avoiding the unusual, rather than that of a reporter who has forgotten it. Whatever its cause, it is a most fruitful source of error in L.

(vii)   361      He come *schygynge* ayen (chasande).

(viii)  592      *Vlonkest* on wede (Worthliest; see (ii) above).

(ix)    647      *An[u]rl[e]d* with ermyn (Furrede).

(x)     1045     He beres [a] *cheef* of aȝour (a schelde).

(xi)    1773     Y rede ȝe *sauȝthle* with þe knyȝth (be frende).

See also 9, 242, 255, 308, 568, 739, 1103, 1125, 1370, L 1474 (C 1475), 1497.

It occasionally happens that the variant in L is so wide of the mark as to make the line irreconcilable with what is said elsewhere in the poem. Numerals are especially liable to confusion.

(xii)   1087     Þre *hundred* knyȝttus of þe best (score).

These numbers describe the size of the retinue that accompanied Sir Degrevant to the tournament. The Earl's party consisted of five hundred according to C, three thousand according to L (1078). In C the disproportion in numbers is reasonable (500 : 300), in L it is quite incredible (3000 : 60). L seems to have deliberately exaggerated the figures in order to make the outcome more creditable to Sir Degrevant. Whatever the motive, one is entitled to prefer the saner version.

Moreover, L shows that he has misinterpreted the meaning of the original, either by confusing pronouns and homonyms, or by clumsy attempts at editing. The result is either banality or rubbish.

(xiii)  771–2    'Þo . . . Shal be fay, and we fyȝth,
                 For all her michel pryde'.
                 ('He sall by it, and I fyghte,
                 For all ȝour mekill pride').

Sir Degrevant is uttering defiance of the Earl to Melidor. In L 771 the subject *he* is weakly repeated from the previous line, and the alliteration has been lost; in C the subject is a whole clause. Since Sir Degrevant has promised to be her man (730–2), to refer to 'ȝour michel pryde' is a tactless way of commending himself to her good graces.

(xiv)   1451     Fyfty mad *of o molde* (on þe molde).

C preserves good sense ('fifty made in one design'); L has taken *molde* to mean 'ground', and has written a tag without meaning.

(xv)    1565–7   And þe bold bachylere
                 Toke þe damysele clere,
                 Þis [han] þei dured þat ȝere, etc.
                 (Than þat bolde bachelere
                 And þe Countase so clere
                 Loued thus al a ȝere, etc.).

L has missed the point by supposing that the passage refers to Sir Degrevant and Melidor, whereas the 'bachylere' is the squire, and the 'damysele' is the waiting maid. L's confusion goes even further: his use of the word 'Countase' is most inappropriate even for Melidor, who was only an Earl's daughter (see note).

(xvi) 1653–5   Þe body syttys opon þe hors
              Hyt was vncomely to þe cors.
              (Þe body satt on þe horse
              Þat was an vnsemly corse).
       L has misunderstood the humour (see note), and has produced
a weak line.
  See also 1305, 1446 and note.
  Arguments based on purely metrical evidence are dangerous in this poem, since, owing to the state of the texts, not as much as could be wished is discoverable about the minutiæ of scansion. Nevertheless, many of the lines in L are rhythmically inferior to the corresponding lines in C. To judge from many of the readings identical in both MSS., terseness of expression was one of the poet's aims, and his technique was appropriately elliptical. L, not being at home with either, sought to mitigate them by filling out lines with syntactically redundant words, which clog and impair the metrical flow. Verse of the kind now to be considered in L cannot surely represent the author's intention.[1]

(xviii) C 1552    And trouþus þei plyȝth
                  (And þare þay trouthes plyghte).
(xix)   C 1630    Blyue his swerde had y-drayn
                  (His swerd hase he owt-drawen).
  See also 107, 220, 292, 473, 478, 481, 541, 553, 561, 598, 1134, 1552, 1712, 1791, 1893, etc.
  When the rime scheme is upset, as it often is, then clearly there has been an attempt to re-write the text.

(xx)    C 480     *Acheue* how hit wold (Proue).
                  C preserves the ornamental device of *concatenatio* (for a fuller explanation, see Section IV). See also 1088–9.
(xxi)   C 1355–6  Þer hys stede stod by-forun,
                  And lenges all þat day.
                  (Whare þaire stedis stode by-forne,
                  Þare als þay þam leuede).
       *Leuede* cannot be defended, as it dislocates the rime. *Þaire* is also an unlikely reading: there is no noun in the two preceding stanzas to which it can refer. C preserves sense and consistency throughout.
  See also 1320, 1623.

(xxii)  L is unaware of the technical device by which the closing lines of the poem repeat those at the beginning. In C the repetition is fairly exact, in L it is a mere echo of sentiment.
  Anticipation and recollection (in the senses already described) are among the commonest textual features of L.

(xxiii) C 48      By sexxty, Y dar say
                  (Sexty, in plyghte).
  A consequential error of an unusually complex type. L 28 is echoed in L 44; this is an error resulting from the inversion of the operative words in the earlier line. Having got the words the wrong way round, the editor has

---

[1] C sometimes has a longer and rhythmically weaker line corresponding to L's shorter and more vigorous one, but not nearly so often (see 53, 524, 1816, 1903).

to re-write the line appearing in its presumably correct form in C 48 in order to make a new rime, and naturally dislocates the true rime scheme. The new line (L 48) anticipates L 140. Stanza XCIX has been similarly dislocated by a line containing a phrase that echoes 620, 652, 780, 1083, etc.[1]

(xxiv)  C 66    A *pousand* poundus worth off land (hundrethe).

Sir Degrevant's wealth is in question. C's account of it must be more nearly right than L's, because it is consonant with the disbursements described later in the poem. He gives the squire a hundred pounds' worth of land in 886, a hundred (in L, three hundred) pounds and a steed to the minstrels after the tournament (1173), and presents worth at least three hundred in 1894. L's reading is an anticipation of 886, 974.

See also 1024 (anticipating 1200), L 1204 (anticipating 1213, itself a dubious reading), 1505 (anticipating 1507), and 1723 (anticipating 1727).

(xxv)  C 316   Þese doughty on dede (Wyse vndire wedis).

L's version, a tag, echoes 236.

(xxvi)  C 1142   Had *y-venkessyd* þe feld (wonnen).

L repeats the verb from 1128, C varies it and produces (apart from the *y*-prefix in a northern poem) a more likely phrase.

See also 184 (rime-word repeating 180, and anticipating 578), 384 (virtually repeating 380, with a different rime-word), 1129–30 (echoing 1061–2), 1148 (echoing 1142), 1416 (echoing 1411), 1519 (echoing 1494) and note.

The following list contains only errors and omissions that may almost certainly be attributed to the scribe. The L-reading is given first.

(i)  296   On gleterand scheldys (geldene).
*Gleterand* repeats a word from the line before. See 1442 for a similar type of error.

(ii)  435   And I gretly gretly anoyede (Y gretly am).
L repeats the adverb and omits the verb.

(iii)  536   Þat lufly in lyre (in lere, *riming with* clere, *etc.*).

(iv)  1305   Þe gud knyghtis aunterous (knyȝht Syre Auntorus).

[1] In both these stanzas, the first pair of tail-rimes is right, and the second pair wrong. In most other stanzas divided into two by the dislocation of tail-rimes it is the second pair that is right and the first pair wrong (XXII, XXV, LXXX, C, CII), and in LXXVI only the first tail-rime line fails to preserve consistency. In nearly all cases when once a tail-rime line has been forgotten and replaced by another, the following tail lines rime with the substitute and do not conform to the original rime sequence. This points to editorial activity of a kind.
As C has been translated into another dialect, what has been described above might be expected to appear more frequently. That it is, in fact, less frequent is another sign of the general superiority of C. Only three stanzas are affected in this way. In one of these (VII), the scribe has re-written the first two tail-rimes in his own dialect. The first of them (*brade*) goes well enough as *brode*; but the second is *grade*, degrade, mechanically translated to *grode*, which can scarcely be called a word at all. At this point he gives up, and leaves the other two tail-rimes (*hade, made*) as they are. The division of the other two stanzas (XX, CXIX) is brought about by wrongly omitting, or wrongly including, an -*s* ending. Of the kind of editorial meddling found in L there is no sign.

The singular is obviously meant. The error may have arisen through the usual MS. contraction for *Sir* closely following the preceding word, and being taken either for a plural contraction or for an -*s*.
See also the variants in lines 29, 504, 632, 727, 767, 1019, 1175, 1547.

4. Much of the evidence considered above, showing that both extant texts depend upon memorized versions, shows also how unsatisfactory are the texts themselves. Errors of copying, and errors due to a reciter's bad memory, abound in both versions, but where the variants are indifferent, as they often are, truth and error are indistinguishable. Many of these are insignificant, e.g., a line in one text may contain an article preceding a noun, and in the other a demonstrative ,pronoun may precede; one may use a plural, the other a singular pronoun or verb; one line may contain a verb in the present tense, and in the other the corresponding verb may be past, and so forth. Sometimes the context will show that one reading is to be preferred, but if so, it will not be possible to find the better reading in the same MS. for many lines together. A reconstructed text would therefore be a patchwork of lines now from one MS., now from the other, and sometimes indeed of lines produced by conflation.[1] Less than a quarter of the total number of lines are identical, syllable for syllable, in both MSS., and frequently there are points of divergence, not of reading only, but of order. More detailed comments on these will be found in the notes; here some examples may be noted.

There are two main sources of variation in order: the first depends on the structure of the complex or multiple sentence, the second is independent of it. In one MS. a main clause will be virtually complete before the adjuncts appear; in the other it will be interrupted by the adjuncts. As the reader's attention is kept in suspense for a moment, the second order is nearly always rhetorically more effective, e.g.:—

    C 197–9    He that seyth þat hit is ryght,
                    Be he squier other knyght,
                    Here my gloue on to fyght.
    L 197–9    Here my gloue with hym to fighte,
                    Be he sqwyare or knyghte,
                    Þat saise þat this es righte.
Also:
    L 1849–51    Of Almayne þe Emperour,
                    With wyrchip and honour,
                    He gaff hir at þe kyrk-dure.
    C 1849–51    And þe ryche Emperour
                    Gaff [hur] at þe kyrke-dore
                    With w[orshi]p and honour.

Cf. also 10–11, 78–9, 341–2, 550–1, 698–9, 1217–8, 1393–4, 1729–31, 1809–10, 1865–6, 1905–6, etc.

[1] In an experimental reconstruction of stanza LXXI in what I suppose to be the original metre and dialect, I found that the most satisfactory text was the result of taking lines 1 and 12 as they stood (practically identical in both MSS.); adopting lines 2, 4, 6, 7, 8, 13 and 16 from L; 5, 9, 10, 14 and 15 from C; and modifying 3 and 11. I have every reason to suppose that a theoretically reconstructed text of the whole poem would involve a similar procedure, though no doubt the proportion of lines contributed to any one stanza by each MS. would vary.

Catalogues of things are presented now in one order, now in another, e.g.:—

    L 42–3        Grewhundes for buk and bare,
                       For hert, hynde, and for hare.
    C 42–3        Grehondes for hert and hare,
                       Both for bokes and the bare.

Cf. also 38–9, 1030–1, 1414–5.

To decide which is the better of these readings is possible, if at all, only on the dangerously subjective basis of individual preference. When such a decision can be reached, the more effective readings are found sometimes in L, and sometimes in C. Neither MS. by itself provides a reliable basis for a text; constant reference must be made to the other.

5. Nevertheless, C provides a somewhat greater number of good readings, though it may be a later copy than L. It has two additional merits: it is more complete, and it shows fewer signs of having been mishandled by an editor. In L, the loss of 802–1008 is an unfortunate accident; but the omission of quatrains here and there is to be imputed to careless transmission. None of them is important to the narrative, but their presence in C helps to confirm the impression of that text's relative integrity.[1] The stanza that C omits (XI) has a function in the narrative: it conducts Sir Degrevant's squire with a letter to the Earl, and describes how the Earl was setting forth to the chase when the squire met him. It is presumably a version of the original; and (as I have argued below) the omission is probably scribal.

At this point, it will be convenient to anticipate the conclusions of Section VII, to unify the necessarily scattered materials of the foregoing Section, and to give as connected an account as the evidence will allow of what the textual history of the poem may have been. Much will necessarily be lacking to give completeness to it, and conjecture must take the place of certainty here and there. At the root of the genealogical tree we suppose the author's original (O) in his own hand, theoretically perfect and complete, but probably containing already a good deal of correction, as is the way of authors' MSS. A written copy (X) was made of this, omitting nothing, but incorporating at least some of the errors common to L and C (e.g., lines 336, 340, 392, 651, 657, 692, and possibly also 1030–1 and 1041). There is no reason to suppose the dialect of X to have been substantially different from that of O.

---

[1] It would be natural to assume that the omission of these quatrains was the accidental result of a reporter's forgetfulness. If so, it is very curious that each of them, as preserved in C, is either a textual crux or contains some exceptional verbal usage. 221–4 is difficult to construe (Luick's punctuation of the passage shows that he has been misled). It is also metrically anomalous, the tail line riming with the triplet lines on the sequence -*ent*. 297–300 contains the phrase *hepene heldus*, which again is easily misinterpreted. 652–6 is the main crux of the poem; two lines of it I have been unable to interpret at all, and the last line contains the word *glemyd* in an unusual sense, with an object. In 1189–92 the word *damysel* occurs in the sense of 'young man'; so far as I know it is not found elsewhere in English with this meaning, and is certainly not common. There may well be more than coincidence in this, and the quatrains may have been omitted because they were not understood. In general, omission is one of the chief characteristics of the reported text, and memorial transmission is the probable cause of it here, but in view of the signs of editorial tampering already observed in L, the possibility that these omissions are both deliberate and scribal must not be ruled out.

At X, the tradition divides into two branches, C and L, of which the various stages of C are more readily reconstructed. Nothing more is necessarily involved than to suppose that X was committed to memory and written out after an interval by a minstrel-scribe Z, who spoke a more southerly dialect with some western features. His text incorporates a number of new errors, but it is relatively intact, his memory being a good one. At least he omitted nothing. He recast the poem in his own dialect, but his MS. may have been illegible here and there, hence the errors in C 765, C 1187, C 1343, C 1885, and elsewhere. It is the immediate original of C, the work of two scribes at least. Jointly, they are responsible for a good deal of the superficial corruption, the textual untidiness, the bad spellings, the confusion of small words like *a*, *in*, *and*, and of different forms of the same word (e.g., the tail-rimes in stanza LIX). And the first of them, having turned over a new page and chosen a new pen, did not observe that two successive stanzas opened with the same words, and so carelessly omitted one (XI).

The L-tradition is more difficult to reconstruct, because we have to deal with several corrupting influences superimposed, and have no means of allocating responsibility for all of them, and even for every example of each one of them, to reporter and copyist. As before, X was committed to memory by a minstrel. He probably transmitted the poem to another of his kind, and the process may have been continued for several generations (in the textual sense). This is the most satisfactory way of accounting for most of the numerous periphrases, anticipations, recollections, upset rime schemes, inconsistencies, insertions of redundant words, and general literary dilution to be found on almost every page of L. On the other hand, the dialect forms were virtually unimpaired. At this stage, the quatrains not found in L may have dropped out, perhaps because they were forgotten, perhaps because in various ways they were thought to be difficult. After the process of dilution had continued for some time, it is to be expected that the text would have diverged very considerably from C, and it may once have contained a larger number of corrupt readings than it now does. Ultimately it was written down by a scribe Y, and this version was copied into the Thornton MS. by L. To these two, Y and L, must be given the credit for having done a considerable amount of tidying-up, since the L-version, in spite of its numerous deficiencies, is a remarkably clean text as we now have it, relatively free from the irritating blunders of C, and giving little trouble to an editor. But, as always happens when a text is emended by hit-or-miss methods, when attempting to set right a passage they did not understand, they sometimes emended away from the true reading rather than towards it, and the result was a series of new errors, e.g., L 651, L 1204, L 1446, L 1467, L 1519. In addition, L himself is responsible for all the purely copyist's errors, i.e., those which, so far as can be seen, are only one generation old, e.g., L 435, L 1101, L 1114–5.

The foregoing discussion is open to objection in one respect: it does not explain how the same MS. X was independently memorized by Y and Z (or Z's ancestor) speaking different dialects, and no doubt natives of different parts of England. It may therefore be necessary to postulate a copy of X (say P) which travelled southward to become the ancestor of all texts not in the L-tradition; but since the existence of such a MS. cannot be demonstrated from the texts as we have them, and at best depends upon extrinsic probability, I have forborne to include it. The following diagram represents the relation between C and L as deduced from the evidence already presented.

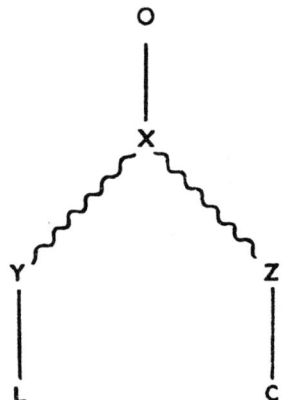

How far the textual history of our two MSS. can be of service to an editor in search of editorial principles is a very dubious question. In the sense that it enables him to decide between them and to choose one as a copy-text, our study has been of no service at all, since neither can be regarded as a consistently reliable witness to the original. Indeed, it has been partly to demonstrate this very point that so much attention has been given to its details. But the only possible conclusion to which it leads is not very helpful: on the whole C is the better text, though here and there L preserves readings that must be original.

Between the memorizing of a text and its final transcription, much can happen to it, for the tricks that a human memory can play are beyond the wit of man to number or to account for. A work related to its archetype by memorial transmission therefore offers great scope for emendation, but since in this case there is nothing to restrain, or to regulate, the editorial hand, the temptation has been resisted.

In the present edition, the texts have been printed side by side, with L on the left-hand page, and C on the right. In this way the different versions of the same passage, and something of the hazards of memorial transmission, can be seen at a glance. No change has been made in the text, even where the rime scheme of a stanza has been dislocated by the scribe's carelessness or the reciter's incompetence. These matters, together with suggestions of what the original may have been, are discussed in the notes following the text. Similarly, no emendation has been made on purely metrical grounds, even where the other MS. has, or points the way to, a more regular line. After much consideration, it has seemed better to preserve a halting line than to reconstruct a smooth one that deviates perhaps widely from the author's intention by an arbitrary change on doubtful MS. authority. In general, emendation has been resorted to only to correct some of the obvious scribal errors. Attention has been drawn to these by enclosing additions or substitutions in square brackets. The removal of a word or part of a word is designated by the sign †. The footnotes give the MS. forms, and items of palæographical interest.

# INTRODUCTION

The capitals of the MSS. and their system of word-division have been altered in conformity with modern usage. The MS. distinction between *u* and *v* has been retained, so also has consonantal *i*, both in compliance with former editorial practice. The punctuation is modern; words divided in the MS. have been joined by hyphens (e.g., *watur-wal* 923).

## IV. METRE

*Sir Degrevant* is written in a tail-rime stanza of sixteen lines, of which the rime-scheme is usually aaab, cccb, dddb, eeeb, as in *Sir Perceval, The Avowing of Arthur*, and the *Disputision bytwene a Cristenemon and a Jew* (Vernon MS. EETS. 117, pp. 484–493).[1] With few exceptions, the sense of each stanza is self-contained; each group of four lines (three triplet-lines and the tail) forms a sub-unit of the stanza, with little over-running. The poet has completely mastered his technique, and handles the stanza with freedom and vigour. His chief additional embellishments are alliteration (which requires a section to itself), modification of the stanza form, and an elaborate series of links between one stanza and the next.

Normally, the stanza requires five rimes, but the poet sometimes flourishes his skill by using only four. The effect of six words riming on one sound in a single stanza is an insistent, inexorable emphasis; the more so as the lines are short. The most common variations in stanza form are a repetition of the third group of triplet-rimes, i.e., aaab, cccb, dddb, dddb, as in stanzas LXII, LXIX, CI, CVIII, CIX; and a repetition of the rime sound of the first group of triplet-lines in the third group, i.e., aaab, cccb, aaab, dddb, as in stanzas XV, LXI, LXIV, LXVII, XCVIII. Less commonly, the rime of the second group of triplet-lines is repeated in the fourth group (i.e., aaab, cccb, dddb, cccb: stanzas XXVIII, LXXXV, CVI); the rime of the first group is repeated in the fourth group (i.e., aaab, cccb, dddb, aaab: stanzas XLIX, LXXVII, CX); the rime of the second group is repeated in the third (i.e., aaab, cccb, cccb, dddb: stanza LXXVI). Sometimes one of the rime-words is repeated as well.

There are two methods of connecting stanzas: what may be called the rime-link, i.e., the rime of one stanza is continued into the next; and the verbal link, i.e., a word or phrase from one line (often the last line) of a stanza is repeated in the first or second line of the next stanza.

Rime-links are of four types.

1. A triplet-rime sound in a stanza is continued in the tail-rime lines of the following stanza: I(3)–II[2]; VII(4)–VIII; XV(1 and 3)–XVI;

---

[1] The effect of the sixteen-line stanza is occasionally achieved in passages written in the more common eight-line form, by combining two stanzas in a common tail-rime (see *Ludus Coventriæ* [ed. Block, EETS.], pp. 26, 319–320).

[2] The symbols need explanation. I(3)–II means that the rime-sound of the third group of triplet-lines in stanza I is carried into the tail-rime of stanza II; CX(1)–CXI(3) means that the rime-sound of the first group of triplet-lines in stanza CX is repeated in the third group of triplet lines in stanza CXI, i.e., an arabic numeral following the roman refers to the triplet group; if no arabic numeral follows, the tail-rime is being referred to. In these lists assonance has not been considered, (though linking by assonance is not infrequent, e.g., XCV(1)–XCVI; CX(1 and 3)–CXI). On the other hand, sequences like *hight, knightes* (i.e., perfect rimes except for the inflexional ending) have been regarded as sufficient to provide a link; to disregard them would not alter the results substantially.

XVIII(4)–XIX; XXIV(1)–XXV; XXVI(2)–XXVII; XLV(1)–XLVI; LXVI(3)–LXVII; LXVIII(3)–LXIX; LXXXIII(2)–LXXXIV; XCVI(1)–XCVII; CXVII(1)–CXVIII; CXVIII(3)–CXIX: 13 examples.

2. A triplet-rime sound is continued in a group of triplet-lines in the following stanza: X(3)–XI(2)–XII(1)–XIII(2); XXVI(1)–XXVII(1); XXVIII(2 and 4)–XXIX(1); XXXIV(2)–XXXV(1); XXXIV(1)–XXXV(4); XLV(3)–XLVI(2); LII(4)–LIII(1); LIV(4)–LV(2); LVI(3)–LVII(3)–LVIII(4); LX(2)–LXI(1 and 3); LXII(3 and 4)–LXIII(1); LXV(4)–LXVI(1); LXXIV(2)–LXXV(2); LXXVII(2)–LXXVIII(4)–LXXIX(1)–LXXX(3); LXXXII(2)–LXXXIII(2); LXXXIV(2)–LXXXV(2)–LXXXVI(3); XC(4)–XCI(1); XCIII(1)–XCIV(2); XCVIII(1 and 3)–XCIX(1)–C(2)–CI(3 and 4)–CII(1)–CIII(3); CX(1)–CXI(3); CXI(4)–CXII(1); CXII(2)–CXIII(3); CXIV(4)–CXV(2); CXV(3 and 4)–CXVI(2 and 4)–CXVII(1): 35 examples.

3. A tail-rime sound is continued in a triplet-rime group of the following stanza: III–IV(1); XVII–XVIII(1); XXV–XXVI(2); XXXII–XXXIII(3); XXXVI–XXXVII(4); XLIV–XLV(1); XLVIII–XLIX(1); LI–LII(1); LIX–LX(3); LXXVII–LXXVIII(1); LXXXIX–XC(3); XCI–XCII(3); XCVII–XCVIII(1); CIX–CX(1): 14 examples.

4. The tail-rime sound is continued in the tail-rimes of the following stanza: XXXI–XXXII; XLII–XLIII–XLIV; LIV–LV; LXXXII–LXXXIII: 5 examples.

In this series of linkages about ninety stanzas, or three-quarters of the poem, are involved. Some stanzas (XXXIV–XXXV; XLV–XLVI; LIV–LV) are linked by two methods and therefore fall into two of the above classes; other stanzas form groups (e.g., XCVII–CII; CXIV–CXIX), each linked to its neighbour by one method or another. An example will show its application. In stanza LXXXII the tail-rime vowel is -a (*twa, swa,* etc.); it is continued into LXXXIII (*maa, gaa,* etc.), thus connecting the two stanzas. The second triplet-rime sequence in LXXXIII is -ide (*pryde, ryde, syde*), which is continued into the tail-rime of LXXXIV (*tyde, abyde,* etc.). The second triplet-rime sequence in LXXXIV is -ight (*hight, knyght,* etc.); it is also the second and fourth triplet rime-sequence of LXXXV, and the third triplet-rime sequence of LXXXVI. The five stanzas LXXXII–LXXXVI are linked together like a chain.

So far as can be determined, the poet uses this embellishment or ignores it at will; it is therefore to be regarded as an ingenious technical device adopted with a view to emphasizing the continuous flow of the action. Viewed in this way, it is neither unpleasing nor obtrusive: the most that the casual reader is conscious of is a certain lack of variety in the rime-sounds. Unlike the intricate and rigid system in the *Pearl*, it is not an integral part of the verse-structure. Indeed, it comes easily and naturally to the author of *Sir Degrevant*, and is brought about by means so simple as to be almost naïve. One of the most useful and the most often drawn upon is the rime-sequence -ight, owing to the large number of Middle English words that it contains.

Verbal linkings are a more occasional form of ornament. Moreover, they are far less pervasive in *Sir Degrevant* than in other Middle English verse tales, notably *Sir Perceval*, where they serve to join almost every stanza to the previous one.

This characteristic of certain Middle English poems was first pointed out by M. P. Medary,[1] on whose conclusions the following remarks are based, but I have preferred to state them in my own way, as the results need correction here and there. Purely verbal stanza-links are found also in *Sir Tristrem*, *The Avowing of Arthur*, *The Awntyrs of Arthur*, in the poems of Laurence Minot and Thomas of Erceldoune, and more occasionally in *The Buke of the Howlat*, *Rauf Coilȝear*, and the *York Plays*. The device appears to have been a particular favourite in the north. Four types of verbal link are distinguished.

1. Repetition of a phrase from the last line of a stanza in the first line of the next.
2. Repetition of a single word in the same circumstances.
3. Repetition of "related words", i.e., different inflexional forms of the same word, or the same inflexional syllable attached to different words.
4. Repetition of a word taken from the penultimate line of a stanza in the first or second line of the next.

Miss Medary finds certain stanzas of *Sir Degrevant* linked together in one or other of these ways. In the article referred to, the numbers of the stanzas are quoted, but not the actual words forming the link. These I have added, transferring from group 3 to group 2 some wrongly classified examples. I have also added comments.

1. (i) XXX–XXXI, cheue how hit; (ii) XLVIII–XLIX, My trouthe I þe plyghte; (iii) LI–LII, met schare; (iv) XCVII–XCVIII, And trouthes plyghte.

   As (ii)–(iv) also involve the rime, they have already been noted in group 3 above.

2. (i) VII–VIII, he; (ii) XXI–XXII, and (not in MS. L); (iii) XLI–XLII, hir; (iv) XLII–XLIII, that; (v) LXVIII–LXIX, was; (vi) LXXV–LXXVI, And; (vii) LXXX–LXXXI, stedes; (viii) CX–CXI, cryid (not in MS. L).

3. (i) IV–V, he, his; (ii) VI–VII, he, him (not in MS. L); (iii) XVI–XVII, lordes, hertes; (iv) XL–XLI, hyr, sche.

4. (i) IX–X, his, were (only *were* in MS. L); (ii) XVIII–XIX, þay; (iii) XXXI–XXXII, I; (iv) XXXIII–XXXIV, love; (v) XLIII–XLIV, Degreuant; (vi) LII–LIII, ysperyd; (vii) LXI–LXII, chartur; (viii) LXII–LXIII, ryng; (ix) LXIV–LXV, the; (x) LXVII–LXVIII, he; (xi) XC–XCI, chaumbur of loue; (xii) CI–CII, hym; (xiii) CVI–CVII, hore (not in MS. L); (xiv) CXI–CXII, bryght; (xv) CXIII–CXIV, ȝorl (not in MS. L); (xvi) CXV–CXVI, I.

It may be doubted whether most of this is of much consequence. The more striking examples (4 (vi), (viii), (xi) and (xiv) ) involve the rime, and have already been classified as rime-links. But the remaining connecting

---

[1] M. P. Medary, *Stanza Linking in Middle English Verse*, Romanic Review, Vol. VII, No. 3. As the author has worked with Halliwell's edition of the poem (which omits stanza XI from the text) it has been necessary to correct the numbering of all stanzas after X.

links consist for the most part of unimportant words like *the, and,* and pronouns. The possibility of the author's having contrived stanza linking after so tenuous a fashion is not denied. But such linking, if deliberate, cannot be anything more than an incidental ornament, subsidiary in interest and significance to the rime-links. The rhetorical and poetic value of such an artifice is negligible.

How the lines of the poem should be scanned is a question that has been debated by those who have written on ME. prosody generally, and specially on the nature of the alliterative line, with which the triplet and the tail-rime line combined are related.

There are three kinds of opinion, sharply divided. The first, represented by Saintsbury,[1] regards the triplet-lines as generally containing six syllables 'with considerable bulgings', and the tail-rime lines as being always 'pretty exactly sixes'.

He scans as follows:—

    The knyth / hoves in / the feld
    Bothe weth / ax and / with sheld;
    The eorl/us dough/dere beheld
        That / borlich / and bolde—
    ffor he / was ar/med so clene,
    With gold / azoure / full schene,
    And with / his trewe/loves betweene
        Was / joy to / behold.

Saintsbury finds little prosodic interest in this, or in any other metrical romance. His conclusion is perhaps natural for one who is sceptical about any conception of continuity in the tradition of English verse rhythms after the Conquest. But exactly for this reason, he is not a sure guide. In the first place, little, if any, insight is gained into the versification of *Sir Degrevant* by counting syllables. Secondly, legitimate exception may be taken to his discussing *Sir Degrevant* and *Libeaus Desconus* together, and ignoring what seems to the present writer to be the fundamental difference in the run of the lines: in *Libeaus Desconus* they are pretty evenly weighted throughout, whereas in *Sir Degrevant* the triplet-lines at least have more weight at the end. Throughout the poem, the tendency seems to be to begin the line with unimportant words, and to end with those of full and distinct meaning, a characteristic which inevitably affects the rhythm.

Of the second variety of opinion, the best representative is Kaluza, whose *Short History of English Versification*[2] provides a useful exposition of his own views and a summary of those of other (mainly German) metrists. He derives the ME. alliterative line from the septenary, and scans it with seven beats, four in the first half and three in the second. He is thus in general agreement with Trautmann, and with Kuhnke, Menniken, and Fischer,[3]

[1] G. Saintsbury, *History of English Prosody* (London, Second edition 1923), Vol. I, pp. 97–8.

[2] M. Kaluza, *A Short History of English Versification* (trans. A. C. Dunstan, London, 1911), §§156–179.

[3] M. Trautmann, *Zur Kenntnis und Geschichte der mittelenglischen Stabzeile* (Anglia XVIII, p. 83); B. Kuhnke, *Die alliterierende Langzeile in der mittelenglischen Romanze Sir Gawayn and the Green Knight* (Berlin, 1900); F. Menniken, *Versbau und Sprache in Huchown's Morte Arthure* (Bonn, 1900); J. Fischer, *Die stabende Langzeile in den Werken des Gawaindichters* (Darmstadt, 1900).

who have applied Trautmann's views in detail to individual poems. The beats are not all of the same value: some are strong, and some weak. Sometimes a single word will take two beats; it then forms 'a foot of two members' (Kaluza, *op. cit.*, p. 200). Kaluza applies this system to *Sir Degrevant*, scanning as follows (p. 231):—

/ With king / Ártòur y / wene
/ And with / Gwénnòur þe / quene
/ He was / knówèn for / kene
That / cómelìche / knight.
In / héthenèsse / and in / Spaine,
In / Fráuncè and / in Brit/taine,
With / Pércevalle / and Ga/waine
For / hérdỳ and / wight
/ He was / dóughtỳ and / dere
/ and ther / névèw full / nere
Ther / he of / dedis / might y/here
Be dayes / or be / night.
For/thy they / name / hem that / stounde,
A / knight / of the / tabull / rounde,
As / maked is / in the mappe/mounde
In / stóryè full / right.

This does not seem satisfactory: it is hard to see how the weak syllables of words like *herdy, doughty*, can take even a secondary accent: and to regard collocations of unstressed syllables like *he of, or be, in þe* (see also p. 202) as feet exaggerates their importance. In any case, the seven-beat theory has lost much of the esteem in which it was formerly held, in England at least.[1]

The third opinion is represented by Luick,[2] who, in spite of opposition, tenaciously held to the traditional two-lift theory (derived ultimately from Sievers and Schipper[3]) for half-lines of ME. alliterative verse. In *Zur mittelenglischen Verslehre* he applied this theory in detail to the scansion of *The Avowing of Arthur*, showing the correspondence between the triplet-lines and the first half of the ME. alliterative line, and between the tail-rime lines and the second half-line.

His consistent advocacy of the two-lift theory in explaining the metre of *The Avowing* led him to some questionable statements[4] that impair the value of an otherwise useful article. The theory does explain the essential continuity of alliterative verse in OE. and ME. as, in the view of most

[1] The most able exposition of it is found in K. D. Bülbring's *Untersuchungen zur mittelenglischen Metrik*, Morsbach's Studien zur englischen Philologie, Heft 50, Halle 1913.

[2] Luick's most important article for its bearing on *Sir Degrevant* is *Zur mittelenglischen Verslehre* (Anglia XXXVII); but see also the same author's *Die englische Stabreimzeile in XIV, XV, und XVI Jahrhundert* (Anglia XI, two parts); *Zur Metrik der mittelenglischen reimendalliterierenden Dichtung* (Anglia XII); and his review of the work of Kuhnke, Menniken, and Fischer (Beiblatt zur Anglia, XII).

[3] It was Schipper who first pointed out how the lines of *Sir Degrevant, Sir Perceval* and *The Avowing of Arthur* corresponded with those of ME. alliterative verse (*Englische Metrik* I. 218).

[4] Particularly, his assumption that reduction of stress takes place in lines containing three important and alliterating words (see Anglia XXXVIII, p. 283, etc.). Similar assertions in Luick's earlier articles had been challenged by Kaluza (*op. cit.*, p. 195).

scholars at least, the half-line in OE. had only two lifts. Whether it adequately explains the metre of *Sir Degrevant* will be part of the purpose of this section to determine.

Finsterbusch applied Luick's ideas with great diligence to the two remaining poems in the group, *Sir Perceval* and *Sir Degrevant*,[1] and came to the same general conclusions. It will be convenient to begin by summarizing them, and to defer comment until exposition is complete. In the first instance, they are based upon those lines in *Sir Degrevant* which, syllable for syllable, are either identical or metrically equivalent in the two MSS. Lines for which they offer divergent readings are separately considered, but are found to belong to the same rhythmic types as the rest, though a line in one MS. does not necessarily belong to the same type as the corresponding line in the other.[2]

In estimating the number of syllables in thesis, he assumes (and rightly) that final inflexional *-e* is not pronounced. The rimes *hilled, felde* (1201–1202), *ground, swouned* (1125–1126, 1329–1330), *y-speryd, afferyd, berd* (833–5) and others to the same effect, show that the inflexional *-ed* can have had no weight as a separate syllable after *l, n, r*.[3] The rhythmic types are as follows:—

TAIL-RIMES[4]

*Type I*

There are two lifts with an intervening dip of two or three syllables; the first lift is usually preceded and the second lift may be followed by an unstressed syllable, i.e., (x) / x x (x) / (x). This is by far the commonest type, and five-sixths of the textually identical or metrically equivalent lines belong to it.

*Examples:*—76, Lyard and soore; 128, And went on hys wey; 308, And lames þe ledes; 1876, Was seruyd in þat sale.

The dip of three syllables is not often found.

*Type II*

The two lifts occur in succession at the end of the line; they are preceded by a dip of two or three syllables, and may be followed by a single unstressed syllable, i.e., (x) x x / / (x).

*Examples:*—60, Was hys most glew; 148, Of his own store; 728, I shal a-non-ry3th; 1484, With here bry3t brondus.

*Type III*

The two lifts are separated by a single unstressed syllable; the first lift is preceded by a dip of two or three syllables, i.e., (x) x x / x /.

*Examples:*—488, That he hath don a-wey; 1040, He shal haue inow; 1604, And non oþur mede.

This type is uncommon.

A few lines have only one naturally strong accent, the second consisting of a less important word at the end of a line. As this is a rime-word, it can carry increased stress without undue distortion, e.g., 1114, So hardy was he.

[1] F. Finsterbusch, *Der Versbau der mittelenglischen Dichtungen Sir Perceval of Gales und Sir Degrevant* (Wiener Beiträge XLIX, Vienna and Leipzig 1919).

[2] Finsterbusch, *op. cit.*, pp. 99–102, 161–169.

[3] *Op. cit.*, p. 80.

[4] *Op. cit.*, pp. 75–106.

A few lines have an introductory dip of two syllables, but rhythmically they (together with 1144 and others like it) belong to Type I, e.g., 1156, o þe castel gan fare.

TRIPLET-LINES.¹

### Type I

In this class are put all lines with two lifts, one in the middle, one taking the rime at the end. They are separated by a dip of two (rarely three, still more rarely four) unstressed syllables. The first lift is preceded by a dip of two (three, or four) unstressed syllables, and the second lift may be followed by a single unstressed syllable. The simplest and commonest rhythmic formula is x x / x x /, but modifications may occur. In its most general form, it is (xx) x x / (xx) x x / (x), but lines containing as many as eleven syllables are not found. Three-fifths of the lines identical or metrically equivalent in both MSS. fall into this class.

*Examples:*—58, Both wyt horne and with hound (*very common*); 63, Bot as an anker in a ston; 1009, Þe Duk ys comen ouer þe see (*rare*); 1039, Whedur he wol tornay or fyȝth; 1295, ȝet wold I sett all on seuen.

Exceptionally, a medial dip of a single syllable is found; it then undergoes lengthening, according to principles expounded hereafter.

*Examples:*—533, She is ware and wyse; 635, Tyll the day wex clere.²

### Type II

There are three natural accents, the first of which undergoes reduction of stress, becoming a dip. The two lifts come in succession at the end of the line. Between the first (reduced) natural accent and the lift there is a medial thesis. This usually consists of two or three unstressed syllables; more rarely only one syllable is found, and on occasion even that is dispensed with. The first naturally accented word may be preceded by an anacrusis. The rhythmic formula is (x) \ (xxx) / /, where \ stands for the first natural accent.

*Examples:*—607, And spek with þat byrde bryȝth; 1395, Fagattus of fyre-tre; 1511, Þat was mad in West-fal; 1726, Þer þe dede men lay.

### Type III

There are two natural lifts, the first at the beginning, the second at the end. An anacrusis of one syllable (rarely more) may precede the first, and an unstressed syllable may follow the second. Several syllables lie between the two lifts. The line is split up into two by means of a pause disposed in such a way that the first half-line corresponds to the second half of lines in Type II, and the second half-line is identical with the first half of lines in Type I.³ The rhythmic formula is (x) / x x ∧ x x / (x), where the two syllables after the first lift replace the second lift in Type II. About one-tenth of the identical or metrically equivalent lines are of Type III.

*Examples:*—333, Þe beste men ∧ þat he hade; 605, Sertanely ∧ þis ilke nyghte; L1475, Þe recheste ∧ þat euer wasse; 1559, Wete ȝe wele, ∧ or þay were wed.⁴

¹ *Op. cit.*, p. 106 ff.
² *Op. cit.*, pp. 106–123, 138.
³ Finsterbusch's explanation of lines of this type is not very full. That given above is the result of combining his remarks on pp. 64, 131-2, with those of Luick (*Verslehre*, p. 333).
⁴ Finsterbusch, *op. cit.*, pp. 131–135.

In order to show how a line of three important and normally stressed words will fit a rhythmic scheme of only two lifts, Finsterbusch explains how the stress on one such word is reduced. Words normally carrying full stress may undergo reduction of stress if they have an auxiliary function in the line (e.g., adjectives preceding nouns, unimportant verbs without full and developed meaning, nouns in apposition to proper names, and the second elements of compounds). A verb of full meaning is subordinated in stress to its grammatical object, as in 40:—

He wane þe pryse aye,

especially if verb and object are combined in a formal collocation. A word introducing an idea already expressed in the immediate context undergoes reduction of stress.

The formula 'he (or she) said' followed by the speaker's actual words is not counted at all if its retention will over-weight the introductory dip, on the ground, presumably, that its rhetorical importance is subordinate to what follows.[1] These principles lead Finsterbusch to conclude, as Luick had concluded before him, that all types of tail-rime line and triplet-line have two lifts and no more, asserting that one word in a line containing three strongly stressed words undergoes reduction of stress, e.g., in 59, To brynge þe dere to þe grounde; 333, Þe beste men þat he hade; *brynge* and *men* are in thesis. The difference between the tail-rime line and the triplet-line is that the tail-rime lines, with the exception of the uncommon Type III, have one dip, the triplet-lines have two.[2]

Medial dips usually consist of two syllables, less usually of three. Exceptionally, only one syllable is found.[3] It is then held to be capable of being lengthened (dehnbar),[4] and of thus doing duty for the normal two

---

[1] A more cogent argument (though it is not used) would be to claim that this formula is no necessary part of the poet's technique; like writers of ballads, he can handle speeches, and even a rapid interchange of dialogue, without it. A speaker's words are introduced without formula in 221, 483, 529, 718, 739, 781, 790 (C 789), 873, 893, 929, 937, 957, 962, 965, 979, 981, 995, 1033, 1189, 1222, 1365, 1393, 1703, 1758, 1789. In addition, one MS. dispenses with the formula (the other unnecessarily inserting it) in C 801, C 1385, L 1746, C 1813. Hence it may not be original even in some cases where both MSS. agree in having it, e.g., 381, 422, 561, 693, 753, 955, 1315, 1325.

[2] *Op. cit.*, p. 138.

[3] For example, in 209, 533, 645, 1659, 1731.

[4] As Finsterbusch's account of the meaning of *dehnbar* is very meagre, reference must be made to Luick's article *Zur mittelenglischen Verslehre* (Anglia 38, pp. 294–6) and expecially the following:—'Steht an stelle der sonst üblichen zwei senkungssilben nur *eine*, so wird sie etwas gedehnt und dafür eignen sich, wie im Neuenglischen, silben mit natürlichem akzent besser als leichte, wofern sie nur bei natürlicher artikulation den sie umgebenden starktönen etwas nachstehen. Mit vorliebe verwendet daher der dichter in diesem falle vollwörter, in zweiter linie auch leichte selbständige wörter wie *and, not, might*, die immerhin noch eine gewisse dehnung zulassen, oder auch wortausgänge mit vollvokal wie -*ly*, für die dasselbe gilt . . . Ganz schwachen silben wären kaum auf jenes mass zu dehnen gewesen, welches zur befreidigung des rhythmischen gefühls des dichters notwendig war.'

Lascelles Abercrombie (*Principles of English Prosody*, p. 23) showing how the quantity of a syllable may occasionally follow the requirements of accent, concedes the same possibility: 'If . . . a monosyllable occurs as the equivalent of a disyllable, its prominence is decided by its accent, but its equivalence will probably be assisted by its length or by an easily imposed lengthening.' He does not imply that unstressed syllables of the order of *and, not, -ly* are capable of being lengthened.

syllables. All kinds of words and syllables apparently have this property with the exception of inflexional *-ed, en, -es*. On the other hand a word in this position suffers reduction of accent if it is normally stressed, e.g.:— 373, When þe Erle come home: 1120, To do swylke dedis.

The statistics of Finsterbusch show that the rhythm of Type I of both tail-rime and triplet-lines (essentially the same rising rhythm, with a general anapæstic movement) prevails in the poem. Both he and Luick claim that some at least of the rhythms are found in ME. unrimed alliterative poetry of the period of the revival. There is, however, an important difference, which neither scholar has pointed out. In the language of the *Sir Degrevant* group of poems, owing to the loss of final inflexional *-e*, the majority of the lines end on a rising rhythm, whereas alliterative poets preferred falling rhythm at the end of the line. The characteristic ending with / x, very common indeed in all poems of the alliterative revival, whether final *-e* has syllabic value or not, is comparatively rare in the tail-rimes of *Sir Degrevant*; while the ending x /, common in both tail-rime and triplet-lines in *Sir Degrevant*, is not often found in unrimed alliterative poetry.[1] With this reservation, a more detailed comparison may be proceeded with.

TAIL-RIME LINES

Type I in *Sir Degrevant* corresponds most closely with the second half-line of alliterative verse when it is in a rising-falling rhythm, ending with an unaccented syllable; e.g., 340, To dethe he tham denges; 396, Hym and xij knythus; C 680, Ladyes and kny3ttus.

This kind of ending is not common in *Sir Degrevant*, but it abounds in contemporary alliterative poetry; e.g., *Purity* 1547, cerues þo for3es; *William of Palerne* 4734, & deedes of armes; *Parlement of Thre Ages* 205, And prouen my strengthes; *Patience* 405, & laften her synnes.

Type I more commonly ends in rising rhythm; e.g., 4, And gestis to fede; 116, Þe sothe for to saye.

Line-endings of this kind are not often met with in unrimed alliterative verse, but they do occur; e.g., *William of Palerne* 4403, for-giue me þis gelt; *Gawain* 644, in melly wat3 stad; *Sege of Jerusalem* 19, hasted he no3t; *Sege of Jerusalem* 462, was craftily ywro3t.

Similarly with *Type II*, the distinguishing characteristic of which is its clashing rhythm. Such tail-rime lines are not common in *Sir Degrevant* whether ending in a weak syllable or not.[2] On the other hand, clashing rhythm is very common in alliterative verse; e.g., *Gawain* 37, vpon Krystmasse; *Gawain* 609, wyth þe best gemme3; *Destr. Troy* 2332, & of grem bryng; *Patience* 401, of oure layth synnes.

Type III is the rarest in *Sir Degrevant*,[3] but again is not uncommon in alliterative poetry; e.g., *Gawain* 692, Þa3 hym no gomen þo3t; *Parlement of Thre Ages* 32, and of body grete; *William of Palerne* 957, 3if þe likes sone; *William of Palerne* 1004, & al middel erþe.

[1] J. P. Oakden, *Alliterative Poetry in Middle English*, Vol. I, 176, regards it as rare in second half-lines.

[2] Finsterbusch enumerates thirty-one examples from the identical or metrically equivalent lines; thirteen more can be found in each MS. amongst the remainder; while L has two (52, 1644), the corresponding lines in C belong to Type I.

[3] About fourteen examples in the whole poem.

## TRIPLET-LINES

*Type I* lines in rising rhythm are usual in *Sir Degrevant* and plentiful in the first half-lines of alliterative verse. It is here that correspondence is closest; e.g., *Gawain* 74, Whene Guenore ful gay; *Gawain* 114, Þise were diȝt on þe des; *Patience* 437, Þer he busked hym a bour; *Patience* 445, When þe dawande day; *Sege of Jerusalem* 787, Made wedes of wolle.

Type II lines are in clashing rhythm, and are very rare[1] in the first half-lines of alliterative verse, though, as we have seen, common enough in the second half-lines. The reduction of stress postulated as the characteristic of this type does not seem to have been practised by alliterative poets.

Similarly with Type III, which Luick himself recognises is not easily paralleled in ME. alliterative verse, owing to its medial pause.[2] One may go further. Neither Luick nor Finsterbusch makes it clear how the composite Type III, made up of the second half of Type II and the first half of Type II, comes into being, nor why the order of its components should be what it is.

We may conclude that with the exception of the Type I triplet-lines, the alliterative rhythms were used by the author of *Sir Degrevant* with some differences: the commonest rhythms in the poem not being those most often found in alliterative verse generally, it is possible to give undue weight to the connexion between them, real though it be.

The criterion that Finsterbusch employs to determine which syllable, if any, is to undergo reduction of stress is that of 'natural speech'; but whether by this he means natural speech in ME. or in ModE. he does not say. The speech rhythms of modern times are often a sure guide to the scansion of alliterative poetry, and of verse like that of *Sir Perceval* and *Sir Degrevant*, which is immediately derived from it. But Finsterbusch seems to assume identity, and scans accordingly. For example, he allocates the line—1480, Owt of sere landus—to Type I, *sere* undergoing reduction of stress; on the assumption, apparently, that it is of less rhetorical importance than the noun that follows it and bears the rime. The objection to this is that in unrimed ME. alliterative poetry, which should be a surer guide than the speech rhythms (real or alleged) of ModE., in a phrase consisting of adjective + noun, the adjective will usually bear the alliteration; and when the initial sounds are different, it must very often bear the stress as well; e.g., In notyng of nwe metes & of nice gettes (*Purity* 1354). Not all adjectives conform to this rule, but *sere* invariably does; e.g., & sette a sakerfyse þer-on of vch a ser kynde (*Purity* 507).[3] Since the tail-rime line (1479) immediately preceding that under discussion alliterates on *s*, a normal and complete alliterative line is produced by writing them together—Kynggus syttyng in þer sete out of sere londus—the second half of which is stressed on the adjective and the noun. It must therefore be regarded as Type II.

Some exception can be taken to his treatment of the triplet-lines; he has not always seen how closely Types I and II approach one another when he employs the principles of stress reduction and lengthening to explain how each verse has only two lifts; e.g., 635, Till þe day wex clere, is regarded as an exceptional form of Type I, with a medial dip of one syllable, which undergoes lengthening. On the other hand, 1726, Whare þe ded men laye,

---

[1] Oaken, *op. cit.*, p. 176.
[2] *Zur mittelenglischen Verslehre*, p. 338.
[3] See also *Purity* 358; *Patience* 12; *Destr. Troy* 1413, etc.

almost identical in rhythm, is relegated to Type II, *ded* undergoing reduction of stress. In the following triplet-lines—66, A hundrethe pondis worthe of londe; 678, Thay wesche and went to þe sete—both belonging to Type I, the principles of stress-reduction must be invoked to remove the accents from *hundrethe*, *worth*, and *went*, each quite an important word in its way. *Went* is parallel in construction to *wesche* and alliterates with it.

In short, the principles of stress-reduction cannot be rigorously applied to these lines,[1] and must be modified when their application conflicts with rhythm and sense. However useful the two-lift theory (to establish which stress-reduction must be freely employed) may be in accounting for the rhythms of the greater part of *Sir Degrevant*, it cannot be employed as a kind of Procrustes' bed, every line in the poem being cut to fit, whatever its natural rhythm may be. To combine with rime a line, or half-line, deriving from the alliterative metre must inevitably affect its rhythm, by attracting a greater weight of emphasis to the end, especially if, as often happens, the rime-word also bears the alliteration. Such a combination will lighten the earlier part of the line: words that in unrimed alliterative verse bear the stress may lose part of it if they are not rimed. This effect has not been allowed for either by Luick or Finsterbusch. Again, in such works as are included in *Scottish Alliterative Poems* (ed. F. J. Amours, STS., 1897), all of which are rimed, lines with more than four alliterating syllables are common.[2] They are also found occasionally in unrimed alliterative poetry There seems no reason why they should not also occur in *Sir Degrevant,* though neither Luick nor Finsterbusch has considered this possibility. It is therefore expedient to admit the possibility of secondary stresses on such lines as: 6, Þare solde men herken and here; 1147, Þe doghtty knyght in þe grene; 1561, Þan spake þe bird bryghte; and of three lifts on: 7, Of beryns þat by-fore were; 45, Fell faukons and fayr; 75, Stedis stabillede in stallis; 287, Wyghtly wepenes þey weld; 1125, Þe Duk dotered to þe ground; 1193, Take for aythir of vs a spere, and many others. Such an admission would be quite in keeping with what is found in ME. unrimed alliterative verse, where first half-lines with three lifts are common enough, and second half-lines, though rare, are not unknown.

To carry analysis any further is scarcely possible, nor would it be profitable, in view of the present state of the texts, and what has been inferred regarding their transmission. As only three tail-rime poems that combine rime with the alliterative long line have survived, it seems likely that the author of *Sir Degrevant* was attempting a metrical experiment; and not being a first-rate craftsman, he allows us to become aware of difficulties imperfectly surmounted. As he chose a form of the tail-rime stanza, he must have been familiar with some at least of the other tail-rime romances, those that had a regular iambic beat. The not infrequent iambic lines in *Sir Degrevant* may be the result of some such influence. It seems more natural to account for them in this way than to try to force them into uneasy conformity with the Types of Luick and Finsterbusch. Those that have the authority of both MSS., e.g., 1559, Wete ʒe wele, or þay were wed,[3] are to be ascribed to the author with more show of probability than those found only in C,[4] which may owe their present form to the transmission.

[1] And others that could be quoted to the same effect (see 46, 601, 1476, 1511).
[2] For a table of metrical statistics, see Amours's Introduction, p. lxxxiii.
[3] See also 601, 762, 1026, 1028, 1383, 1660, 1887.
[4] For example, C 82, C 303, C 393, C 699.

## V. ALLITERATION

The author of *Sir Degrevant* has employed alliteration much more freely than most writers of romance in which it is only an inessential ornament. He has alliterated more than a third of his poem, and the remarks that follow in this section refer mainly to this third. The greater part of it is alliterated like the half-lines of unrimed alliterative poetry, i.e., there are two principal staves, forming the lifts. Many of the lines alliterated in this way consist of or contain the phrases widespread in ME. poetry (*For soth Y you say* 116, 436; *houed and by-held* 329, 1255; *see with syȝth* 606, 760, etc., etc.), but often enough, like any other poet, he is his own phrase-maker. Most of the alliterating sounds occur at the beginnings of words, though occasionally an alliterating syllable has an unstressed prefix (e.g., 47, 703, 1048, C 1500). There is a good deal of what appears to be deliberate alliteration of stressed and unstressed syllables (e.g., L 104, C 360, 1099, 1268, 1312, 1400, 1695, 1724), but as the author's alliteration is not essential to the verse, it cannot be presumed *a priori*, and it is difficult to be sure that the device was cultivated as often as it is suspected. For the same reason, it is impossible to compile statistical tables showing the incidence of alliteration.

Three points may be noted in connexion with the alliteration of *w*: (i) *w* nearly always alliterates with itself (204, 212, 439, 440, 449, 1887, 1888, etc.); (ii) it does not habitually alliterate with *wh*: the only example found (1523) is dubious, as the *wh* is unstressed; (iii) alliteration of *w* and *v* in C 592 may be of dialectal significance (cf. Wyld, *Coll. Eng.*, p. 292).

Not infrequently, three strongly stressed alliterating words are found in a single line, showing clearly (as has been said already) that some lines have three lifts, and also that the poet consciously varied his methods. Examples are:—34, L 43, C 45, L75, C 110, 287, C 297, C 309, 322, 323, 338, L 406, C 510, 517, 523, 591, C 1103, 1106, 1114, C 1115, 1138, 1149, 1381, 1418, 1459, 1499, 1559, 1626, 1634, C 1722, and possibly 1523.

Another, and more important, characteristic of the author's use of alliteration is his habit of linking two or more consecutive lines with the same alliterating sound, e.g.:—

  L 405-6 Sir Degreuant, þat hende knyght,
       With heghte helmys on hyghte
  41-2  Oþer gammenes he louede mare:
       Grewhundes for buk and bare.

Two-thirds of the lines connected by continuous alliteration consist of the last triplet-line of a group and the following tail-rime. Since the triplet-line corresponds metrically to the first half and the tail-rime to the second half of the unrimed alliterative line, an approximation to such a line is produced when the alliteration is continuous through both of them. It is often a reasonably correct one, having four lifts, three alliterating syllables, and medial pause, e.g.:—

  1395-6 Fagotes of fyr-tree . fett you vs ȝare,

with the important difference alluded to: owing to the loss of final *-e*, all such composites end in rising rhythm. But as the distribution of pairs of lines continuously alliterated is usually as described, and as the resulting alliterating type aa/ax is one of the commonest, the author probably had the older verse in his mind as he wrote. Variants of the type often found in alliterative poetry, xa/ax, ax/ax, occur also in *Sir Degrevant*, though infrequently (four times each).

Other alliterative types in the poem deviate more or less widely from normal alliterative practice: thus aa/bb, aa/aa, usually either avoided or rare, are here among the commonest (17 examples; 7 examples). But deviation is most apparent in the large variety of unorthodox or rarely used types such as aax/ax, aax/bb, aax/aa, axx/aa, aba/bb, or ab/ab. Many of these are used only once each, but their diversity is so great as to suggest the conclusion that the author knew contemporary alliterative poetry and was deliberately experimenting with it in a conscious effort to see how far its rhythms and its alliteration would combine with rime.

Sometimes a common alliterating sound links three lines together (82–4, 275–7, 1195–7, 1394–6, 1519–21, 1834–6), four lines (1058–61, 1402–5, 1453–6), or even five lines (1635–9).

The following list gives details of the alliterative types produced by combining the last triplet-line of a group with the tail-rime line when the two are in continuous or double alliteration.

*aa/ax:*  3–4, 83–4, 159–60, 439–40, 611–2, 647–8, 855–6, 931–2, 1139–40, 1395–6, 1403–4, 1479–80, 1495–6, 1555–6, 1591–2, L 1635–6, 1707–8, 1919–20 (17 examples).

*aa/xa:*  C 615–6, 739–40, C 775–6, C 1227–8, 1295–6 (5 examples).
*Example:*
1295–6  I sold haf sett all on seuen ffor Mildor þe swete.

*aa/aa:*  19–20, 255–6, 339–40, C 839–40, 1339–40, C 1411–2, 1443–4 (7 examples).
*Example:—*
19–20  He was knawen for kene, þis commly knyghte.

*aax/aa:*  15–6, 1655–6 (2 examples).
*Example:—*
1655–6  Þe stede strak ouer þe force, and strayed on straye.

*aaa/ax:*  295–6, C 323–4, 563–4, 1311–2 (4 examples).
*Example:—*
295–6  Gleves gleteryng glent opon geldene scheldus.

*aax/ax:*  L 519–20 (1 example):—
Grete geddis i-nowe  gate he vn-talde.

*aaa/aa:*  C 1115–6 only:—
Bryȝthe browus and b[r]ent brodelyche bledus.

*aaa/xa:*  L 1383–4 only:—
Sexty sythes, are he stynt, he kyssed þat swete.

*ax/aa:*  C 1415–6, C 1447–8, C 1509–10, 1751–2, 1779–80, 1835–6 (6 examples).
*Example:—*
1751–2  What deþe þat I take, or dool þat I drye.

*ax/ax:*  27–8, L 139–40, 631–2, C 1191–2, 1319–20, L 1407–8, 1455–6, C 1639–40 (8 examples).
*Example:—*
27–8  Whare he of dedis myghte here, be daye or be nyghte.

*xa/ax:*  283–4, L 763–4, 1471–2, C 1635–6, 1651–2 (5 examples).
*Example:—*
283–4  He was na-thyng affrayede of þe fers knyght.

## INTRODUCTION

*xa/xa:*  L 263–4, L 1047–8 (2 examples).
    *Example:—*
    L 263–4  Why will noghte Sir Degreuant come rescu his dere?

*xa/aa:*  415–6, C 1047–8, 1059–60, 1379–80, L 1875–6 (5 examples).
    *Example:—*
    415–6  Hit semes as that dowghty Sir Degreuaunt drede.

*ax/xa:*  719–20, 1035–6, 1527–8, C 1683–4, 1891–2 (5 examples).
    *Example:—*
    1891–2  Cortays and auenaunt,  ladyes and kny3thus.

*aa/bb:*  L 35–6, C 47–8, 511–2, C 691–2, 703–4, C 1275–6, 1279–80, 1391–2, C 1451–2, 1491–2, C 1543–4, 1675–6, L 1731–2, 1811–2, 1855–6, C 1895–6, C 1903–4 (17 examples).
    *Example:—*
    1491–2  With a bright bordure, cumpaste ful clene.

*aaa/bb:*  523–4, 591–2, 1255–6, 1499–1500 (4 examples).
    *Example:—*
    1499–1500  Brad besantes full bryghte, and tressours by-twene.

*aax/bbx:*  1399–1400 only:—
    Clathes couerde þer wore, swylke saw I neuer are.

*aab/bb:*  1143–4, 1787–8.
    *Example:—*
    1143–4  Many man hym by-helde, sa hardy was he.

*aax/bb:*  L 1863–4 only:—
    Bright byrdis and schene, and frely to folde.

*ab/ab:*  C 139–40, C 1695–6 (2 examples).
    *Example:—*
    C 139–40  Hys husbondus that yaf rent was y-hery3ed dounryght.

*abx/ab:*  1359–60 only:—
    To speke with Myldor þe bryght, spede if he maye.

*aab/bx:*  1219–20 only:—
    To Mayd Myldor he ches, and chalangys þat fre.

*aba/bb:*  C 655–6 only:—
    Off rede golde þe rybanne glemyd hur gyde.

*ab/ba:*  C 763–4 only:—
    Go feche all hys many with me for to fy3th.

*xxa/xa:*  59–60, L 1147–8 (2 examples).
    *Example:—*
    59–60  To brynge þe dere to þe grounde was his maste glewe.

*axx/ax:*  87–8, C 519–20, C 1407–8 (3 examples).
    *Example:—*
    87–8  He gafe þam robis of palle, bothe golde and fee.

*axx/aa:*  L 99–100, C 807–8, C 1875–6 (3 examples).
    *Example:—*
    99–100  Of brade londis and wyde, and borowes full brade.

*axa/xa:*  C 1147–8, 1195–6 (2 examples).
    *Example:—*
    1195–6  Greyþ myn hors on hor gere, and lok þat þei be gay.

*axa/ax:*  107–8, 1607–8 (2 examples).
    *Example:—*
    107–8  And brak hys parkes about, the best that he hade.

*xxaa/aa:*  1887–8 only:—
    Þey tok her leue and [went] her way, thys worþely to w[ale].

INTRODUCTION                                            xlv

It frequently happens that the readings of the two MSS. are not identical. Sometimes the divergence is not great enough to affect the above classification, but frequently the passage corresponding to a complete alliterative line in one MS. is lacking in the other, or is so corrupt as to produce doubtful sense, or the alliteration fails altogether. In the following nine examples, divergent alliterative types are produced. All these have been entered under each type in the foregoing list.

|    |          | C       | L       |
|----|----------|---------|---------|
| 1. | 139–40   | ab/ab   | ax/ax   |
| 2. | 519–20   | axx/ax  | aax/ax  |
| 3. | 763–4    | ab/ba   | xb/bx   |
| 4. | 1047–8   | xa/aa   | xa/xa   |
| 5. | 1147–8   | axa/xa  | xxa/xa  |
| 6. | 1407–8   | axx/ax  | ax/ax   |
| 7. | 1635–6   | xa/ax   | aa/ax   |
| 8. | 1695–6   | ab/ab   | xb/xb   |
| 9. | 1875–6   | axx/aa  | xa/aa   |

## VI. VOCABULARY

In *Sir Degrevant* some of the commoner words and phrases typical of alliterative poetry are used. So the synonyms for 'man' (used either for variety or for metrical convenience), frequent in alliterative poets, are found here: *beryn* 317, 516,[1] *freke* L 1381, *gome* 318, *renk* 1105, 1314, etc., *sege* C 291, and *wy* 579. In addition, there is *ledes* C 308, common also in non-alliterative poetry.

The poetic synonym for 'woman', *byrde* 607, etc., common enough in alliterative poetry and the ballads, is often found here, usually in the phrase *þat byrde bright* or some variant of it. *Wight*, person, is not exclusively or even mainly an alliterative word; though usually applied to people of either sex, is here used only of Melidor (479, etc.).

With the exception of *renk*, *byrde*, and *wight*, all the above words are alliterated whenever they occur; the three exceptions are sometimes alliterated.

Adjectives preceded by a demonstrative or other adjective are frequently used as nouns in such phrases as *þis dowghty*, *þat frely to fold*. More rarely, the phrases have a plural application. This device of style is taken from alliterative poetry.

*Examples:* *þat amerous* C 671, *that aunterous* C 421, *þat bryghte* 1223, *þat cheualerouse* L 421, *that hend* C 11, *many bolde* 359, *alle þe balde* 1178, *many dowghty* 310, *þat (ilk) doghety* 415, 1141, *þat (þis) free* 429, 761, 1220, 1737 (all referring to Melidor), C 959, 1140 (referring to Sir Degrevant), *þis (þat) semly* 1391, C 1411, *þat swete* 1384, *þat wis* 449, *my wylde* 440.

*Þat borly and bolde* 468, *þis (þat, a) frely to folde* 476, 528, *þese doughty on dede* C 316, *þat lufly in lere* L 536.

[1] In this Section, lists of references are not meant to be exhaustive; additional examples may be found in the Glossary. To avoid the difficulty of the divergent readings and displacements of lines, the following notation has been used: 317 means that the word is found in both MSS., either in the same line or in one near by: unless indication is given to the contrary, L 1381 implies that the word is not found anywhere in C but that there is no reason to suspect its originality in the line given, as the other text offers either an inferior reading or none at all. (L 1381) implies that some element of doubt attaches to the reading.

The periphrastic expression denoting God:—
                304 He þat alle weldys,
is also in the manner of some ME. alliterative poets, and may have been borrowed from them.[1]

A striking characteristic of the poem is the large number of adjectives of complimentary meaning used to describe the chief actors or their retainers. As in all romances, the words have no sharply defined meanings, and have come to be as conventional in use as the characters they describe. To say that a knight is *bold*, or that a lady is *fair* implies neither more nor less than saying that he is *aunterous, dowghty, chivalrous* (in the special sense in which the word is used in 1593, etc.), *fierce, freck, hardy, kant, keen, sterne, stowte, stiff, stithe, wight*, and *worthy*, or that she is *clere, clene, bryght, lovesome, schene, schyre, wlonk*, and so forth. Adjectives describing the conduct and manners of both knight and lady are plentiful: *avenant, bounteous, courteous, free(ly), gentle, good(ly), gracious, hende, kind*; they are far more numerous than those describing their intelligence: *wise, ware*.

Verbs denoting movement and resting or stopping are also plentiful. Here again, one is impressed rather by their number than by the fine shades of meaning expressed. The author, like the alliterative poet, found it convenient to avail himself of a varied assortment of such words to alliterate and strengthen his line, or for purposes of rime.

*Examples:—*
1. *Movement in general: bowe* C 55, *busk* 167, etc., *chese* 1123, etc., *come* 89 and *passim, doter* C 1125, *dight* 683, *found* 57, 241, 505, etc., *go* 1320 and *passim, helde* C 300, *lede* C 933, *pass* 78 and *passim, repayre* 47, etc., *ride* 130, etc., *(a)stray* 1656, *strike* (C 1656), *wade* (in the modern sense) C 938, *walk* 412, etc., *wend* 90, etc., *wyn* 918, and the past tenses *ȝede, ȝoud* 626, C 942.

    In addition, the auxiliary *will* (*shullen*) alone suffices to express movement in 603.

2. *Rapid movement: frouschen* C 1103, *lepe* 631, 770, *press* (L 1103), *run* 510, *schased, chased* 357, etc., *stir* 1281, *syle*, fall 359.

3. *Standing still, resting*, etc.: *(a)bide* L 129, 172, etc., *dwel* C 1204, *hove* 1311, etc., *lend* 1576, etc., *leng* C 1356, *lie* 687, *lyght* 256, etc., *let* C 837, *logge* C 244, *rest* 513, 634, etc., *stand* 1689, etc., *sesse*, cease 267.

A remarkably large number of French words are found throughout the poem, but these are clustered especially thickly in the ornate passage describing Melidor's chamber, and the banquet (1409–1520), and to a lesser extent in that describing Sir Degrevant's coat of arms (1045–56). A concentrated distribution of this kind may be paralleled in the descriptive passages of other romances, especially where the author, with the true mediæval love of catalogue, is specifying the details of a feast, a castle, or someone's clothes (cf. *The Squyre of Lowe Degre* 317–26, 741–852, 1069–78; *Emaré* 90–168; *Gawain* 568–622, 787–802).

[1] Cf. *Gawain* 2441–2:—
              Þe wyȝe hit yow ȝelde
        Þat vpholdeȝ þe heuen and on hy sitteȝ;
    *Patience* 111:—
              Þat wyȝ þat al þe world planted;
but also *Song of Roland* 509:—
              he that heaven wields (see Oakden, *op. cit.* II, 394).

# INTRODUCTION

All the French words in *Sir Degrevant* are appropriate to the courtly life they depict: most of them group themselves naturally according to the aspects of it they set forth, particularly to the arts at which the French themselves excelled, and which they succeeded in implanting permanently in England: government, warfare, heraldry, building and domestic ornament, clothing, eating and drinking, amusement, and courtly love and sentiment. In addition, there are words in *Sir Degrevant* that may be conveniently grouped together as denoting ideas connected with religion, social and moral conduct, and with the ranks of society.

The words in the following lists are derived immediately from French (a few, especially in list II, are taken directly from Latin), their ultimate etymology not being taken into account. Some of them have taken English formative affixes. They are classified according to their contexts in the poem, hence *lyon* is found among the heraldic words. There are about four hundred in all, i.e., a new word for every five lines, and the lines are short.

*Examples:—*
1. *Administration and Government (state and domestic).*
   *Bouche of court* 1014, *chartur* C 266, C 975, *costage* 1013, *contre* 135, etc., *(de)maynus* 69, *hospitall* 1833, *lyuere*, livery 1019, *manere*, manor 137, *ordyr* 891, *purvayed* 245, *purueance* 1825, etc., *rent* 139, etc., *roberyse* C 498, *sesyd* 65, etc., *store* 72, *tenandrye* 141, *tonage* (L 1014), *wage* (C 1014).
2. *People, Ranks of Society.*
   *Archers* 239, 277, *bachelere* 1098, etc., *ban(e)rett* C 474, etc., *baroun* 179, L 1860, etc., *botelere*, butler, 1665, *cheftayne* 259, *contasse* 1761, etc., *dame* 18, *damesels* L 710, C 873, *doseperes* 1870, *duk* 1026, etc., *emperoure* 858, etc., *foster* 1598, etc., *gyant* 262, etc., *hauraud*, herald 1157, *ayere*, heir, 570, *madame* 483, *mayster* 1833, *marchal* (C 1678), *menʒe* 134, etc., *messengere* 186, etc., *minstrel* 1877, etc., *nevew* C 26, *officers* 1595, *oste*, host 245, *page* 1015, *pant(el)ere*, pantler 1665, *perys*, peers 1904, *portere* 397, etc., *prese*, crowd 1122, *pypere* 1585, *remenant* 1669, *reten(ans)* C 946, 1163, *rout* 106, *semble*, assembly (L 1084), *seruant* 731, *seruitourus* C 1081, *Sir* (*passim*), *soldan* 1914, *squiere* 883, etc., *trompers* C 677, *vschere* (L 1678), *waytis* 1581.
3. *Fighting.*
   *Arey* (n. and v.) C 492, 703, C 865, etc., *avaunt* 275, *assayle* 1034, etc., *battle* 346, etc., *(en)buschement* 1597, etc., *chalange* 1220, etc., *cheualrye* 1031, *conquerour* 1545, *course* 1306, etc., *coursurs* 609, *delyuer* 394, *endure* 555, *enemys* 578, *(en)joined* 289, *fayled* (L 1303), *feraunt(s)* 387, 1262, etc., *fewtir* 1282, etc., *ferres*[1], fierce, C 248, etc., *fray* 253, 500, *frouschen*[1] C 1103, *foynede* 290, *gre* 1148, etc., *hurtes* C 829, *joust* 1267, etc., *lyarde*, grey 76, *maystry* L 303, 112 etc., *(de)pertede*, divided, 346, *pavilyons* 243, *pesse*, peace 1194, etc., *playtede* (C 342), *recouer* 1289, *rescu* 264, etc., *sore*, reddish brown 76, *stoure* 1061, *stroyed* 433, *tornament* 95, etc., *tornay* (v.) 1100, etc., *trompis* 276, *victory* C 303, *vencust*, vanquished, 426, etc., *war* 1267, etc., *warreyed* L 437.

[1] These words have already been included in other lists of this Section.

xlviii                    INTRODUCTION

4. *Arms and Armour (Man and Horse).*
   *Armed* 1094, etc., *armere* C 298, *armes* 118, *basenetis* 322, etc., *banere* 275, 1052, *colere*, collar 1651, *dress* (v.) C 1321, *gambassowne* 318, *glayue* 295, *habirgeon* 1638, *hawberk* C 294, *japon* 307, *jesseraunt* 307, etc., *maylis* L 294, 311, *mantelete* 1198, *trapped* 1197, *topteler* (C 1198).

5. *Heraldry.*
   *Archede* (L 1048), *cheef* C 1045, *creste* C 1210, *dolphyn* 1054, *engrelyd* 1046, *gowlys* L 1052, *lyon* 1051, *resoun*, motto 1239, *sayntour*, *satur*, saltire 1046, *scochenes*, escutcheons C 1497, *tressoure* 1047.

6. *Buildings, Domestic Ornament and Decoration, Furnishing.*
   *Barnekynch*, outwork (C 391), *barresse*, outwork (L 391), *besantes* 1444, 1499, *bordure* 1491, *castle* 73, etc., *celure*, canopy 1490, *chambir* 74, etc., *champed*, adorned (L 1510), *chapell* (C 638), *chayers* 1389, *chymney* 1393, *chekir* (L 1490), *condyth* 1865, *cordis* 1517, *cornere* (L 1501), *crystal* 532, 1486, *cyprus*, cypress-wood C 1498, *dese*, dais 1218, *fagotes* 1395, *gabelettes*, little gables 1478, *gete*, jet L 1197, 1477, *grese*, stairway 1375, *moyneles*, mullions C 1475, *orloge*, clock 1469, *(ouer)chowchid* L 646, L 1487, *ouerkeueryd*, covered over (C 1487), *palesse* L 163, *pall* 87, etc., *papeiayes* 1496, *parpon*, binding stone C 1446, *paynted* (L 1465, etc.), *pelers* 1458, *posterne* 615, *poyned*, embroidered C 1507, *quyltes* (C 1507), *quyssyns*, cushions 1390, *riddels*, curtains 1514, *ruel*, ivory 1445, *salere*, salt-cellar 1405, *sanappis*, table-cloths 1403, *sendale*, silk 1509, *tasselde* L 1508, *tester* C 1490, C 1501, *torches* C 890, *toure*, tower C 1131, *towels* 1401, *trestellus* (C 1398), *fristis*, trestles (L 1398), *yuore*, ivory 1397, etc.

7. *Clothes, Jewels and Toilet.*
   *Anamelde* 650, *anurled*, trimmed C 647, *aʒoure* 650, etc., *basyn* 1406, *beralle* 531, *bosys* 663, *botouns* 649, *broche* 572, *courchefs* 669, *couerde* (L 648), *croune* 1418, etc., *coronal* C 658, *curious* 669, *endent(ed)* 665, etc., *ermyne* 647, *ewer* 1406, *euerrose*, rose-water C 1407, *fausoned*, fashioned 543, *fyne* 1199, *furrede* (L 647), *frount(ell)* 665, *garnementes*, *germentes* 1880, *gyde*, raiment 656, *ouert*, open C 648, *payr*, pair 663, *perle* 642 etc., *perry*, jewellery 1495, *rybanne* C 655, *robis* 1878, *saphyrus* C 643, *topyes*, topaz 651, *veluet* (L 641, etc.), *vyolet* (C 641, etc.).

8. *Eating and Drinking.*
   *Chere* C 881, *conynges*, rabbits 1421, *curlewe* 1422, *deyntese* 811, 1427, *fesant* 1422, *galentyne* 1415, *hastelettes*, pigs' entrails 1415, *Maluesyne* 1431, *maungery*, feast 1159, etc., *pantry* 1410, *paste* 1418, *payndemayne*, white bread 1291, etc., *plouerys* 1418, *powdird* 1418, *Roche* 1430, *souppe* (v.) C 1006, 1159, *sopere*, supper 882, 1426, *spyces* 1428, etc., *vernage* 1292, etc., *vytayled* C 935.

9. *Pastimes: Music, Hunting and Outdoor Life, etc.*
   *Abaye*, (at) bay 254, *arbere* 711, *ayere*, brood 46, *best*, beast 503, *cetoyle*, stringed instrument L 35, *chase* 377, *daunce* 371, 1869, *fawcon* 1896, etc., *forest* 1206, etc., *geterne*, zither C 36 (*gytternyng* L 36), *grese* 265, *heue*, shout L 252, *laund*, glade 255, etc., *luces*, pike L 519, *melody* L 92, *note* 38, *playn* 71, 258, *revay* 50, 322,

etc., *rose* 534, *rosere*, rose-tree 634, *ryuere* C 810, *reuelle*, 1883, etc., *romance* 1886, *sawtree*, psaltery 35, *schalmouse*, shawm 1102, *stabillede* L 75, *story* 1467, etc., *vncuppilde* 249, *veuers*, fishponds L 113, L 434.

10. *Courtly Love and Chivalry.*
    *Amorous* 1027, *bewte* 475, *chyualry* C 826, etc., *cheualrous* 1026, 1593, *cortayse* 1587, *cortesy* C 802, *erraunt* (C 1327), *gay* 1027, etc., *gentryse* 497, 747, *gentle* 419, etc., *gracyous* 670, etc., *nobulle* C 92, *lelely* 529, *paramour* 1063, 1150, etc., *pervenke*, paragon C 746, *pryse* 746, *recumaunde* 893, 897, *Table Rownde* 30.

11. *Religion.*
    *Archangells* 1450, *doctorus* 1463, (*en*)*soyn* 291, *fay* 120, etc., *grace* 1615, etc., (*gra*)*mercy* 801, *lay*, faith 1843, *parabylls* 1455, *pistills* 1454, *pontifical* 1846, *pocalyps* 1453, *repent* 270, *saue* 721, *sent*, *sayne*, saint 713, *Trinite* 1817, etc., *vow* 229.

12. *Social and Moral Conduct: Moral Qualities, Pain and Pleasure.*
    *Accord* (n. and adj.) 1783, 1801, etc., (*a*)*mend* 203, *anoyed* 435, (*as*)*sent* 863, C 1551, *atent* L 1795, *avaunt*, declaration 1889, *blame* (n. and v.) 715, 785, *comandment* 1794, *coumforde* 1803, *countenauns* 1182, *cruel* 1596, etc., (*de*)*grade* 104, *delay* C 1200, *descure*, reveal 554, *deseruyd* C 1148, *disdayne* L 101, *disonowre* (n.) C 859, *doel*, pain C 576, *dured* 1567, (*en*)*payre* 1903, *ensent* consent 869, *ensure* C 553, *envyous* L 423, *false* 1740, *foly* 585, etc., *fouchesaff* C 959, *graunt* 719, etc., *greue* 1341, *gyle* C 832, *gyne*, trick 722, etc., *honore* C 299, *joye* 1234, *marriage* 1536, *maugre* 431, etc., *mescheue* 1342, *pay*(*d*) (n. and v.) 281, 796, *pain* 548, *plight*, evil state L 140, *pray* 155, etc., *preually* 1409, *preferrys* C 857, *profird* 1291, *prow*, advantage 230, *pruest*, most valiant C 1188, *quite* (v.) 443, *rebuke* C 879, *recreaunt* 1263, *redressyde* 1818, *restored* 487, *rewarde*, award 447, *serued* 1404, 1411, *seruyce* L 1875, *skorne* 1069, *socoure* C 911, *solas* (C 1084), *spyt* C 101, *trayne* 1740, *traytour* 733, *trauelus*, troubles oneself C 850, *vayn* C 850, *velany* 755, etc., *waryson* 782.

13. *Miscellaneous.*
    (*A*)*cheue* 480, 481, *alas* 377, *aley*, garden-path 690, *ankyre* 63, *avyse* C 184, C 577, *bargayne* 454, *barrayne* 438, *case* 526, etc., *cause* 750, *certys* C 693, *chaunce* C 200, *compasyd* 1056, *conselle* 554, *cost*, direction 246, *count* 206, *colour* L 535, *dyuerse* 1717, *draye*, noise L 1200, *dure*, hard (L 649), *face* L 670, *haste* 1417, *lettre* 121, etc., *manere*, manner 368, *mappemounde* 31, *meruel*(*ous*) 1513, etc., *message* (L 211), *moue* C 1438, *ordayned* 1398, *pace* 799, *persayued* 1364, *place* 138, etc., *precious* 537, *proue* (L 480), *ryally* 674, etc., *semblaunt* C 815, *semble* (v.) L 1084, *sertaynly* C 871, C 969, *sesse*, cease 267, *symplust* C 795, *sort*, fate C 1670, *space* 697, *touchest* C 1534, *turne* 727, *vsep* C 822, *vyssag* C 670.

As the words of Scandinavian origin are far less numerous they may be dealt with more briefly. For the most part they express common ideas, and are found quite frequently in other poems and prose writings of the late fourteenth century. A few, e.g., *anger, tydandis, wyndows, carp*, by this time have become so widespread as to be used by writers in areas where

# INTRODUCTION

Scandinavian settlement was relatively sparse. Most of the remainder, e.g., *bowne, gar, gayne, grayth, menske, rade, sere, thra, tyte, wale*, and *witterly* seem by the fourteenth century to have a distinct northerly flavour, that is, they belong exclusively to the north and midlands (especially the north midlands), so far as reliance can be placed in the lists of illustrative matter in the OED., and in my own supplementary observations. At least it can be claimed that they are used far more commonly in these than in other areas. But the north and the midlands together represent a large proportion of England; it is impossible to employ these words as evidence for determining with any precision the original dialect of the poem. The most that they can help to prove is that it is not southern.

Two words of Scandinavian origin are purely northern. *Coddis*, pillows (L 1505, L 1507, C 1509) is found in both MSS. and is therefore presumably original. *Geddis*, pike, L 519 occurs in only one, the textual accuracy of which, as we have had abundant occasion to notice, is uneven. As the other MS. at this point has the French equivalent *luces*, the authority of *geddis* is questionable, though it has the support of the alliteration. It has a more restricted currency than *luces*, which was known to more southerly writers like Chaucer,[1] and for that reason is just the kind of word that a scribe might replace by another when translating into a more southerly dialect. On the whole, the balance of probability inclines in favour of *geddis* as the original, and *luces* as the substituted word. The originality of *slyk*, such (ON. *slíkr*), L 1216 is also open to question on the same grounds; but like *geddis*, is probably authentic enough.

Another word of severely limited currency (its etymology is obscure; it is perhaps of echoic origin) is *schygynge*, trotting C 361, which according to the OED. is found only in Norfolk. This occurs only once in the poem, and in one MS., L having *chasande*. The fact of its rarity is an argument for regarding it as original; in view of the commonness of *chase* (the number of examples of the verb and noun is considerable in *Sir Degrevant* alone) it is a powerful argument. The likelihood of *chasande* being the original word is still further diminished by the fact of its repeating *schased* four lines earlier. Its occurrence here may be due either to lapse of memory or to deliberate substitution.

The occurrence of a pure Norfolk word in the same poem as others just as purely northern shows that its vocabulary, though a confirmatory test of dialect, must be used with caution and with due regard to its limitations.[2] *Sir Degrevant* is not in the Norfolk dialect, but there are reasons why the poet should have known something of the country, hence the presence of an expressive Norfolk word is not difficult to account for. East Anglia, and Norfolk especially, was the centre of the main group of poets using the various tail-rime stanzas; according to a recent critic,[3] their influence was widespread. The author of *Sir Degrevant* must have known some of their work; he may also have known their country, and perhaps even some of the poets themselves. The only English place-name in the poem is the Norfolk town of Aylsham (1401), which he knew to be an important centre for the manufacture of textiles. The Norfolk word may therefore be a purely literary borrowing, or may be the result of a more personal intimacy with the county or with its people.

---

[1] *Prologue to Canterbury Tales* 350.
[2] Examples of *shig-shog*, v, trot or amble in riding, are quoted by the EDD. from nothern and midland counties. *Shig* may once have had a wider currency than Norfolk.
[3] A. McI. Trounce, *The English Tail Rhyme Romances* (Medium Ævum, Vols. 1-3)

INTRODUCTION                                                li

## VII. LANGUAGE

### A. SPELLING.

In neither text is the spelling regular; in the Cambridge MS. it is chaotic, particularly in the representation of short and long vowels.

*The Lincoln MS.*

The following are some of its peculiarities:—
1. A redundant *h* sometimes precedes an unstressed prefix beginning with a vowel: *habade* 129, etc.; *habyde* 1336; *haby* 454, etc.
2. Initial *h* is sometimes omitted from French words: *oste* 282; *ayere* 570, etc.; but *hauraud* 1157; *hospitall* 1833.
3. A consonant is often doubled:—
    (*a*) After a short stressed vowel: *gyff*, give 1066; *hunttyd* 515, *thritty* 1906.
    (*b*) After a short unstressed prefix: *appon* 385, etc.; *affrayede* 283,
    (*c*) After a long vowel: *wysse*, wise 180, etc.; *whytte*, white 1402; *schott*, shoot 280; *pesse*, peace 1585.
    (*d*) In an unstressed word having an originally short vowel: *haffe* 1028; *off*, of 1760, etc.
4. In French words *s* is sometimes used initially and medially to represent the voiceless dental spirant usually spelt *c*: *sesse* 267; *sertys* 589; *sertanely* 605; *seloure* 1490; *plase* 1495.
5. Conversely *c* is used for English *s* in *face*, foes 426; *celly* 1707.
6. *sch* is used:—
    (*a*) For *s* in *redrischt* 1818.
    (*b*) For normal French *ch* in *schased* 357; but *chasande* 361.
7. Unaccented *e* is represented:—
    (*a*) by *y*: *withowtyn* 690, 1369; *chambyrs* 1439.
    (*b*) by *i*: *chambir* 1376; *mowthis* 1392; *sanappis* 1403; *powdird* 1418.
    (*c*) by *e*: *kyssed* 1384; *clathes* 1399; *serued* 1416.
    (*d*) by *o*: *vndron* 636, 1225.
    (*e*) by *u*: *coursurs* 609.
8. A redundant *e* is sometimes added after a short vowel: *blane* 1133; *mete* 689; *whate* 546.
9. There is the usual fifteenth-century confusion between *þ*, *ʒ*, *y*, e.g., *þou* (?*you*) 1230, 1342, 1396; *tyʒandis*, tidings 1736, 1796.

*The Cambridge MS.*

The notable spelling peculiarities are:—
1. The symbol *ʒ* is rarely used by hand A; hands B and C use it frequently.
    Hand A uses it to represent:—
    (*a*) The sound of Mod. E. consonantal *y* (OE. front spirantal *g*, and the first element in the rising diphthong *ēo*: *ʒoode* 127; *y-heryʒed* 140.
    (*b*) The sound of *z*: *aʒour* 470.

Hands B and C use ȝ to represent:—
(a) The sound of *y* (as above, with the possible addition of ON. *j*) *ȝede* 626; *ȝour* 740; *ȝatt* 629; *ȝowlus* 781; *ȝorle*, earl (hand C only) 1737, 1753, etc.
(b) The sound of *z*: *aȝour* 650; *asȝure* 1489.
(c) OE. *-h*, especially in *-ht* combinations after front and back vowels: *myȝthe* 590; *knyȝth* (*passim*); *wrouȝth* 1607.
(d) OE. back-voiced spirant *-g*: *wouȝh* 739; *louȝh* 954. The sound *w* may be implied in the rime *wouȝh*, *bow* 738–9.
(e) *ȝ* is redundant in *a-bouȝt* 1521; *stonyȝed* 1108; *trouȝth* 696, etc. (cf. *troupus* 889, etc.); *seyȝne*, since 1724.
2. *gh* is redundant in *whyght* 518.
3. *ff* is used frequently, especially by hand A:—
(a) Medially: *lefft* 195; *swyfftly* 1126; *soufft* 1727.
(b) Finally after both long and short vowels: *off* 9; *yaff* 51, etc.; *gyff*, if 957; *wyff* 983; *cheff* 1666.
4. Other doubled consonants are often though not regularly used as a sign of shortness in the preceding vowel: *wentten* 683; *styrres* 1281; *hadd* 675; *mornne* 1603; *oppon* 781; *fryppus* 1732; *messaggere* 211; *fforesstus* 190.
5. Double *r* is found after a long vowel in *berre* 1623 (r.w. *werre*, war, *spere*). This may be a sheer mis-spelling: the scribe substituted *werre* for *were*, and then wrote *berre* to match it.
6. French *ch* is represented by *ch* in *chalangys* 1220; by *sch* in *schased* 357; by *sh* in *shaunce* 1095; and by *sc* in *scalmuse* 1102.
7. *s* is used for usual French *c* in *sese* 267; *sertaynly* 871; *plas* 1495.
8. Length in vowels is indicated by:—
(a) Doubling: *moo* 452; *goo* 456; *feet* 1380; *see* 976; *soore*, sorrel 76; *nooke* 181.
(b) Addition of final *-e* after an intervening consonant:—*qwene* 1504; *mede* 1346; *wise* 180.
These are the usual methods in ME. The following are less orthodox:—
(c) Addition of *-e* to the vowel *knyef* 556.
(d) Often no indication is given: *swet*, sweet 1384; *stak*, stake 1060; *dred* 916; *wis* 449; *ensur* 553; *slep* 784; *ned* 354[1], etc.
9. Unaccented *e* is represented by *e, i, y, u*; *e* predominating in both hands: *maystries* 112; *rydys* 1243; *folkys* 390; *rachis* 510; *vndir* 1032; *watyr* 1407; *dedus* 312; *kynghus* 314; *robus* 1879. The spelling *o* is also used for unstressed vowels of various origins: *emporour* 846; *commolych* 704; *proford* 1291; *wepon* 1323; *geton* 1366; *bassonett* 1635.
10. Etymological *i* in an unaccented syllable is written *-e* in *heyle* 1601.
11. The diphthongs *ei, ai* are confused and levelled sometimes under the spelling *ei*, sometimes under *ai*; *mey* 124, 501; *wey* 128, 212; *sey*, say 486; *way* 214; *may* 215, etc.

---

[1] Irregularity in methods of showing vowel length is found also in the Lincoln text, but it is only sporadic (see *weile* 1537; *wod* 1577; *ham* 1603).

INTRODUCTION  liii

## B. Phonology.

As the dialect of L gives a better idea of the original than that of C, the linguistic features of this text, particularly those of which the rime gives evidence, will be considered first. They will establish the conclusion discussed more fully at the end of Section C below, that the poem was written and has been transmitted in a north-eastern dialect. As C can offer no important evidence to the same conclusion that is not already found in L, this text will be discussed more briefly.

1. ME. *ă* remains before nasals: *man* 1134 r.w. *blane, wane*. As might be expected, ME. *ă* also remains when lengthened in an open syllable before a nasal: *lame* 375, r.w. *hame*; and before *-nd*: *vndirstande* 1839 r.w. *lande, offerand*; *hande* 15 r.w. *fande, Scotlande*. Occasional *o*-forms are scribal: *londe* 66, r.w. *hande, sittande*; *mony* 343.

2. OE. *ǣ* develops to *ă*: *was* 1493, r.w. *Amadase, plase*; *glase* 1473, r.w. *brase, wasse*. *Eftyr* 1794 is probably scribal.

3. OE. *ā*, ON. *á* usually remain, riming with OE. *ă, ĕa, ǣ* lengthened, with OE. *ǣġ*, and with Fr. *ā*: *are*, before 1236, r.w. *bare, bore, ʒare, ware*, were; *mare* 41, r.w. *bare, hare*; *stane* 1447, r.w. *bane*, bone, *Vrbane*; *face*, foes 426, r.w. *grace, place*; *fame*, foam 562, r.w. *name, blame*; *ake*, oak 1051 r.w. *blake, for-sake*; *sare* 1264, r.w. *fare, bare*, boar; *onane* 1029, r.w. *slayne*.[1]

Occasionally *ǭ*-forms are found: *stone* 1465, r.w. *ilkone, Absolone*; *more* 68, r.w. *sore*, sorrel, *store*; *ylkone* 1454, r.w. *John, Salomone*; *wote* 39, r.w. *rotte, note*.

The rime *onone* 219, *sone*, soon, must be regarded as doubtful, since OE. *sōna* should give a close vowel in ME.

4. OE. *ǣ* (non-WS. *ē*) becomes *ẹ̄* and rimes with ME. developments of original *ē*; *ē* the *i*-mutation of *ō*; non-WS. *ē* the *i*-mutation of *ēa*; *ēo*; and AN. *ẹ̄*: *wedis* 408 r.w. *stedis, nedis*; also with *bledis* 1112; *strete* 1107, r.w. *fete, mete*, OE. *mētan*; *dede* 1608, r.w. *mede*, OE. *mēd, spede*; *bere*, OE. *bǣr* 1731, r.w. *Gaymere, sqwyere*; *ʒere* 1897, r.w. *clere, fere*, OE. (*ge*)*fēra*; *drede* 441, r.w. *dede, mede*; *nere* 540, r.w. *clere, lere* OE. *hlēor* (MS. *lyre*), *dere*, dear.

5. *ẹ̄* is found for *ę̄* before *d, n*: *clene* 469, r.w. *schene, by-twene*, and with *wene, grene* 1056; and with *kene, sene* 1080; and with *qwene* 1492; *manhede* 83, r.w. *dede, fede*; *lede* 1314, r.w. *stede, mede*.

6. *ę̄* (OE. *ĕ* with ME. lengthening) rimes with *ę̄*(OE. *ēa*), with *ę̄* (OE. *ǣ*, *i*-umlaut of *ā*) and with OFr. *ę̄*: *schede* 309 r.w. *dede*, dead, *rede*, red; *swere* 581, r.w. *were*, war, *here*, army; *mete* 677 r.w. *sete, grete* (adj.); *were*, war 709, r.w. *dere*, injure; *lese*, falsehood 1121, r.w. *chese*, chose; *spere* 1189 and 1322, r.w. *were*, war, *gere*; *lese* 1229, r.w. *cesse, pesse*; *teres* for *tere* (v.) 1704, r.w. *dere*, injure, *pere*, pear, *spere* (MS. *swerdis*); *grete* (adj.) 1785, r.w. *mete* (n.), *swete*, sweat.

*Notes*

(a) Since words having an undoubtedly tense *ę̄* are kept apart in rime from those having slack *ę̄*, the following must be regarded as doubtful: *manere*, manner 368, r.w. *dere*, injure, *spere*, *pere*,

---

[1] *Schewe* 149, r.w. *drawe, lawe* has been substituted by the scribe for *schawe*.

pear; *were*, war 395, r.w. *were*, were, *þere*; *cheue* 481, r.w. *leue* (n.), *greue*, grief; *stede*, place 565, r.w. *rede* (n.), *dede*, death; *lepe* 631, r.w. *slepe, kepe*; and rather less certainly, *see*, sea 133, r.w. *menȝe, contre*, country, and with *menȝe, free* 1009.[1]

(b) Words riming on slack *ę̄* are always spelt *e* (see 6 above); those riming on northern *ā* are always spelt *a* (see 2 above). Since words in these groups never rime with each other, although the older *ā* must have been fronted by the date of the poem, and since they are kept apart in the spelling, the *ę̄* of group 5 words must have been of a different quality from the *ę̄* of words in group 2.

7. OE. *ȳ* is unrounded to *ī*: *by* (v.) 753, r.w. *hardy, velany*; *kyn* 1363, r.w. *gyn, in*; *hill* 618, r.w. *styll, till*; *syn* 721, r.w. *gyn, wyn*; *hill* 744, r.w. *will, spill, ill*; *gylte* 741 and 1790, r.w. *spylte, wylt*; *kyssed* 1819, r.w. *wist, redrischt; fullfill* 1536, r.w. *till, will, ill*; *knylle* 1472, r.w. *will, till*; *pryde* 98, r.w. *syde, wyde*; and 163, r.w. *ryde, habyd*; *hyde* 196, r.w. *be-syde, wyde*; *kythe* 315, r.w. *wrythe, frythe*; and 380, r.w. *swythe, blythe*; *lyte* 1111, r.w. *smyte, tyte*.

8. ME. *ę̄ȝ* (OE. *ēag, ēah*, Anglian *-ēg, -ēh*) is raised to *ī*: *ly*, tell lies 1748, r.w. *drye*, suffer, *dy*, mercy. This and the rime *dy* 463, *trewly, lyghtly* establishes the raised sound also in *ly* 564, r.w. *bey* (OE. *bēag*), *drey*.

9. The development of OE., ON., and EME. *ǭ* is doubtful as this sound rimes with itself: *stod* 1689, r.w. *flode, ȝode*; *loghe* 737, r.w. *boghe, woghe*; *flode* 1579, r.w. *wod*, wood, *ȝode*.

Traces of over-rounding to [*ȳ*] are found in the *u*-forms that occur occasionally in rime: *fune*, earlier *fone*, few 195, r.w. *sone, done*; *tuke* 182, r.w. *luke, noke*. *gud(e)* is frequently found in other parts of the text: 54, 240, 354, 450, etc.

10. OE. *ēo* becomes *ę̄*: *glee* 3, r.w. *see* (v.), *Trynite*; *dere*, deer 264, r.w. *here, sqwyere; fre(e)* 33, r.w. *glee, sawtree*; and 84, r.w. *fee, melody*; and 1140, r.w. *he, gree, see*; *tre* 734, r.w. *see, be*; *by-twene* 471, r.w. *clene, schene*.

11. Lengthening in open syllables.

There is clear evidence for the lengthening of *a, e, u*:

*ă*: *fare* 502, r.w. *spare, mare*; *lame* 375, r.w. *hame*; *make*, mate 1132, r.w. *stake, strake*.

*ĕ*: *fele*, OE. *fela*, 341, r.w. *stele*; *stede*, OE. *stede*, place 565, r.w. *dede*, death; *mete* 677, r.w. *sete, grete*.

*ŭ*: *wod* OE. *wudu* 1577, r.w. *flode*. The spellings *come* 1119, 1226, *sone*, OE. *sunne*, 1077, and *gomes* 318 may represent orthographical *o* for *u* before nasals.

*ĭ*: the evidence for lengthening is less clear. *wiete* 1420, r.w. *crete* seems to point to such a lengthening, the spelling with *ie* here and in 160, 546, etc. indicating the long vowel. *leue* 1342, riming tense with *greue*, grief, may be from OE. *lēofian*.

---

[1] According to ten Brink (*Language and Versification of Chaucer* p. 16 § 24) *see*, sea always rimes tense in Chaucer.

# INTRODUCTION lv

12. The following points are of more occasional occurrence or are less important:—

(a) ME. *ĕ* becomes *i* before *nt*, as is shown by the rime sequence *flynt* 1381, *hent, stynt*; *hent* is obviously scribal (see Luick, *Hist. Gram.* §379c).

(b) ME. *ĕ* becomes *i* before *ng*: *hynge*, ON. *hengja*, 736, 1514, r.w. *thynge, rynge*; *Yngland(es)* 583, 1826.

(c) The same development also occurs before *s*: *cresse* 206, r.w. *i-wys, mysse*.

(d) On the other hand, it does not apparently occur between *r* and *st*, and the following *i*-forms are probably scribal: *riste* 513, r.w. *beste, foreste*; *risted* 634; *brist* 1525, r.w. *ryste, beste*. (On the change, see Luick, *op. cit.*, §379b and Note 1.)

(e) Traces of ME. *i* lowered to *ĕ* are found: *preualy* 699, 712, 1369, etc.; *recheste* 1475; *velany* 455, 587, 755, etc.; *rechere* 1503, *steraps* 1287; *feftene* 1680. As the stem vowel of the following words may have been lengthened, it is uncertain whether they should be included here or in 11 above: *prekid* 1122; *gleterand* 295; *glemerand* 656; *stekid* 320. There is no evidence that any of these forms are characteristic of the author's dialect. *es* for *is* 535, 546 (stressed) is a scribal substitution of ON. *es* for ME. *is*. *es* in 531, 544, may represent the same substitution, but the example is probably unstressed.

(f) OE. *æg* > *ai*, though the development is obscured by the MS. form in *drawen* 681, r.w. *layne, agayne*; and 1630, r.w. *slayne, layne*; and 758, r.w. *slayne, fayne*.

(g) ME. *er* > *ar* is rare, but see *hard* 1724 beside *herd* 1723, etc.; *gare* 399, etc.

(h) ME. *seþen*, perhaps influenced by ON. *siðan*, is contracted to \**syne* and rimes with words having long *ī*, though the development is obscured by the MS. form: *sythen* 1724, r.w. *wyne*, *Ryne* (river), *hyne*. This is a northern rime sequence (see OED. *s. v.* Syne).

(i) Parasitic vowel-glides between *a* and a following *l* and between *l* and *f* are probably indicated by the spellings *haull(e)* 86, 401, 538, and *tweluft* 1016. These may be merely scribal.

(j) The northern and north midland forms *mase, tane* are both certified by rime: *mase* 1763, r.w. *Allas, faas*; *tane* 765 and 1297, r.w. *grane, ane*; and 1031, r.w. *slayne, onane*. The older *take* is also found 1068, r.w. *strake, make* (n.), *sake*; also 383, etc.

(k) The development of *sch* to *s* in accented and unaccented syllables is found in the rime-sequence *fysche* 113, *i-wysse, this*, and in the very common *sall* 229, 491, etc., *sold(e)* 187, 211, 270, 479, etc., *suld* 1801, *Alsame* 1401, and possibly *vencuste*, vanquished 426.

(l) Unvoicing of *v, d*, is found in *haf(e)* 267, 294, etc., *lufe, lufly, lufsome* 420, 477, 479, 536, etc.; and *stont* 242.

(m) *k* for OE. *c* is found in *ilk(e)* 415, 1507, r.w. *mylke, silke*; *ylk(e)* 89, 93; *swylke* 112, 1120. See also *slyk* 1216 (ON. slíkr).

13. The following rimes show that final inflexional -*e* was silent:—
1110 *tyte* (ON. *tytt*), *lyte* (OE. *lȳt*), *smyte*; 601 *wele* (OE. wĕl), *stele*; 620 *tyde*, *habid*; 689 *mete*, *met*, *let*, *gret*. See also 161, 789, 1133, 1221, 1245, etc. Owing to the free rhythm of the poem, it is impossible to collect certain evidence regarding final -*e* not at the end of a line, but in all probability it was also silent.

C. ACCIDENCE.

14. *Nouns*
Most nouns conform to the str. masc. type, and have the following inflexional endings:—
 Sing. Nom. Acc. —, -*e*. Gen. -*es*, —. Dat. -*e*, —.
 Plural. -*es*, -*is*, -*s*.
Genitive without inflexional ending: *Erle* 467. Datives without inflexional ending: *day* 756; *chambir* 777; *west* 1085; *forest* 1086; *heuen* 1212, 1293.
*Survivals:*
 (*a*) OE. str. neut. pls.: *horse* 1195 (cf. *horses* 1017, 1201), *ȝere* 1906 (after a numeral), *childir* 1907.
 (*b*) OE. str. masc. pl. of stems in -*nd*: *frende* 1816.

15. *Adjectives*
Owing to the loss of final -*e*, no distinction has been preserved between the str. and the wk. form of the adj., or between the sg. and the pl. Each form of the adj. is found either with or without final -*e*.
*Examples:*—Strong Singular, *grete* 1010; *gud* 602. Strong Plural, *calde* 524; *hend* 1459. Weak Singular, *grete* 208; *bryght* 1359. Weak Plural, *mare* 278; *bryght* 1484.

16. *Pronouns*
The following points call for notice:—
 (*a*) The 3rd fem. sg. is always *scho* 421, 473, 475, etc.
 (*b*) The 3rd pl. forms are *þay*, *thay* 233, 1079, etc., *þayre*, *þaire* 308, 1553, etc., *þam* 2, 109, etc.
 (*c*) The forms of the demonstrative pl. are *thir* 1273, 1391, etc. (the commonest) together with *þase* 1300, and *þose* 274.
 (*d*) In conversation the distinction between the 2nd sg. and the 2nd pl. forms is fairly consistently maintained. The pl. form is used for the sg. when the Countess addresses her husband (378, 1773); when the squire addresses Sir Degrevant (577); and when the maid addresses her mistress (782). The sg. form is used in talking to an inferior (e.g., Melidor and the maid, 1366), to an equal (e.g., the Duke and the Earl 1038, 1042), and in moments of passion (the Earl and his daughter 1738, 1756). Melidor's addressing the Duke in the sg. may be put down to her contempt for him or to sprightliness of character (1325, 1336). It is more difficult to account for the Duke's use of the sg. in reply (1341), and particularly for the use of sg. and pl. forms in the same speech (Degrevant to Melidor 723, 730; 763, 768, 772; 1523, 1526; Melidor to Degrevant 1530, 1537; the Squire to Degrevant 552, 560), except when the inconsistency is due to the transmission.[1]
 (*e*) *hym-selfe* 1592 is emphatic, not reflexive (cf. C 976 *þi-self*).

[1] C is more consistent in this respect.

# 17. Verbs

(a) *Infinitive.* The usual ending is -*e* (e.g., *here* 6, *telle* 9, *ryde* 162, etc.); forms without ending are frequent (e.g., *herken* 6, *sitt* 15, *syng* 38, etc.). There are only two forms in -*ne*, *sene* 1084, 1592 (MS. *see*) and *bene* 1588 (MS. *be*) both certified by rime.

(b) *Indicative, Present.* Sg.: 1, -*e*, —; 2, -*s*, -*es*; 3, -*es*, -*se*, -*ys*, -*is*, rarely -*e*. Pl.: -*s*, -*es*, -*ys*, -*e*, —.
Examples:—Sg.: 1, *wene* 17, *cownt* 206; 2, *wakyns* 739, *knawes* 1042; 3, *lays* 306, *prayes* 155, *gose* 127, *weldys* 304, *beris* 1045, *me-thynke* 1386. Pl.: *luffes* 3; *mase* 1763, *berys* 266, *bledis* 1116.

(c) *Pret.-Pres. Verbs.* The form of the 2nd sg. pres. has been levelled under that of the 1st and 3rd: *will* 748 and (probably) *sall* 1230. The pl. has been levelled similarly in *will* 267, *may* 486, *sall* 463.

(d) *Indicative Past; Strong Verbs.* Sg.: 1, -*e*; 3, -*e*, —. Pl.: -*e* (usual), —.
Examples:—Sg.: 1, *spake* 1779; 3, *schane* 1570; *laye* 1329. Pl. *rane* 510; *satt* 1627.
*Weak Verbs.* Sg.: 1, -*e*; 3, -*e*, —. Pl. -*e*, —.
Examples:—Sg.: 1, *mett* 1538; *werreyde* 437; 3, *louede* 41; *lyued* 64. Pl.: *synned* 1560; *louede* 1150.

(e) *Subjunctive, Present.* Sg.: 1, *fyghte* 771; 2, *neuen* 1530; 3, *saue* 721. Pl.: *gete* 587; *halde* 1785.

(f) *Imperative.* Sg.: -*e*, —: *thynk* 202; *thynke* 578. Pl.: -*e*, -*s*, -*is*: *make* 1200; *herkyns*, *heris* 1459.

(g) *Present Participle.* -*and*(*e*): *sittande* 67, r.w. *hande*; *gleterand* 295, etc.; *standand* 1458; *chasande* 361, but also *rydyng* 1262 in a similar construction.

(h) *Past Participle.* Strong verbs have -*en*, -*yn*; -*ne* if the stem ends in a vowel or -*r*: *wonnen* 1142; *haldyn* 326; *slane* 450; *torne* 1710.
Weak verbs frequently end in unetymological -*e*: *wed* 1559; but *leuede* 334; *wounde* has a past participle *wondid* 374, beside the contracted form \**wounde* 336, fixed by the rime but obscured by the spelling. The prefixes *i*-, *y*- are not found.

(i) *Verbal Noun.* Usually -*yng*(*e*): *rehersyng* 1821; *saghtelyng* 1822; *offerynge* 1829; but *offerand* 1838; all forms secured by rime.

(j) *The Verb 'to be'.* Infin. is usually *be* 211, etc.; but there is one example, secured by rime but obscured by spelling, of \**bene* 1588 (see (*a*) above).
Pres. Indic., 3rd Sg.: *es* 31, 123, etc., is the MS. form, but the rimes *i-wysse*, *es*, *pis* 545 imply *is* in the original. Pres. Indic., 3rd Pl.: usually *are* 285, etc.; but occasionally the sg. *es* is used (192, 403).
Past Indic., Pl.: the sg. form *was* is sometimes found: 1188, 1426, 1427, 1900.

It will be convenient to summarize the important characteristics of the language for the purpose of determining the poet's dialect.
1. ME. $\breve{a}$ remains before nasals.
3. OE. $\bar{a}$ remains; exceptionally it becomes $\bar{\varrho}$.
4. OE. $\bar{æ}^1$ rimes tense.
5. OE. $\bar{æ}^2$ rimes tense before *d*, *n*.
7. OE. $\bar{y}$ is unrounded to $\bar{\imath}$.
8. ME. $\bar{e}_\jmath$ is raised to $\bar{\imath}$.

9. OE. ǭ remains in the spelling, but may have become [ȳ].
10. OE. ēo becomes ē.
12. (h) The rime sequence *syne, wyne, etc., 1724.
    (j) The verb forms mase 1763, tane 765, etc.
    (k) Occasional s for sch.
    (l) The forms haf(e), lufe, etc.
    (m) k for OE. c; slyk 1216, etc.
13. Complete loss of final -e in rime; probable loss of it in other positions.
17. (b) -s endings in pres. indic., 2 and 3 sg., -s ending in pl.
    (f) Imperative plural in -s.
    (g) Present participle in -and(e).
    (i) One analogical verbal noun in -and.

These points, mostly certified by rime, may be assumed to be characteristic of the original. Point 4 shows the language of the poem to have developed from Old Angl.; points 1, 7, 10 are characteristic features of the eastern part of the area; 12 (m), 17 (g) and (i) might be found in any region of strong Scandinavian influence; 12 (a), (b) point to the northern or north midland areas; but 3, 9, 12 (h), (j), (l), 17 (b) and (f) point very clearly to the north. Though 8 is regarded as mainly a midland development, raised forms are not confined to texts of midland writers;[1] and as Miss Serjeantson has pointed out,[2] the test cannot be said to be thoroughly reliable. Hence the occurrence of these forms in *Sir Degrevant* is not necessarily out of keeping with its other phonological features. Similarly the raising of ę̄ to ē before dentals and nasals has been claimed[3] to be an Old Merc. development. As the place-names of the East Riding[4] also have tense e for OE. ǣ (any source) this characteristic in the phonology of *Sir Degrevant* need not exclude it from the northern area; indeed Luick (*Hist. Gram.* §361, Note 2) claims that ē-forms apparently preponderate in the north. The occasional ǭ-forms for OE. ā (point 3) are probably used for convenience in riming rather than because the poet habitually spoke a mixed dialect: two of these forms rime with proper names, and two more with relatively uncommon French words. The original dialect was therefore clearly north-eastern, with some slight admixture of Midland forms. This result is confirmed, or at least is not contradicted, by the remaining features of the phonology and and accidence, and also by the evidence afforded by the vocabulary. (See Section VI). The phonology and accidence of those parts of the text not certified by rime are much the same as those that are, hence we may conclude that the original north-eastern poem has been transmitted in a north-eastern dialect. It is not, however, quite the same dialect. There are rather more unsecured than secured ǭ-forms for OE. ā, and the MS. forms show considerable divergences between author and scribe in the treatment of ME. ĕ in association with combinations of consonants.

[1] Minot VII 79 has *ine*, eyes, r.w. *pine*.

[2] M. S. Serjeantson, *The Dialects of the West Midlands in ME.*, RES., Vol. III, No. 10, p. 186.

[3] See Tolkien and Gordon, *Sir Gawain and the Green Knight*, p. 123, and Bülbring's article in the *Miscellany presented to Dr. Furnivall* there referred to.

[4] See A. H. Smith, *Place Names of East Riding*, pp. XXVIII–XXXI, for a list of the phonological features of this dialect.

## D. Linguistic Features of the Cambridge Text.

Though its textual value is considerable, MS. C can supply but little information of importance for the study of the original dialect. The copyists have translated the poem into their own dialect, which was more southerly and westerly than the original. The result, including the rime-words, is a medley of forms that could scarcely have co-existed in the spoken language of any region. Apart from the textual alterations that transmission and translation have involved (for which, see Section III), the northern rimes remain much the same (the chief difference being that OE. $\bar{a}$ is sometimes written *o*); but changes have been made in the phonology and accidence of the unrimed words, which have taken on a more southerly character.

A striking point of difference between the two versions is that whereas the dialect of L on the whole preserves the forms of late northern Middle English, that of C has certain occasional features that are characteristic of a later period. Though the two MSS. were written probably about the middle third of the fifteenth century, these occasional spellings reflect the state of the language at that time rather more faithfully than do the more conservative forms of L.

A list follows of the linguistic features of C in so far as they differ from those of L. Some have a bearing on the dialect of C, others on its date, others again are of general philological interest. The words are usually taken from those parts of the line where the copyists have been free to substitute their own dialect forms for those of the original. Differences have been noted between the forms of words employed by the various hands in so far as they may reflect differences in speech habits. Northern characteristics, which are assumed to have been inherited from the original, have as a rule been excluded.

*General Midland Feature*
  1. Plural Pres. in -*en*: *han* 202; *styken* 297; *resten* 634; *weshen* 678; *rysen* 682; *vschen* 1078; *frouschen* 1103.

*Features Common to Midland and Southern*
  2. *ch* for OE. *c*: *muchell* 72; *mechell* 98; *ych* 89, 93; *syche* 799; *swych* 1534; *euerychon* 1454.
  3. 2nd Sg. Pres. in -(*e*)*st*: *hast* 426, 757, 851; *dost* 707; *comyst* 709; *taryest* 1328.
  4. 3rd Sg. Pres. in -(*e*)*th*: *seyth* 197; *chalangeth* 432; *syȝthe* 819; *vseþ* 822.
  5. Past Plural of 'to be': *weren* 1284.
  6. Imperative Plural in -*eþ*: *herkeneþ* 1459.
  7. The following plural forms of the 3rd pers. pronoun:—
     Acc.: *hem* 120, 948; *hom* 233, 324, 684; *home* 1516.
     Gen.: *her* 342, 772; *here* 889, 943; *hor* 1118, 1195; *hore* 1695.
     Dat.: *hem* 87, etc.
     (Forms in *th*- are plentiful in the Nom. Acc. and Gen. but these have been excluded. English forms would scarcely be found in a pure northern text at this date).
  8. The following forms of the Demonstrative pronouns:—
     Sg.: *þus* 403; *þo* 865, 904, 1561.
     Pl.: *þo* 770; *þese* 1112, 1278.

The Demonstrative Pronoun *þo* is used with the weakened force of the Def. Art. in 942 (sg.) and 1475 (pl.). (Note the survival of OE. instr. *þӯs, þis* in *þis* 1349.)

*Typical Features shared by West Midland and Southern*
9. OE. ӯ remains, and is spelt *u, uy: dud* 360, *dude* 1252, 1374; *duden* 679; *burd(e)* 785, 825, 1529; *kunred* 851; *hull* 1209; *suche* 1120; *hurde* 637; *fuyre* 1381, 1394.
    *Note.* There are occasional *e*-forms: *mechell* 208; *seche* 499; *dede*, did 442, 455; *ment* (OE. *myntan*), intended 1285; *berde*, maid 775; *ferste* 1538; *fersted*, thirsted, 1714.

These may be due to south-eastern influence, but are perhaps better explained in other ways: *dede* may have a long vowel, and in the remaining words the vowel may have been lowered from *i*. (See Wyld, *History of Mod. Colloquial English*, p. 226, and 18 below.)

10. OE. *ă* before nasals; the rounded form prevails: *honged* 758 (cf. *hanged* 736); *þonke* 899; *þonked* 1095; *lond, hond* 14, 15; *erond* 920; possibly *gon* 1157, 1302, etc. Also *schom* 127, r.w. *nom, com*, but these may be derived from lengthened forms.
11. Past Participle in *i-, y-: i-gon* 980; *y-sen* 1592; *y-sent* 121; *y-went* 123; *y-heryʒed* 140; *y-born* 317; *i-sett* 643; *y-deryd* 829; *y-speryd* 831, 833; *y-lauʒth* 843, etc.
    *Note.* There is a *y*-form in the infinitive *y-her* 27.
12. The following forms of the Feminine Pronoun:—
    Nom.: *hoo* 702; *ho* 1723, 1793; *hoe* 1801.
    Acc.: *hoe* 779.
    The north midland and northern *sho* is found once (733).
13. Loss of final *-n* in strong Past Participles and other words: *slawe* 349; *go* 630; *be* 796; *gyf* 973; *slay* 1667; *opo*, upon 154; *aʒe*, again, 1354.

*Southern Features*
14. Pres. Part. in *-yng: harpyng* 1434; *lowynge* 1452; *syttyng* 1458, 1479.
15. Plural Present in *-eþ: louethe* 3; *bereth* 266; *wyteþ* 739; *lepeþ* 770; *lyʒth* 1574; *makeþ* 1889.

The prevailing complexion of the dialect is thus midland (points 1–8) and is west midland rather than east (9–13); 3 and 4, however, are found also in east midland texts, and the presence of these features here may indicate slight influence from this area, though not necessarily. If 13 is to be regarded as a midland and not a southern feature (and it probably is, in view of the majority of the remainder), it points to the south-west midlands. The originally southern present participle in *-yng* (14) is probably significant of nothing except date and the gradual spread of what was to become the standard form.[1] I therefore suggest tentatively that the scribes of C spoke a west midland dialect, or at least were working on a text containing a considerable number of west midland forms, though it may also have contained some admixture of east midland (3, 4, 9 [*e*-forms], possibly 14), and southern (15).

---

[1] According to Wyld (*Short History of English*, p. 258), *-yng* forms are found in *Handlying Synne*, written about a century before *Sir Degrevant*.

## INTRODUCTION

*Further points of general interest*

16. Unstressed endings *es, er* spelt *us, ur: justus* 95; *kynghus* 314; *hytus* 400; *pedur* 1083; *dyntus* 1700; *mowthus* 1718; *robus* 1879, etc.
    This characteristic, though not confined to the west midlands, is more common there than in other areas.[1]
17. ME. *er* > *ar: marvelus* 423; also implicit in the inverted spelling *herdy* 24.
18. The raising of $\bar{e}$ is implied by the spelling *mele*, mile, r.w. *whyll syle* 358. The same vowel is also used for the fronted development of OE. $\bar{a}$ in *hem*, home 90; cf. also *ples*, place 427. These spellings are confined to hand A.
19. Lowering of ME. $\check{\imath}$ to $\check{e}$: *weste* 302; *well*, will 457; *freth* 502; *breng* 507; possibly also *dent* 356; *ment* 1285; *berde* 775; *ferste* 1538; *fersted* 1714. These forms are noticeably more frequent in the part of the text written in hand A.
20. Over-rounding of ME. tense $\dot{\varrho}$: *south*, sooth 436; *flour*, floor 1485 (cf. *flore* 1488); *ʒoud* 942; *soufft* 1727. For an interpretation of these spellings, see Wyld, *History of Mod. Colloquial English*, p. 234.
21. Parasitic vowels are occasionally found before and after *r: perow, porow* 1122, 356; *scorun* 1069, r.w. *i-swrun, to-mowrun; morwoun* 1353, r.w. *porun, by-forun*. See Wyld, *op. cit.*, p. 299. Examples of parasitic vowels in other positions are *stalloworþ* 1061 (cf. *stalworʒth* 1129); *nobulle*, nobility 92.
22. Loss of spirant *ʒ* after front vowel and before *t: hytus* 400. The following inverted spellings also testify to this loss: *whyʒth* 642, 1402, 1446; *brghtenes* for *bryttenes*, hews to pieces 322.
23. Loss of spirant *ʒ* after back vowel: *þo* 1533. Inverted spelling: *trouʒth* 768, 769 (see Wyld, *op. cit.*, p. 305).
24. Loss of *t* after consonant: *laf*, left 349 (see Wyld, *op. cit.*, pp. 303–4).
25. Development of *w-* initially before ME. slack $\bar{\varrho}$: *whome*, home 945 (see Wyld, *op. cit.*, pp. 306–7).
26. Loss of *w* before an unstressed vowel or *h*; after a consonant before a rounded vowel: *hammard*, homeward 1249; *ho*, who 1449, 1868; *to*, two 474 (see Wyld, *op. cit.*, pp. 296-7; Jespersen, *MEGr*.7.32; Luick *Hist. Gr.* §716(2).
27. *wh* is found for etymological *w* in *whan*, won 96.
28. Loss of *l* before *t: satur*, saltire 1046 (see Wyld, *op. cit.*, p. 297).
29. *f* for *þ: fersted* 1714 (see Wyld, *op. cit.*, p. 291).
30. Voicing of *t: herd*, heart 196, 1104, 1340; *doughder* 467; *counforde* 1782, r.w. *lorde, a-corde; send*, sent 1265; *wend*, went 367; *herdus*, harts 71 (probably).
31. Unvoicing of *d: prout* 1575 (? perhaps from LOE. *prūt*).
32. Metathesis of *r: worng(es)* 384, 558; *hawþrone* 944; *dere-wroþe* 1447; *worth*, angry 209; *þryd* 1306; *þrytty* 1905. (Metathesized forms occur also in L, but are not so frequent, e.g., *thristid* 1714; *thritty* 1906.)

[1] See Serjeantson, *op. cit.*, pp. 8, 12.

33. Survivals, etc., in the accidence of nouns:—
   (a) Gen. sg. -r stems: *fadyr* 1550.
   (b) Northern (uninflected) genitive: *Englond* 583; *devyl* 792; *damysel* 1190.
   (c) Neuter pl.: *hors* 1017, 1195, 1201; *thyng* 487.
   (d) Fem. pl.: *dede* 118.
   (e) *menne* (gen. pl.) 1476 may be explained as a development of OE. plural *manna* with mutated vowel from the nominative.

## VIII. ANALYSIS AND SOURCES

The basic pattern on which the story is moulded is as follows:—

A man falls in love with a woman above him in rank. They are accustomed to meet in a secret place, but their love is discovered and is reported to the lady's father. In spite of this and other obstacles provided by convention or the author's fancy, the ending is happy and the two are united in marriage.

In *Sir Degrevant* this theme, which lies at the root of many romances ancient and modern, is elaborated and modified. The following elements may be distinguished:—

1. The Earl's hunting raid, the consequent bitterness between the hero and himself, and the hero's retaliation.
2. Sir Degrevant's love for his enemy's daughter (a lady somewhat above him in rank), his secret wooing, and his marriage.
3. The meeting in the garden.
4. The three days' tournament in which he shows himself to be worthy of her.
5. The loyal squire, who receives the knight's confidences; the waiting maid, whose co-operation is secured.
6. The description of Melidor's chamber, which may further be analysed into a number of contributory details:—
   (a) The hero first received by the waiting-maid.
   (b) The secret entrance to the castle.
   (c) The washing.
   (d) The meal.
   (e) The adornments of the chamber.
   (f) The bed.
7. The wicked servant who betrays the lovers.

No other romance is known that combines all these elements and that therefore may be looked upon as the source of the poem. Since most of them have been used before, in the first instance the question of sources resolves itself into finding parallels for one or more of them in the stock of tales to which the author may have turned for material. When the survey is complete, nothing more will have been proved about the poem than that it is a composite product, presenting well-worn ideas in a new combination. The problem of estimating the extent of the author's reading so far as it is reflected in this poem will still remain. One hopes to be able to show, or at least to make it seem probable, that he owes a debt to specific romances, even though one can infer little or nothing of how the debt was incurred.

The wrong done by the Earl in raiding Sir Degrevant's lands provides a reason for much that follows: Sir Degrevant's retaliation, his chance meeting with the Earl's daughter, the necessity for wooing in secret, the forester's betrayal, and its consequences both violent and happy. Incidents similar to this are found in both the history and the romance of the Middle Ages, but in view of the realistic treatment of this part of the story, it may be inferred that the author looked no further for details than to his own observation of what was going on round him. The germinal idea of the dispute about lands between the hero and his feudal superior was probably obtained from some romance (the point is more fully discussed later), but the manner of its presentation seems to imply more special knowledge of how an estate was run than is usual in romances. As a northern man, the author must have been familiar with border raids such as are re-told in the spirited verse of *The Hunting of the Cheviot*; but local acts of lawlessness (such as are found recorded in the bald prose of the Parliamentary records)[1] must have been known throughout the realm. Given a hint from the romance, and the author's knowledge of the hazards of mediæval life, there is nothing in the situation that is so striking, or so boldly original, as to be beyond the competence of a minstrel to work up into a story.

Most of the remaining themes, and many of the incidental details, are romantic commonplaces. Love is usually secret, either because the lady is married (as with Lancelot and Guinevere, or Tristram and Iseult), or because she is a paynim (as in *Octovian* and *Generydes*), or because of the difference in rank, real or supposed, between the lovers (as in *King Horn*, *William of Palerne*, *Amis and Amiloun*, *Roswall and Lilian*, *The Squyr of Lowe Degre*, etc.), or because the hero and the lady's father are enemies (as in *Torrent of Portyngale*), or for a combination of such reasons.

---

[1] The following account shows that lawless invasions of a man's property by his enemies (the owner being away at the wars) were known in real life. The events occurred, of course, in a locality far removed from that in which *Sir Degrevant* was written:—A no*s*tre seign*ur* le Roi mus*t*re Alisot la femme Henr*i* de Uphatherle [Up Hatherly, near Cheltenham] q*ue* come jadis le dit Henri son baroun esteit pr*is* ove les Escotes en bataile Estriveling *et* illeoq*ue* detenu en p*ri*son un *et* plus *et* raunsoné p*ur* xl liv*res*. Thomas de Uphatherle *et* Robert de Presteburi tan come le dit Henri eust demoré en Escoce luy deseiseru*nt* de sa terre en Uphatherle cest a saver de deus charwes de terre ove les apertenances *et* depa*r*teru*nt* mesmes ceux tenements entre eux *et* ses mesones abateru*nt et* de illeoq*ue* remueru*nt* tanq*ue* a Presteburi *et* la le dit Robert fist faire edifieme*n*s sur son soil domeine. Et les biens le dit Henri [ensement] emporteru*nt* a la value de CC. liv*res*. Et puis le dit Henri veint hors de Escoce entra en ses dites tenements *et* en eux ne demora for [ke] un nuyt . . . Apres ceo les dites Robert *et* Thomas . . . [bat]eru*nt* le dit Henri en le vile de Glouce*st*re cest a saver debruseru*nt* ses deus braaz ses deus quises *et* ses deus jambes *et* sa teste de chescune part *et* son corps tut naufré *et* vilement treté q*ui* a grant peine eschapa le mort (*Ancient Petitions*, P.R.O. File 179, No. 8929. The petition was presented in 1330).

*The Calendar of Patent Rolls*, 1340, p. 101, mentions a Commission of oyer and terminer to Richard Wylughby, etc. . . . on complaint by Ralph Basset of Drayton that Alan, etc. . . . broke his hedges, dykes, and hays at Drayton Basset, entered his park there, carried away his deer, and assaulted . . . his servants. See also *Year Books of Edward III*, Rolls Series, 12v: Index of Matters s. v. Trespass; Caxton *Fayttes of Armes and of Chyualrye* (ed. Byles, EETS, 1932), pp. 221–2. The commonness of the offence makes one hesitate to accept Miss Rickert's virtual identification of Degrevant and James Douglas, with estates in S. W. Galloway (*Romances of Love*, Intro., pp. xlvii–viii), just as it is difficult to regard him as a western man with estates in Wales (Hibbard, *Medieval Romance in England*, p. 307; see below). I see no valid reason for supposing that the author had in mind any locality more remote than the Yorkshire dales, or any historical personage.

The steward, especially the wicked and tale-bearing steward, is a familiar figure in English romances. This conception of his character may originate in Sir Kay, the boorish and uncourtly seneschal of King Arthur's hall.[1] In *Amis and Amiloun* the steward betrays Amis and Belisaunt to her father and thereby incurs the author's disapproval,[2] even though, according to any reasonable way of looking at the incident, the man was only doing his duty in telling the father of his daughter's lasciviousness. In *The Squyr of Lowe Degre* it is the jealous steward that betrays the love of the hero and heroine. *King Horn* is yet another story of the hero's love for a maiden above him in rank, and the betrayal of that love to her father.

*Sir Degrevant* varies this theme slightly. The difference in rank between the knight and the Earl's daughter is alluded to (in a passage of only subsidiary importance) but is not insisted upon. The Earl does not urge it as an obstacle to their marriage, probably because it suited the author's purpose in the introductory part of the poem to make the hero a wealthy man, well endowed with lands.[3] Again, it is the forester, and not the steward, that reports their love to the lady's father. The steward is brought a little later into the story to conspire with both of them in plotting the ambush. But in spite of the variation, the conventionality of the incident is plain enough.[4]

The three days' joust with a lady as the prize is a variant of a very common theme—the tasks that a man has to perform as a test of his fidelity and worthiness. Some obstacles are always put in the path of the hero of romance before he can win his heart's desire. Jousting was a pastime common to most romances, and though it is probably to be considered as forming part of the test in *Sir Degrevant*, once again the author lays no emphasis upon this aspect of it. There is a tournament in *Roswall and Lilian* wherein the hero wins the lady by jousting three times each in armour of a different colour. In *Ipomedon* there is a three days' tournament; in *Sir Gowther* there is another, the issue of which is watched by the lady from her bower.[5] The ballad of *Thomas of Potte* (*Percy Folio MS.*, Vol. III, 137) tells how the low-born lover wins the Earl's daughter by overcoming the high-born rival in a tilting match.

The faithful squire and the waiting-maid are provided by writers of French and English romances to receive the confidences of their master or mistress and to share their adventures. There is a loyal squire in each of the romances of *Eglamour, Partonope, Ipomedon*, and *Libeaus Desconus*. Of these, Sir Eglamour's squire approaches most nearly to Sir Degrevant's. In so far as the squire is his master's confidant in love, he is to be related to Amis in the *Romance of the Rose*.

[1] Sir Aymere, the steward in *Sir Degrevant*, is referred to in C 1594 as *þe Kayous*, which may mean that he resembled Sir Kay (see note). The word is not recorded in the OED.

[2] See *Sir Degrevant* 1585–8, where the minstrel's discreet silence is commended, and by implication the forester and the steward are condemned.

[3] The waiting-maid (857–864) is more explicit on the point than anyone else in telling him that the Duke of Gerle is a far more suitable match than he for Melidor, who would be lowering herself in taking him.

[4] For further examples of the part played by stewards, good and bad, in the romances, see note to 1593.

[5] Miss J. L. Weston has shown it to have originated in folk-stories (*The Three Days' Tournament*, London, 1902).

The waiting-maid is his counterpart. She is to be found especially in romances of courtly sentiment, where the chief characters are given to introspection, and in particular to discussing at length what it feels like to be in love. Examples are *William of Palerne* (and of course its French original), and the story of *Tristram*. In the *Yvain* of Chrétien de Troyes, as in *Sir Degrevant*, she receives the hero in a room of the castle, and undertakes to help him in winning over her mistress.

The castle garden is a favourite place in the romances for protestations of love. In *William of Palerne* it is there that the love-sick hero wanders every day in order to be as near as possible to Melidor's bower. The Squire of Low Degree wanders frequently in the garden, where his soliloquies are overheard by the lady in her bower. It is there that Belisant first makes her declaration of passion for Amis, and the bastard Sir Gowther is begotten. Alternatively, as in *King Horn* and *Sir Beues*, the lovers meet in the lady's bower. In *Sir Degrevant*, as in *The Squyr of Lowe Degre*, they meet in both places.

The question still remains whether there are romances, preferably of early date, in which some of these recurrent themes are already in combination, and which the author of *Sir Degrevant* may have known. In this connexion, Miss Hibbard (*Mediæval Romance in England*, p. 307) considers that the possibility of Celtic, and especially Welsh, influence must not be lost sight of. This is true, though not perhaps quite in the sense in which she intended it, and though some of the evidence upon which she bases her conclusion is of dubious value.[1] There are at least three such tales, each having some association with Celtic literature. Let it be said at once, however, that the possibility of direct Celtic influence or direct translation from Celtic sources must be ruled out. There is not a shred of evidence that the author knew anything of Celtic literature at first hand. The exact way in which this influence has made itself felt in the poem is obscure, and may always remain so.

[1] Three of Miss Hibbard's points may here be dealt with.:—

1. In 1557–60 there is an allusion to the folk-custom known as 'bundling': the lovers do their courting in bed, but refrain from sexual contact. Miss Hibbard thinks that the author may have obtained his information on the subject from some Welsh source, on the ground that later authorities speak of the custom as of long standing in Wales. But it is so widespread that it is doubtful whether any such conclusion can be drawn. Even the authorities cited by Miss Hibbard speak of the practice not only in Wales, but also in England, Ireland, Holland, Afghanistan, New England, and among Slavonic peoples. For list, see note on 1557.

2. Sir Degrevant's retinue is spoken of in 1367 as 'wylde men of þe west.' This, Miss Hibbard thinks, may imply that they were Welshmen. She might also have added that Sir Degrevant is represented as riding out of the west towards the Earl's castle in C 1085. The geography of the poem, however, has not been clearly thought out as a whole. In 1205 Sir Degrevant is said to have ridden westwards (i.e., out of the east) towards the Earl's castle. These statements cannot be reconciled; but even if C 1085 and 1367, being consistent with each other, be accepted against 1205, the most that they can be taken to mean is that the Earl's lands and castle lay to the east of Sir Degrevant's.

3. The place name *Westwale* (L 1511) Miss Hibbard quite wrongly assumes to mean western Wales. The true meaning is Westphalia, less ambiguously spelt in C. In *Morte Arthure* 621, in a context that leaves the meaning open to no possible doubt, Westphalia is spelt *Westwale*; in 2656 it is *Westuale*; in 2826 it is *Westfale*. I have found no evidence for either a silk-weaving or a glass industry in Wales in the Middle Ages, but the German glass industry had long been established. It is significant that *knoppes* (C 1510) is of Low German origin.

The first story to be considered is the English romance of *The Erle of Toulous*[1], one text of which is to be found in the Thornton MS[2]. Towards the close of the poem we are told that the author has been working on a Breton tradition. Though *The Erle of Toulous* is a version of the Persecuted Wife story, another common romance theme, it is remarkably similar to *Sir Degrevant* both in situation and detail. There is the initial act of lawlessness committed against the hero's lands by his feudal superior. Both aggressors are defeated, and both their wives protest against the wrong done. The Earl of Toulous begins by loving his enemy's wife with a kind of chivalrous and distant regard, Sir Degrevant at once falls passionately in love with his enemy's daughter. In both poems the hero secretly visits the lady at the castle, with a single companion. The Earl of Toulous sees her in a chapel; Sir Degrevant lies hidden in the garden and sees her pass into the chapel. In both poems the ringing of the Mass bell is specially mentioned. Each lady is richly clothed for the service, and goes about accompanied by two noblemen. On his way from the castle, the hero is led into an ambush, but routs it utterly in spite of the odds against him. At another point in the story, the hero makes his way back to the castle to fight on behalf of the lady, in *Sir Degrevant* to take part in a tournament against a rival, in the *Erle of Toulous* as her champion in an ordeal by battle against false accusers. The action ends with the hero's triumph over all his foes, with the reconciliation of the contending parties brought about by the intervention of a woman, and with the hero's marriage. The length of his married life and the number of his children are specified (see note on 1905–7), and the poems conclude almost in the words with which they began—a pious prayer for salvation (see note on 1). There are occasional resemblances in expression and phraseology as well, but these are not numerous enough or close enough to make it certain that the author of *Sir Degrevant* was working over *The Erle of Toulous* in its present form, though it is not known to exist in any other.

It does not seem to have been pointed out before that there are a number of detailed resemblances between *Sir Degrevant* and the *Lay of Guigemar* by Marie de France. In one important respect, the two are entirely different, for the *Lay* is a tale of faerie; but the similarities are sufficiently striking to suggest the conclusion that the author of *Sir Degrevant* knew the story, whether or not in Marie's version is impossible to say. It will be convenient to present the points of resemblance in the form of a list, and to refer in brackets to the appropriate passages in *Sir Degrevant*. This method will remove the necessity of dwelling upon the numerous differences, which have nothing to do with *Sir Degrevant*.

1. Guigemar was a brave knight (9–12), who had distinguished himself in many countries.
2. He was fond of hunting (49–60), and indifferent to the charms of women (61–4).

[1] Miss Hibbard discusses this parallel, *op. cit.* p. 310.

[2] The fact is given for what it is worth, but it is difficult to say whether or not it has a bearing on the question of whether the poem was known to the author of *Sir Degrevant* as it was to the scribe. In the MS., the two poems are almost contiguous, being separated only by the short *Metrical Life of St. Christopher*. The similarities may therefore have impressed the scribe.

INTRODUCTION lxvii

3. The castle to which he was taken in the magic boat had one entrance only, from the sea (933–938). (The Earl's castle has more than one, but there is also a water-gate opening on to the sea, and Sir Degrevant passes through this gate when he is visiting Melidor secretly.)
4. The lady is in the garden of the castle when she catches sight of her destined lover (685–692).
5. The garden is associated with the chapel in the same passage of description (637–40).
6. The hero interviews the waiting-maid who informs her mistress of his arrival, and conducts him to her (805–836; 1361–1376).
7. The maid becomes the knight's confidante, and he tells her of his love (837–880; 897–920).
8. The wooing is continued secretly for about eighteen months (1565–1568).
9. The intrigue is discovered by a servant who informs the lady's husband (1589–1592).
10. The hero wins his right to the lady in a tournament at which, it is expressly stated, the jousters are given food at the castle (1157–1160).

Much of this, of course, is common romantic material, and could easily be paralleled elsewhere. But some of the points mentioned (particularly 2, 3, 8) are not at all common. Taken singly, again, the points of resemblance prove little, but the cumulative effect of a number proves at least that at the end of the twelfth century, there existed a French story, derived from Celtic sources, that the author of *Sir Degrevant* could have known, and from which he might have obtained hints for his poem. In view of the large number of French words in *Sir Degrevant* (some of them recorded only here), there is no difficulty in supposing that the author knew the language well.

So far, no important parallel has been adduced for one of the more striking passages in the poem—the scenes, one can almost say the ritual, in Melidor's chamber. Full-length descriptions of interiors with elaboration of pictorial detail are uncommon in Middle English romance, but they are much after the French manner. Such descriptions[1] are generally ablaze with gold and colour and precious stones. Scenes from well-known stories are painted on the walls. Statues also contribute to the opulence of the total effect but, as in *Sir Degrevant*, are not usually described in detail. French writers are particularly fond of describing mechanical toys: dancing figurines, automatic sentinels, gold and silver birds that whistle when the wind blows, and so forth.[2] So characteristic a feature is this that the presence of some mechanical device of the kind is almost to be looked for. Melidor's chamber is free of such gewgaws, but the author has installed a clock there (as in the *Sept Sages*[3]) and we

[1] See B. de Sainte More, *Roman de Troie* (ed. Joly, Paris 1870) 14583 ff.; *Roman d'Alexanlre* (ed. Armstrong, Princeton and Paris 1937) Branch III, st. 48–51, etc.

[2] See *Roman de Troie* 14662 ff.; Chrétien's *Perceval* (ed. Potvin, Mons 1865–71) 13352 ff.; *Ipomedon* (ed. Kölbing and Koschwitz, Breslau 1889) 3294 ff.; *Roman d'Eneas* (ed. J. Salverda de Grave, Halle 1891), paragr. 389–90; *Floire et Blanceflor* (first version ed. du Méril, Paris 1856) 1731 ff.

[3] *Sept Sages* (ed. Keller, Tübingen 1836) 3958 ff.

may be sure it was no ordinary clock, for it had bells to strike the hours, and four lines are devoted to it. If the chamber is a bedroom, much care is lavished on the description of the bed, its ornate hangings and embroidered coverlet.[1]

In one respect (it is, I think, important) the interior decorations of the French romances differ significantly from what is found in *Sir Degrevant*. A French poet will adorn the walls of a room with scenes from the Trojan Wars, or from the life of Alexander the Great, or David, or with allegorical figures like the Seven Liberal Arts, but not usually with pictures or statues of saints, or indeed with anything of predominantly religious, as distinct from Biblical, colouring. The passage from *Sir Degrevant* (1450–68) portraying the archangels, the Four Doctors, and scenes from both Old and New Testaments thus stands in contrast to what our poet could have found in possible French originals, and to the purely secular tone of French interiors.[2]

Close parallels, both in general situation and in detail, to the incidents leading up to the description of Melidor's bower are found in the Welsh romance of *Owein and Lunet*, sometimes called the *Lady of the Fountain*. The story itself depends upon a French original (possibly the *Yvain* of Chrétien de Troyes, more probably upon some other romance now lost) based ultimately upon Celtic tradition. The English version of *Sir Degrevant* is considerably nearer to the Welsh than to the French of Chrétien, or to the English romance of *Ywain and Gawain*. The following passage is taken from Ellis and Lloyd's translation of the *Mabinogion*, II, 43–4. In both *Sir Degrevant* and the Welsh story, the knight is received first of all by the waiting-maid:—

And Owein looked all over the upper chamber, and there was not in the upper chamber a nail which was not coloured *with priceless colours*, nor was there a panel without *gilded carvings of divers designs* upon it.

And the maiden *kindled the firewood*, and took a *silver bowl with water in it, and a towel of white lawn* on her shoulder, and *gave water for Owein to wash*, and placed a silver *table*, inset with gold, in front of him, and upon it a *cloth* of yellow lawn, and *she brought him his dinner*. And Owein felt certain that he has never seen *any kind of food, which he did not see plenty thereof there* ... And he had never seen anywhere such an abundance of *rare courses of food and drink* ... And worthy of Arthur was the excellence of the *bed* that the maiden made for him. It was of scarlet with furs and brocaded silk, and sendal and lawn.

---

[1] See *Karls des Grossen Reise nach Jerusalem und Constantinopel* (ed. Koschwitz, Heilbronn 1883) 430 ff.; *Roman de Troie*, 1535 ff.; *Perceval* 9054 ff., 22420 ff.; *Escanor* (ed. Michelant, Tübingen 1886) 15832 ff.

[2] The recently discovered painted chamber in Longthorpe Tower, near Peterborough, also preserves the kind of decoration described in *Sir Degrevant*. The murals, which must once have completely covered the walls and the vaulted roof, are of the early 14th century, and must at one time have been quite as sumptuous as those of the poem. Not all the individual figures have been identified, but there is the same combination as in *Sir Degrevant* of sacred, didactic, and secular. In spite of wide differences in detail and a difference of emphasis in conception (the poem being more ecclesiastical), both Melidor's chamber and Longthorpe Tower include the Evangelists (1457), a number of crowned figures (1479) varied with diaper-work (1444), birds (1496), and heraldic ornaments (C 1497), the last two embroidered on the bed-hangings. (See E. C. Rouse, *Medieval Paintings at Longthorpe Tower*, Country Life, Vol. CI, pp. 604 ff.)

In Chrétien's *Yvain* there is no unified description at all, but a few details about the room, the feast, and the bed are scattered through the passage (970 ff.) describing the interview with the damsel and her gift of the ring. The corresponding passage in the English romance of *Ywain and Gawain* is a mere couplet (1131–2).

Regarding this passage, we seem to be faced with two alternatives, since direct adaptation cannot be seriously considered. The first is that the common stock of romance themes must have been larger than has been supposed, and must have included a conventional way of describing a lady's bower, and what went on when the lady, or her maid, or both together, entertained the young knight to a meal. In view of the pervasive conventionality of mediæval romance literature, this possibility must always be kept in mind. What appears to be quite as likely an hypothesis is that the author had access to, and adapted from, the French original of the *Lady of the Fountain*, or to some other French poem related to it. Any more certain or precise conclusion does not seem possible on the evidence, but it is borne out by the fact that two French poems are alluded to during the course of the passage (*Amadas et Idoine*, 1494, *Les Vœux du Paon*, 1519, and probably also 1481. See notes on these lines).

Some account will now be given of the parallels that can be found elsewhere to the phraseology of the poem, though this is a matter that can be treated more briefly. As with the author's material, so with his turns of phrase and expression: many of them are conventionality itself, found so frequently in Middle English poetry, especially tail-rime poetry, that it is quite impossible to trace their origins, or to do more than give some indications of the wide currency they enjoyed. Expressions like *clear crystal, spear and shield, war and wise, red gold, the sooth for to say, fair and free*, and scores of others can be found almost anywhere in the popular poetry of the fourteenth and fifteenth centuries, and the author is heavily indebted to them.

On the other hand, some are more individual in form, and embody ideas that are less stereotyped. For most of them, the author was no doubt indebted to his own inventiveness, but occasionally he shows signs of having borrowed from the alliterative *Morte Arthure*, especially in the catalogue of food and wines consumed at the supper in Melidor's chamber (1409–1432). This passage reads like a condensed account of the banquet given by the King in honour of the Roman embassy (*Morte Arthure* 182–204). The individual items can be paralleled in description of mediæval fare in poetry or prose:[1] these were the things that our mediæval forefathers ate and drank. But no less than nine of the items mentioned in *Sir Degrevant* are common to the list in *Morte Arthure*, a considerably larger number than are common to any other two Middle English bills of fare. The following quotation will show the manner and extent of the imitation at this point:—

> Pacokes and plouers in platers of golde,
>
> . . . . . .
>
> Seyne bowes of wylde bores with þe braune lechyde,
>
> . . . . . .

---

[1] See *The Weddynge of Sir Gawen* 611 ff.; *Iohn de Reeue* (Percy Folio MS. II 576) 464, etc.; *The Squyr of Lowe Degre* 319 ff., and Mead's note; *Two Fifteenth Century Cookery Books* (EETS.); and Mead, *The Medieval Feast*.

> Þan cranes & curlues, craftyly rosted,
> Connygez in cretoyne, colourede full faire,
> Fesauntez enflureschit in flammande siluer,
>
> . . . . .
>
> Rynisch wyne and Rochell, richere was neuer;
> Vernage of Venyce vertuouse and Crete.

Another detail from the same banquet:—
> Þane clarett and Creette clergyally rennen
> With condethes full curious, all of clene siluyre
>               (*Morte Arthure* 200–201)

is paralleled in the account of Sir Degrevant's wedding feast:—
> Þe wyne in condyths rane
>            (L 1865, C 1866).

A list follows of further phrases that may be regarded as borrowings. It does not include clichés:—

1. Deg. 83.     With menske and with manhede
   M.A. 399.    My menske and my manhede.
2. Deg. C 266.   Bereth no chartur of pes
   M.A. 3058.   I gyf ʒow chartire of pes.
3. Deg. C 290.   With speres ferisly þey foynede
   M.A. 1897–8. With ferse men of armes . . . we foynede with sperys
        (See also M.A. 2163, 3689).
4. Deg. 387.    Appon a stede feraunt
   M.A. 1811, 2140, 2259, 2451. One feraunte stedez.
5. Deg. 409.    He askis justyng of were
   M.A. 1657.    We seke justynge of werre.
6. Deg. 463.    Ma doghety sall dy
   M.A. 4241.    That euer þat doughtty sulde dy.
7. Deg. 557.    Þat I sall faythfully fyghte
   M.A. 1735.    Bot luke ʒe fyghte faythefully.
8. Deg. C 941, also 1579, 1690. Fayir þei passed þat flode
   M.A. 3718.    Thane was þe flode passede.[1]
9. Deg. 1110.    Þay teme sadils full tyte
   M.A. 1801.       and temez theire sadills.
10. Deg. 1123.   Vn-to þe cheftane he chese
    M.A. 2954.   Cheses to sir Cheldrike, a cheftayne noble.
11. Deg. 1323, also 1622. A scharpe wapyn for þe were
    M.A. 2137.   wyghte wapynez of werre.[2]

Lastly, it is probably significant that the only examples quoted in the OED. of the rare verb *revay* (see Glossary) are taken from *Sir Degrevant* and *Morte Arthure*, where it occurs several times.

In order as far as possible to unify the material of this section, I tentatively put forward a hypothesis regarding the genesis of the poem. It must be regarded as provisional.

---

[1] The phrase is also found in the *Wars of Alexander* 3844, where it may represent an independent borrowing from *Morte Arthure*.

[2] The alliteration is obvious enough to have occurred to two writers independently. The phrase is therefore of less value as evidence than most of the others cited.

An author familiar with the ordinary themes and motives of romance, and impressed by the tale of *The Erle of Toulous*, decided to adapt that poem afresh, and to give it an English setting. He expanded at length the initial episode of the dispute over lands, filling in details from his own experience. He suppressed the Persecuted Wife, and substituted the high-born and spirited but dutiful daughter in love with her social inferior and father's enemy. At this point a difficulty had to be met; for if the disparity in rank and position were great enough, the interest in the quarrel would diminish, indeed the whole reason for it would disappear. The less the social importance of the hero, the less likely he would be to have lands to defend. So the low-born hero was replaced by the valiant and wealthy young knight, the equal in renown of Perceval and Gawain, and a member of the Round Table. In crediting these adventures to Sir Degrevant (Agravain, see note on Title) the author was giving prominence to one of King Arthur's less celebrated knights, and one whose character had suffered depreciation at the hands of some French romance writers (followed by Malory), who represent him as a knight of inferior prowess, a spy, and a tale-bearer: constantly being unhorsed in battle, and betraying Lancelot and Guinevere to the King.[1] Our author rebuts the charge of tale-bearing against Agravain by condemning the same fault in the forester; he represents the hero as a knight of great skill in battle, endowed with the *dures mains* that Chrétien had ascribed to him (*Perceval* 9510; see also *Gawain and the Green Knight* 110). In these circumstances, his inferiority in rank to the Earl's daughter could be kept in the background. Such a change of emphasis enabled the poet to spread himself over the quarrel, which, unlike that in the *Erle of Toulous*, is never lost sight of; and set him free to describe its consequences, and in particular the battle between the Earl's retainers and Sir Degrevant's.

By making the hero fall in love with the daughter, instead of the wife, of his enemy (a theme never popular in English romance), the author avoided an awkward moral question. But the wife is retained to play the part of mediator, and to point the moral to her husband when his violence brings defeat and shame. The faithful squire, the waiting-maid, the tournament, the secret meetings, the wicked servant, and the betrayal—indeed most of the stock characters and episodes in the middle of the story—follow in sequence as part of the conventional working out of the love motive. Only at the end, when describing the obvious and inevitable outcome of the preceding events, does the author gravely tell us that he is reproducing an older story:—

>In romance als I heard saye,
>He tuk hir in Goddis laye

(1842–3; see also 1886).

To invoke his authority at this point, as though he were revealing something very important and so marvellous that he scarcely hoped that his unsupported word would be taken, is either a nice touch of irony, or a piece of crass ineptitude.

Narrative details, particularly those relating to the character of the knight, the entrance to the castle, and the description of Melidor's chamber,

---

[1] Another tradition of Agravain's character is preserved in Lovelich's *Merlin* (ed. Koch, EETS.) where he is represented as a courageous and responsible commander. See esp. ll. 19429–19603, 26915 ff.

were taken over from French romances (depending, as it happens, upon Celtic tradition), supplemented from the author's knowledge or fancy. The whole is cast into an unusual tail-rime stanza form, strongly influenced by Middle English alliterative verse, and particularly by *Morte Arthure*. In this or in some such way, the tale of *Sir Degrevant* came into being.

## IX. AUTHOR; DATE

Nothing of the author is known positively, but it is reasonable to infer that he wrote for minstrels, and even that he was a minstrel himself. The poem is directly adapted for recitation: the pious prayer at the opening and close pre-suppose an audience and a host 'sitting in fere'; the break at the close of the first fit (C 368) points in the same direction. When the interest is in danger of flagging after a long descriptive passage, the audience is directly appealed to (1459–60). Minstrels and their craft are periodically commended or advertised, as when the Earl's minstrel is praised for his discretion in keeping to himself his knowledge of Sir Degrevant's wooing and the manner of it. We are told that minstrels are all as 'cortayse' as he (1585–8). The hero's repeated and lavish generosity to minstrels is given prominence (86–8, 1173–6, 1345–6, 1877–80), but since gifts on this disproportionate scale cannot have been seriously expected by a popular minstrel, the author's intention in recounting them cannot have been wholly serious either. They may be taken as his half-humorous estimate of how such people were treated in 'arethede'. The hero's skill in music is singled out for special commendation: it almost makes him an honorary member of the craft.

The author appears to have been a man of some education, acquainted at least with a wide range of romantic literature. In the previous section, he has been shown to have possessed some knowledge of contemporary English poetry, and probably of French poetry as well. In addition, he appears to have known, or at least to have known of, the story of Amadase and Edoyne (not extant in English), that of Betyse and Ydore (1518–9), and the legend of the Rhine gold (542). Though *Sir Degrevant* is not a courtly romance, the author was sufficiently familiar with the ways of polite society to portray the manners of a gentleman, and to distinguish them from those of a boor.

Any date assigned to the poem must be conjectural in the absence of unambiguous internal evidence. If the poet borrowed from *Morte Arthure* and the *Erle of Toulous* (and there is ample reason for supposing that he did), then obviously he must have written after the later of these (i.e., probably the *Erle*). The outside limits of date are thus c. 1400[1] and 1446, the latest possible date for the compilation of the Cambridge MS. So far as linguistic criteria can be used, they point to the earlier of these, for the phonology is that of the fourteenth rather than the fifteenth century. Thus there are no examples in rime showing diphthonging of ME. long vowels $\bar{a}, \bar{\imath}, \bar{u}$, or to the raising of $\bar{e}$.[2] In *The Squyr of Lowe Degre* ME. $\bar{e}$ (tense or

---

[1] The date assigned to the *Erle* by Trounce (Medium Ævum II, 190; III, 48), though Emerson (*Middle English Reader*, p. 279) considers that it was originally composed about the middle of the 14th century.

[2] An apparent exception (*fre* L 84, r. w. *fee, melody, hardy*) is undoubtedly due to corruption (see notes to 92, 96).

slack) rimes with words in unstressed or weakly stressed -*y*, -*ly* (e.g., *chyvalry* 471, r.w. *sea*; *kne* 467, r.w. *gentely*), and this fact is used as an argument for a mid-fifteenth-century date.[1] But in *Sir Degrevant* such rimes are not found: words ending in -*y* rime with ME. $\bar{\imath}$ (e.g., *hy* 412, r.w. *redy*, *doghety*; *hy* 453, r.w. *haby*, *velany*). Unless, therefore, the author used only rimes that were exceptionally archaic, we shall not err greatly in putting the composition of the poem in the first ten years of the fifteenth century, or even earlier.

## X. LITERARY ESTIMATE

Our survey of the contributory themes and analogues of the poem has shown that the author had few original ideas: the material, or most of it, is derivative, and it is presented in a very familiar form. The events work out with practically no surprises, according to a recipe that has been provided by countless previous romance-writers. The characters fit into the design quite easily: their modes of thought and action are those of straightforward, simple-minded folk, who move as the author pulls the strings. The hero and heroine are endowed with the obvious virtues of bravery, kindliness, and beauty, and the usual obstacles are put in the way of their final happiness. From the moment of Sir Degrevant's first avowal of love for Melidor, we realize that her father's objections to the marriage have to be overcome; he must either be killed off, or undergo a change of heart. The author chooses the second course.[2] After having carried on the feud with Sir Degrevant for more than seventeen hundred lines, the Earl is brought from thoughts of murder to thoughts of forgiveness in thirty-two. In little more than another stanza, reconciliation is complete, and he is induced to give up the struggle for no other reason, apparently, than that his wife asks him to. In other ways besides, the ending is unduly hurried, as though the author had tired of puppetry. Thus after the marriage we are told of the death of the Earl and the Countess, Sir Degrevant's succession to the lands, thirty years of married life, the birth of children, Melidor's death and then Sir Degrevant's. All this is passed over with disproportionate haste, even for a story that moves swiftly throughout.

Yet in spite of all that can be said against it, *Sir Degrevant* can be read with pleasure, for the old theme is vigorously presented; within the conventional framework of warfare and wooing the characters are very active, and are always busy about something fresh. There is a great deal of coming and going of various kinds, hunting, fighting, tilting, the paying of secret visits and the taking of messages. All this contributes movement and variety, and there is none of it without purpose. Thus the Duke is brought from over the sea to be Sir Degrevant's rival in love. After his inglorious share in the tournament his work is done; he is sent home again in discomfiture, and out of the poem. The squire, also a shadowy figure, has little to say, but he is useful as the hero's confidant and messenger, constantly moving to and fro between Sir Degrevant's castle and the Earl's. When he can serve in this way no longer, he is promised in marriage to the waiting-maid,

[1] *Squyr of Lowe Degre*, ed. Mead, p. lxxii.

[2] The author of the *Erle of Toulous* takes the other way out (see line 1207 Lüdtke's ed., Berlin 1881.

and we hear little more of either of them. The wicked steward precipitates the crisis by setting the ambush, and is soon disposed of. Seeking to make an end of true love, he succeeds only in bringing about its consummation, his life being the penalty of his interference. There is poetic justice, and a touch of irony, in the situation.

The author's deftness in manipulating his characters, moving them in and out of the story and tying off loose ends, is but one aspect of that sense of proportion with which he has built his poem. Though there is much movement and action, there is also much conversation and description. The balance between them is maintained very fairly, and all tastes are gratified. For the cultured, there are the occasional allusions to courtly sentiment and behaviour, and the passages of pure description, especially the scene in Melidor's bower with its Pre-Raphaelite elaboration of detail.[1] For the unsophisticated, there are the battle-scenes, the love-story, and the wedding feast. This last, relating how gifts and lavish hospitality were available for all comers, is described as a guest would enjoy it, not from the viewpoint of him who pays for it.

*Sir Degrevant*, then, is a popular romance in the best sense; it is addressed to the whole of the people. How far it succeeded in capturing their interest we have naturally no means of knowing, but at least two scribes thought it worthy of preservation.

Since the author has seen with great clearness all that he describes, it is as descriptive writing rather than as narrative that he would probably want his work to be judged. In this respect, he had the right sort of skill for what he set out to do, for the descriptive passages are felt more vividly than the details of the story, the moral qualities of the hero, or the charm of Melidor's presence. He has lavished care on the description of the bower; he has made a list of all the most beautiful things he can call to mind, and the result is a striking passage of considerable pictorial quality, full of colour and variety. It is not perhaps quite as good as it might be, for it is intended to fulfil the same purpose as Acrasia's Bower of Bliss, or the description of Madeline's chamber: to stupefy the hero's senses, and to make credible his attempted seduction of Melidor. The idea is ambitious, but it does not quite succeed, partly because of a lack of unity and congruence in the details, and partly because the stanza form is unsuitable for such work.

On the whole, the poem is at its best when Sir Degrevant leaves his love-making and heeds the call to battle. The expression, usually direct and vigorous, takes on a new power—

> Þe styward Syre Eymere
> Com a lytyl to nere,
> Hys hede by þe colere
> He kerues away.
> (1649–52)

---

[1] The Pre-Raphaelites themselves were sufficiently interested in the poem to publish it and to paint scenes from it. The Kelmscott edition printed by William Morris and containing an illustration by Burne-Jones has been noticed in Section II of this Introduction. J. W. Mackail (*Life of William Morris*, London 1899, I 158) relates how Morris had the drawing-room of the Red House, Upton, decorated with three scenes (again executed by Burne-Jones) from the poem. This was in 1862, thirty-four years before the Kelmscott edition.

Or again, when Melidor, her former resistance broken down, realizes her destiny and leads a horse to her lover in the midst of the fray—

> ʒet she spekys a word of pride:
> 'On þis stede wol I ryde
> By my lemmanes syde
> In lond whare he go.'
> (1317–20)

This is unanswerable; it has the simple forthright determination and finality of some of the best moments in the ballads, with which indeed the poem more than once challenges comparison—

> 'I'd rather be Chiel Wyet's wife,
> The white fish for to sell,
> Before I were Lord Ingram's wife,
> To wear the silk so well.'[1]

For this brief space, Melidor ceases to be the conventional romantic heroine of rather shrewish temper,[2] and becomes a human being.

The author did well, too, in contriving a natural setting for the action. It is a pleasant, wild landscape near the sea—a sun-lit country of forest, frith, and fell, park and chase, heath, woodland glades, and lakes. Though it is so constantly in his mind that no main incident is recounted without some reference to it, the place is never described in set terms, but is lightly touched in here and there, serving to set off more important matters.

Alliteration combined with three pouncing triplet-rimes is a useful device for securing emphasis in the writing; and the use of short lines and occasionally elliptical syntax contributes much to its speed. The poem is alliterated throughout, though not uniformly; there is at least some attempt at concentrating the alliteration or relinquishing it as occasion warrants. Thus it is fairly continuous in the battle and the tournament scenes (see especially 285–350, and 1105–1120), but is not so insistent in the idyllic passage describing how Melidor sang love songs to Sir Degrevant after supper (1433–40). The verbal and rime links are a typical product of mediæval ingenuity, but like the alliteration they are not used merely as ornament. They mitigate the effect of what might otherwise be a source of weakness. A narrative in stanzas is in danger of telling itself in isolated units, each incident being made to fill a stanza irrespective of its importance to the whole, but there is little of this in *Sir Degrevant*. The linking serves to carry the attention from one stanza to the next, and thus to assist the flow of the action until the end. Sir Degrevant, the lover of mirth and minstrelsy, died in defending the Holy Land. As the Lord loves all such, may Heaven be his reward—a thought that brings us back to the starting point. The wheel has come full circle, the tale is told, and the writer bids you farewell.

---

[1] *Lord Ingram and Chiel Wyet* in *English, Scottish, and Popular Ballads*, Student's Riverside ed., London 1904, p. 132.

[2] She belongs to the same tradition of character as Floripas in *Sir Ferumbras*.

## SELECT BIBLIOGRAPHY

*Note.* ME. texts supplying parallels to the phraseology of the poem have not been included. Standard editions, usually those of the EETS., have always been used. For works cited only incidentally, see the footnotes to the Introduction, and the Notes.

1. EDITIONS

   Halliwell, J. O. (ed.), *Early English Metrical Romances of Perceval, Isumbras, Eglamour, and Degrevant, selected from manuscripts at Lincoln and Cambridge,* Camden Soc., London, 1844.
   Luick, K. (ed.), *Sir Degrevant,* Wiener Beiträge XLVII, Wien und Leipzig, 1917.
   Rickert, E., (trans.) *Early English Romances in Verse,* 2v., London and New York, 1908.

2. LITERARY HISTORY

   Wells, J. E., *A Manual of the Writings in Middle English,* Yale Univ. Press, 1916, with six supplements.
   Hibbard, L. A., *Mediæval Romance in England,* New York, 1924.
   Bruce, J. D., *The Evolution of Arthurian Romance From the Beginnings Down to the Year* 1300, 2v., Second ed., Göttingen and Baltimore, 1928.
   Taylor, A. B., *An Introduction to Mediæval Romance,* London, 1930.
   Oakden, J. P., *Alliterative Poetry in Middle English,* 2v., Manchester, 1930, 1935.
   Trounce, A. McI., *The English Tail Rhyme Romances,* Medium Ævum, Vols. 1–3, 1932–4.

3. ANTIQUITIES, SOCIAL BACKGROUND

   Turner, T. H., *Domestic Architecture of the Middle Ages,* 4v., London, 1851 ff.
   Wright, Thomas, *The Homes of Other Days,* London, 1871.
   Schultz, A., *Das höfische Leben zur Zeit der Minnesinger,* 2v., Leipzig, 1879–80.
   Söhring, O., *Werke bildender Kunst in altfranzösischen Epen,* Romanische Forschungen, Erlangen, 1900.
   Turner, G. J., *Select Pleas of the Forest,* Selden Soc., London, 1901 for 1899.
   Mead, W. E., *The English Medieval Feast,* London, 1921.

4. ANALOGUES

   Lüdtke, G. (ed.), *The Erl of Toulous and the Emperes of Almayn,* Berlin, 1881.
   Foerster, W. (ed.), *Der Löwenritter (Yvain) von Christian de Troyes,* Halle, 1887.
   Mead, W. E., Introduction to edition of *The Squyr of Lowe Degre,* Boston, 1904.
   Ellis, T. P. and Lloyd, J., *The Mabinogion, A New Translation,* 2v., Oxford, 1929.
   Harris, J. (ed.), *Marie de France: the Lays of Gugemar, Lanval, and a fragment of Yonec,* New York, 1930.

## 5. LANGUAGE

Tolkien, J. R. R., *The Devil's Coach-horses*, RES. I., 331.
Tolkien, J. R. R. and Gordon, E. V. (eds.), *Sir Gawain and the Green Knight*, Appendix on Language, and Glossary, Oxford, 1925.
Wyld, H. C., *History of Modern Colloquial English*, Third ed., Oxford, 1936.

## 6. METRE

Luick, K., *Die englische Stabreimzeile im XIV, XV, und XVI Jahrhundert*, 2 parts, Anglia XI, 1888–9.
Luick, K., *Zur Metrik der reimendalliterierenden Dichtung*, Anglia XII, 1889.
Bülbring, K. D., *Untersuchungen zur mittelenglischen Metrik*, Morsbach's Studien zur englischen Philologie, Heft 50, Halle, 1913.
Luick, K., *Zur mittelenglischen Verslehre*, Anglia XXXVIII, 1914.
Medary, M. P., *Stanza Linking in Middle English Verse*, Romanic Review VII, No. 3, 1916.
Brown, A. C. L., *Origin of Stanza Linking in English Alliterative Verse*, Romanic Review VII, No. 3, 1916.
Finsterbusch, F., *Der Versbau der mittelenglischen Dichtungen Sir Perceval of Gales und Sir Degrevant*, Wiener Beiträge XLIX, Wien und Leipzig, 1919.

## SIR DEGREUAUNTE

### [I]

JHESU, Lorde in Trynite,
   Graunte þam heuen for to see
   Þat luffes gamen and glee
      And gestis to fede.     4
Whare folkes sittis in fere,
Þare solde men herken and here
Of beryns þat by-fore were
      Þat lyffed in arethede.     8
I will ȝow telle of a knyghte:
Sir Degreuante for-sothe he highte,
He was hardy and wyghte
      And doghty in dede;     12
Was neuer knyghte þat he fande
In France ne in Scotlande
Mighte sitt a strake of his hande
      One his styff stede.     16

### [II]

With Kyng Arthure, I wene,
And Dame Gaynore þe quene,
He was knawen for kene,
      Þis commly knyghte;     20
In Haythynnes and in Spayne,
In France and in Bretayne,
With Perceuelle and Gawayne,
      For hardy and wyghte.     24
He was doghety and dere:
Euer he drewe hym full nere
Whare he of dedis myghte here
      Be daye or be nyghte;     28
For-thi þay named [him] þat stownde
Knyghte of þe Table Rownde,
As it es made in mappamonde,
      In story full ryghte.     32

---

L *Heading: in red, but not in capitals.* 1. *A red initial capital.* 10. *Small* d *in* Degrevant *throughout.*

C *Title:* & theynke and thanke *added in another hand.* 2. to *inserted above the line.* 4. *The scribe wrote* Gestus. *The MS. now reads* Gesstys *owing to correction by hands that may be a century later.* 7. hem *inserted above the line in a later hand.* 12. of dede

## SIR DEGREUUAUNT

### [I]

Lord Gode in Trynite,
Yeff home hevene for to se     *I will tell you the story of Sir Degrevant,*
That louethe gamen and gle
    And gestus to fede.
Þer folke sitis in fere
Shullde men herken and here
Off gode that be-fore [hem] were
    That leuede in arþede.
And Y schall karppe off a knyght
That was both hardy and wyght:     *a brave knight*
Sir Degreuaunt that hend hyght,
    That dowghty was of dede;
Was never knygh that he fond
In Fraunce ne in Englond
Myght sette a schafft of hys hond     *distinguished in war.*
    On a styþe stede.

### [II]

Wyth Kyng Arrtor, Y wene,     *the nephew of Arthur and Guinevere,*
And wyth Gwennor the Quene,
He was known for kene,
    That comelych knyght,
In Heþenesse and in Spayne,
In Fraunce and in Bryttayne,
Wyth Persevall and Gawayne,
    For herdy and wyght.
He was dowghty and der,
And ther nevew full ner,
Þer he of dedys myght y-her
    By days or by nyght;
For-þy they name hem þat stounde
A knyght of Tabull Round,     *and a member of the Round Table.*
As maked is in þe mappe-mound,
    In storye full ryght.

---

added above, and wyght *cancelled.* 13. he *inserted above.* 14. *Above the line,* In ffraunce *written after a smudge, and cancelled. Above* nglo *a long stroke, without significance.* 15. *Above* ond *a long stroke, without significance.* 23. Gawayne: *over* yne *a long stroke, without significance.* 25. he was herdy and wyght *written above the line, and cancelled.* 27. myght *cancelled after* he.

[III]

He was faire and free,
And gretly gaf hym to glee:
To cetoyle and to sawtree
 And gytternyng full gaye;  36
Wele to playe on a rotte,
To syng many newe note,
And of harpyng, wele I wote,
 He wane þe pryse aye.  40
Oþer gammnes he louede mare:
Grewhundes for buk and bare,
For hert, hynde, and for hare,
 By dayes and by nyghte;  44
Many fawcouns and faire,
Hawkis of nobill ayere,
On his perke gun repayre,
 Sexty, in plyghte.  48


[IV]

f.130b

He walde be vp or daye
To hunt and to ryvaye;
Gretly gafe hym to playe
 Ilke a day newe;  52
To here messe or he went
Trewely in gud entent,
And sythyn buskede to þe bent
 Whare gamnes in grewe.  56
To his foreste to founde
Both with horne and with hunde;
To brynge þe dere to þe grounde
 Was his maste glewe.  60
Certis, wyfe wolde he nane,
Wenche ne no lemman,
Bot als an ankyre in a stane
 He lyued here trewe.  64

---

C 37. in. 39. *Inserted later by scribe A in a smaller hand.* 41. mare: *Luick reads* mere, *erroneously.* 42. Grehondes: *over* hond *a long stroke, without significance. After* for, *a* t *cancelled; the* a *of* hare *badly made, and much resembles a type of* e. 47. parke: *the spelling with* a *is normal to this scribe when he writes the word in full; cf.* 70, 107.

## [III]

  He was fayre man and free,
  And gretlech yaff hym to gle:
  To harp and to sautre
36    And geterne full gay;
  Well to play [o]n a rote,
  Off lewtyng, well Y wote,
  And syngyng many seyt not
40    He bare the pryes aey.
  Yet gamenes hade he mare:
  Grehondes for hert and hare,
  Both for bokes and the bare,
44    Be nyght and be day;
  Fell faukons and fayr,
  Haukes off nobull eyre,
  Tyll his parke ganne repeyr,
48    By sexxty, Y dar say.

*He was fond of music*

*and hunting,*

## [IV]

  He wold be vpp or the day
  To honte† and to revay;
  Gretly yaff hem to pley
52    Eche day to newe;
  To† here hys mas or he went
  Trewly in gode entaunt,
  And seþþe to bowe into þe bente
56    Þere games ine grewe.
  Now to forest he founde,
  Both wyt horne and with hound;
  To breyng þe deere to þe grond
60    Was hys most glew.
  Certus, wyff wold he non,
  Wench ne lemon,
  Bot as an anker in a ston
64    He lyved ever trew.

*but would have nothing to do with women.*

---

ganne: *over* ann *a long stroke, without significance.* 50. honte and: *MS.* honte to and. *First* to *cancelled.* 53. Tho; mas: *possibly* mes. 54. to *cancelled after* trewly. 56. *Over* ine *a long stroke, without significance.*

## [V]

Þare was sessid in his hande
A hundrethe pondis worthe of londe
Of rent wele sittande,
    And somm-dele more;      68
Many ploughes in þe maynes,
Grete hertes in þe haynes,
Faire bares in þe playnes,
    And mekill tame store;      72
Castells with heghe walles,
Chambirs with heghe hallis,
Stedis stabillede in stallis,
    Lyarde and sore;      76
Whare he herde any crye,
He passede neuer for-by,
Þat he ne† was ay redy
    In landis ay-whare.      80

## [VI]

He louede almous-dede,
Poure folke for to fede
With menske and with manhede;
    Of mete was he fre;      84
Gestis redy for to calle
To here mynstralls in haulle,
He gafe þam robis of palle,
    Bothe golde and fee;      88
In ylke lande whare he come,
When he went oghte fra home,
Thay hafe haldyn vp his name
    With mekill melody;      92
In ylk lande whare he went
Many man hase he schent;
In fightis and in turnament
    Þe knyghte was hardy.      96

---

L 79. ne he.

C 65, 66. *Over* hand, land *long strokes, without significance.* 68. muchll. 69. houndered: *over* dere *a long stroke, without significance.* 73. heygh: *over* eygh *a long stroke,*

## [V]

    Ther was sesyd in hys hand  
    A þousand poundus worth off land  
    Off rentes well settand,  
68         And much[e]ll dell more;  
    An houndered plows in demaynus,  
    Fayer parkes in-wyth haynus,  
    Grett herdus in þe playnus,  
72         Wyth muchell tame store;  
    Castelos wyth heygh wallus,  
    Chambors wyth noble hallus,  
    Fayer stedes in the stallus,  
76         Lyard and soore;  
    Wher he herd of anny cry,  
    Ever he was redy;  
    He passede never forth by  
80         In lond wher þey were.

*f.96$^v$a*  
He was a wealthy landowner,

and was very generous

## [VI]

    He lovede well almosdede,  
    Powr men to cloth and fede  
    Wyth menske and manhede;  
84         Off met he was fre;  
    And also gestes to call,  
    And mensteralus her in halle,  
    He yaff hem robes off palle,  
88         Off gold and off fee;  
    In ych place whaer he come,  
    When he wente fram hem,  
    They hade halowed hys name  
92         Wyth gret nobulle;  
    In ych lond wher he wentt  
    So many men he hadd schennt;  
    In justus and on tornament  
96         He whan ever the gre.

especially to minstrels.

---

*without significance.* 77. he *inserted above the line.* 84. *Joined to the last* f *of* Off *is an illegible stroke, possibly meant for* e. 88. Off: *three cancelled letters* (Gad?) *follow.* 89. come: *over* ome *a long stroke, without significance.*

## [VII]

f.130ᵛa

There wonnede ane Erle hym by-syde,
A grete lorde of mekill pryde,
Of brade londis and wyde,
  And borowes full brade;   100
Hym thoghte desdeyne of þe knyghte
(For he was hardy and wyghte),
And thoghte þe beste how he myghte
  Þat doghety degrade.   104
The Erle was steryn and stowte,
And rade with a grete rowte,
And brake his perkes al abowte,
  Þe beste þat he hade;   108
In þam he made a sory playe,
The fatteste he fellyd aye,
Righte by sexty on a daye,
  Swylke maystris he mad.   112

## [VIII]

He drew his veuers of fysche,
He slewe his fosters, i-wysse;
Þe knyghte wist not of this,
  Þe sothe for to saye:   116
He was in þe Haly Lande
Dedis of armes for to fande,
Hethyn folke with his hande
  He fellid in faye.   120
His stewarde hase a lettre sent,
A messangere hase it hent,
Forthe on his way es he went
  Als fast als he maye;   124
When he to his lorde come,
Þe lettre sone he hym nome,
And sayde, 'Alle gose to schome,'
  And went on his way.   128

L 126. nome: *original word (?nen) struck through, and* nome *written after it.*

C *At the top of* 96ᵛb. *the following lines have been copied (cf.* 77–9) *and cancelled—*
  Wher he herd of anny Cry
  Ever he was redey
  he passede never forth b

## [VII]

  Ther wonede an Eorl him be-syd,    f.96ᵛb
  3e, a lord off mechell pryd,    His neighbour the
  That hadd viij forestes ful wyd,    Earl trespassed on Sir Degrevant's
100    And bowres full brode;    lands,
  He hade a grete spyt of þe knyght
  That was so hardy and wyght,
  And thought howe he best myght
104    That dowghty to gr[a]de.
  He was sterne and stoute,
  And rode in a gay route,
  And brak hys parkes about,
108    The best that he hade;
  Ther-inne he made a sory pley,
  The fattest he feld, in fey,    hunted his beasts'
  By sexty on a day,
112    Suche maystries he made.

## [VIII]

  He drowhe reueres with fysh,
  And slogh hys forsteres, y-wys;    and slew his foresters,
  The knyght wyste not of thys,
116    For soth Y you say,
  For he was in þe Holy Lond    while the owner was in the Holy Land.
  Dede of armes for to fond,
  The heþene men with hys hond
120    He feld hem offten in fey.
  Hys steward hadd a lettre y-sent,    The steward sent for Sir Degrevant
  A mesynger hath hyt hent,
  And forth hys wey ys y-went
124    As fast as ever he mey;
  When he tyll hys lord com,
  The lettre in hys hand he nom;
  He sey[de] all 3oode to schom,
128    And went on hys wey.

---

98. mechell: *first* e *smudged, possibly* o. 104. Grode. 111. on: *over the* n *a curved stroke, probably without significance.* 113. drow he. 113–160. *The character of the hand changes somewhat, as though the scribe had chosen a thicker pen.* 116. you: *the* u *with final curl;* Luick *reads* yow. 119. heþenemen: *second* e *inserted above.* 127. sey.

## [IX]

Þe knyghte no lengare habade,
Bot on his waye faste he rade
Fra Flaundres vn-to† Granade
    Fast als he myghte;    132
Sone he passede the see,
He and his menȝe,
And come to his contre
    With-in þe twelt nyght.    136
To his manere he wente:
A faire place was þer schent,
His husbandes þat gaffe hym rent
    Heryede in plighte:    140
His tenandrye was alle downe,
Þe beste innes in ylke towne,
His nobyll perkes comowne,
    And fowly by-dyghte.    144

## [X]

He closed his perkes agayne
(Alle his husbandis were fayne),
He lent þam oxen a-gayne
    Of his awen store;    148
Alsua, þe sothe for to schewe,
He lent þam aueres to drawe;
He thoghte to wyrke by þe lawe
    And by no noþer schore.    152
There-fore a lettre hase he dyghte
To þe Erle of gret myghte,
And prayes hym to do hym ryghte
    Or telle hym whare-fore;    156
With a sqwyere he it sent,
Of ten powndis worthe of rent,
Forthe on his way es he went
    To wiet his ansuare.    160

L 131. Degranade. 133. Sone: *possibly* sonne; *the MS. has a curled stroke over the* n.
152. schore: *the* r *has a faintly showing tail, as though a* ȝ *had been partially erased.*

C 131. off *cancelled before* frount; of þe. 137. maner *inserted over* masynges (?) *cancelled.*

## [IX]

      Wyth þe knytht was non abad,
      He buskyd hym forth and rade       *f.97a*
      Fram þe frount of† Garnad       *who returned,*
132         As faste as he myght;
      Son he pased the see,
      He and hys meney,
      And com in-to hys contre
136         By the twelþe nyght.
      Tyll hys maner he went:       *inspected the*
      A feyr place he fond schent,       *damage,*
      Hys husbondus that yaf rent
140         Was y-heryȝed doun ryght:
      His tenantrie was all doun,
      The best in every toun,
      His fayr parkes wer com[ou]n,
144         And loþlych by-dyght.

## [X]

      He closed hys parkes ayen
      (His husbondus þey were fyen),
      He lent he[m] oxon and wayn       *recompensed his*
148         Of his own store;       *tenants,*
      And also sede for [to] sowe,
      Wyght horse for to dr[a]w,
      And thought werke be lawe
152         And wyth non oþer schore.
      For-thi a lettre has he dyght       *and sent a letter*
      To this Eorl opo myght:       *demanding redress*
      He preyd hem to do him ryght       *from the Earl,*
156         Ar tell hym wher-fore;
      And wyth sqwer he hi[t] sent
      Off an honderd pond of rent,
      And forth hys wey ys he went
160         To wytt hys answer.

---

143. comen. 144. *At the end of the stanza a single slanting stroke.* 147. hen. 150. horse *after* hose *cancelled*; drow. 153. For thi: th *smudged.* 155. preyd: e *inserted with caret by (probably) later hand.* hem: *over* em *a stroke without significance.* 157. him. 159. wey: e *indistinct.*

## [XI]

The sqwyere wold noghte habyd,
Bot forthe faste gun he ryde
Vn-to þe palesse of pryde
    Þare þe Erle wonnde;    164
Sone so he of hym had syghte
(Sir Sere of Cypirs he highte,
Was buskede with many knyghte
    In þe foreste to hunte;    168
He was steryn and stowte
With many knyghtes hym abowte),
The sqwyere thoght gret dowte
    To byde his firste brount;    172
There-fore wold he noghte lett;
Sone with hym als he mett,
Euen to hym was he sett
    With his horse front.    176

## [XII]

The sqwyare wold noght lighte,
Bot haylsede þe Erle appon highte,
And sythyn baron and knyghte
    With wordis full wysse;    180
He had þe letter by þe noke,
To þe Erle he it tuke,
The Erle gan þer-one luke,
    And saide, 'Art þou wysse?'    184
He saide to þe sqwyere:
'Ne ware þou a messengere,
Þou solde by righte here
    Vndir þe wode-rysse;    188
I will for þi lordis tene
Hunt in his woddis grene,
Breke his perrkes alle by-dene,
    Þat proudeste es of pryse.'    192

## [XI]

(Missing)

## [XII]

Þe squier nolde nat down lyght,      f.97b
Bot haylis this Eorl opon hyght,
And sethe[n]s b[arow]n and kynyght
180      With wordes full wise;
He held the lettre by the nooke,
And to þe Eorle he hit toke,
And he ther-on gan loke
184      And seyde his avys.
And spake to the squiere:
'Ne were thou a messengere,     who threatened to
Thou shuld abey ryght here     hang the messenger
188      Vnder this wode-rys;
I wull, for thy lordes tene,
Honte hys foresstus and grene,
And breke his parkes by-dene,
192      Proudeste of prys.'

C 177. *After* nolde *one cancelled letter* (?d). down: *over* wn *a long stroke, without significance.* 178. opon: *over* on *a long stroke without significance.* 179. sethes bowron. 181. nooke: *the first* o *inserted above the line.*

## [XIII]

The sqwyare ansuerde full sone:
'Sir, þat es euyll done,
Thou hase lefte hym full fune,
  In hert es nott to hyde;    196
Here my gloue with hym to fighte,
Be he sqwyare or knyghte,
Þat saise þat this es righte,
  What-so-euer be-tyde;    200
Sir, if þat it be thi will,
Thynk þat þou hase done ill;
I rede þou mende it with skill,
  For wathes walkes wyde.'   204
The Erle ansuerde, 'I-wys,
I cownt hym noghte at a cresse,
I will noghte mend my mysse
  For all his grete pryde.'    208

## [XIV]

Sone þe Erle wexe wrathe
And sware many grete athe,
He solde his message be lathe
  Bot he a-waye went.    212
He tuk his leue with-owten nay,
And went forthe on his waye
Als faste als he maye
  Ouer the brade bent.    216
He come hame at þe nonne;
His lorde askede hym sone
And he talde hym onone
  What mendis he hym sent.   220

  . . . . . .
  . . . . . .
  . . . . . .

L 202. hase: *possibly* hafe: *the MS. character has a short cross stroke on each side the thickened downstroke.* 220. *There is no indication in the MS. of a hiatus.*

 C 193. sono.   195. bot: t *followed by smudge; final* e *may have been cancelled.*

## [XIII]

Thanne the squier seyde son[e]:
'Syre, that is nat well done,
Ye haue lefft hym bot whone,
    In herde is nat to hyde;
He that seyth þat hit is ryght,
Be he squier other knyght,
Here my gloue on to fyght,
    What chaunce so be-tyde;
Syr, yeff hit be your well,
Þenkes þat ye han don ylle;
Y rede ye amend to schkyll,
    For wothes is ever wyde.'
Þe Eorl answeryd, 'Y-wyse,
Y woll nat amend þat mese,
Y counte hym nat at a cres
    For all hys mechell pryd.'

*and discourteously refused.*

## [XIV]

Than the Eorl wax w[ro]th
And swor many a gret owth,
He schold be messaggere lothe
    But he hys wey wente.
He toke his leue with-outen nay,
And wendus forth on his way
As fast as ever he may
    Over the brode bent.
He com hom at the none
And told how he hade done;
The knyght asked him as sone
    What answer he sent.
'Sir, and he may as he ment,
His game woll he never stent;
Thy-self, and he may the hent,
    I tell the for y-schent.'

f.97ᵛa

*When Sir Degrevant was told the Earl's answer,*

---

209. worth. 216. *At the end of the line two strokes: one slanting, one curved (/~).* 222. woll: *Halliwell reads* wolt, *Luick* wolle (*extending* lł). *The final letter is not clear, but as the last two letters have been crossed, and as the scribe never crosses a single medial* l, *a final* l *may be inferred.*

[XV]

Than Sir Degreuant hase hight
To Hym þat maste es of myghte:
'Jhesu, safe me my ryghte,
    And Mary me spede! 228
I sall gyff God a vowe:
It sall noghte be for his prowe;
Þe tane of vs sall it rewe,
    And I can righte rede.' 232
Now to armes þay þam dighte,
Bathe sqwyere and knyghte,
And many worthily wyghte,
    I-wysse vndir wedis; 236
Thare warre armed in hye
Tene score full redy,
And thre hundrethe archers þam by
    Gud at alle nedis. 240

[XVI]

Now to foreste þay founde,
Þay stont stilly a stownde,
Þay putt vp pavilyons ronde,
    And lendid þere þat nyghte; 244
The Erle purvayed hym an oste,
He come in at a coste
With his brage and his boste,
    With many kant knyght; 248
He vncuppilde hys hundis
Till his rachis rebundys;
Gromys and grewhundis
    Þay heue appon hight; 252
Thus þe forest þay fraye,
Þe hertis bade at a-baye;
On a laund þer þay laye
    Lordis downe lyghte. 256

f.131b

L 235. *This line has been written twice. The first attempt originally read* **Many worthyly wyghte**; many *was then struck out, and* bathe (*doubtless from the line above*) *written in the margin. The line adopted here is written underneath its uncancelled predecessor.*

## [XV]

Þan Syr Degreuuaunt syght,
And by-held the heven vp-an hyght:    *he commended his cause to God,*
'Jhesu, saue me in my ryght
228   And Mare me spede!
And Y schall yeff Gode a vow:
Som of vs schall hyt r[o]w;
Hyt schall not be for his prow,
232   And Y may right rede.'
Anon to armus they hom dyght,    *and gathered his retinue.*
As fast as ever they myght,
Both squier and kynyght,
236   Wys vnder wede;
Ther wast† y-armed on hye
Ten score knythis redy,
And iij hondred archerus by,
240   Full goode at her nede.

## [XVI]

Anon to the forest þey found,    f.97ᵛb
Ther they stotede a stound,
They pyght pauelouns round,
244   And loggede that nyght;
The Eorle purveyede him an ost,
And com in at an-oþur cost
Wyth his brag and his bost,
248   Wyth many a ferres knyght.
He vncouplede his houndus
Withinne the knyghtus boundus;    *When the Earl committed his next act of trespass,*
Bothe the grene and þe groundus,
252   They halowede an hyght.
Thus þe forest they fray,
Hertus bade at abey;
On a launde by a ley
256   These lordus doune lyght.

C 225. degreuuaunt: *two cancelled letters, probably* sw, *follow.* 229. avow. 230. Raw. 231. schall *inserted above.* 232. Y *inserted above.* 233. they *corrected from* them. 237. was: *a cancelled letter* (W?) *precedes, and another* (y) *follows, originally belonging to* armed (*restored in my text*). *The* r *inserted into* armed, *and the* y *cancelled, by a later hand.*

[XVII]

Sexty hertis were slayne
And broght forthe on þe playne
By-fore þe chefe cheftayne
    Of þat contre. 260
Þan spake þe Erle on þat launde:
'Whare es now þis geaunte?
Why will noghte Sir Degreuant
    Come rescu his dere? 264
Me thynke his hertys of grese
Berys na letters of pese;
We will hafe or we sesse;
    I walde he ware here. 268
Trewly, or he went,
He solde þe gamen repent,
Þe proude lettre þat he sent
    With his sqwyere.' 272


[XVIII]

Sir Degreuant was þan sa nere
Þat he þose wordis myght here;
He said, 'Auant banere,
    And trompis on hight.' 276
His archers þat ware þare,
Bathe þe lesse and þe mare,
Als so swythe were þay ȝare,
    To schott ware þay dighte. 280
Þare-of þe Erle was payede,
Sone his oste hase he grayede,
He was na-thyng affrayede
    Of þe fers knyght. 284
Now are þay mett in þe felde
Bathe with spere and with schelde;
Worthy wapyns þay welde,
    And freschely þay fyghte. 288

## [XVII]

Sexten hertus wase y-slayn
And wer brought to a pleyn;
Byfore þe cheff cheuenten
260     Y-leyd wer y-fere.
Þane seys þe [Eorl] on þe land:    *in defiance of the letter,*
'Wher ys now Sir Degreuuaund?
Why wol not com þis gyant
264     To re[s]cow his dere?
Hys proud hertes of grese
Bereth no chartur of pes;
We schall haue som ar we sese;
268     Y wold he wer here.
Trewely, ar he went,
He schuld þe game repent,
Þe proud lettre þat he sent
272     By hys sqwer.'

## [XVIII]

Syr Degreuuaunt was so nere    *f.98a*
That he the wordes can her;
He seyd, 'Avaunt baner,
276     And trompes apon hyght.'
Hys archarus þat wer thare,
Both lase and the mar,
As swythe wer they thare,
280     To shote wer þey dyght.
Thane þe Eorle was payd,
Sone his batell was reyde,
He was no-thyng afreyd
284     Off that feris knyght.    *the two sides joined battle,*
Now ar they met on a feld
Both with spere and sheld;
Wyghtly wepenes þey weld,
288     And ferysly þey fyght.

C 257. wase: se *smudged, the* s *having been written with a very thick down stroke.* 261. dukes. 264. rescow: s *inserted into the word by corrector.* 267. sese *inserted above the line.* 287. wepenes: *a long stroke, without significance, over* wep. 288. ferysly: ys *smudged: upper part of* y *indistinct; Halliwell and Luick read* fersly, *erroneously.*

[XIX]

When þe batells were iunede
With speris freschely þay funede;
Þare myghte no sydis be soynede
 Þat faghte in þose feldis;  292
With suerdis bright on þe bent
Brighte maylis hafe þay rent,
Glayues gleterand þay glent
 On gleterand scheldys.  296

 . . . . .
 . . . . .
 . . . . .
   . . . .  300

f.131ᵛᵃ   Þay faghte þan so frekly
Þare wiste nane witterly
Wha solde hafe þe maystry,
 Bot He þat alle weldys.  304


[XX]

Doghty Sir Degreuant
Lays þe Erle on þe launde;
Thorow japon and jesserant
 He lamed þaire knyghttis.  308
Bryghte scheldys ware schede,
Many doghety were dede,
Brighte maylis wexe rede,
 So many doghety bledis.  312
Þus þay fighte in þe frythe,
With waa wreke þay þaire wrythe,
Þe kynde knyghtis in þaire kythe,
 Wyse vndire wedis:  316
Beryns are borne down,
Gomes with gambassowne
Lyes on þe bent so browne,
 Stekid vndir scheldis.  320

---

L *At the foot of f.* 131, *in the same hand:*—Vt dicunt multi Cito transit lancea stulti. 296. *There is no indication in the MS. of a hiatus.*

C 289. Enꞃioined: *a short thick slanting stroke over the first* n, *unlike the usual suspension.* 291, 293. ensoynd, on: *over* oynd, on *long strokes, without significance.* 296. geldene: *over* ene *a long stroke, without significance.* 300. heþᵉne: *see note.*

## [XIX]

And whan þe batell ennioined
With speres ferisly þey foynede;
Ther myght no sege be ensoynd
    Þat faught in þe feld;
Wyth bryght swerdus on þe bent
Rych·hawberkes þey rent,
Gleves gleteryng glent
    Opon geldene scheldus.
Þey styken stedus in stour,
Knyghtus thorow her armere;
Lordus off honor
    Opon þe heþet heldus.
The[y] foughten so ferisly
Þer weste non so myghty
Who schold haue þe victory,
    Bot He that all weldus.

## [XX]

Þe doughty knyght Sur Degrevaunt     f.98b
Leys þe lordes on þe laund
Þorw jepun and jesseraund,
    And lames þe ledes.
Schyr scheldus they schrede,
Many dowghty was dede,
Ryche maylus wexen rede,
    So manye bolde dedus.
Þus they fowghten on frythe,
Kene kynghus in-with kyth,
Wo wrekes thare wryth
    Þese doughty on dede!
Burnes he hadde y-born doun,
Gomes wyth gambisoun
Lyes opon bent broun,
    And sterff vnder stede.

301. Then. 305. doughty: *a long stroke from the* u *to the* y, *without significance.* Degrevaunt: *the* a *much resembles* e. 306, on, laund: *over each a stroke, probably without significance.* 313, 314, 317. frythe, kythe, kynghus, born, doun: *long strokes above the whole of* frythe *and* doun; *the* yth *of* kyth, *the* n *of* born, *and the* yng *of* kynghus. *All without significance.*

## [XXI]

Sir Degreuant þe knyghte
Brittyns basenetis brighte;
His feris freschely gan fighte
    And stirred þam on þaire stedis.    324
Knyghtis of þe Erlis house
Þat were haldyn cheualrouse
And in batelle bownteuous,
    Þay dyede in þat stownde.    328
Þe Erle houed and hym by-helde,
Bathe with spere and with schilde
How þay farede in þe felde,
    And sone þay s[at]t vn-sownde.    332
Þe beste men þat he hade
He had leuede þer in wede;
With fyfty speris he flede,
    And wathely was wondide.    336

## [XXII]

Sir Degreuant with his men
Folous faste in þe fen,
Als þe dere in þe den
    To þe dede he þam dyghtis.    340
He bristis bacenettis fele
With scharpe axis of stele,
Mony knyghte gart he knele,
    And many worthy wight;    344
Sir Degreuant was full thra,
He pertede his batelle in twa,
Þe Erle fled and was full waa,
    [On] a stede gan he sprynge;    348
He lefte slayne in a slake
Ten score in a pakke,
Wyde opyn on þe bake,
    Lyand in lynge.    352

L 332 satt: at *conjectural, owing to smudge.* 345. thra: *MS.* wa *crossed through and sub-puncted*; thra *written beside it.*

C 321. Knyght: *the* t *is written so closely to the* h *as to be almost indistinguishable.* 322. Brghtenes. 323. ferysly: *the* y *is badly made, without the curve in the tail usual in this hand, and may possibly be an* r. 324. hom: *over* om *a smudged stroke.* 325. knyghtus: *over* gh *a short stroke, without significance.* 326. chyualerus: e *not clear, and*

## [XXI]

Sir Degreuaunt þe gode knyght
Br[yt]tenes þe basnettus bryght;
Hys feris ferysly þey fyght
    And felles hom to grond.
Þe knyghtus of þe Eorlus hous
Þat wer y-halden so chyualerus
And in batell so bountyveus,
    Þey deyden all þat stond.
The Eorl houede and be-held,
Both with sper and with scheld
How they fayr in the feld,
    And syght vn-sound.
Þe best men that he ledde
He hadd y-lefft hom to wedde;
With fyffty spers is he fledd,      *in which the Earl*
    And wodelech was y-wounded.      *was put to flight.*

## [XXII]

Syr Degriuuant and his men
Feld hom faste in the fen,
As the deer in the den
    To dethe he tham denges.      f.98<sup>v</sup>a
Wyth scharpe axus of stell
He playtede her basnetus well;
Many a knygh gart he knell
    In the morny[n]g;
Sir Degreuua[n]t was full þro,
Departed her batell atwo,
Þe Eorl fley and was wo,
    On a stede can he spryng;
He laf slawe in a slak      *leaving many dead*
Forty scor on a pak,      *on the field.*
Wyd open on her bake,
    Dede in the lyng.

---

*may be* o; r *followed by curl, usually without significance.* 333. *After* men, *a single letter* (I?) *cancelled.* 341. axus: *Luick reads* exus *erroneously.* 343. knygh; *a long stroke over the first four letters, without significance.* 344. mornyg. 345. degreuuant: *usual* n *suspension omitted; cf.* 353, 385. 346. *After* departed *two cancelled letters* (hr?). 347. fley: *Luick reads* sley; *there is a preliminary tick to the long* s, *but it is not carried right across the down stroke.*

## [XXIII]

Sir Degreuant gat a stede
Þat was gud at þe nede,
Many sydis garte he blede
    [With þe dynt of his spere];    356
He schased þe Erle in a while
Mare [þan] halfendele a myle;
Many balde garte he syle
    [Þat are did þam dere];    360
He come chasande agayne,
Alle his men ware full fayne,
Fande he neuer ane slayne,
    Ne þe werse by a pere.    364
He knelid down in þat place
And thanked God of His grace
Alle went þat þare was
    To his manere.    368

## [XXIV]

To þe soper þay are dighte,
Bathe baron and knyghte;
Þay dawnesid and reueld þat nyghte,
    In herte ware þay blythe.    372
When þe Erle come hame
He was wondid all to schame;
Þe lady sawe þat he was lame
    And syghed full swythe.    376
Ofte scho cryed, 'Allas!
Had ȝe noghte perkes to chase?
What did ȝe in þat place
    Swylk maystris to kythe?'    380
'Dame,' he said, 'I was þare,
And þat me rewis full sare,
I take my leue for euer-mare
    Swilk maystres to dyghte.'    384

L 356, 360 *have changed places.* 358. amyle. 363. slaynee, *first* e *smudged.*

C 358. Mele. 360. *The first* d *of* dud *written in another hand over original* d. 361. schygynge: *the first* y *written over* e *in the same hand.* 368. *After this line is written in hand A —*
    Her endyth þe first fit

## [XXIII]

|     |                                             |                              |
| --- | ------------------------------------------- | ---------------------------- |
|     | Syr Degreuua[n]t gat a sted                 |                              |
|     | Þat was gode in ilk a ned,                  |                              |
|     | Many a side grat he bled                    |                              |
| 356 | Þorow dent of his spere;                    |                              |
|     | And schased þe Eorl with-in a whyll         | He was pursued by            |
|     | Mor þen enleue m[y]le;                      | Sir Degrevant,               |
|     | Many bold gert he syle                      | whose men were               |
| 360 | Þat by-fore dud hym dere;                   | unwounded.                   |
|     | He com sch[y]gynge ayen,                    |                              |
|     | And of hys folk was fyen,                   |                              |
|     | And fond never on slayn,                    |                              |
| 364 | Ne worse be a pere.                         |                              |
|     | He knelyde doun in that place               |                              |
|     | And thankyd God of His grace;               |                              |
|     | And all wend that þere was                  |                              |
| 368 | Tyll his feyr manere.                       |                              |

## [XXIV]

|     |                                             |                              |
| --- | ------------------------------------------- | ---------------------------- |
|     | Bleue to soper they dyght,                  |                              |
|     | Both squier and knygh[t];                   |                              |
|     | Þey daunsed and revelide þat nyght,         |                              |
| 372 | In hert wer they blythe.                    |                              |
|     | And whan þe Eorl com ham                    | When the wounded             |
|     | He was wonded to scham;                     | Earl arrived home,           |
|     | Þe lady ses he was lam                      |                              |
| 376 | And swouned full swyth.                     |                              |
|     | Offte she cryed, 'Alas!                     | f.98ᵛᵇ                       |
|     | Haue ye nat parkus and chas?                |                              |
|     | What schuld ye do at is place               |                              |
| 380 | Swych costus to kythe?'                     | he resolved never to         |
|     | 'Dame,' he seys, 'Y was thare,              | do anything of the           |
|     | And me rews now full sar,                   | sort again.                  |
|     | Y take m[y leve] for eueremare              |                              |
| 384 | Swych wornges to wrythe.'                   |                              |

*and in hand D —*
      Howe say ye? will ye any more of hit.
370. knygh, *with long line over* ygh. 373. whan: *re-written after smudge.* 379. at is: *the original MS. reading, corrected by a later hand to* athis *by inserting* h. *Luick reads* a this. 381. was: *altered from* wys. 383. leve: *written above the line in another hand to replace* lyfe *cancelled.*

## [XXV]

Appon þe morne Sir Degreuant
Busked hym at his ownn auant
Appon a stede feraunt
    Armyd at ryghte. 388
To þe castelle he rade
With þe folke þat he hade;
At þe barresse he habade
    And bawndonly down lyghte. 392
He asked if any swylke were
Þat wold delyuer hym þere
Thre courses of were
    For hym and twelue knyghtis. 396
Þan he prayed þe portere
Þat he wold be his messynger,
And gare hym hafe an ansuere,
    On-ane he hym hightis. 400

## [XXVI]

The porter went to þe haulle,
On þe Erle gan he calle:
'Here es comen to þe walle,
    Wele armed on stedis, 404
Sir Degreuant, þat hende knyght,
With heghte helmys on hyghte,
With many bald man and wyghte,
    And wyse vndir wedis. 408
He askes justyng of were,
And prayes the of answere,
He mad me his messagere,
    To walke on his nedis.' 412
The Erle ansuerd in hy,
'Here es nane so redy
Þat schames þat ilk doghety
    Sir Degreuant dedis.' 416

C 386, 387. auennaunt, Ferraunt: *possibly* auennannt, Ferrannt. 394. delyver: l *corrected, probably from* h. 395. *Above* cors *a long stroke, without significance.* Luick *reads* corses, *while stating that the long stroke is meaningless.* 410. *After the line is found* —

## [XXV]

On the morow Sir Degreuua[n]t  
Dyght him at is auennaunt  
On a sted ferraunt  
388   Y-armed at ryghtes.  
To þe castell he rad  
With folkys þat he had;  
At þe barnekynch he abad  
392   And lordelych doun lyght;  
And axed yef þer eny were  
Þat wold hym delyver him þer  
Off þre cors of wer,  
396   Hym and xij knythus.  
He prayd þe porter  
For to ben his mesenger,  
And to wit an answer,  
400   And anon he him hytus.

*The next day, Sir Degrevant rode armed to the Earl's castle*

*to challenge the Earl to renew the combat,*

## [XXVI]

The porter went to þe hall  
And to þe Eorl he can call:  
'Her is comen to þus wall,  
404   Y-armed apon a sted,  
Sir Degreuuant þe gode knygt,  
With hey helmes bryght,  
Many bold men and wyght,  
408   Wyse vnder wede.  
He axit justes of were,  
And prays þe of answer,  
He mad me his mesager,  
412   To walk on his ned.'  
Þe Eorl answerd an hy,  
'Here is non redy.'  
Hit semes as that dowghty  
416   Sir Degreuaunt drede.

*f.99a*

*but the offer was declined.*

---

he mad me hys mesger,  
*the last word being crowded against the edge. The whole line cancelled, and the more correct form written below.*

[XXVII]

The Countas went to þe walle,
And hir dogheter with-alle
Þat was bothe gentill and smalle
 And lufsome of syghte;  420
Scho lokide on þat cheualerouse
And said, 'Knyghte aunterus,
The semys to be envyous,
 My trouthe I þe plyghte.  424
Sir, God hase sent þe þat grace
Þat þou hase vencuste thi face;
Seke vs noghte in oure place
 Be day ne by nyghte.'  428
The knyghte spake to þat fre:
'Ma-dame, wite noghte me;
Mekill maugre hafe he
 Þat chalanges vn-righte!  432

[XXVIII]

'Luk, my perrkes are stroyed,
And my veuers are drawed,
And I gretly [am] anoyde,
 For sothe als I say.  436
When I werreyde in Spayne,
He mad my landis barrayne,
My woddis and my warrayne;
 My wylde are awaye.  440
Dame, I do ȝow owt of drede,
He þat did me þat dede
I sall qwyte hym his mede,
 Als so sone als I may,  444
Or I sall dy in þe payne;
He þat my fosters hase slayne
I sall rewarde hym agayne,
 I telle ȝow in fay.'  448

L 435. *MS. repeats* gretly.

C 418–9. *In the MS., these lines are in the reverse order, corrected by means of marginal letters* b, a. 420. seyght: *over* yght *a long stroke, without significance.* 421. aunterous: *the* o *much resembles* e. 422. seygh; kynghtes. cheualerus: *the word has been heavily cancelled, for no apparent reason. It seems to have been corrected before cancellation, and its original form is irrecoverable. Luick relates it to* 460 (*written opposite* 422

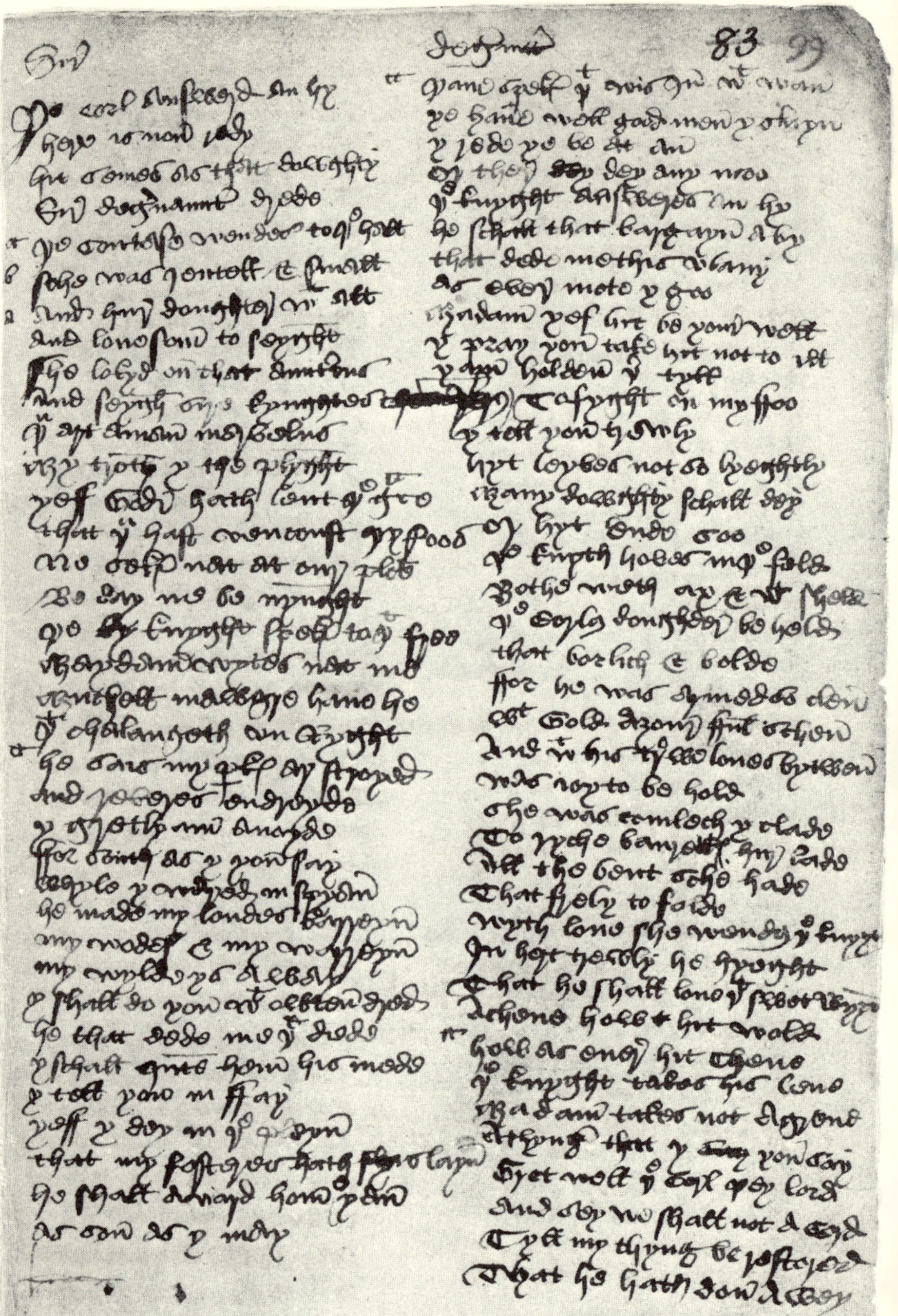

MS. Cambridge Univ. Lib. Ff. i. 6, folio 99
(ll. 413–488).

## [XXVII]

Þe Contase wendes to þe hall,  *The Earl's wife saw Sir Degrevant,*
And hur doughter with-all,
Sche was jentell and small
420     And louesom to seyght;
She lokyd on that aunterous
And sey[t]h, 'Sire k[ny]ghte cheualerus,
Þou art a man marvelus
424     My troth Y the plyght.
Yeff Gode hath lent þe grace
That þou hast vencoust þy foos,
Ne sekes nat at our pl[a]ce
428     Be day ne be nyght†.'  *and asked him to cease from molesting them any further.*
Þe knyght spekes to þat free:
'Maydam, wytes nat me;  *'Do not blame me,*
Muchell mawgre haue he
432     Þat chalangeth vn-ryght'.

## [XXVIII]

He sais, 'My parkes ar stroyed,
And reveres endreyde,
Y gretly am anoyde,
436     For south as Y you say.
Whyle Y wared in Spyan,  *'the Earl has done me great wrong,*
He made my londes barreyn,
My wodes and my warreyn;
440     My wylde ys a-way.
Y shall do you with-owten dred,
He that dede me þat dede
Y schall quite hem his mede,
444     Y tell you in fay.
Yeff Y dey in þe pleyn,
That my fosteres hath slayn,
He shall award hom eyan,
448     As son as Y may.'

*in f.99b), but it undoubtedly belongs here.* 424. troth, plyght: *over* roth *and* plyght *long strokes, without significance.* 425. Gode: *the* e *carelessly made, resembling* r. 427. plee; *a peculiar stroke (inserted* c?) *above second* e. *Luick reads* ples, *erroneously.* 428. nynght, *with long stroke, without significance, over* nyng. 429. *After* þe *two letters* (ky) *cancelled.* 443. qute, *with a long stroke over* ute. 446. *After* hath *four cancelled letters, probably* flyi. 447. eyan: e *inserted above, with stroke to show point of insertion.*

## [XXIX]

Than spekes þat wyese in wane:  
'Þou hase oure gude men slane,  
I rede ȝe be at ane  
    Or þar dy any ma.'      452  
The knyghte ansuers in hy:  
'He sall þe bargan haby  
Þat did me þis velany,  
    Als euer mot I ga.      456  
Ma-dam, if it be ȝour will,  
I pray ȝow takes it to nan ill;  
I am haldyn þer-till  
    To fyghte on my faa.      460  
I telle ȝow reghte trewly  
It leues noghte so lyghtly,  
Ma doghety sall dy  
    Or it end swa.'      464  

## [XXX]

The knyghte houed in þe felde,  
Bathe with spere and with schelde,  
The Erle doghter hym by-helde,  
    Þat borly and balde;      468  
He was armed full clene  
In gold with asure full schene,  
Alle sett with bagges by-twene,  
    Þis frely to falde.      472  
Scho was full comly clede,  
Twa riche barons hir lede,  
Alle þe bewte scho hade  
    Was gay to be-holde.      476  
With lufe scho wondid þe knyght;  
With hert trewely he hir highte  
Þat he sold lufe þat swete wyghte,  
    Proue how it wolde.      480  

L 470. clene (*repeated from line above*) *crossed through, and* schene *written after it.*

## [XXIX]

 Þanne spekes þat wis in-with wan:   *f.99b*
'Ye haue well good men y-slayn,
Y rede ye be at an
452   Or ther dey any moo.'
Þe knyght answeres an hy:
'He schall that bargayn aby
That dede me this v[i]lany,
456   As ever mote Y goo.
Madam, yef hit be your well,
Y pray you take hit not to ill;
Y am holden þer-tyll
460   To fyght on my foo.
Y tell you trewly
Hyt leyves not so lyeghtly,
Many dowghty schall dey   *'and many a brave*
464   Or hyt ende soo.'   *man must die because of it.'*

## [XXX]

Þe knyth hoves in þe feld,
Bothe weth ax and with sheld,
Þe Eorlus doughder be-held   *The Earl's daughter*
468   That borlich and bolde;   *was impressed by his bearing,*
For he was armed so clen
With gold [and] aȝour ful schen,
And with his trowe-loues bytwen
472   Was ioy to be-hold.
She was comlech y-clade,
To ryche banre[ttes] hur lade,
All the beut[e] sche hade   *and he by hers; he*
476   That frely to folde.   *fell in love.*
Wyth loue she w[o]ndus þe knyȝt;
In hert trewly he hyeght
That he shall loue þat swet wyȝt,
480   Acheue how hit wold.

C 452. dey *written twice, the first being cancelled.* 455. vlany. 471. trowe: *the* o *written above the* r *in the same hand; Luick reads* trewe *erroneously.* 474. banrettes: *the two ts and plural contraction written over in a later hand.* 477. wendus. 480. *After* how, *a letter* (t?) *cancelled.*

## [XXXI]

How-som-euer þat it cheue,  
Þe knyght takis lis leue:  
'Madame, tak it noghte to greue  
    A thyng I ȝow saye:             484  
Grete wele þe Erle ȝour lorde,  
And say þat we may noghte accorde  
Or my thynges be restorede  
    Þat he hase don a-waye.        488  
Here by-fore he myghte ethe  
Sone hafe mad me asethe;  
Þat sall he, mawgre his tethe,  
    For alle his gret draye.         492  
Trewly, I vndir-take,  
If it ne ware for ȝour sake,  
I sold hym vnwynly wake  
    Or to-morne daye.            496  

## [XXXII]

'Bot I lett for my gentryse  
To do swylke reueryse,  
For swylke gud ladyse  
    This castell to fraye;          500  
Bot sen I may do na mare,  
To his foreste will I fare,  
I will na wylde best spare,  
    For sothe† all þis day.'       504  
Now to þe forest þay funde  
Bathe with horne and with hunde,  
To bryng þe dere to þe gronde  
    On laund þer þay laye.        508  
I-wysse þe gamnes by-gan,  
Hertis ryally rane,  
Sexty bukkes, or þay blan,  
    Þay fellid, in fay.            512  

L 504. sothe: *MS. adds* of.

C 484. *After* y, say *cancelled.* 485. þey. 489. he *inserted above the line.* 490, 491. aseyth, tyeth: *long strokes, without significance, over the last four letters of each.*

## [XXXI]

|     | | |
|---|---|---|
| | How as euer hit cheue, | Sir Degrevant's answer: |
| | Þe knyght takes his leue: | |
| | 'Madam, takes not agreue | |
| 484 | A thyng that Y you say; | |
| | Gret well þe Eorl þy† lord, | |
| | And sey we shall not a-cord | 'There will be no peace between us unless I am given restitution.' |
| | Tyll my thyng be restored | |
| 488 | That he hath don a-wey. | |
| | Her afore myght he eyth | f.99ᵛa |
| | Son haue made me aseyth; | |
| | Nowe schall he, magre his tyeth, | |
| 492 | For all is grete arey. | |
| | Trewly, Y vndertake, | |
| | Wer hit not for your sake, | |
| | Y schall hym wynly wake | |
| 496 | Or to-morrow it wer day. | |

## [XXXII]

|     | | |
|---|---|---|
| | 'Y lette for my gentriese | |
| | To do swych roberyse, | |
| | For seche fayr laydes | |
| 500 | Ther Casteles to fray; | |
| | Sen Y mey do no mare, | |
| | Tyll his freth wyl Y fare, | |
| | Y woll no wyld best spare, | |
| 504 | For soth all this day.' | |
| | Anon to forest þey founde | |
| | Both with horn and with hound, | |
| | To breng þe dere to þe grond | Sir Degrevant hunted on the Earl's land, and killed his beasts, |
| 508 | Alaund þer þey lay. | |
| | Thus this games he be-gan, | |
| | Rachis reyally ran, | |
| | Sexti bockes, ar he blan, | |
| 512 | Hadde he felde, in fay. | |

497. Gentriese: *the* e *is badly made, and is thickened at the top*; Halliwell *and* Luick *read* o. 506–7. *In the MS., these lines are in reverse order, corrected by means of letters* b, a *in the margin.* 509. G *cancelled after* this.

## [XXXIII]

Sir Degreuant, or he riste,
He sent þe Erle of þe beste,
He hunttyd in his foreste
  With beryns full balde.   516
His depe dykis he drewe,
His qwykke swannes he slewe,
Grete geddis i-nowe
  Gate he vn-talde.   520
Bot now hym lyste noght playe,
To hunt ne to ryvaye,
For Maydyn Myldor þat may
  His caris are calde.   524
Als he hunted in the chase
He tolde his sqwyere þe case:
Þat he luffed in a place
  This frely to falde.   528

## [XXXIV]

'My lufe es lelely lyghte
On a lady wyghte,
Þare es no beralle so brighte,
  Na cristalle so clere;   532
Scho es warre and wysse,
Hir rod as þe rose on ryse,
Hir coloure full white it es,
  Þat lufly in lyre.   536
Scho es precyous in palle,
Scho es fayreste in haull,
I sawe hir ons on a walle,
  I neghede na nere;   540
Me ware leuer þat scho war myn
Þan alle þe golde in þe Ryn,
And also in floreyne,
  Scho es me so dere.   544

C 514. temede. 515. forste. 516. bernus: *re-written after smudge.* 521. no *written twice, the first then cancelled.* 525, 527. honted, place: *over* ont, plac, *long strokes without significance.*

## [XXXIII]

Sir Degreeuant, ar he reste,
Te[n]ede þe Eorl on þe beste,
And hontede his for[e]ste
  Wyth bernus full bolde.
His depe dychys he drowe,
Hys whyght swannes he slow,
Grete luces y-nowe
  He gat hom [in] wold.
Now hym lykys no pley,    *but took no pleasure*
To honte ne to revey,      *in the chase,*
For Mayd Melidor þe may
  His care wax all cold.
As he honted in a chas
He told his squier his case:
Þat he loued in a place
  A frely to folde.

## [XXXIV]

'My loue is leliche y-lyeght    f.99ᵛb
On a worthly wyeght,    *because his thoughts*
Ther is no berell so bryght,  *had turned to love.*
  Ne cristall so clere;
She is ware and wyse,
Rode ronne hit ys,
As the rose in þe ris,
  Wyth lylye in lere.
She ys precious [in] pall,
Fere feyrest of all;
Y say hur ones on a wall,
  Y ney3ed hur so nere;
Y hade leue[re] she were myn
Than all þe gold in þe Reyn,
Fausoned on floren,
  She is myn so der†.'

---

534. his *cancelled after* ronne. 537. &. 539, 543. *Over* on, *curved strokes without significance.* 544. drer.

## [XXXV]

The sqwyere ansuerd, 'I-wysse,
I wold wiet whate scho es;
I solde seke hir whare scho es
    In payne of my lyfe;      548
I sall do þat I may
Iff I kan by any waye
Bathe by nyghte and by daye
    To wyn hir to ȝour wyfe.      552
And I sall to ȝow an athe suere
Ȝour concell sall I neuer discouer,
Ȝif my body may endure,
    With suerde or with knyfe,      556
Þat I shall faythfully fyghte
Bathe in wrang and in righte,
With sqwyere and als with knyghte,
    Þat agaynes the will stryfe.'      560

## [XXXVI]

'Myldor,' he said, 'es hir name,
Scho es white als þe fame;
Balde beryns wald me blame
    (What bot es to ly?),      564
Thus to wowe hir in þat stede
Agayne alle hir frendis rede;
Bathe my lyfe and my dede
    In hir es lokyn in hy.      568
Scho es frely and faire,
And þe Erls awn ayere,
I will no-thyng of þaire,
    Broche ne no bey.      572
I wolde aske hym no mare
Bot hir body alle bare,
And we frendis for euer-mare,
    What-so-euer I drey.'      576

C 546. *Below the line, the following has been written in error and cancelled* (*cf.* 548–9) —
    In payn of my lyue
    That
547. y *and.* 553. y *inserted above line.* 554. descur: c *badly made, and resembles* o.

## [XXXV]

His squier answered, 'Y-wyse,  
Lat me wyte what she is,  
[And Y] wol syker þe þis  
548    In payn of my lyff;  
That Y woll do þat Y mey  
Both be nyght and be day  
Yeff Y can be any way  
552    Wyn hur to your wyf.  
And here Y shall the ensur  
Thi consell never descur,  
Whyll my body may endur,  
556    Wyth swerd and wyth knyef,  
That Y shall faythly fyeght  
Both in worng and in ryght;  
Or he be squier or knyght  
560    Ayenese þe woll str[y]eff.'

*His squire promised his help in winning Melidor,*

## [XXXVI]

'Melydor ys hur naume,  
Whyegh[t] as þe seys fame;  
My bolde burnes wold me blam  
564    (What bot is þat Y ley?),  
Þat I shoulde wow in a stede  
A3eyn alle mene rede;  
And boþe my lyff and my dede  
568    Ys loken in hur tye.  
For she is frely and fair,  
And þe Eorlus owun eyer,  
I wolde noþing off þeir,  
572    Broche ne bye.  
I wolde aske þam na mare  
But hyr body all bare,  
And we frendes for euermar,  
576    What doel þat I drye.'

f.100a

557. fyeght: *a long stroke, without significance, over the whole word.* 563. me *inserted above.* 564 *is written at the bottom of the page. A blank leaf (unfoliated) follows, and the poem is continued by hand B on fol.* 100. 565. shoulde: l *inserted above the line by means of caret; cf.* molde 1451. 573. namare.

## [XXXVII]

The sqwyare said, 'Are ȝe wyse?
Thynke þat ȝe are enemys,
And late some wy þat es wysse
 Walke on ȝour nedis.    580
I dare sauely swere,
And he take ȝow on were,
All Ynglandes here
 Sall speke of ȝour dedis,   584
And say it es foly
For to lufe ȝour enemy
Ȝife ȝe gete a velany
 And mawgre to ȝoure mede.   588
Sertys, ladys will saye
Þare myght no noþer ȝow pay
Bot Mayden Mildor þe may,
 Worthliest in wede.'    592

## [XXXVIII]

Than said Sir Degreuant:
'Þou sall noght make þin auant
That I sall be recreaunt,
 For frend ne for faa.    596
Thow wold holde me drade,
And for þe Erle full rade;
Trowes þou þat I be made
 To leue my lufe swa?    600
At euen arme the wele
In gud iryn and in stele,
For we will to þe castelle
 By-twix vs ane twa.    604
Sertanely, þis ilke nyghte
I mon se hir with syghte,
And speke with þat bird brighte,
 For wele or for wa.'    608

L 595. recreaᵃunt. (*See note to* L 593–4.)

[XXXVII]

Þat sqwyer seyde hys avyse:  
'Þink þat ȝe er enemys,  
Lat some wye þat ys wys  
580     Walk on þus nede.  
For I dar saffly swere,  
Gyff he take þe in werre,  
Alle Englond here  
584     Wold spek of þi dede,  
And say hyt ys a folly  
For to louet þin enemy  
Gyf þou gett a vylony  
588     But maugre to mede.  
Oþer ladyes wolde say,  
"Myȝthe no womman þe apay  
B[o]te Maiede Mylder þe may  
592     Vlonkest on wede?" '

*but tried to dissuade him from the folly of loving his enemy's daughter.*

[XXXVIII]

Þen saide Syr Degriuaunt:  
'Þou shal not mak þin avaunt  
Þat I shall be recreaunt,  
596     F[or] frende ne for foo.  
Þou woldest halde me ful made,  
For þe Erle ful rade;  
Troust I be so made  
600     To leue my loue so?  
At euen arme þe well  
Boþe in yren and in stel,  
And we shullen to þe castel  
604     Bytwyx vs owun two.  
Sertenly, þis ylke nyȝth  
I wyll see hyr with syȝth,  
And spek with þat byrde bryȝth,  
608     For wel or for wo.'

*f.100a*

*At nightfall,*

C 580. on: *short stroke over* n; *scribe may have intended* ouer. 586. Forto. *After* loue *a single letter,* i *or* l, *mis-written, and left uncancelled.* 591. Bete. 596. Fro.

## [XXXIX]

Twa faire coursurs þay hent,
To þe castelle are þay went,
On a laund are þay lent
    By a forest syd. 612
Till it drewe nere day,
Þe Erle busked hym to playe,
Owt a[t] posterne he tuk þe waye
    With knyghtis of pryde. 616
Sir Degreuant held hym styll
Whils he was passed þe hill,
Þan spake þe sqwyere hym till,
    Preualy þat tyde: 620
'I rede we hy vs full ȝerne
In at þe posterne,
And late vs hald vs in derne
    Þe byrde to habid.' 624

## [XL]

Sir Degreuant tuk gud hede,
In at þe posterne he ȝede;
Þe porter had ben in drede
    Had he bene þare! 628
He þat þe ȝatis solde kepe
He was gane for to slepe;
In-to ane orcherde þay lepe,
    Armed als þay were. 632
The knyghte and his sqwyere
Risted vndir a rosere
Till þe day wex clere,
    Vndron and mare; 636
Be þat þay herde a belle
Ryng in þe castelle,
And þe gay dameselle
    Busked full ȝare. 640

L 615. at: t *conjectural, owing to a small hole in the MS.* 634. rosere *after* rosrere (*second* e *incomplete*) *cancelled.*

## [XXXIX]

|     |                                      |                          |
|-----|--------------------------------------|--------------------------|
|     | Tow ryche cou[r]sers þei hente,      | they went to the         |
|     | And forþe here weys þei wente,       | Earl's castle            |
|     | Vndir a lynd or þei lente            |                          |
| 612 |     By a launde syde.                |                          |
|     | Whyle hyt dawed ly3th day,           |                          |
|     | Þe Eorle buskede on hys way,         |                          |
|     | Out at a posterne to play            |                          |
| 616 |     With kny3th of pryde.            |                          |
|     | Sir Degriuaunt helde hym styll       |                          |
|     | Whyle þe Eorle passyde þe hyll,      |                          |
|     | And seid hys squier hym tyll,        |                          |
| 620 |     Pryualy þat tyde:                |                          |
|     | 'I rede we hye vs ful 3erne          |                          |
|     | In at þe 3ond posterne,              |                          |
|     | And let vs halde vs in derne         |                          |
| 624 |     Þe burde tyll a-byde.'           |                          |

## [XL]

|     |                                      |                          |
|-----|--------------------------------------|--------------------------|
|     | Syr Degriuaunt tok non hede,         |                          |
|     | In at þe posterne he 3ede;           |                          |
|     | Þe porter hade ben in drede          |                          |
| 628 |     Hadd he ben þare!                |                          |
|     | He þat þe 3att shulde kepe           | f.100ᵛa                  |
|     | He was go for to slepe;              |                          |
|     | In at an orcherd þei lepe,           | and into his orchard     |
| 632 |     Y-armede as þei ware.            |                          |
|     | Þe kny3t and þe squiere              |                          |
|     | Resten in a rosere                   |                          |
|     | Tyll þe day wex clere,               |                          |
| 636 |     Vndurne and mare;                |                          |
|     | Whyle þat hurde þei a bell           |                          |
|     | Ryng in a chapell,                   |                          |
|     | To chyrche þe gay dammisel           | from which they          |
|     |                                      | caught sight of          |
| 640 |     Buskede hyr 3are.                | Melidor on her way       |
|     |                                      | to Mass.                 |

C 629. shulde: *ornamental flourishes, to the right of* h, l. *Luick reads* schulde.   632. y *corrected over* In

## [XLI]

Scho come in a veluet
With white perle ouerfret,
And faire were þay in sett
    On euer-ylke a syde;    644
Alle of palle-werke fyne
Cowchide with newyne,
Furrede with ermyne,
    And couerde with pryde.    648
To telle hir botouns were dure:
Þay were anamelde with asure;
With t[o]pys and with tre[ch]oure
    . . . . . . .    652
. . . . . . .
. . . . . . .
    . . . . . . .
    Glemerand hir gyde.    656

## [XLII]

Hir here hillyd on [m]olde
With a coroune of golde;
Was neuer made on this molde
    So worthy ne so mylde.    660
Scho was frely and fayre,
Wele semyd hir a chayere
With riche bosys and fayre
    And derely by-dyghte.    664
With a frountell endent
With perle of þe Oryent,
Owt of Cyprese was it sent
    To þat bird brighte;    668
Hir courchefs were curious,
Hir face gay and gracyous;
Sir Degreuant was amorous
    And had joy of þat syghte.    672

f.133b

L 651. terepys; tredoure. *There is no indication in the MS. of a hiatus.* 657. holde.

C 642. perl: r *inserted above the line.* 646. *Luick reads* miche (*see note*). 647. an erlud.
651. &. 656. Gyde: *Luick reads* syde, *but the first letter has the same form as the G of*

## [XLI]

  Sche come in a vyolet
  With why3th perl ouerfret,
  And saphyrus þerinne i-sett
644    On eueryche a syde;
  All of pall-work fyn
  With n[o]uche and nevyn,
  An[u]rl[e]d with ermyn,
648    And ouert for pryde.
  To tell hur botenus was toor,
  Anamelede with a3our;
  With topyes [hur] trechour
652    Ouertrasyd þat tyde.
  Sche was receuyd a spanne
  Of any lyuand manne;
  Off rede golde þe rybanne
656    Glemyd hur gyde.

## [XLII]

  Hyr here was hy3thtyd on [m]old
  With a coronal of golde;
  Was neuer made vpon mold
660    A worthelych[er]e wy3th.
  Sche was frely and fair,
  And well hyr semed hyr geyr,
  With ryche boses a payr
664    Þat derely were by-dy3th.
  With a front endent
  With peyrl of Orient
  Out of Syprus was sent
668    To þat burd bry3th;
  Hur kercheuus was curyus,
  Hyr vyssag ful gracious;
  Sir Degriuaunt þat amerus
672    Had joy of þat sy3th.

f.100ᵛb

---

Glemyd. 657. hold. 660. *A sequence of smudged letters (indecipherable) follows* worthely; *the rest of the line has been re-written below.* 670. vyssag: *the last three letters inserted above the line.*

## [XLIII]

By þat þe messe was sayde
The haulle was ryally arrayed;
The Erle þan had revayde,
    And in hert was lyghte.    676
Than þay tromped to þe mete,
Thay wesche and went to þe sete,
Bothe þe smale and þe grete,
    Lady and knyghte.    680
When þe borde was drawen
The ladyse rase, noghte to layne,
And went to chambir agayne,
    On-one þay þam dyghte.    684
Myldore and hir maye
Went to ane orcherde to playe;
Whare Sir Degreuant laye
    Þay come onon-ryght.    688

## [XLIV]

Sir Degreuant þan hir mete
In an alay with-owtyn let;
Ferly faire he hir gret,
    Þat worthily wyghte.    692
He said, 'Curtayse lady and fre,
Jhesu Criste safe the;
Thy seruant will I euer be,
    My trouthe I þe plyghte.    696
I wald speke, had I space;
My lufe es lent in thi grace,
Preualy in þis place,
    Thou worthily wyghte.'    700
The birde was gretly affrayed,
Neuer þe lesse scho was payed,
He was so ryally arrayede,
    Þat comly knyghte.    704

L 686. orcherde: *the first* r *corrected from* y *or* þ. 688. MS. þat worthily wyght *crossed through, and* Þay come, *etc., written above it.*

## [XLIII]

By þat þe masse was i-seid
Þe halle was ryaly areyd;
Þe Eorlle hadd i-reuayd
676        And in hys ȝerd lyȝthus.
Trompers tromped to þe mete,
Þey weshen and went to sette,
So duden all þe grete,
680        Ladyes and knyȝttus.
When þe [b]ordys were drawin
Ladyes rysen, was not to leyn,
And wentten to chaumbur aȝeyn,
684        Anon þei hom dyȝthus.
Dame Mildore and hyr may     *When she appeared in the orchard*
Went to þe orcherd to play;
Þer Syr Degriuaunt lay
688        Þei com anon-ryȝthus.

## [XLIV]

Syr Degriuaunt withouten lett     *Sir Degrevant intercepted her,*
In an aley he hyr mete,     *saying, 'I love you*
And godlyche he hyr gret,     *very much.'*
692        Þat worþelych wyȝth.
And seyd, 'C[orte]ys lady and fre,     f.101a
Jhesu saue þe and see;
Þi seruaunt wold I be,
696        My trouȝth I þe plyȝth.
I wold spek, hadd I space,
Preuely in a place;
My lyff ys loken in þi grace
700        Þou worþilych wyȝth.'
Þe byrd was gretely affraid,     *She was very frightened, though his*
But naþeles hoo was wel paid,     *appearance pleased*
He was so ryally arayd,     *her,*
704        Þat commolych knyȝth.

C 681. lordys. 692. þat: a *smudged and almost illegible.* 693. certys.

## [XLV]

The bird ansuerde on highte:
'Whethir þou be sqwyere or knyghte,
Me thynke þou dose noghte ryghte,
    Þe sothe for to saye,      708
That comes thus armed on were
Thus damesels for to dere
Þat walkes in þaire arbere
    Preualy to playe.      712
By God and by Sayne Jame,
I ne knowe noghte þi name,
Bot þou ert gretly to blame
    I swere the in fay.'      716
The knyght knelyd hir till:
'Damesell, if it be þi will,
I grant wele I hafe done ill,
    I may noghte gaynesay;      720

## [XLVI]

'Als God saue me fra syn,
I myght with na noþer gyn
To ȝour speche for to wyn
    Be day ne by nyghte;      724
Fra I telle ȝow my name,
I ame noghte gretly to blame,
And [e]f it turne me to grame
    I sall onone-righte.      728
It am I, Sir Degreuant;
And I were to þe auenant,
I wald be thi seruant
    Als I am trew knyght.'      732
Scho sayd, 'Traytour, lat be!
By Hym þat dyed on þe tre,
My lorde hym-selfe sall þe see
    Hynge appon hyghte.'      736

L 718. if *written in the margin, inserted by means of caret.* 727. Of.

C 707. not: o *smudged.* 709. comyst: *Luick reads* commyst, *interpreting the tail of a* y *in the preceding line as a suspension.* ys *of this form are found elsewhere e.g.* 756 (day).

## [XLV]

Þe byrd answerus on hyȝth:
'Wheþur þou be squier or knyȝth,
Me þenkus þou not dost ryȝth,
708         Soþely to say,
Þat þou comyst armid on werre
To maydenus to afferre
Þat walkes in her erbere
712         Priuely to play.
By God and by Sent Jame,
Y know not þi name,
Þou erte gretely to blame
716         I tell þe in fay.'
Þe knyȝt kneled hyr tyll:
'Medame, yf hit be ȝour wyll,
I graunt I haue done yll,
720         I may not a-geyn-say;

## [XLVI]

'As God saue me of synne,
I myȝth with non oþer gynne
Tyl ȝour spech for to wynne
724         By day ne be nyȝth;
Fro I tell þe my name,
I am not for to blame,
And yf hit turne me to grame       f.101b
728         I shal a-non-ryȝth.
Hyt is I, Syr Degryuaunt;
And hit wer ȝour auenaunt,
I wold be ȝour seruaunt
732         As Y am trew knyȝth.'
Sho seyd, 'Tratur, lat be þe!       and threatened to
Be Hym þat dyed on tre,       betray him to her
My lord hym-self shal þe see       father.
736         Hanged on hyȝth.'

*Luick makes the same error in* 807. 713. and (&): *in a footnote Luick wrongly claims that the MS. reads* in. *The form of the* & *is unusual, in that it lacks the preliminary bold curve enclosing the rest of the character; but it lacks also the final hook of the in in* 711. *Another example of this type of* & *occurs in* 1173. 723, 726. forto.

## [XLVII]

Than Sir Degreuant loghe  
Þer he stode vndir þe boghe:  
'Ma-dame, þou wakyns my woghe  
    If it be thy will.          740  
I had neuer na gylte  
Of all þe blode þat was spylte;  
Þat will I proue, als þou wylt,  
    Onnon on ȝone hill.      744  
Curtayse lady and wyse,  
Als þou art proudeste of pryse,  
I do me in thi gentryse.  
    Why will þou me spill?    748  
If I be slane in this stede,  
Þou sall be cause of my dede,  
Ȝit will it rewe þe in thi rede,  
    And lyke it full ill.'      752

## [XLVIII]

Scho sayd, 'Traytoure, þou sall by!  
How was þou swa hardy  
To seke me with velany  
    By daye or by nyghte?    756  
For þe folke þat þou hase slayne  
Þou sall be hanged and drawen;  
Þar-of my lorde will be fayne  
    To se þe with syghte.'    760  
Than spake þe knyghte to þat fre:  
'Sen it may na better be,  
Gase fett forthe ȝour menȝe  
    With me for to fyght.     764  
Here my trowthe: or I be tane,  
Many of ȝour gestis sall grane,  
[E]f þer come fourtty for ane,  
    My trouthe I þe plyght.    768

L 764. for: *a small hole in the MS., just before the* f. 767. Of.

## [XLVII]

<blockquote>

Þan Syr Degriuaunt lou3h  
As he stod vndur þe bow,  
'Madame, 3e wyteþ me with wou3h  
740      Gyf hyt be 3our wyll.  
I had neuer no gylt  
Of al þat blod þat was spylt;  
Þat wyll I proue, as þou wylt,  
744      Aboue þe 3ondur hyll.  
Corteys lady and wyse,  
As þou arte peruenke of pryse,  
I do me on þi gentryse.  
748      Why wolt þou me spyll?  
And I be slayn in þis stede,        'If you do, you will  
Þou shalt be cause of my dede,    be responsible for  
3et wolt þou rew þat rede,         my death,  
752      And lyke hyt ful yll.'

</blockquote>

## [XLVIII]

<blockquote>

Sche said, 'Tratur þou shalt bye!  
Why were þou so hardye  
To do me þis vylanye  
756      By day ar by ny3th?  
For our folk þat þou hast slayn  
Þou shalt be honged and drawyn;  
Þerof my fadyr wol be fayn         f.101ᵛa  
760      To see þat with sy3th.'  
Þe kny3t spak to þis fre:  
'Seþþe hyt may no bettur be,  
Go feche all hys many  
764      With me for to fy3th.  
And here my trou3th: er I [b]e ton,   'but I will sell my  
Þe geyest of hem shal gron,        life dearly.'  
Gyf þer come fourty for on,  
768      My trou3th I þe ply3th.

</blockquote>

C 747. do *re-written after smudge.* 749. *After* and *a single vertical stroke, uncancelled.* 751. rew: w *smudged.* 764. forto. 765. be ton: *MS.* leton (*see note*).

## [XLIX]

'Here my trouthe I þe plyghte:
He þat leppis full lyghte,
He sall by it, and I fyghte,
 For all ȝour mekill pride.'    772
Þe stowte man in hert was stirred,
His sqwyere raght hym his swerde,
Þan was þe maydyn afferde,
 No lenger durst scho byde.    776
Till hir chambir scho went
And swore þe knyght sold be schent;
Hir maydyn hir hode of hent
 And knelid þat tyde:    780
'Madame, appon ȝole-nyghte
My waryson ȝe me highte;
I aske noghte bot ȝone knyghte
 To slepe be my syde.'    784

## [L]

Sone þe birde gan hir blame,
Bot scho wolde lett for no schame,
Þat scho ne askede the same,
 Þe sothe for to saye.    788
Þe may bad hir do hir beste:
'Ga glade þe with thi geste;
Þou lett me noght of my rest
 In twentty deuell way;    792
For, als so God me saue,
Had þou askede me a knaue —
The werste of alle þat I haue —
 Hade bene mare to my pay.    796
I swere þe by Goddes grace,
Come he euer-more in this place,
He passede neuer swilke a pace,
 'By nyghte ne by day.'    800

## [LI]

'Now, ma-dame, gramercy

## [XLIX]

'And her my trouȝth I þe plyȝthe:
Þo þat lepeþ now ful lyȝth,
Shal be fay, and we fyȝth,
  For all her michel pryde.'
Þe stout man was astered,
Hys squier rauȝth hym hys swerd,
Þanne þe borlych berde
  No lenger durst byde.
Tyl hyr chaumbur sche went
And swor þe knyȝth shulde be schent;
Þe mayde hur hood of hoe hent   *Melidor's chamber-*
  And knelyd þat tyde:      *maid declared*
'Meydame, oppon ȝowlus-nyȝth
My waryson ȝe me hyȝth;
Y ne axe þe bote ȝonde knyȝth   *that she would*
  To slep by my syde.'     *gladly take him for*
               *her lover.*

## [L]

Blyue þe burde gat a blame,
Bot sche ne let for no schame,
Þat sche ne asked þe same,
  Soþly to say.
'Damesel, go do þi best,      '*Do what you like*
I pray þe let me haue my rest,
Go and glad þi gest
  In all þe devyl way.      *f.101ᵛb*
For, as euer Gode me saue,
Haddest þou asked a knaue —   *but I had rather you*
Þe symplust þat I haue —    *had asked for some-*
  Hadd be more to my pay.   *one else.'*
I swer þe by Godus grace,
Come he euert in þis place,
He passed neuer syche a pace,
  By nyȝth ne by day.'

C 798. neuer. 799. pace: c *smudged*.

## [LI]

'Maydame,' sche seid, 'gramercy  
Of þi gret cortesy.'  
Blyue a chaumbur þer-by  
    Busked was ȝare,      804  
And in sche feches þe knyȝth,  
Priualy, withouten syȝth,  
As wymen conn mychel slyȝth,  
    And þer wylles ware.      808  
Sche dyȝt to hys sopere  
Þe foules of þe ryuere,  
Þer was no deynteþus to dere,  
    Ne spyces to spare.      812  
Þe knyȝt sat at hys auenaunt  
In a gentyl jesseraunt;  
Þe mayd mad hym semblaunt,  
    And hys met schare.      816

## [LII]

Of all þe met þat she schar,  
Þe knyȝt ete neuer þe mare;  
Whan he syȝthe ful sare  
    Þe mayden gan smyle.      820  
Sone aftyr he seys:  
'What vseþ þe Eorl adayes?  
Hontes he ar reuayes?  
    What does he þis whyle?'      824  
Þe burd answerus agayn:  
'Seþþe hys chyualry was slayn  
He passed neuer out on þe playn  
    Haluendel a myle;      828  
Hys hurtus has hym so y-deryd  
He has byn gretely afferyd;  
Þe ȝatus has byn ay y-speryd  
    For dred of þi gyle.'      832

---

C 807. wymen: *Luick reads* wymmen. *See footnote to* 709. 825. burd *inserted above the line.* 829. hys: s *smudged.*

## [LIII]

'Or hys ȝatis be y-speryd,
I shal mak hym afferyd,
I shal schak hym by þe berd
    Þe nexte tyme we mete;        *he confessed his*
But I let for hur sake                          *love for Melidor;*
Þat I haue chosen to my mak;
Sche doys me vnwynly to wak
    With wongus ful wete.
I had leuere sche wer sauȝth
Þen all þe golde in hys auȝth,
And I in armus hade y-lauȝth
    Þat commely and swete.
Þann durste I saffly syng
Was neuer emporour ne kyng
More at hys lykyng,
    An† honde I þe hete.'

## [LIV]

Þe mayd answerus aȝeyn:
'Me þink þou trauelus in vayn,        *but the maid dis-*
Þou hast our kunred y-slayn,          *couraged it;*
    How myȝt hit so be?
I swer þe by Godus myȝth,
Com þou euer in hur syȝth,
Þou bes honged on hyȝth
    Hyie on a tre!                *his rank was not*
Hyr proferrys par amoure              *high enough.*
Boþ dukes and emperoure,
Hyt were hyr disonowre                *f.102b*
    For to taken þe.
Þe Duke of Gerle for hir has sent     *The Duke of Gerle*
Þat he wol haue a tornament,          *was soon to come to*
Hyt ys my lordys assent               *joust for her.*
    With-ynne for to be.

C 848. And. 860. forto.

## [LV]

'Þo Duke comes of so gret arey
To iuste and to tornay;
Þou comes nat at þat play
  By counsayl of me.    868
Hyt is my lordys en-sent,
Come þou to þat torniment,
Sertaynly þou be schent,
  And all þi meynye.'    872
'Damesele, withouten drede,
Þou hast warnyd me of þis dede;
Of þis gret gentyl rede
  God for-ȝelde þe.    876
And Y swer be Sent Luke
I shal iuste with þat Duke,
Or I gete a rebuke,
  How-euer þat hyt be.    880

*Sir Degrevant undertook to attend the tournament.*

## [LVI]

'And, damesel, for þi chere,
And for my god sopere,
Þou shalt haue my squiere,
  Lok yf þe paye.    884
Here I gyf † ȝow be band
An .c. pownd worþ of land;
Do tak hyr by þe hond
  And do as Y þe saye.'    888
Whan here trouþus were plyȝth,
Sone torches were i-lyȝth,
And gaff hym ordyr of knyȝth,
  For soþe as I say.    892
'Recumaunde [me], for Godys Pyne,
To my lady and þine,
As þou wolt þat I be þin
  To my deþus day.    896

*Sir Degrevant promised her his squire in marriage,*

f.102ᵛa

*and bade her greet his lady for him.*

---

C 874. þis: is *superscribed*. 878. shal: l *smudged*. 883. squiere: *over the second e a short vertical stroke, without significance*. 885. I gyf l: *Luick reads* igyf I. *See note*. 887. Do: *Luick reads* To *erroneously*. 894. þine: *suspension over* in.

## [LVII]

'Recumaund me pryvaly
To þat fayr lady,
Or hur þ[e]nke lyȝthely
900     Þat I am pore;
Þer shal emporour ne kyng
Þat shal hyr to bed bryng
Þat I shall make a lettyng —
904     I sey þe þo soþe.
Here my trouþ I þe plyȝth:
Seyn fyrst I see hyr with syȝth,
I sleped neuer o nyȝth
908     Haluendel an hour.
Pray þat corteys and hende
Þat sche wold be my frend,
And some socour me send
912     For hyr mychel honowre.'

## [LVIII]

Þe maid seis, 'I take on hand
Þat I shal do þyn errand;
Or I be flemyd out of lond,
916     Y lete for no dred;
I shall teche þe a gyn      *The maid showed him out of the castle by a secret way,*
Out of þis castel to wyn,
And how þou shal come in
920     Þyn erond to spede.
Þer ys a place in þe wall
By-twyne þe chaumbur and þe hal;
Þor lyȝth a mychel watur-wal
924     Of fourty feyt brede;
Þer shalt þou come in a nyȝth      f.102ᵛb
Preualy withouten syȝth,
And here þi chaumbur shal by dyȝt,
928     And I can ryȝth rede.'

C 899. þonke.

## [LIX]

'Damesel, for Godus grace
Teche me to þat ylke place.'
Þe maid priualy a-pace
    Passes by-fore,     932
And ledes hym out at a gate,
In at a watur-ȝate
Þer men vytayled by bate
    Þat castel with cornes.     936
'At ebbe of þe see
Þou shalt not wad to þe kne.'
Þe knyȝt kyst þat fre.
    Erly at þe morow, .     940
Fayir þei passed þat flode,
To þo forest þei ȝoud,
And toke here stedus wher þei stod
    Vndur þe hawþrone.     944

## [LX]

*and he went home to prepare for the tourney.*

Syr Degriuaunt ys whom went,
And aftyr hys reten[ue] sent;
To þat gret tornament
    Þei busked hem ȝare.     948
But leue we now þat gentyl knyȝt,
And spek we of þat byrd bryȝt,
How þei gestened þat nyȝt
    Carp wyll we mare.     952
Erly on þe mowroun
Þe lady louȝh hyr to scorn;
Sche seys, 'Þi maydynhed is lorn;
    God gyf þe care.'     956

*f.103a*
*The maid told Melidor*

'Maydame, gyff hyt so be,
Hyt deres no man but me.
I fouchesaff on þat fre,
    And hyt so ware.'     960

C 943. stod *written above* wor *cancelled.* 946. reten.

## [LXI]

Þo lady louȝhwes vppon hyȝt;
'Damesele, for Godys myȝt,
How peyis þe þat knyȝt,
964    As euer mote þou the?'
'I dar make myn avaunt
For my lord Syr Degriuaunt,
Corteys and auenaunt,
968    I know non so fre.
Sertaynly þis ylke nyȝth
Hys squier ys mad knyȝth;
He and I ys trouþe-plyȝth
972    My housbond to be.
And he haþ gyf vs by band    *that she herself was*
An .c. pownd worþ of land;    *betrothed to the squire,*
Here þe chartur in þi hand,
976    Þi-self may hyt see.'


## [LXII]

Þan þat lady was glad
By sche þat chartur had rad.
'Had þou Syr Degriuaunt† had,
980    Þen had þou wel i-gon.'
'Nay, Meydame, so mot I þryue,    *and asked her to*
Þer ys not† lady on lyue    *relent towards Sir*
Þat he wol wed to wyff,    *Degrevant;*
984    But only þe allon.
Y warne þe of o þing —
Þer shall be emperour ne ky[n]g
Þat shal þe to bede bryng —
988    I owt-take non —
Þat he wol mak a lettyng;    f.103b
He sendys þe syche a gretyng,
Lo! here ys a rede gold ryng
992    With a ryche ston.'

C 979. deg*r*iuaunant.  982. now.  986. kyg.  988. non: *over on a suspension mark, without significance (cf. also* allon 984).

(Missing)

### [LXIV]

| | |
|---|---|
| The Duke es comen ouer the see | |
| With a grete menȝe; | |
| The Erle curtayse and free | |
|     Faste gan hym praye | 1012 |
| To duelle at his costage, | |
| At bouche of court and tonage, | |
| Bothe sqwyere and page, | |
|     To the tweluft daye; | 1016 |
| A thowsand horses and three | |
| Of þe Dukes menȝe | |
| Ilke nyghte to lyuere | |
|     Bathe corne and haye. | 1020 |
| The knyghtes of þe Erles howse | |
| Helde þe Duke cheualrouse, | |
| For he was gaye and amorouse, | |
|     And made so mekill draye. | 1024 |

## [LXIII]

|   |   |   |
|---|---|---|
| | Þe lady loked on þat ryng; | |
| | Hyt was a gyfte for a kyng: | |
| | 'Þis ys a merveylous þing, | |
| 996 | Wenus þou I be wode | but in vain. |
| | To do syche a foly, | |
| | To loue my lordys enemy, | |
| | Þow he were to so dowȝty? | |
| 1000 | Nay, by þe Rode! | |
| | Y do þe wele for to wyte | |
| | Y nel non housbond haue ȝyte: | |
| | Seye þe knyȝth, whan ȝe mete, | |
| 1004 | I wol hym no gude. | |
| | Þe Duk of Gerle hase i-hyȝt | |
| | Þat he wol soupe here þis nyȝt, | |
| | And gyf my chaumbur wer i-dyȝt, | |
| 1008 | Noþing for-ȝ[oo]d.' | |

## [LXIV]

|   |   |   |
|---|---|---|
| | Þe Duk ys comen ouer þe see | The Duke arrived |
| | With a ful grete meyne; | with his retinue, |
| | Þe Eorl cortays and fre | |
| 1012 | Fayr hym gan praye | |
| | To dwel at hys costage, | |
| | At bouche [of] court and wage, | |
| | With knyȝt, squier, and page, | |
| 1016 | Tyl þe tent day. | |
| | A þousaund hors and þre | |
| | Of þe Dukus meyne | |
| | Ylke nyȝt tok lyuere | |
| 1020 | Off cowrun and off hay. | |
| | Þe ryche Duk, whan he eet, | f.103ᵛa |
| | Þe Eorle hertely hym hete; | |
| | And with Mayd Myldore þe swet | |
| 1024 | To haue hyr for ay. | |

C 1008. ȝeed, *possibly* ȝeod. 1014. &.

## [LXV]

    Þe riche Duke, when he gun mete  
    With Mayden Mildore þe swete,  
    Þe Erle baldly he hym gun hete  
        To haffe hir for ay.        1028  
    The Erle tolde hym onane  
    How his cheualrye were slayne,  
    And whate harmes he had tane  
        Vndir þe wod-boghe:        1032  
    'The baron wonnes hereby  
    Þat will assayle this cry;  
    Þat did me þat velany,  
        And wroght me this woghe.'    1036  
    The Duke ansuerde þis knyght:  
    'Here my trouthe I þe plyghte,  
    Whethir he will tournay or fyght,  
        He sall haf ynoghe.'        1040

## [LXVI]

    The Duk ansuerd on hight,  
    'Whare-by knawes þou þat knyght?'  
    Þe Erle t[alde] hym full right  
        With wordis, I wene:        1044  
    'He beris a schelde of asure  
    Engrelyde with a sa[w]tour,  
    With a dowbyll tressoure,  
        And archede by-twene;        1048  
    Bot his bagges are blake;  
    For he will nane for-sake,  
    A lyon tyed till an ake  
        Of gowlys and grene;        1052  
    A helme riche to be-holde,  
    He berys a dolphyn of golde,  
    With a trewelufe on þe molde,  
        Cumpaste ful clene.        1056

L 1043. t . . . . : *a hole in the MS., with space for four letters. The lower parts of* a, d, e *just visible.* 1046. sayntou*r*r.

## [LXV]

  Þe k[n]yȝthus of þe Eorles house
  Held þe Duk so chyualrous,
  For he was gay and amorous,
1028    And made hyt so tow.
  Þe Eorl tol[d] hym a-non    *and learned about*
  What armes he hadde tonn†,    *Sir Degrevant,*
  And how hys chyualre was slon,
1032    Vndir þe wod-bowe:
  'Þe Baneret þat wonnes here-by
  Wol a-sayl þe cry;
  He wroȝthe me þis vylany,
1036    And dud me þis wouȝh.'
  Þe Duk answerus on hyȝth:
  'Here my trouþ I þe plyȝth,
  Whedur he wol tornay or fyȝth,
1040    He shal haue inow.'

## [LXVI]

  Þe Duk answerus on hyȝth,
  'Whereby k[n]owus þou þe knyȝth?'
  Þe Eorle tauȝth hym ful ryȝth
1044    With wordys, I wene:
  'He beres [a] cheef of aȝour    *who was to be*
  Engrelyd with a satur,    *recognized by his*
  With doubule tressour,    *coat-of-arms.*
1048    And trewelouus by-twene;
  Hys bagges is† blake;
  For he wol no man for-sake,
  A lyoun tyed to an ake
1052    Off gold and of grene;
  An helme ryche to be-hold,
  He beres a dolfyn of gold,
  With trewelouus in þe mold,
1056    Compasyd ful clene.

---

C 1030. conn. 1030–1 *are written in the reverse order in the MS.; the correction is made by means of letters* b, a *in the margin.* 1039. fyȝth: *the* f *is badly made, and closely resembles* s. 1045. a: *MS.* s; *Luick reads* in, *erroneously.* 1049. þis. 1050. noman.

## [LXVII]

'He es bown to þe felde,
Bath with spere and with schilde,
The helme sall be wele stelyd
    Sall stande hym a strake;      1060
He es stalworthe in stowres,
By Sayne Martyn of Towres,
And he luffede paramours,
    I knewe noght his make.      1064
Alle þe land þat I welde
I wold gyff in my elde·
To see hym fellede in þe felde,
    Wha wolde it vndir-take.'      1068
Þe Duke loghe hym to skorne,
Thus hastyly þam hase he sworne,
'He sall habye to-morne,
    Sir, for þi sake.'      1072

## [LXVIII]

ONE þe morne þe Duke hym dight
Als fast als he myght,
Þe Erle hardy and wyght,
    Crowell and kene.      1076
The sone schane full clere;
Thre thowsand in fere
Thay helde with þe banere,
    Armed full clene.      1080
Þay þat were aunterous by-syde
In a cuntre full wyde,
Þay come thedir þat tyde
    Þat semble to sene.      1084
Sir Degreuant of þe west
He broghte owt of þe forest
Thre score knyghtis of þe best
    Graythed wele in grene.      1088

L 1073. *A red capital.*

## [LXVII]

'He ys a lyoun in feld,     f.103ᵛb
When he ys spred vndur scheld,
Hys helme shal be wel steled
    Þat stond shal as stak;
He ys so stalloworþ in stoure,
By Seynt Martyn of Toure,
Couþe he loue par amoure,
    I k[n]ew neuer hys mak.
All þe londes þat I welde
Wold I gyf in my ȝelde
To se hym falde in þe feld,
    Ho wold hyt vndur-take.'
Þe Duk louȝh hym to scorun,     The Duke was not afraid
Hys oþ heyly has i-sw[o]run,
'He shal a-bye to-mowrun,
    Syre, for þi sake.'

## [LXVIII]

And on morow þe Duk hym dyȝth     and made ready for the battle.
Also fast as he miȝth,
Þe Eorl hardy and wyȝth,
    Cruel and kene.
Þe sonnet† schonne en clere;
Þey vschen in with banere
.V. hunderyd knyȝtus in fere
    I-armed ful clene,
And þer seruitourus by-syde.
All þat contray so wyde
Come þedur þat tyde
    Þat solas to sene.
Sire Egriuaunt out of þe west     Sir Degrevant arrived,
Brouȝth out of þe forest
Þre hundred knyȝttus of þe best,
    Was greyþed al on grene.

C 1064. kew. 1069. scorun: *over* u *a suspension mark, without significance.* 1077. sᶜonne (*see note*).

## [LXIX]

Þare was none so hardy
Þat durste assayle þat cry;
Þay helde þe Duke so doghety
    For his mekill pride.     1092
Bot when þay saw Sir Degreuant
Cum armede on a feraunt,
Þay thanked God of his sant
    Alle þe toþer syde.     1096
Than drewe þay full nere,
Baron and bachelere,
To be vndir his banere,
    To tournaye þat tyde;     1100
With trompis, and with nakerere,
And with þe schalmous full clere,
Folkes pressed in fere,
    In hert es noghte to hyde.     1104

## [LXX]

When þe renkes gan mete,
Fay were fellid vndir fete,
Knyghtis tombled in þe strete,
    Stonayde vndir stedis;     1108
With swerdis swyftly þay smyte,
Þay teme sadils full tyte;
Þare was n[e] langare lyte,
    Thies worthy in wedys.     1112
Of alle þe beryns of þe bent,
[Schuldirs schamesly þay schent;
Bryghte crounes and brent]
    And brathly bledis.     1116
Many armys were tynt,
Þat were neuer at þe sent
To come to þat tournament
    To do swylke dedis.     1120

L 1111. ne: *a cut in the MS.*; *possibly* no *or* na. 1114. *This line is written after* 1115 (*see note*).

## [LXIX]

 Þer was non so hardy
 Þat durst asayl þe cry;
 Þe held þ[i]s Duk so douȝty
1092   For hys mychel pryd.    f.104a
 But when þei se Syr Degriuans
 Com armed vp a ferauns,
 Þei þonked Gode of her shaunce
1096   Al þat oþer syde.
 Þen þei drowe hym ful nere,
 Baneret and bachelere,
 To ben vndur hys banere,
1100   To tornay þat tyde;
 With trompe, and with naker,
 And þe scalmuse clere,
 Folke frouschen in fere,
1104   In herd ys not to hyde.

## [LXX]

 And when þe renkus gan mete,    and the tournament
 Fele was fouled vndur fete,    began;
 Knyȝthus strewed in þe strete,
1108   Stonyȝed with stedys;
 With swerdus smartely þei smyt,
 Þe temes sadel[us] ful tyte;
 Þer was no lengur delyte,
1112   Þese worþely in wedus.
 Baronus syttys on þe bent
 With shuldrys shamly shent;
 Bryȝthe browus and b[r]ent
1116   Brodelyche bledus.
 Manye harmus has þei hent;
 Þat was neuer at hor asent
 To come to þat tornament
1120   To do suche dedus.

C 1105. gan: *over* n *a suspension mark, without significance.* 1110. sadely. 1113. syttys: tt *smudged.* 1115. *MS.* bent, *with small ornamental tick over* b.

## [LXXI]

Sir Degreuant with-owttyn lese
Prekid faste in þe prese;
Vn-to þe cheftane he chese,
    And raughte hym a strake;    1124
Þe Duke [dotered] to þe gronde,
And þan swyftly he swounede;
Sir Degreuant in þat stownde
    Wane his stede blake.    1128
He was staleworthe in stowres,
Be Sayne Martyn of Towres;
Þe lady laye in hir bowres
    Þat solde be his make.    1132
Sir Degreuant, or he blane
(Þat see myghte many a man),
Fourty stedis he wane,
    And broghte þam to stake.    1136

## [LXXII]

Sir Degreuant þat ilke daye,
Þe certayne sothe for to saye,
Alle þe pryce of the playe
    Es putt on þat fre;    1140
Sone þe doghety vndir schelde
He hase wonnen þe felde;
Many man hym by-helde,
    Sa hardy was he.    1144
Þan þay sayde al by-dene,
Bathe kynge and qwene,
'Þe doghtty knyght in þe grene
    Hase wonnen þe gree.'    1148
Bryghte birdis in þe boure
Louede þe knyghte paramoure:
Ladyse of honoure,
    And all þat hym see.    1152

L 1125. Þe doghety duke.

## [LXXI]

Syre Degriuaunt with-outen les
Prykkus fast þerow þe pres;
To þe cheuentayn he ches,
1124     And rauȝth hym a strok;
Þe Duk dotered to þe ground,
On erþe swyfftly he swouned;
Syre Degriuaunt with-in a stound
1128     He wan hys sted blak.
He was stalworȝth in stoure,
For he loued par amoure;
Þe lady lay in þe toure
1132     Þat shuld be hys mak.
Syre Degriuaunt, ar he blan
(Þis sey many a man),
Syxty stedus he wan,
1136     And brouȝth to stak.

*the Duke was un-horsed,*
*f.104b*

## [LXXII]

Syre Degriuaunt euery day,
Þe sertayn soþ for to say,
Al þe prys of þe play
1140     Was put on þat fre;
Sone þat douȝty vndur sheld
Had y-venkessyd þe feld;
Many a man hym by-held,
1144     So hardy was he.
Ladyes seyden al by-dene,
Boþe contasse and qwene,
'Ȝond gentyl knyȝt on grene
1148     Haþ deseruyd þe gre.'
Bryȝth burdus in þer boure
Loued þat knyȝth par amoure:
Gret ladyes of honoure,
1152     And [alle] þat hym seyen.

*and Sir Degrevant was victorious.*

## [LXXIII]

Þe Duke was horsede agayne,
He prikked faste in þe playne,
Þe riche Duke with a trayne
 To þe castelle gan fare.   1156
A hauraud faste gan crye,
And prayes all þat cheualry
To souppe at þat maungery
 If þaire will ware.   1160
The gud knyght Sir Degreuans
Had made his awen purueance
Tyll all his retenans
 For thre dayes and mare,   1164
In the syde of a felle,
Whare hym lyked for to duelle,
In a fayre castelle,
 For to slaa care.   1168

## [LXXIV]

The steryn knyghte and þe stowte
Þat tournayde þat daye with-owte
Ledd a-waye in a rowte
 Thre hundrethe and ma;   1172
A hundrethe pownde and a stede
He sent mynstrals to mede;
Of gyftis was he [n]euer gnede
 In wele na in waa.   1176
A ryche mawngery he made,
Alle þe balde þat habade
To þe castelle þay rade,
 Withskapid nan hym fra.   1180
At evyn sayde Sir Degreuans,
'I will see þe contenans
Of þe cheualrye of France,
 Als euer mot I gaa.'   1184

L 1153. agayne: *the g partially obscured by a brown stain.* 1175. neucr: *MS.* eu*e*r, *with a considerable space between it and the preceding word.*

## [LXXIII]

  Þe Duk was horsed agayn
  And prycked fast þorw þe playn;
  Þe Eorl and he with a trayn
1156    To þe castel gan fare.
  Þane an heroud gon crye,
  And prayd al þe chyualrye
  To soupe at þe maungerye
1160    Gyff þer wyllus ware.
  Þe good knyȝt Syre Degriuaunce   f.104ᵛa
  He had y-made repurueaunce
  For al hys retenaunce
1164    Fourty days and mare,
  In þe syde at a fel,
  At a wel feyre castel,
  Whyle hym was left† for to dwel,
1168    For to sle care.

## [LXXIV]

  Þe sterne knyȝthus and þe stout
  Whylk þat torn[ayde] with-out
  Ryden a-way in hys rout
1172    Þre hundred and mo;
  And c pound and a stede
  He send þe mynstralus to mede;   He rewarded the minstrels lavishly,
  Off gyffte was he neuer gnede
1176    For wele nor for wo.
  Tyl hys castel he rade,   and rode off to his castle.
  A ryal maungerye he made,
  Alle þe bold þer a-bade,
1180    Þer scapyd non hym fro.
  At euen seyd Syr Degriuauns,
  'I wol se þe countenauns
  Of þe chyualrye of Frauns,
1184    As euer mote I go.'

C 1154. playn: *over* n *a suspension mark, without significamce.* 1167. lefte. 1169. knyȝthes: n *inserted above.* 1170. tornyment.

## [LXXV]

Syr Degreuant at euen-lyghte
Callid to hym a knyghte,
And armed þam bathe ryghte
    Þat proudest was aye.     1188
. . . . . . .
. . . . . . .
. . . . . . .

. . . . . .
'Take for aythir of vs a spere,
Bathe of pese and of were,
Graythe vs horse and my gere,
    Loke þat þay be gaye;     1196
Þat þay be trapped in gete,
Bathe telerer and mantelete,
Ryghte of a fyne veluete,
    And make we na draye.'     1200

## [LXXVI]

When þaire horses were hilled
Þay prikkede fast thorow þe felde,
Bathe with spere and with sch[el]de,
    Na langare habade þay.     1204
Sythen þay rade euen weste
Thorgh a fayre foreste
With twa trompets of þe beste
    Þat range als a belle.     1208
On a hill þay gan reste,
He tuke his helme and his creste,
He was þe stowteste geste
    Fra heuen in-till helle.     1212
Sir Degreuant na langare bade,
To þe Erles castelle he rade,
He fand þe ȝatis opyn brade,
    Slyk happe hym by-felle.     1216

L 1188. was *corrected from* waþ *or* way; s *written on top of last letter. No indication given of hiatus (see note).* 1203. schelde: *a hole in the MS. makes the fourth letter illegible, and cuts off the bottom of the* 1.

## [LXXV]

|      | |       |
|---|---|---|
|      | Syr Egriuaunt aȝ euyn-lyȝthus | That evening, |
|      | Armed hym at al ryȝthus, | |
|      | And callyd to hym to[w] knyȝthus | |
| 1188 | Þat preuest† were ay. | |
|      | 'Ha dyȝt ȝow on stedus | |
|      | In two damysel wedus, | |
|      | For I wol found in my nedus | |
| 1192 | As fast as I may. | |
|      | Tak eþer of ȝow a spere | |
|      | Boþe of pes and of were, | f.104ᵛb |
|      | Greyþ myn hors on hor gere, | |
| 1196 | And lok þat þei be gay; | |
|      | Þat þey be trapped a get, | |
|      | In topteler and in mauntolet, | |
|      | In a fyn vyolet, | |
| 1200 | And makes non delay.' | |

## [LXXVI]

|      | | |
|---|---|---|
|      | And whan here hors wer held | |
|      | Þei toke þer sperus and þere scheldus, | |
|      | And prycked fast on þe felde, | |
| 1204 | No lengur wolde þei dwel. | |
|      | And syen þei ryden euen west | |
|      | Þorw a fayr forest | |
|      | With two trompess of þe best | |
| 1208 | Þat range as a bell. | |
|      | On an hull he gan hym rest, | |
|      | Þei gaf hym hys helm [and] hys [c]rest, | |
|      | He was þe sternest gest | |
| 1212 | Fro heuen to helle. | |
|      | Syr Degriuaunt with-outen a-bad | he rode with two |
|      | To þe Eorlus castel he rade, | knights to the Earl's castle, |
|      | He found þe ȝat so brad, | |
| 1216 | Swyche hap hym felle. | |

C 1187. tolly. 1188. pryuest. 1189. *After* ha *two letters* (dd?) *cancelled. Luick reads* have *erroneously*. 1203. on: *MS.* oñ, *as in* 1237, 1245, 1257, *etc.* 1206. *Below the line*, 1209 *has been copied in error, and cancelled.* 1210 *in* hys rest.

## [LXXVII]

Als þay were seruede of þe first mese  
He rade vp to þe dese;  
Mayden Mildore he chese,  
    And chalanges þat free.      1220  
The Duke styrte þan vp on highte:  
'Sir, here my trouthe I the plyght,  
I sall delyuer þe þat bryghte,  
    To-morne sall it be.      1224  
By-twene vndron and pryme,  
Luk þou come at þat tyme,  
And ane of vs sall ly in swyme,  
    The lady sall see.      1228  
Trewely, with-owtten lese,  
Þou sall be seruede, are I cesse,  
Bathe of w[er]e and of pesse —  
    Of aythir, courses thre.'      1232  

## [LXXVIII]

Þe knyghte was dressed sa free  
It was joye for to see,  
So fayre a horse-man as† he  
    Sawe I neuer are.      1236  
Sum luked on his stede,  
And sum on his riche wede,  
And sum þe resouns gan rede  
    Þat the knyght bare.      1240  
He lowtted down to þam alle,  
Bathe to ryche and to smalle,  
He rade owte of þe haulle,  
    He busked full ȝare.      1244  
Of alle þat luked on þe knyght,  
Nane wyste what he highte  
Bot Mayden Mildore þe bryght,  
    Of all þat þare ware.      1248  

---

L 1230. þou: *Luick reads* you, *which is palæographically just as acceptable, owing to the similarity in this MS. of* y *and* þ. *The singular pronoun is here adopted in order to conform with* 1226. 1231. *MS.* w . . e *owing to tear, repaired by a small piece of paper obliterating the first* e, *and cutting off the bottom of the* r. 1235. was. 1239. resons: *MS.* resous, *over* u *a curved suspension-mark, with dot underneath it.*

## [LXXVII]

|||
|---|---|
| | And rydes vp to þe des |
| | As þei were seruid of her mes; |
| | To Mayd Myldor he ches, |
| 1220 | And chalangys þat fre. |
| | Þe Duk sterte vp an hyȝt: |
| | 'Here my troupe Y þe plyȝt, |
| | I shal delyuer þe þis bryȝt, |
| 1224 | To-morow shalt þou se. |
| | By-twene vnderun and prime, |
| | Loke at þou come at þat tyme, |
| | O[u]þer swowne shal i[n] sweme, |
| 1228 | Þe lady shal i-se. |
| | And trewly, with-outen les, |
| | Þou shalt be seruid, or I sess, |
| | Boþe of werre and of pess — |
| 1232 | Of ayþur, cours þre.' |

*up to the dais where Melidor was, and claimed her as his prize.*

*The Duke asserted that they would joust the next day.*

f.105a

## [LXXVIII]

|||
|---|---|
| | Þe knyȝth was so dresse |
| | Hytt was gret ioye to se, |
| | So fayr an hors-man as he |
| 1236 | Seye þei neuer are. |
| | Some loked on hys stede, |
| | And some on hys rych wede, |
| | And some þe resoun gan rede |
| 1240 | What þe knyȝth bare. |
| | He loutes down to þem alle, |
| | Boþe to þe [grete] and to þe smalle, |
| | And rydys out of þe halle, |
| 1244 | And buskys hym ȝare. |
| | Of all þat loked on þe knyȝt, |
| | Was non þat knew hym with syȝt |
| | Bot Mayden Myldor þe bryȝt, |
| 1248 | Of all þat þer ware. |

C 1228. *A stroke cancelled after* lady. 1248. þer: þ *smudged.*

## [LXXIX]

Hamwardes he rydis ryghte
Als faste als he myghte;
And on þe morne he hym dighte
    Als þat he did are.     1252
He fyndis þe Duke in þe felde,
Bathe with spere and with schelde,
þe Erle houede and by-helde,
    Bryme als a bare.     1256
Than spake þe Duke on þe laund:
'Whare es now þat gyant?
Whi will he noghte hald conand
    For all his mekil fare?'     1260
Bot when he saw Sir Degreuant
Com rydyng on a ferawnt,
His hert wexe recreawnt,
    And syghed full sare.     1264

## [LXXX]

The Duke sent a sqwyere
To wiete whate his will were:
To juste on pese or on were,
    Sa sore he hym drede.     1268
The knyght ansuerde þer-till
Bathe with reson and skill:
'It sall be at his awen will,
    As euer God me spede.'     1272
Than thir doghety þam dyght,
And sett helmys on highte
Als faste als þay myghte —
    Thir worthily vndir wedis:     1276
Twa speris of pese
Bathe þe schaftis þay chese,
And prikked faste in þe prese
    Appon styfe stedis.     1280

## [LXXIX]

  Hammard he rydes ryȝth,
  And as fast as he myȝth;
  On þe moro[w] he hym dyȝth   *When the next day came,*
1252     Ryȝth as he dude are.
  And fyndys þe Duk in þe feld,
  Boþe with spere and with sche[l]d,
  þe Eorl houed and by-held,
1256     Brem as a bare.
  Þan seid þe Duke on þe land:
  'Whare ys now þis geand?
  He wol hald no couenand
1260     For alle hys gret fare.'
  But when he say Syr Degriuaunt
  Come armed vp a feraun[t],
  Hys hert wex recreaunt,
1264     And syȝth ful sare.

## [LXXX]

  Þe Duk send a squiere   *f.105b*
  To wytt what hys wyll were:
  To iuste o pesse or off were,
1268     So sore he hym dredus.
  Þe knyȝt answerd þertyll
  Boþe with resoun and with skyll:
  'Hyt shal be at hys wyll,
1272     Tak hap what ledus.'
  Þen þe douȝthy h[e]m dyȝth   *they met in single combat;*
  As faste as þei myȝth;
  Þei set helmus on hyȝth,
1276     Þes douȝty on dedus:
  To gret sperus of pese
  Boþe þese lordes hem chese,
  And prikes fast þorw þe prese
1280     Opon stout stedus.

C 1251. mowro. 1257. on: *over* n *a suspension mark, without significance.* 1262. a *written twice, the first cancelled*; Ferauns. 1273. hy*m*. 1274. *After second* as, *a single stroke like long* s, *uncancelled.*

## [LXXXI]

Thaire stedis stirred þam fast,
Thir knyghtis in fewtir þay caste,
Thaire gud speris al to-braste
    On molde when þai mett.    1284
Sir Degreuant, als he mynt,
He gafe þe Duk suylke a dynt
Þat bathe his steraps he tynt,
    On hand I ȝow hete.    1288
Bot he recouerd agayne,
All his frendis wer fayne,
Þay profird hym payndemayne,
    Vernage, and crete.    1292
The Duk suerres by Heuen:
'Had my horse gane euyn,
I sold haf sett all on seuen
    For Mildor þe swete.'    1296

## [LXXXII]

Twa grete speris hafe þay tane,
And gyrdis þe stedis to þay grane;
Wete ȝe wele many ane
    Loked on þase twa.    1300
Thorgh þe renkes gan þay ride,
Thir doghty knyghtis of pride
Fayled bathe at þat tyde;
    Þaire happe fell swa.    1304
Þe gud knyght[e Sir] Aunterous
Come in at þe third course,
For he loued paramours;
    In hert was he thra.    1308
He strak þe Duk in þe schelde,
Wyde opyn in þe felde;
Þe Erle houed and by-helde,
    In hert was he waa.    1312

L 1305. knyghtis. *I insert* Sir.

C 1281. styrres: e *smudged.* 1282. knyȝthes: *the* e *followed by an illegible smudge: the ink has run into the* rr *of* styrres *in the line above.* 1283. alto. 1286. And gaf.

## [LXXXI]

Þer stedes styrres hom faste,
Þe kny3the[s] iusset or þy cast,
Þer good speres al to-brast
  Þat weren gode at nede.
Syr Degriuaunt, as he had ment,
†Gaf þe Duk swych a dynt
Þat boþe styroppus he tynt,
  An† hond I þe hete.
Þe Duke rekyuered a3[a]yne,
Hys frenchepys were fayn,
Þe proford hym payn-mayn,
  Vernage, and crete.
Þe Duk swore by gret God of heue[n]:
'Wold my hors [g]o euene,
3et wold I sett all on seuen
  For Myldor þe swet.'

## [LXXXII]

Tow gret sperus ha þey ton,
And gerd þere stedus w[h]yll þe gron;
Wytt 3ow wel þat many on
  Lokede on þem two.   f.105ᵛa
Þe dou3ty kny3thus of pryde
Þorw þe renckus gon þei ryde,
Bote þey myssede at þat tyde;
  Þorw hap hyt fell so.
Þe good kny3th Syre Auntorus
Come in at þe þryd cours,
For he loued paramours;
  In hert þat he was þro,
And strykus þe Duk þorw þe scheld,   Sir Degrevant was
Wyd opon in þe feld;   victorious.
Þe Eorl houed and by-held,
  In hert he was wo.

---

1288. And. 1293. heue. 1294. so. 1295. on: *over* n *a suspension mark, without significance.*
1298. w[h]yll: *a letter* (h?) *inserted above between* w *and* y.   1310–11 *are in the reverse order in the MS.; corrected by means of letters* b, a *in the margin.*

## [LXXXIII]

The† damesele tuk þe stede,
Thorow þe renkes scho gan it lede.
Scho sayd, 'Tak þat to thi mede
    Whils þou gete maa.'  1316
Than spake scho a word of pryde:
'On this stede will I ryde
Right by my leman syde,
    In lande whare he fare.'  1320
The knyghtis dight hym in his gere,
Þe mayden raght hym a spere,
A scharpe wapyn for þe were,
    Þe Duk for to sla.  1324
Scho said, 'Sir Duke auenant,
I pray þe holde thi conant,
Ȝondir es a knyght byddand;
    Why taries þou hym swa?'  1328

## [LXXXIV]

The Duk lay on þe ground,
In hert swyftly he swunned,
He stotyede sore in þat stownde,
    Trewly þat tyde.  1332
Ȝit scho cries on heghte:
'Ȝondir es an armyd knyght,
Alle redy for-sothe es he dyghte,
    Thi come to habyde.'  1336
The Duk ansuerd hir till,
Bathe with reson and skyll:
'I am hurte full ill,
    In hert es noght to hyde.  1340
I pray the tak it to na greue
Þou sese me in mescheue;
I hope noghte I may leue,
    Swa sare es my syde.'  1344

---

L 1313. The ta damesele. 1342. þou: *possibly* You (*see* 1230, *and note*).

C 1314. gon: *over* n *a suspension mark, without significance.* 1320. I. 1326. couenaunt:

## [LXXXIII]

  þe damessel toke þe stede,
  And þorw þe renkus gon hym lede,
  And seys, 'Haue þis for þi mede
1316    Tyl þou gete mo.'
  ȝet she spekys a word of pride:
  'On þis stede wol I ryde
  By my lemmanus syde,
1320    I[n] lond whare I go.'
  Þat knyȝt dressyd hym in hys gere,
  Hys felawe rauȝth hym a spere,
  A scharpe wepon of were,
1324    þe Duk for to slo;
  And seis, 'Syre Duke auenaunt,
  I pray þe hold couenaunt,
  ȝondur ys a knyȝth erraunt;
1328    Why taryest þou hym so?'

## [LXXXIV]

  þe Duk lay on þe grownd,
  On erþe swyftely he swound,
  He was stonyed þat stownd,
1332    Trewly þat tyde.
  And ȝit she cryes vpon hyȝth:
  'ȝondur ys armed a knyȝth
  All redy and y-dyȝth,
1336    Þi comes for to a-byde.'
  þe Duk answerd þer-tyl,    f.105ᵛb
  Boþe with reson and skyl:
  'I am y-hurte ful yl,
1340    In herd is not to hyde.
  Pray hym tak hit nat a greff,
  He ses I am at myscheff;
  Y h[op]e nat Y m[a]y lyff,
1344    So sore ys my syde.'

*over* o *a suspension mark, without significance.* 1327. knyȝth: n *inserted above the line, with caret to mark point of insertion.* 1333. vpon: *over* on *a suspension mark, without significance.* 1343. y haþe nat y my lyff.

## [LXXXV]

Sir Degreuant tuke þe stede,
Gaff hym mynstrals to mede,
Sythyn hamward he ȝede
    Als fast als he may.      1348
The Duk þat was sa dyghte
Tuk his leue þat ilke nyght
Bathe at baron and knyghte,
    And went on his waye.      1352
Sir Degreuant, on þe morne,
Come agayne to þe thorne
Whare þaire stedis stode by-forne,
    Þare als þay þam leuede.      1356
And preualy, on þe nyghte,
He come with his knyght
To speke with Myldor þe bryght,
    Spede if he maye.      1360

## [LXXXVI]

The may wist by a gyn
Þat þe knyght was comen in;
The lady of heghe kyn
    Persayued and thoghte.      1364
'Damesele, sa haf I rest,
Þou hase getyn a geste
With wylde men of þe west,
    Layne þou þam noghte.      1368
Preualy, with-outtyn sight,
Do me speke with the knyght;
Here my trouthe I þe plyght,
    Dere he hase me boghte.'      1372
Þan þe damesele was glade,
And did als þe lady hir bade;
Vp at a grese scho hym lade,
    To chambir scho hym broghte.      1376

L 1366. hase: s *closely resembles* f.

## [LXXXV]

  Syre Degriuaunt toke his stede,
  And gaff þe mynstrelus to mede,
  And to forest þei spede
1348     As faste as þe may.
  Þe Duke þat was þis y-dyȝt
  He toke his leue þat ylk nyȝt    *The Duke departed*
  Boþe with baroun and with knyȝt,   *that night.*
1352     And went on hys way.
  Sir Degriuaunt, on þe morwoun,
  Come aȝe to þe þorun
  Þer hys stede stod by-forun,
1356     And lenges all þat day.
  Priuayly, at þe nyȝth,    *The next night Sir*
  He come in with hys knyȝth   *Degrevant visited*
  To spek with Myldore þe bryȝth,   *the Earl's castle in secret,*
1360     Spede yf he may.

## [LXXXVI]

  Þe mayde wyst by a gynn
  Þat þe knyȝth was comen in;
  Þe lady of heye kynn
1364     Perseued þe þouȝth.
  'Damesele, so haue I rest,
  Þou hast geton þe a gest
  Off wylde men of þe west,
1368     Layne† þou hom nouȝth.
  Preuayly, withouten syȝth,
  Do me carp with þat knyȝth;
  Here my trouȝth Y þe plyȝth,
1372     He has dere y-bouȝth.'    f.106a
  Þanne þe mayden was glade,
  Sche dude as þe lady bade,
  And vp at þe grese hoe him lade,
1376     And to chaumbur hym brouȝth.

C 1352. on: *over* n *a suspension mark, without significance.* 1368. Delayne.

## [LXXXVII]

The lady of honowre  
Met þe knyght at þe dore,  
And knelid down in þe flore,  
 And felle hym to fete.   1380  
Þe frek, als fyre of þe flynt,  
In his armes he hir hent;  
Sexty sythes, are he stynt,  
 He kyssed þat swete.   1384  
'Welcome,' scho said, 'Sir Aunterous,  
Me thynke þou art meruelous;  
Wist my lorde of þis house  
 With grame he wold the grete.'   1388  
Swythe chayers þay fett,  
Qwyssyns of veluett;  
And þare thir semly wer sett  
 With mowthis to mete.   1392

## [LXXXVIII]

'A fyre in the chymney  
Loke, damesele, þat þer bee,  
Fagotes of fyr-tree  
 Fett þou vs ȝare.'   1396  
Scho sett a borde of yvorye,  
Tristis ordayned þer-fore;  
Clathes couerde þer wore,  
 Swylke saw I neuer are.   1400  
With towels of Alsame,  
Whytte als þe see-fame,  
And sanappis of þe same,  
 Serued þay ware.   1404  
With a gylte salere,  
Basyn and owere,  
Þat ware of þe ryuere  
 Þat was righte þare.   1408

---

L 1378. dore: *the MS. has been torn, and the surface of the paper rubbed; the upper part of the* e *is indistinct.* 1396. Luick reads *you, but it is unlikely that the plural form would be used in addressing an inferior.*

## [LXXXVII]

|||
|---|---|
| | þe lady of honowre |
| | Metes þe [knyȝt] in þe doure, |
| | Knelyd doun in þe floure, |
| 1380 | And fel hym to feet. |
| | Frek as fuyre in þe flynt, |
| | He in armes had hyr hynt; |
| | And þrytty syþes, ar he stynt, |
| 1384 | He kyst þat swet. |
| | 'Welcome, Syre Aunterous, |
| | Me þenkus þou art mervelous; |
| | Wyst my lord of þis hous |
| 1388 | With grame wolde þe gret.' |
| | Swyþe chayres was i-sete, |
| | And quyschonus of vyolete; |
| | Þus þis semely was i-sete |
| 1392 | With mouþ for to mete. |

*and saw Melidor, who returned his love.*

## [LXXXVIII]

|||
|---|---|
| | 'Damesele, loke þer be |
| | A fuyre in þe chymene, |
| | Fagattus of fyre-tre.' |
| 1396 | Þat fec[c]hyd was ȝare. |
| | Sche sett a bourd of yuoret†, |
| | Trestellus ordeyned þerfor; |
| | Cloþus keuerede þat ouur, |
| 1400 | Swyche seye þei neuer are. |
| | Towellus of Eylyssham, |
| | Whyȝth as þe seeys fame, |
| | Sanappus of þe same, |
| 1404 | Þus seruyd þei ware. |
| | With a gyld saler, |
| | Basyn and ewer, |
| | Watyr of euerrose clere, |
| 1408 | Þey wesche ryȝth þare. |

*They had supper in her bower,*

f.106b

C 1378. þe: *possibly* þo. 1386. k *cancelled after* me. 1395. Fagattus: *MS. possibly* Fagactus. 1396. fecthyd. 1397. yuorere. 1402. see ys.

## [LXXXIX]

Paynedemayne preualy
Scho fett fra þe pantry,
And serued þam semly,
 On hand I þe highte.   1412
Scho fechede of þe kytchyn
Hasteletes in galentyn,
The schuldir of þe wyld swyne,
 And serued þam full ryghte;  1416
And sythen scho broght in haste
Plouerrs powdird in paste,
Þat was of þe maste,
 I do ʒow to wiete;   1420
Fatt cunyngs y-nowe,
Þe fesant and þe curlewe,
Riche wyne scho þam drewe,
 Vernage and crete.   1424

## [XC]

To tell þe metis were to tere
Þat was at þat sopere;
Þare was no dayntese to dere
 Na spyces to spare;   1428
And euer scho drewe þam þe wyne,
Bathe þe roche and þe ryne,
And of þe gude maluesyne
 Filled scho þam þare.   1432
And euer Mildor sett
And harped notys full suete,
And oþerwhile scho ete
 Als hir will ware.   1436
Scho sang songes a-boue,
And oþer mirthis ynewe,
In þe chambyrs of loue
 Þus þay sla kare.   1440

## [LXXXIX]

  Paynemayn priuayly  
  Sche brouȝth fram þe pantry,  
  And serued þat semely  
1412    Same þer þei seet.    *with delicacies of all kinds,*  
  Sche brouȝt fram þe kychene  
  A scheld of a wylde swyne,  
  Hastelettus in galantyne;  
1416    An hand Y ȝow hete;  
  Seþþe sche brouȝt hom in haste  
  Plouerys poudryd in paste;  
  Þer ware metus with þe maste,  
1420    I do ȝow to wytte;  
  Fatt conyngus and newe,  
  Fesauntus and corelewe,  
  Ryche she þam drewe  
1424    Vernage and crete.

## [XC]

  To tell here metus was ter  
  Þat was serued at her soper;  
  Þer was no denteþus to dere  
1428    Ne spyces to spare;  
  And euere sche drow hom þe wyn,   *and rare wines,*  
  Boþe þe roche and þe reyn,  
  And þe good maluesyn  
1432    Felde sche hom ȝare.  
  And euere Myldore sche sete  
  Harpyng notus ful swet,  
  And oþer-whyle sche et  
1436    Whan hur leueste ware.  
  Songe ȝeddyngus aboue,  
  Sw[y]che murþus þey moue,  
  In þe chaumbur of loue  
1440    Þus þei sleye care.

C 1414. swyne: *over* n *a suspension mark, without significance.* 1436. *The second minim of the* n *in* whan, *and the first stroke of the* h *in* hur *are missing owing to a hole in the MS.* 1438. swyche: y *lost, owing to hole in the MS. All later lacunae (e.g.,* 1569–74) *are due to the same cause.*

## [XCI]

Þare was a ryalle roffe
In þat chambir a-boffe;
 It was busked a-bowe
  With besantes full bryghte;  1444
All of rewelle-bane,
Off Egir, and of Vrbane,
 With many worthy stane
  Endentid and dighte;  1448
Þer men myght, who so wolde,
Se archangells of golde,
 Fefty made on þe molde,
  Gleterand full bright;  1452
With þe Pokalypps of John,
Paulis Pistils ylkone,
 The Parabylls of Salomone
  Paynted full righte.  1456

## [XCII]

And þe foure Gospellers
Standand on þe pelers;
 Hend, herkyns and heris,
  Giff it be ȝoure will.  1460
Austyn and Gregorius, ·
Jerome and Ambrosius:
 Thir are þe foure doctours;
  Lystyn þam till.  1464
Thare was paynted in stone
[Þe fele[so]feris ilkane,
 The storye of Absolone],
  Þat l[a]iked full [il]le;  1468
With a norloge on highte,
To rynge þe curse of þe nyght,
 To wakyn Mildore þe bryght
  With belles for to knylle.  1472

L1466-7 *reversed in MS.* 1467. fele feris. 1468. liked; wele.

## [XCI]

  Þer was a ryal rooffe  
  In þe chaumbur of loffe;      f.106ᵛa  
  Hyt was buskyd a-boue      *It was a splendid*  
1444    With besauntus ful bryȝth;  *apartment,*  
  All off ruel-bon,  
  Whyȝth oge[e] and parpon,  
  Mony a dere-wroþe stone  
1448    Endentyd and dyȝth;  
  Þer men myȝth se, ho þat wolde,  
  Arcangelus of rede golde,  
  Fyfty mad of o molde,  
1452    Lowynge ful lyȝth;  
  With þe Pocalyps of Jon,  
  Þe Powlus Pystolus eueuychon,  
  Þe Parabolus of Salamon  
1456    Payntyd ful ryȝth.

## [XCII]

  And þe foure Gospellorus    *adorned with*  
  Syttyng on pyllorus;      *statues,*  
  Hend, herkeneþ and herus,  
1460    Gyf hyt be ȝoure wyll.  
  Austyn and Gregory,  
  Jerome and Ambrose:  
  Þus þe foure doctorus;  
1464    Lysten† þa[m] tylle.  
  Þere was purtred in ston  
  Þe fylesoferus eueuychon,  
  Þe story of Absolon  
1468    Þat l[a]yked ful ylle;  
  With an orrelegge on hyȝth,  
  To rynge þe ours at nyȝth,  
  To waken Myldore þ[e b]ryȝth  
1472    With bellus to knylle.

---

C 1446. og*er*. 1450. Arcange*lu*s: c *inserted above*. 1451. molde: l *inserted above, with caret to mark point of insertion*. 1463. doctorus: ct *smudged*. 1464. lystened þan. 1469. on: *over* n *a suspension mark, without significance*. 1470. rynge: g *smudged*.

## [XCIII]

Corven wyndows of glase,
With joly bandis of brase,
Þe recheste þat euer wasse
    Made with mannes hande;      1476
Ale þe walle was of gete,
[With] gaye gabelettes and grete,
Knyghtes syttand in þaire sete
    Owt of sere landes:      1480
Kyng Charles with croun,
Godfraye de Boloyne,
Sir Arthure de Bretayne,
    With þaire bryght brandes.      1484
Þe floure was paynted ouer-alle
With a clere cristalle,
And ouer-cowchid† with palle,
    On floure þer scho standes.      1488

## [XCIV]

Hir bed was of asure
With a chekir seloure,
With a bright bordure,
    Cumpaste full clene;      1492
Also a story þer was
Of Edoyne and Amadase,
With perry in ilk a plase,
    And papeiayes of grene.      1496
Þe stowt dedis of many a knyght
With gold of Sypirs was dight,
Brad besantes full bryghte,
    And tressours by-twene;      1500
Þar was at ylk a cornere
Þe Erles awen banere;
Was neuer bed rechere
    Of emperours ne qwene.      1504

L 1478. Of. 1487. chowchid. 1504. qwne, *with* e *inserted by means of a caret.*

## [XCIII]

  Square wyndowus of gl[a]s,
  Þe rechest þat euer was;
  Þo moynelus was off bras,     f.106ᵛb
1476     Made with menne handus;
  Alle þe walƚus of geete,
  With gaye gablettus and grete,
  Kynggus syttyng in þer sete
1480     Out of s[e]re londus:
  Grete Charles with þe croune,
  Syre Godfray [d]e Boyloune,
  And Arþur le Bretoune,
1484     With here bryȝt brondus.
  Þe flour was paued oueral
  With a clere crystal,
  And ouer-keueryd with a pal,
1488     A flore where she stondes.

## [XCIV]

  Hur bede was off asȝure     and with rich hang-
  With testur and celure,       ings.
  With a bryȝt bordure,
1492     Compasyd ful clene;
  And all a storye as hyt was
  Of Ydoyne and Amadas,
  Perreye in ylke a plas,
1496     And papageyes of grene.
  Þe scochenus of many knyȝt
  Of gold and cyprus was i-dyȝt,
  Brode besauntus and bryȝt,
1500     And trewelouus by-twene;
  Þer was at hur testere†
  Þe kyngus owun banere;
  Was neuere bede rychere
1504     Of empryce ne qwene.

---

C 1473. glas: a *illegible owing to hole in the MS.* 1480. sure. 1481. croune: *over* un *a suspension mark without significance.* 1482. þe. 1484. brondus: *over* on *a suspension mark, without significance.* 1485. paued: *Luick reads* paned. 1488. Afflore. 1498. gold *written to the left of the text, and inserted by means of a caret after* &. 1501. test*ur*ere.

## [XCV]

Faire coddis of silke,
Chalke†-whyte als þe mylke,
Coddis paynted of þat ilke,
    Tasselde þay ware; 1508
And oþer of sendale
Champed with cristalle;
Thay were wroght in Westwale
    With women of lare. 1512
That was a meruelle thynge
To se þe riddels hynge
With many red golde rynge
    Þat þam vp-bare. 1516
The cordis þat þay on rane
The dere Duke þam wane,
Maydyn Edoyne þam spane
    Of mery-maydyns hare. 1520

## [XCVI]

Righte a-bowte midnyght
Sayd Sir Degreuant þe knyghte:
'When will ȝe, swete wyghte,
    Lystyn me till? 1524
For lufe myn hert will brist;
When þou gase to thi ryste
Lady, wysse me the beste,
    Giff it be thi will.' 1528
The birde answerde ful ȝare:
'Neuen þou it any mare,
Þou sall rewe [it] full sare,
    And lyke it full ill. 1532
Certis, sir, [e]f þou were a kyng,
Þou solde do me no swylke thing
Or þou wede me with a rynge,
    And maryage full-fill. 1536

L 1506. Chalked. 1533. of.

## [XCV]

Fayr schetus of sylk,
Chalk-whyȝth as þe mylk,
Quyltus poyned of þat ylk,
    Touseled þey ware;
Coddys of sendal,
Knoppus of crystal
Þat was mad in West-fal
    With women of lare.
Hyt was a mervelous þing
To se þe rydalus hyng
With mony a rede gold ryng
    Þat home vp-bare.
Þe cordes þat þei on ran
The Duk Betyse hom wan,
Mayd Medyore hom span
    Of mere-maydenus hare.

## [XCVI]

Ryȝt a-bouȝt mydnyȝt
Seyd Syre Degriuaunt þe knyȝt:
'When wolt þou, þe worþely wyȝt,
    Lysten me tyll?
For loue my hert wyl to-brest;
When wylt þou bryng [m]e to rest?
Lady, wysse me þe [best],
    Gyf hyt be þi wyll.'
Þe burde answered [full ȝa]re:
'Neuene þou þat eny mare,
Þou schalt rew hyt ful sare,
    And lyke hyt ful ylle.
Sertes, þo þou were a kyng,
Þou touchest non swych þing
Or þou wed me with a ryng,
    And maryage ful-fylle.

*About midnight, Sir Degrevant asked for the privilege of a husband;*

*but she bade him wait till their marriage*

C 1517. on: *over* n *a suspension mark, without significance.* 1521. *After* a bouȝt, myþd *cancelled.* 1526. me: *owing to a hole in the MS., the* m *lacks the entire first minim, and the lower parts of the second two.*

### [XCVII]

'Wete ȝe weile, with-owttyn lett,  
Þe firste tym þat I ȝow mett,  
Myn hert was hally on ȝow sett,  
    And my luf on ȝow lyghte;     1540  
I thoght neuer to hafe nane,  
Lord ne no lemmane,  
Bot þe sekirly allane,  
    Als I ame trewe wyghte.     1544  
Kyng ne no conquerour,  
Ne no lorde of honour,  
[E]f he ware an Emperour,  
    Þat mast es of myghte.     1548  
For-thi, sir, halde the styll  
Till ȝe gete my fadirs wyll.'  
Þe knyght grauntid þer-till,  
    And þare þay trouthes plyghte.     1552

### [XCVIII]

When þayre trowthes were plyght,  
Þan were þaire hertes lyght;  
Was neuer fawcon of flyght  
    Sa fayn als þay ware.     1556  
Thay lay down on the bedd,  
With riche clothes was it sprede,  
Wete ȝe wele, or þay were wed,  
    Synned þay na mare.     1560  
Þan spake þe bird bryghte  
To Sir Degreuant þe knyghte:  
'Leue sir, come ylke nyghte,  
    And luke how we fare.'     1564  
Than þat bolde bachelere  
And þe Countase so clere  
Loued thus al a ȝere  
    And a quarter, and mare.     1568

L 1547. Of.

## [XCVII]

'Leff þou well withouten lette,
þe ferste tyme Y þe mette,
Myn hert on þe was sette,
1540   And my loue on þe ly 3th;
I þou 3the neuer to haue non,
Lord noþur lemman,
Bot onely þe allon—                     f.107b
1544   Caysere ne kny 3th,
Kyng ne non conquerour,
Ne no lord of honour,
And gyff hyt were þe Emperour,
1548   Most proued of my 3th.
For-þy, syr, hald þe stylle,
Whyle þou get my fadyr wylle.'
Þo kny 3t sentus þer-tylle,
1552   And trouþus þei ply 3th.

## [XCVIII]

And whan here trouþus was ply 3t,
Þan here hertus were ly 3th;
Was neuer faukon† off fly 3t
1556   So fayn as þei ware.
Þai lay doun in þer bede,
In ryche cloþus was spred,
Wytte 3e wel, or þei wer wed,
1560   Þei synnyd nat þare.
Þan spekus þo burd bry 3th
To Syre Degriuaunt þe kny 3th:
'Swet syre, come ylke ny 3th,
1564   And loke how we fare.'
And þe bold bachylere
Toke þe damysele clere,
Þis [han] þei dured þat 3ere,           He repeated his
1568   Þre [qua]rterus, and mare.        visits in secret for
                                         more than a year,

C 1552 *cancelled in the MS., apparently because the scribe, unaware of the device of linked stanzas, thought there was an error in the text (see next line, and Introduction, p. xxxiii).* 1555. faukon: *MS.* faukons (u *inserted above*), *the long* s (*not normally used to end a word*) *being cancelled. Luick reads* faukons.

## [XCIX]

At missomer, on an nyght,
þe mone schane full bright;
Sir Degreuant and his knyghte
  Busked þam to wende;    1572
Þis doghety knyghte and fre
Lyghted down vndir a tree;
A prowd foster gan þam see
  On launde þer þay lende.    1576
He folowed þam þorowe þe wod
Alle þe gatis þat þay ȝode,
And how þay passede þe flode,
  He sawe wele þat tyde.    1580
The waytis blewe one þe walle,
Þe Erlis awen mynstralle
How þay went to þe haulle,
  And þare þay gun habyde.    1584

## [C]

The mynstralle helde his pesse,
To no man he it sayse
(Mynstrals are ay curtayse
  Als þay ere kende to be).    1588
The foster talde on highte
To the Erle of myghte
How þay come armed on nyght;
  Hym-selfe gun it see.    1592
The stewarde es cheualrous,
Sir Aymere þe gracyous,
With þe officers of þe house
  Was crouelle and kene.    1596
A gret enbuschment þay sett
Þare þe foster þam mett;
Þay thoght Sir Degreuant to lett
  Þe gatis so grene.    1600

L 1575. þam: *MS.* þa̅y, *with* m *written over last letter.*

## [XCIX]

At [mi]ssomere, in a ny3th,
þ[e mo]ne schone wondur bry3t;
S[yr De]griuaunt and hys kny3t
  [Bus]ked to wend;
[þe] dou3ty kny3thus so fre
[L]y3th doun by a tre;
A prout foster ga[n] þam se    until he was seen by a forester,
  A laund þer þei lende;    f.107ᵛa
And folewes hom þorw þe wode
Alle þe weyes þat þei 3ode,
And how þei passed þe flode,
  þe kny3thus so hende.
So dud þe weyt on þe wall,
þe Eorlus owne mynstrall
Sey þam wende to þe hall,
  And wyst neuere what hyt mende.

## [C]

þe pypere haldus hys pays,
Tyl no man he hyt says
(Mynstralus shuld be cortays
  And skyl þat þei ben).
þe foster tolde anone-ry3thus    who told the Earl.
To þe Eorle and hys kny3thus
How þei come armede any3thus,
  As he hadde y-sen.
þe styward was chyualrous,
Syre Eymur þe kayous,
With offycyrus of þat hous
  Cruel and kene.
A gret buschement hadde he [sette]    His steward set an ambush.
Per þe foster hom mette,
And þou3th Syre Degriuaunt lette
  þe wayes ful grene.

C 1575. gan: MS. gam, *with a tail (cancelling stroke?) after the last minim.* 1581. on: over n *a suspension mark without significance.* 1586. noma*n.* 1593. st *of* styward, *and* ch *of* chyualrous *smudged.*

## [CI]

Þe stewarde hase his athe sworne:
'Come he by þe hawthorne,
We bryng his hed ham to-morne
 And no noþer mede.'   1604
Mildor wist righte noght
What thir men had thoghte;
Scho wend no-thyng þat was wroghte
 Had wyste of þaire dede.   1608
When Sir Degreuant had hight,
Righte als he was trew knyght,
To speke with Mildor þe brighte,
 He lettis for na drede.   1612
God, als þou ert mekill of myght,
Saue Sir Degreuant þe knyghte,
And lene hym grace in þat fyghte
 Wele for to spede!   1616

## [CII]

SYR Degreuant, þat hend knyght,
Armed hym and his knyght,
And tuk preualy I ȝow highte,
 And couerde þam fra syghte.   1620
Now-þer schelde ne spere,
Na no wapyns of were,
Bot scharpe swerdis [þay bere]
 Of Florence ful bright.   1624
When þay come to þe slake,
Þe balde buschement brake;
Þay satt appon stedis blake,
 Armed full clene.   1628
Sir Degreuant, es noghte to layne,
His swerd hase he owt-drawen;
He þat come forþermast es slayne
 In þat schawe schene.   1632

L 1603. ham: a *superscribed*. 1607. no thynk, *with* g *written over* k. 1617. *A red initial capital.* 1623. of were, *repeated from previous line.*

## [CI]

Þe stywarde heyle haþ swornne:
'And he come be þi[s þor]nne,
We bryng hys he[d on] þe mornne
  And non oþur mede.'
Dame Myldor wy[st n]ouȝth
What al þis folkys [hade þ]ouȝth;
She wende no man þat ha[d ben]e wrouȝth
  Hadde wyten of hor de[de].
And Syre Degriuaunt hadde y-[hiȝ]th,
Ryȝth as he was trew k[n]yȝth,
To speke with Myldore þat nyȝth,    f.107ᵛb
  And lette for no drede.
God, as ȝe ar muchel of myȝt,
Saue Syre Degriuaunt þe knyȝt,
And lene hym grace in þat fyȝt
  Wel for to spede!

## [CII]

Syre Degriuaunt at euene-lyȝth
Armede hym [and] hys knyȝth,
And toke on priuayly for syȝth
  Two gownes off grene.    *Sir Degrevant and the squire were only lightly armed;*
Noþur schelde ne spere,
Ne no wepen of werre,
Bot twey swerdus þei berre
  Off Florence ful kene.
Whan þei come to þe slac,
Þe bolde buschement brac,    *they were taken by surprise,*
[Sto]ute opon stedus bac,
  [Ar]mede ful clene.
[Sy]re Degriuaunt, ys nat to layn,
[B]lyue hys swerde had y-drayn;
He þat come formast was slayn
  In þe schaw schene.

C 1606. þis: is *superscribed.* 1607. noman. 1618. *After* hys, ky *cancelled; only part of* & *visible owing to hole in MS.*

## [CIII]

When þay Sir Degreuant mett,
Seuen speris on hym sett;
On his bacenett þay bett,
    Þay bryssed it in twa.    1636
Sonne bare þay thorgh þe gown,
And braste his bright habirgeon;
His bachelere was borne down,
    His swerd lay hym fra.    1640
Than Sir Degreuant down lyght
For to rescu his knyght,
And cryed to hym on hyghte,
    'Why lies þou swa?'    1644
The best man þat þay hade
By þe schuldirs þay hym s[ch]rade;
He was neuer sa harde stade
    In wele ne in wa.    1648

## [CIV]

The stewarde Sir Aymere
Come a lyttill to nere;
Þe heuede by þe colere
    He cuttid a-waye.    1652
Þe body satt on þe horse
(Þat was an vnsemly corse);
Þe stede strak ouer þe force,
    And strayed on straye.    1656
So Sir Degreuant faride,
He mad þam in hert sterid;
With his twa-hand swerde
    He made swylk pay,    1660
Þat fourty lay in þe felde,
Bathe with spere and with schelde,
Þat na wapyns myght welde,
    Ne noghte wynn a-waye.    1664

L 1646. strade.

## [CIII]

Whan þei Syr Degriuaunt mett,
Seuene sperus on hym y-sett;
Euene in hys bassonett
    Brasten a two,
Some bare hym þorw þe gown,
Some brast on hys haberiown;
Hys sqwyer was born down,
    Hys swerd cast hym fro.
Þen Syre Degriuaunt lyȝth
And rescowede hys knyȝth,
And cryed to hym an hyȝth,
    'Why wolt þou lyen so?'
Þe beste stedes þat þei hade
By þe scholders he þem sch[ra]de;
He was neuer so hard y-stade
    For wele ne for wo.

*and the squire was almost overcome,*

*but his master rescued him.*

*f.108a*

## [CIV]

Þe styward Syre Eymere
Com a lytyl to nere;
Hys hede by þe coler
    He kerues a-way.
Þe body syttys opon þe hors
(Hyt was vncomely to þe cors);
Þe stede stert ouer a fosse,
    And strykys a-stray.
Y wyst neuer how hyt ferde —
He betus hom fast to þe erþe,
With hys two-honde swerde
    He made swych paye,
Þat syxty lay on þe feld,
Boþe with sper and with sche[ld],
Þat neuer wepen myȝth [weld]
    Sen þat ylke day.

*The steward was killed, and many of the Earl's men with him.*

C 1633. Whan: *a smudge has spread over both* a *and suspension.* 1634, 1638, 1639, 1661. on: down: *over* n *a suspension mark, without significance.* 1644. wolt: lt *smudged.* 1646. scharde.

## [CV]

Þe pantelere, and þe botelere,
And þe Erles awen sqwyere —
Þay lay slayne alle in fere
    In þat schawe schene.    1668
Than þe remenant flees
For þe fyght þat þay sees,
And sum lurkede vndir trees,
    And couers þam full clene.    1672
Thankid be God of His grace
Of þat cheualrouse case!
He hase vencust his fase,
    Þe crouele and kene.    1676
Noght fourty fote fra þe walle
He slew þe vschere of þe halle,
And of þe sqwyers with-alle
    Ma þan feftene.    1680

## [CVI]

By þat it drewe nere daye
He had endid þis playe;
Sum passede a-waye,
    Bot many ware slayne;    1684
Þan spak Sir Degreuant to his knyght:
'Here my trouthe I þe plight,
I speke with Mildore þe bryght,
    To dy in þe payne.'    1688
Thay sett þaire stedis þer þay stod,
And fayrly passed þe flode,
To þe chambir þay ʒode
    Þaire gatis so gayne.    1692
Than þe lady bryght
Faire scho welcomd þe knyght;
Scho wist noght of þe fighte,
    Þer-of were þay fayne.    1696

## [CV]

Þe panter, þe boteler,
Þe Eorlus cheff sqwyer —
Þer lyes slay y-fer
    In þe schawe schene.
Þan þe remenaunt fles
On þe sort þat þei sees,
And some lorkus vndur tres     *The rest fled.*
    In slowes vnshene.
Þonkede be Godes grace,
He has venkest hys face,
And made a chyualrous chace,
    Þat crewel and kene.
Nouȝth fourty fot fram þe wal
He slowe þe marchal of þe hal,
And oþer gode sqwyers withal
    Mo þen fyftene.

## [CVI]

By þat hyt dawed ney day     f.108b
By þat he hade endyd þis play,
Some scaped a-way,
    And many on was slayne;
Þan sayd Syre Degriuaunt þe knyȝt:     *Sir Degrevant and the squire made their way to Melidor,*
'Here my troupe Y þe plyȝt,
I shal speke with Myldore to-nyȝt,
    To dey in þe payn.'
Þei set here stedus þer þei stode,
And fayr passede þe flode,
To þe Eorlus castel þe ȝode
    Þe gatus ful gayn.
Þan þe lady so bryȝth
Fayr sche welcomed þe knyȝth;
She had nat hard hore fyȝth,
    Þerof wer þei fayn.

C 1672. *After* In, *a long* s *cancelled.* 1673. godes: *the first three letters smudged.*
1692. gates: at *smudged.* 1695. hard: d *smudged.*

## [CVII]

Bot scho meruelle[de] of itt,
Why þaire clothis were so slytt,
As þay˙in hurtelyng had ben hitt
  With dynttis of swerdis;  1700
Þaire gaye gownnes of grene
Schamesly were þay ryuen:
'Leue sir, whare hafe ȝe bene,
  Ȝoure clathes þus to tere†?'  1704
The knyght sayd gayly,
And sayde to þat semly:
'We sawe no celly
  Þat solde vs oght dere;  1708
Bot als we come by þe thorne
Thus oure clothis were torne;
We sall hafe newe to-morne —
  We cownt þam noght at a pere.'  1712

## [CVIII]

f.137ᵛa

Þe knyghte† had foghten als a bare
And þerfore hym thristid sare;
Þe mayden broghte hym full ȝare
  Þe spyce and þe wyne;  1716
Dyuerse spyces þay ete,
Ofte with mouthes þay mete;
Scho broghte þam vernage and crete
  And wyne of þe Ryne.  1720
He tuke his leue at þe daye
At Mildor þe faire maye;
Ȝit scho herd not of þe playe
  Þat scho hard sythen.  1724
Þe knyght went on his waye
Whare þe ded men laye,
And says oft, in his playe,
  'Thir were stoute hyne.'  1728

L 1697. meruelle. 1702. ryuen: y *written over first* e. 1704 *written in body of text, not in margin.* teres. 1713. knyghte: knyghten; had foghten *inserted by means of a caret.*

## [CVII]

|     |     |     |
| --- | --- | --- |
|      | She had wondur in hyr wyt | who wondered at their untidy appearance, |
|      | Why here clopus war to-slyt, | |
|      | As þei in holtus had byn hyt | |
| 1700 | With dyntus of spere; | |
|      | [H]ere gay gownus of grene | |
|      | [W]ere ful schamely be-sene: | |
|      | '[Le]ue syre, where haue ȝe bene | |
| 1704 | [ȝ]oure c]lopus to tere?' | |
|      | Þe knyȝth sat semely | but was put off with an excuse. |
|      | And seide tyl hyr priuely: | |
|      | 'We sey n[euer selly] | |
| 1708 | Þat sh[old vs] auȝth dere. | |
|      | But as [we passed] by a þorn | |
|      | Þus [wer ou]r gownus to-torn; | |
|      | We sh[alle] haue new to-morn — | |
| 1712 | We [cownt]e hyt not a payr.' | |

## [CVIII]

|     |     |     |
| --- | --- | --- |
|      | Þe [knyȝ]th had fouȝten as a bar | |
|      | S[o þat] hym fersted ful sare; | |
|      | [Þe m]ayde brouȝth hym ful ȝar | They had supper. and Sir Degrevant went home. |
| 1716 | [Þe s]pyces and þe wyn; | f. 108ᵛa |
|      | Dyuerse spices þei ete | |
|      | And ofte with mowthus þei mete; | |
|      | Sche brouȝthe hem vernage and crete | |
| 1720 | And wyne of þe Reyn. | |
|      | He toke his leue at þe day | |
|      | At Mayde Myldore þe may; | |
|      | Ȝet wyste ho note of þe fray | |
| 1724 | Þat she harde seyȝne. | |
|      | Þe knyȝth wendys on his way | |
|      | Þer þe dede men lay, | |
|      | And seyde soufft, on his play, | |
| 1728 | 'Ȝondur was stout hyne.' | |

C 1700. dyntus: nt *smudged*. 1701. gay: a *smudged*. 1709. *There is room for six letters and two spaces between the* s *of* as *and the* b *of* by. *Hence Luick's reconstruction* (we come) *is improbable*. 1724. harde: r *inserted above*. 1725. wendys *inserted above*; *the caret indicating point of insertion wrongly put between* on *and* his.

## [CIX]

Þe steward Sir Gaymere,
And mony gud sqwyere
Þay broght hame on bere
    Fra frythis vn-fayne.    1732
Þay blewe owt ouer-alle,
Bathe þe grete and þe smalle;
Þe mayden rynnes to þe haulle
    Tyȝandis to frayn.    1736
The Erle said to þat fre:
'I witt Sir Degreuant and the
Þe slagheter of my menȝe;
    Þis es a false trayne.    1740
By Hym þat dyed on þe tre,
This daye sall þou ded be;
Now wate I wele it es he
    Þat hase the for-layne.'    1744

## [CX]

The mayden ansuerd agayne:
'Be my faythe, I am fayne
Þat þe knyght es not slayne;
    What bote es to ly?    1748
Sen he hase chosen me to make,
I sall hym neuer for-sake,
Whatkyns dede þat I take,
    What dole þat I drye.'    1752
Þan þe Erle wexe wode,
And swore by bane and by blode:
'Þar sall na mete do me gud
    Or I se þe dy!'    1756
Þe Cowntas knelid down onane:
'Sir, we hafe no childe bot ane,
For þe lufe of Sayne Jame
    Off hir haff mercy.'    1760

## [CIX]

Þei brou3the hom on bere     News of the ambush
Þe stywarde Syr Eymer,     reached the Earl,
And oÞer gode sqwyer
1732        Off fryÞÞus vn-fayn;
And cryide out ouerall,
Both gret and small;
Þe mayde wyndus to Þe hall
1736        Tythyngus to frayn.
Þe 3orle spekus to Þat fre:
'Y wytt Syr Degriuuant and Þe     who blamed
Þe slau3thtur of my mene;     Melidor for the
                                             disaster, and threat-
1740        Þis is 3owr false treyn.     ened to kill her.
By Hym Þat dyede on tre,
Þis day shall Þou de[de] be;
I wat well, hit [is he]
1744        Þat hase Þe be[layn].'

## [CX]

Þe mayde answer[de a3ayn]
And seis, 'Petur! I [am f]ayn
And Þat kny3th be n[ot sla]yn;
1748        What bote is Þat I l[ye]?
Sene he was chosen my f[yrst m]ake,
Shall I hym neuer for-sake,     'I shall always be
What deÞe Þat I take,     loyal to him.'
                             f.108ᵛb
1752        Or dool Þat I drye.'
Þan Þe 3orle wax wode,
And swor be bonus and blode:
'Mete ne drynk shall do me gode
1756        Ar I se Þe dye!'
Þe Contasse knelyd Þ[o] anon:     The Countes
'Gode schylde, syr, Þat he be slon,     pleaded for her,
We hade neuer chyl but hyr on,'
1760        And cryid ful hye.

C 1741. *After* dyede, *two letters* (of?) *cancelled.* 1742. *Before* be *two letters* (bj?) *cancelled.* 1748. is *inserted above; the last visible letter of the line is possibly* b. 1756. Ar *originally* An: r *cancelled, and* n *written above the line.* 1757. *Most of the line smudged;* Þo: *MS.* Þe.

## [CXI]

Þe Countas said: 'Allas!
ȝe hafe bene lang faas;
Wikkid tunges it mase,
 God gyff þam scham!   1764
I dare hardyly saye
Þat he went hym to playe;
Þay withsett hym þe waye,
 He was noghte to blame.   1768
When he werid in Spayne
ȝe made his landis barrayne,
His woddes and his warrayne,
 His wylde and his tame;   1772
I rede ȝe be frende with þe knyght
Þat es sa bolde and sa wyghte,
And grant hym þat bird bryghte
 By hir righte name.'   1776

## [CXII]

Than spake þat byrde so bryght:
'Þare was bot he and his knyght,
I spake with þam this nyghte,
 Why sold I spare?   1780
He es my lufe and my lorde,
My joye and my comforde;
It ware gud ȝe ware accorde,
 If ȝowre will ware.   1784
And ȝe halde it so grete,
I sall neuer ete mete.'
Þe Erle for angre gun swete,
 And syghede full sare.   1788
'Now, dameselle, are þou be spilt,
I for-gyffe þe thi gylte;
It sall be ryghte als þou wilt,
 I may do no mare.'   1792

## [CXI]

The Contasse cryed: 'Alas!
ȝe haue ben to longe foas;
Wycked tonge hit mas,
  God ȝif þem shame!
I dar sauely say
þe knyȝth went on his way;
[O]wre men by-sett hym þe way;
  [He] was not to blame.
[W]as not his fosteres slayn
While he werred in Spayn?
Hys woddys and hys waryn
  ȝe made hem all tame.
Y rede ȝe sauȝthle with þe knyȝth
Þat is so hardy and wyȝth,
And graunte hym Myldore þe bryȝt
  By hyr ryȝth name.'

*and urged reconciliation with Sir Degrevant.*

## [CXII]

Þan spekus Myldore þe bryȝth:
'Þer was but he and a knyȝth,
I spake with hym þis nyȝth,
  Why shulde I spare?
He is my loue and my lorde,
Myn hele and my counforde;
Hyt is gode ȝe be a-corde,
  And ȝowre wyllus ware.
And giff ȝe holde vs a gret,
Shall I neuer ete mete.'
Þe ȝorl for angur gan swet,
  And syȝthe ful sar.
'Damesele, ar þou be spylte,
I for-giff þe þe gylte;
Hit is all as þou wylte,
  I can say na mar.'

*f.109a*

*The Earl agreed,*

C 1792. namar.

## [CXIII]

A riche lettre scho hym sent,
Eftyr hir lordis commandment,
And talde hym alle hir atent
 With tyȝandes full newe;  1796
And prayed hym [come] preualy
With his beste cheualrye;
Trow it righte trewely,
 And trow it for trewe.  1800
And scho suld make swylke **accorde**
By-twyx hym and hir lorde
Þat it solde be comforde
 To all þat þam knewe.  1804
Ȝitt Sir Degreuant h[ym] drede:
Sexty knyghtis he clede,
And to þe castelle þay spede
 When þe daye dewe.  1808

## [CXIV]

Þe steryn knyght and þe stout,
Þe Erle met hym þer-owt;
Wondir lawe gun he lowte,
 And haylsede þat hende:  1812
'Welcome, sir, to this place!
I swere þe, by Goddis grace,
We hafe bene lange fase,
 Now will we be frende.'  1816
Or any man þat wist,
Alle wranges ware redrischt:
Þe Erle and þe knyght kyssed,
 And to the castelle þay wende.  1820
With-owttyn mare rehersyng,
Twyse þay made þaire saghtelyng;
He grauntis hym Mildor þe ȝynge
 To hys lyues ende.  1824

L 1797. full. 1805. hir.

## [CXIII]

  Bylyue a lettur ho sent      *Sir Degrevant was sent for,*
  Þorw þe ȝorlus comandment;
  A messenger has hyt hent
1796     With typingus ful newe.
  She bad hym cum priuely
  With hys best chyualry,
  As he was gode and douȝty
1800     And holden for trewe.
  And hoe shuld make swych a-cord
  Bytwene hym and hur lorde
  Þat shulde be a counforde
1804     Tyll all þat hym euer knewe.
  Ȝet Syr Degriuuant hym drade:
  Syxty knyȝthus he clade;
  Tyl þe ȝorlus castel he spede
1808     By þe day dewe.

## [CXIV]

  Þe ȝorle metus hym with-oute    *and peace was made outside the castle.*
  With sterne knyȝthus and stoute;
  Wonder low gan he loute,
1812     And haylus þat hende,
  And says, 'Syr, by Goddys grace,
  Welcome to þis place,
  We haue ben to longe fase,
1816     Now wyl I be þi frende.'
  Priuely, þat no man wyste,
  All wrongus was redressyde:
  Þe ȝorle and he hade keste,
1820     And to chaumbur þei wende.
  With-outyn mor rehersyng      f.109b
  Made was þe sauȝthlyng,
  And grauntyd hym Myldor þe ȝing
1824     Till hys lyues ende.

C 1817. noma*n*.

## [CXV]

Was neuer slyke† a purueance
Made in Yngland ne in France
Als was for Sir Degreuance
    And Mildore þe schene.     1828
Þare come to þat offerynge
Bathe Emperour and Kynge,
Ersbechops with many a ryng
    Filly fyftene.     1832
The Mayster of þe Hospitalle
Come with a cardenalle,
Þe riche Kynge of Portyngale
    With knyghtis full kene;     1836
Alle þe lordis of þat lande
Þay were at þat offerand,
Sothely to vndirstande,
    Bathe Emperour and Qwene.     1840

## [CXVI]

Sone appon þe third daye,
In romance als I herd saye,
He tuk hir in Goddis laye
    Till his lyues ende.     1844
Solemply a cardenalle,
With a rynge pontyfycalle,
He dyd a messe ryalle
    And weddid þat hende.     1848
Of Almayne þe Emperour,
With wyrchip and honour
He gaff hir at þe kyrk-dure
    Als for his awen frende.     1852
Þay sew golde in þat stownd:
Mare þan thre hundreth pounde
Laye gleterand þer on þe grounde
    In wayes whare þay wende.     1856

L 1825. slylke. 1831. a *inserted*.

## [CXV]

  Was neuer sych a puruyaunce  
  In Englond ne in Fraunce  
  As was at Sir Degriuua[n]ce  
1828    And Myldor þe schene.  
  Þer com tyl hir weddyng  
  An emperour and a kyng,  
  Erchebyschopþ₃ with ryng  
1832    Mo þen fyftene.  
  Þe Mayster of Hospitall  
  Come ouer with a cardinall,  
  Þe gret Kyng of Portyngall  
1836    With kny₃thus ful kene;  
  All þe lordys of þat lond  
  War holy at þat offorand,  
  And ladyes, Y vndyrstond,  
1840    Emperyce and qwene.

*Sir Degrevant and Melidor were married*

## [CXVI]

  On þe Trinite day,  
  Þus in romance herd Y say,  
  He toke hyr in Godus lay  
1844    Tyll hys lyuys ende.  
  Solempnely a cardinal,     *by a cardinal.*  
  Reuestyd with a pontifical,  
  Sang þe masse ryal  
1848    And wedded þat hend.  
  And þe ryche Emperour  
  Gaff [hur] at þe kyrke-dor  
  With [worshi]p and honour,  
1852    As f[or hy]s owne frend,  
  And [se]w gold in þat stonde:  
  W[elle] a thowsand pounde  
  Lay glyteryng in þe gronde  
1856    By þe way as þei wende.

C 1846. Reuestyd: *Luick reads* c *for* t; *this is unlikely.* 1856. *Below, as the last line of the page, is found:*
   þen þei semeled þe sale  
þe *having been altered from* ye. *The whole line cancelled.*

## [CXVII]

Sone þay sembled in sale,
Bathe kynges and cardenale,
þe Emperour so ryalle
    With barouns full bolde.     1860
Gaye ladyse by-dene,
Bathe countase and qwene,
Bright byrdis and schene,
    And frely to folde.     1864
þe wyne in condyths rane
Fra þe mawngery by-gan
þat was fre to ilk a man
    To tak wha sa walde.     1868
þare come in a daunce
Alle þe Dugepers of France;
Me thynk swylke a purueance
    Was gay to be-halde.     1872


## [CXVIII]

ȝitt knew I neuer nan so wysse
To telle þe metis of pryce;
Ne couthe of þat seruyce
    Was serued in þat sale.     1876
Alle þe mynstrals in þe haulle
He gaffe þam robis of palle,
And oþer gyftis with-alle —
    Germentes alle halle.     1880
Ilk a daye þat fourtnyghte
þe lorde come with a knyghte,
Reuelle wha sa best myght
    Aboute in þat haulle.     1884
Appon þe fyftened day,
In romance als I herd saye,
þay tuk þaire leue and went a-waye,
    With wirchip tuk alle.     1888

L 1871. Methynk. 1881. foutnyghte, r *inserted*.

## [CXVII]

|      | |      |
|---|---|---|
|      | Þan þe semelede þe sale, | f.109ᵛa |
|      | Kyng and cardynale, | The wedding festivities |
|      | And þe Emperour ryale | |
| 1860 | With barnus ful bolde. | |
|      | So dud ladies by-dene, | |
|      | Both contasse and qwene, | |
|      | Bryȝth burdys and schene | |
| 1864 | Was joye to be-holde. | |
|      | Fro þe mangery by-gan | |
|      | Wyn in condyt ran, | |
|      | Redy tyll ylke man, | |
| 1868 | Take ho so wolde. | |
|      | Þer com in a daunse | |
|      | IX Doseperus of Fraunce; | |
|      | Me thowȝth syche a countynaunce | |
| 1872 | Was joye to be-holde. | |

## [CXVIII]

|      | |      |
|---|---|---|
|      | I knewe neuere man so wys | |
|      | Þat couþ tell þe seruise; | |
|      | Ne scrye þe metys of prys | |
| 1876 | Was seruyd in þat sale. | |
|      | Mynstrallus hade in halle | |
|      | Grete gyftys with-alle — | |
|      | Ryche robus of palle | |
| 1880 | With garnementus hale. | |
|      | Ylke day þat fourtynyȝth | lasted a fortnight. |
|      | Justyng of seryd knyȝthus, | |
|      | To reuele he best myȝth | |
| 1884 | With wyn and with ale. | |
|      | And on þe fyfte[n]þe day, | |
|      | Þus in romaunce h[erd Y] say, | |
|      | Þey toke her leue and [went] her way, | |
| 1888 | Thys worþely to w[ale]. | |

C 1857. þan: *over an* a *suspension mark, without significance.* 1874. seruise: *second* s *smudged.* 1885. fyfteþe. 1888. Thys: h *smudged.*

## [CXIX]

Alle þay mad þaire auant  
Of þe lord Sir Degreuant,  
Curtase man and auenant,  
    Bathe† lady and knyghte.       1892  
He gaffe sum stede in þat stownd  
Better þan thre hundreth punde,  
With-owttyn hawkis and grewhund,  
    And fawcon of flyght.           1896  
Þe Erle dyed þat same ȝere,  
And þe Countas so clere;  
Bathe þaire beryels in fere  
    Was gayly dyghte.             1900  
Þan was Sir Degreuant ayere  
Of all þat lande so fayre;  
Might na perys enpayre  
    Be skill ne by righte.          1904  

## [CXX]

Þan þay lyffed in fere  
Mare þan sex and thritty ȝere:  
Ten childir scho hym bere  
    Worthily in wede.            1908  
Sythyn scho dyede, I vndirstand;  
He made his ayere with his hand  
And went to þe Holy Land:  
    Heuen be his mede!          1912  
Sertanly he was slayne  
With þe justyng of a sowdane;  
Now to God es he gane,  
    Þat doghty in dede.           1916  
Jhesu, Lorde in Trinite,  
Graunt vs all in Heuen to be  
Thy worthy face for to see,  
    And gyff vs wele to spede. Amen.   1920  

    Amen. Explicit Sir Degreuant.

L 1892. bathe day lady.

## [CXIX]

Al þei makeþ þer avaun[t]
Off þe lord Syr Degriuua[nt],
Cortays and auenaunt,
    Ladyes and kny ʒthus.      f.109ᵛb
He gaff stedus þat stound
Worþ a þousand pound,
Withouten haukus and hound,
    And faukun of fly ʒthus.
Þe Ʒorle dyede þat same ʒer,
And þe Contasse cler;
Boþe hor beryelus y-fer
    Was gayly by-dy ʒth.
Syr Degriuaunt by-lefte þer eyr
With brod londus and fair;
Was neuer peres† my ʒth hym peyr
    By reson ne ry ʒth.

1892
1896
1900
1904

## [CXX]

Þrytty wyntur and mare
Þei lyuede to-gydur with-out care:       *They lived together more than thirty years;*
And seuen chyldur she hym bare
    Þat worþly in wede.
And sene sche dyed, Y vndurstond;        *then she died, and he went to the Holy Land,*
He seysed hys eyr with hys hond
And went in-to þe Holy Lond:
    Heuen be hys mede!
At Port Gaff was he slon,                *to be slain in the Crusades.*
For-iustyd with a soudon;
Þus to Gode is he gon,
    Þus douʒty in dede.                  *May Heaven reward him!*
Lord Gode in Trinite,
Gyff hem Heuen for to see
Þat loues gamen and gle,
    And gestus to fede.

1908
1912
1916
1920

C 1903. perues? 1920. *Below the line is written in the same hand*
    here e (*cancelled*),
    Elisabet Koton *enclosed in roughly drawn rectangle.*
    Elisabet frauncys
*and to the right of these, in a later hand*
    e
    Rokeldo (?)
    u

# NOTES

A line-number preceded by L. or C means that the following note refers only or principally to the version of the text preserved in that MS. Notes referring to L precede those referring to C. If no letter precedes, the note refers equally to both versions. Such notes precede L- or C-notes.

The meanings of the abbreviations employed are usually self-evident. The exceptions are —
1. C. Brown (13): *English Lyrics of the XIIIth Century*, ed. Carleton Brown, Oxford 1932. Quoted by page and line.
2. C. Brown (14): *Religious Lyrics of the XIVth Century*, ed. Carleton Brown, Oxford 1924. Quoted by page and line.
3. *Gawain: Sir Gawain and the Green Knight*, ed. Tolkien and Gordon, Oxford 1925.
4. *Ipomydon, Ipomedon* B: couplet version (ed. Kölbing as above, pp. 255–319; or Weber, *English Metrical Romances*, Edinburgh 1810, Vol. 2).
5. *Octouian:* ed. Weber as above Vol. 3.
6. *Octavian:* tail rime version, ed. Halliwell, Percy Society, Vol. XIV.

Title. **Degreuante.** Halliwell (*Thornton Romances* pp. 288–9) suggested that the hero is to be identified with 'Agravayn a la dure mayn', (Chrétien's *Perceval* 9510; *Gawain* 110), the son of King Lot of Lothian, and of Belisent, the half-sister of Arthur. This name was given the form of *d'Egrivauns, d'Egrivaunt*, and the English romancer, or scribes, misunderstanding the significance of the *d*, joined it to the name. This would be almost inevitable in a memorially transmitted text.

The first suggestion is supported by the following facts —
(i) In our poem (C 26) the hero is spoken of as the nephew of Arthur and Guinevere.
(ii) The distinctively, not to say exclusively, Scottish coat of arms given him in 1045–55 is appropriate to the King of Lothian's son.
(iii) There is no recorded knight of the Round Table whose name even approaches the form *Degrevant*.

In the poem, the hero's name is not spelt consistently.
(i) In C 1085, C 1185, it appears in the form *Egrivaunt*.
(ii) In 1093, 1161, 1181, etc. the forms *Degriuans, Degriuaunce*, etc. are found certified by rime. (For complete list of forms, see Index of Proper Names.)

Another example of misapprehended *d* is found in the name *Degare, Diggory* for *d'Egaré*, the lost one.

1. **Jhesu, lorde**, etc. The conventional opening of tail-rime poems, often echoed at the close. Cf. 1917–20 and *Erle of Toulous* 1–6, 1222–4; *Emaré* 1–6, 1033–5; *Eglamour* 1–6, 1340–1; *Amis and Amiloun* 1–2; *Avowing of Arthur* 1–8, 1145–8; *Sir Gowther* 1–6, 25–7, 754–6; *King Edward and the Shepherd* 1–3; *Isumbras* 1–3, 793–4. The minstrel-narrator of *Emaré* thinks that the worthy custom should always be observed —

> Menstralles þat walken fer and wyde
> Her and þer in euery a syde,
> In mony a dyuerse londe,
> Sholde, at her bygynnyng,
> Speke of þat ryghtwes Kyng
> That made bothe see and sonde
> (*Emaré* 13–18).

5–8. Cf. *Sege off Melayne* 1–3 —
> All werthy men that luffes to here
> Off cheuallry þat by fore vs were
> Þat doughty weren of dede.

*Sir Isumbras* 4–6 —
> Now, hende in haule, and ȝe wolde here
> Of eldirs that by-fore us were
> That lyffed in arethede.

*Morte Arthure* 12–15; *Sir Cleges* 1–2; *Cursor Mundi* 2225; *Horn Childe* 4–6.

8. **arethede:** an uncommon word which the OED. records only here and *Isumbras* 6. For another example, see *Pearl* 711.

Two etymologies are possible:—
(i) OE. *ǣrþēod, with change of ǣr to ar due to Scandinavian influence.
(ii) OE. * ærgeþēod (cf. ingeþēode) > ęrʒe- or arʒe-.

L 10. **Sir Degrevant, for sothe, he highte.** Cf. *Sir Beues* (MS. Chetham) 7; *Guy of Warwick* (MS. B) 49–50, 631, 11837–8; *Launfal* 27; *Rowlande and Ottuell* 151–2.

C 13. MS. **kynġh**: *knyght* is obviously meant. Scribe A's forms of this word are peculiar and inconsistent: **knytht** 129, **kynyght** 179, **kynġhus** 314, **knyġh** 343, **knyġt** 405. As they may represent an attempt to reproduce an altered pron. of *ʒt* (noted by Sir William Craigie, *Bellenden's Translation of Livy* II, 334, STS. 1903), they have not been emended.

14–15. Cf. *Horn Childe* 292–3 —
þer was no kniʒt in jnglond
þat miʒt a dint stond of his hond;
also *ib.* 406–7, 781–2; *Sir Gowther* 151–2; *Guy of Warwick* (MS. B) 7583–4; *Perceval* 1186–7; *Octavian* 1063–4.

L 18. **Gaynore.** The form of the name as in *Avowing of Arthur* 455.

21. Cf. *Triamour* (MS. A) 136, where this line occurs at the beginning of a similar, though briefer, enumeration of the countries where the hero's valiant deeds had been done. In *Sir Beues* (MS. Chetham) 20–28 the knight is introduced by lauding his prowess in foreign lands —
> He was kyd a doughty knyght
> In yche lond, that he rideth and goos,
> For to wynne price and loos,
> In Fraunce, in Flaunders and in Allmayn
> In Braban, in Cesile and in Bretayn
> In Denmarke, in Walis and in Gascon,
> In Hungry, in Calabre and in Burgayn,
> In Englond, in Norway and in Pecardye,
> In Scotland, in Walis and in Lumbardye.

At the end of the *Wars of Alexander* there is a similar list of all countries conquered by Alexander the Great (5656 ff.).

26. Confusion in both versions is suspected; **nevew** (C) seems to be an original reading, but þer as it stands in the following line is meaningless. The poet may have written —
> He was þer nevew full nere,
> And was doghety and dere
> Whare (*or* þer) he of dedis myghte here, etc.

C 26. **ther:** i.e., Arthur's and Guinevere's, as he was the son of Arthur's half-sister. He is thus full brother to Gawain. In *Gawain* 111 the hero and Agravain are described as being —
> Boþe þe kynges sistersunes and ful siker kniʒtes.

31–2. These lines, and especially the meaning of **mappemonde,** have puzzled earlier commentators. Miss Rickert suggests that some kind of chart or list of Arthur's knights is being referred to, as though the word had come to mean not so much 'map' as 'the material on which a map might be painted'. Her case is difficult to maintain in the absence of parallel examples of such a usage.

E. Smirke, in the course of an interesting article *On the Hall and Round Table at Winchester* (Proceedings . . . of the Archæological Institute of Great Britain and Ireland for 1845, published London 1846), points out that —

> 1. The Winchester Round Table, the existence of which is attested by John Hardyng (1812 ed., p. 146) has such a chart painted upon it.
>
> 2. King Henry III ordered a *mappa mundi* to be painted in the same hall (see *Calendar of Liberate Rolls* 1226–40, p. 405).

Smirke refrains from identifying the *mappa mundi* and the Table on the ground that the *mappa mundi* (in the literal sense of the term) was a fairly well-known domestic ornament. This is a tempting suggestion, but even if the *mappa* and the Table were identical, is open to the objection that neither of them could properly be called a **storye.**

The lines take on more coherent meaning if **mappemonde** is interpreted less strictly than hitherto. In contemporary or nearly contemporary English poetry it means not so

much 'map of the world' as 'the world' itself in the vaguer sense implied in the phrases 'man upon *molde*' or 'What on *earth* are you doing?' In the following example —
        Goiss Halkis war governouris of the gret oist,
        Chosin chiftanis, chevalrus in charge of weris
        Marchonis in the mapamond
           (Holland, *Buke of the Howlat*, 326–8)
it may well be questioned whether the word does much more than fill up the line, and this may be its function in *Sir Degrevant*. One will then translate:—'Therefore they nominated him to be a Knight of the Round Table, as is written in story in this world'.

A possible alternative is to take **storye** to mean 'representation of a story in pictures' (see OED. *s. vv.* Story *sb.*¹ 8; Storied 1), and translate 'as is represented in the "mappemonde" by means of pictures'.

33–64, 81–96. For a parallel, but more elaborate account of mediæval diversions, see *Squyr of Lowe Degre* 739–852, and the shorter lists in *Horn Childe* 40–48, *Parlement of the Thre Ages* 199 ff.

35–40. The author has endowed his hero with skill in the instruments of the minstrel's craft. See J. J. Jusserand, *English Wayfaring Life in the Middle Ages*, London 1920, p. 207 ff.; A. Schultz, *Das höfische Leben zur Zeit der Minnesinger*, Leipzig 1879, I 429 ff.

36. The gittern is illustrated in F. W. Galpin, *Old English Instruments of Music*, London 1910, p. 82, fig. 15, and plate facing p. 22.

37. In the OED. the **rot(t)e** is defined as 'a mediæval musical instrument, probably of the violin class'. Fuller and more accurate information is available in F. W. Galpin, *op. cit.*, pp. 4–6; and in Gustav Reese, *Music in the Middle Ages*, London 1941, pp. 124, 384 ff. Both these later authorities agree that the *rote* was a lyre-shaped instrument, usually played like a harp, but occasionally bowed. The number of strings varied from four to seventeen. For illustrations of the earliest types, see Galpin, *op. cit.*, p. 75, fig. 11, and plates facing pp. 6, 192.

38. **new note:** cf. *Pearl* 879; *Squyr of Lowe Degre* 55; and (with *note* in a different sense) *Pearl* 155.

42–3. Cf. *Avowing of Arthur* 25–6 —
        To hunte atte buk and atte bare
        To þe herte and to þe hare.

L 44, 48. A clear example of memorial transmission: the nouns of the phrase (preserved in C) in 44 have been inverted, and an attempt has been made to repair the damage by re-writing 48. This upsets the rime, and produces two half-stanzas of eight lines instead of one of sixteen (the same has occurred also in XV, XXII, XXV, XXX, XXXVI, XXXVII, LXXX, LXXXIX, C, CXVII, all from MS. L).

47. **perke.** The writer had effective knowledge of the distinctions between the various kinds of demesne land and of the technical words relating to forest law.

A *forest* was a game reserve, not necessarily wooded. Most forests in England belonged to the King, but by the end of the fourteenth century large tracts of forest land had been alienated to his subjects. According to C 99 (probably the original reading), the Earl possessed eight such tracts: he was therefore a considerable landholder.

If a forest passed by royal grant into the hands of one of the King's subjects, it was referred to in official documents as a *chase*. It was no longer regulated by forest law, though some of the King's rights over the beasts and the timber of the forest became vested in the new owner.

A *park* was a piece of land enclosed by a paling erected either for the purpose of keeping the owner's deer in, or other people's deer out. Liberty to impark an area usually involved an obligation to maintain the fences so that the King's beasts might not stray into the park. C 70 implies that Sir Degrevant's fences were in good repair. As private property, a park was not protected by forest law, but it was an act of trespass to enter park or chase for the purpose of taking or hunting beasts *feræ naturæ*. The legal provision against such acts seems to have been settled about 1276; the punishment included imprisonment, and compensation to the owner. The writer presumably had such a statute in mind when he makes Sir Degrevant say that he intended 'to wyrke by þe lawe' (151). Clearly, the Earl had broken down the fences, and had killed the beasts (107–10).

A *warren* (439, 1771) was unenclosed land over which the owner had the right of hunting certain beasts *feræ naturæ*. Free warren was often made the subject of a special grant: i.e., the mere possession of land did not necessarily include the right of hunting over it. If an owner had the right of free warren, he was obliged to keep a warrener or warden to prevent the intrusion of unauthorised people, on pain of losing the warren. The hero's warrener appears in the poem with the title of **stewarde** (121). The legal remedy for trespass and the procedure for obtaining it varied according to the seriousness of the offence, but always seems to have included reparation to the owner. The main beasts of the warren were the hare and the roe deer; the red and the fallow deer were beasts of the forest. A warren might lawfully be entered in pursuit of beasts which were not beasts of the warren. The equivalent term in *Sir Degrevant* to beasts *feræ naturæ* is **wylde** (440).

48. **Sexty**: here and in 111, 501, C 1135, L 1383 used to denote a round number of impressive size. For other examples, see Kölbing's note to his ed. of *Sir Beues*, p. 249.

50. Cf. 522; C 823.

C 52. **to newe**: an unusual expression. **to** is probably an inadvertent repetition from the line above.

56. For the association of **games**, and **grew**, see *Sir Tristrem* 1273 ff. —
> In warld was non so wiis
> Of craft þat men knewe
> Wiþouten Sir Tramtris
> Þat al games of grewe
> On grounde.

57–8. Cf. 505–6; a parallel to the first line occurs in 241.

61. With the combination of generosity in almsgiving, valour in war, and diffidence in love by which the author characterises Sir Degrevant, cf. the following —
> Gugemars se part de le cort;
> Molt i dona ains qu'il se'en tort.
> En Flandres ala son pris querre
> U ot tous iors estrif et gerre,
> En Laëraine n'en Gascogne,
> En Alemagne n'en Borgogne.
> A cel tans ne pot on trouver
> Meillor cevalier ne son per.
> De tant i ot mespris nature
> Ke de nul amor n'avoit cure:
> Sou siel n'a dame ne pucele
> Ki tant fust avenans et bele,
> Se il d'amour la requesist
> Que volentiers nel retenist!
> Plusors l'en requissent souvent,
> Mais il n'en avoit nul talent.
> Nus ne pooit apercevoir
> Que il vousist amor avoir.
> Pour çou le tiennent a peri
> L'estrange gent et si ami.
> Marie de France, *Lay of Guigemar* 49–68.

63. **an ankyre in a stane**: 'an anchorite in a cell', *stane* having one of the senses of ON. steinn.

65. **sessid in his hande**, bestowed into his possession. Not a common phrase, but cf. *Erle of Toulous* 1205; *Prophecies of Merlin* quoted in Minot's Poems (ed. Hall) 103/202; *Wars of Alexander* 5313.

C 69. 'A hundred measures of land in his possession'. This I take to be the meaning, though the usual form of the phrase is *in demeyne* (sg.), except when there is more than one owner (see OED. *s. v.* Demesne 1, especially the quotation from Pecock *Repr.* III, iii, 290: Tho whiche thei helden in her owne demenys). Perhaps the author has made the noun pl. to fit the rime. Þe **maynes** (L) is probably a corruption of this.

L 74. **heġhe:** the scribe has repeated the adjective from the previous line. The hall was the principal room in the mediæval house; the chamber was a smaller, more private apartment. The distinction in sense is faithfully preserved in *Gawain* 48 —
     Al wat3 hap vpon he3e in halle3 and chambre3.
 75. **stedes in the stalles:** cf. *Perceval* 1545. The L-version increases the alliteration by combining another phrase: **stedis stabillede** (cf. *Awntyrs off Arthure* 447).
 L 79. Þat he ne is the usual ME. order; that in the MS. (Þat ne he) inverts it. Þat . . . ne practically means 'but' (See *Havelok* 57, etc.).
 81. **almous**⟨ON. almusa; **almos**⟨AFr. almosne (see OED. *s. vv.* Almose, Almous).
 83. Cf. *Morte Arthure* 399.
 L 85–7. The sense is, 'He was prepared to invite guests to hear minstrels in the hall, to whom (i.e., to the minstrels) he gave robes of fine cloth and rich rewards'.
 86. The theme of Sir Degrevant's generosity to minstrels is introduced three times into the poem (see also 1173–6, 1877–80) as a broad hint to the audience. The same hint was constantly being dropped elsewhere, and similar gifts were expected: food, horses, gold, silver, and rich clothes. See *Coer de Lion* 671 ff.; *Syre Gawene and the Carle of Carelyle* 643–4; *Ipomedon B* 549 (at the end of a tournament: cf. *Sir Degrevant* 1173–5); *Octouian* 1269–70 (at Florient's wedding: cf. *ib.* 1298; *Sir Degrevant* 1877–80); *Sir Cleges* 46 ff., 496; *Isumbras* 19–20; *Eglamour* 1327–9, 1336–8; *Guy of Warwick* (MS. B) 7104–5; also *Gunnlaugssaga Ormstungu* (ed. L. M. Small, 1935), pp. 36, 39–40; John de Bromyard, *Summa Prædicantium*, Antwerp, 1614, *s. vv.* Eucharistica, Part I, p. 257, Nativitas, Part II, p. 107.
 92, 96. **melody, hardy / nobulle, ġre.** There is no doubt that C, preserving the continuity of the tail-rimes in the first half of the stanza (**fre, fee**), has the original reading. Since L's *melody, hardy* apparently made passable rimes with *fre, fee* in his dialect, this sequence is interesting as showing how ME. $\bar{e}$ was raised to $\bar{\imath}$ in the northern dialect by the mid-fifteenth century at latest; and since it is corrupt, it shows that the raising probably had not occurred in the dialect of the original. This fact has an important bearing on the date (see Introduction, Section IX). The example is unique in the poem.
 C 104. See Introduction, p. xxvi, footnote.
 107–115, 137–144. With the picture of desolation here described, cf. *Tale of Gamelyn* 74–5, 83–7 —
    [He] leet his londes for-fare . and his houses bothe,
    His parkes and his woodes . and dede nothing wel;
    He thoughte on his londes . that layen vnsawe,
    And his faire okes . that down were i-drawe;
    His parkes were i-broken . and his deer byreued;
    Of alle his goode steedes . noon was him byleued;
    His howses were vnhiled . and ful yuel dight;
also *Eger and Grime* 1421 —
    They brake his parkes and killed his deere.
In *The Erle of Toulous* 25–36, 55 ff., the general situation resembles that in *Sir Degrevant* more closely, but specific details of damage done are not given.
 C 110. Cf. 120, 512. **Feld in fey** (with its variants) may be an adaptation of *feallan fæge* (*Beowulf* 1755; *Maldon* 105), which survived into ME. in *Gawain* 1067; *Wars of Alexander* 4002.
 112. See note to L 380, L 384.
 117–8. Cf. *Guy of Warwick* (MS. B) 787–8 —
    And went far into straunge londe
    Dedis of armes for to fonde;
also *ib.* 4351–2.
 127. The identical phrase is found in the *Tale of Gamelyn* 99 in a similar context: the hero is lamenting how his father's patrimony is being neglected by his own brother.
 131. Possibly intended as a paraphrase of Chaucer's line (*Prol.* 56), 'In Gernade at the seege eek hadde he be'; like Chaucer's Knight, Sir Degrevant had fought in the Holy Land (see 117). He alludes to his Spanish campaign in 437, but how he got to Granada from Palestine we are not told. **Frount** is therefore being used in the military

sense of 'line of battle'. **Flaundres** (L) is a corruption of this; a journey from Flanders to Spain is clearly in the wrong direction for a traveller from Palestine to England. **Degranade** (L) is another corruption, perhaps due to confusion of *de* and *þe* as in L 1483. I therefore read **(þe) Granade**, assume that the def. art. in C and restored to L was an error of the archetype, and remove it from the text.

C 143. **com[ou]n**: MS. **comen**, with final curl after the *n*. The original probably read *comoū*; if the *ou* was indistinct, and open to misinterpretation as *en*, the word would then be taken to be the pp. of *come*.

C 146. **fyen**: an exceptional spelling for 'fain', influenced by the form **ayen** in the line above. The repetition of the forms in rime at 361–2 points to deliberate intention on the scribe's part: there is no strong case for emendation.

L 147. **a ǵayne**, probably a scribal dittography from 145.

L 150. For the etymology of **aueres**, see J. R. R. Tolkien, RES. I 331.

160. **ansuare / answer**. As it stands, the rime is imperfect. The obvious course is to emend to *ansuore / answor*, but forms of the word in *-o-* appear not to have been used in the written language after the twelfth century. In OE. they are not uncommon, both as noun and verb (at least two are found in the Northumbrian part of the Rushworth Glcss), the rounding being due to the loss of stress in the second element of the compound, and to the preceding *w*. Though the existence of the *o*-form in the spoken language may be fairly inferred, scribes seem to have been hesitant to acknowledge it, hence the MS. forms have been left unemended.

161. The omission of a whole stanza in C is probably scribal rather than memorial. At 113 the character of the handwriting changes: the downstrokes become much thicker, as though the scribe was using a different pen. At 161 the hand becomes normal again; i.e., the work of copying was almost certainly interrupted when he had finished f.97a., and he reverted to his original pen, or one like it. Taking up the work again, he began in the wrong place. The error was natural, since the two lines 161, 177 (the first two of stanzas XI, XII) begin in an identical fashion (**þe squiere . .**), and are very similar in meaning.

163. Cf. *Purity* 1389.

L 180 etc. **wysse**: the *ss*-spelling after a long vowel, not uncommon in the north, indicates a voiceless consonant. For further examples, see OED. *s. v.* Wise *a*.

184. The line in L is difficult in this context for two reasons —
1. Unambiguous examples of identical words riming together are very rare in either text (in L 147, L 251, L 546, C 934, C 1391, L 1617, and L 1664, the other MS. either has a different, and a better reading, or else the line is wanting).
2. It is unlikely that the Earl, a man of violent and predatory nature, would receive the emissary's letter so mildly.
Assimilation to the rime-word in 180 is almost certainly the cause of the corruption. Once the line is in the text, it exerts an assimilating influence in its turn, and as such is repeated in L 577.

192. Cf. *Avowing of Arthur* 742.

193–4. Cf. *King Horn* 483–4 —
    Þe King sede sone
    'Þat is wel idone'.

195. **fune / whone**: C has the rarer, and presumably original reading, though the words are synonymous. *Fone* is not uncommon in northerly texts, where it rimes tense, e.g., *Cursor Mundi* 19782 *fon, vtedon; ib.* 18246 (Gött.) *fordone, fone*. In 23922, MS. Cotton has *quone* (*whone*); Fairf. and Gött. *fone* (r. w. *bone*, boon), a parallel variant reading to that in *Sir Degrevant*. It is a dialectal form of OE. hwŏn, influenced by *f*-types, Norse or English. The original tense vowel is shown by the form **fune** in L, representing the northern raising of OE. ō to [ȳ].

204. See *Squyr of Lowe Degre* 520 —
    For treason walketh wonder wyde.

209–10. Cf. *Sir Triamour* 97–8 —
    Then was the quene wonder wrothe
    And swere mony a grete othe.

C 211–12. I take **lothe** in the sense of 'unwilling' (to come a second time), and hence 'regretful' (that he had been at all), and paraphrase 'Unless the squire went away, he would regret ever having come with such a message'. L corrupts these lines.

L 236. **Wedes:** the sixteen-line stanza is split up into two eights; C preserves both the rime scheme and the more common ME. idiom **at nede.**

237. **Thare warre armed,** etc. Although most of the battle between Sir Degrevant and the Earl is commonplace romance material, it is similar, both in substance and arrangement, to that between the Erle of Toulous and the Emperor (*Erle* 61–156). In particular the following resemblances may be noticed; viii and ix are especially significant —
    (i) The cause of the fight is a dispute about land (*Erle* 28–9).
    (ii) A description is given of the gathering of forces on each side (*Erle* 61–9).
    (iii) The special mention of the aggressive confidence of the Earl (*Degrevant* 247) and of the Emperor (*Erle* 82).
    (iv) The description of the battle itself (*Erle* 83–108).
    (v) The rout of the tyrant (*Erle* 109), who is pursued (*Erle* 118).
    (vi) Many are slain on the defeated side (*Erle* 121–6), few or none on the other (*Degrevant* 363; *Erle* 127).
    (vii) The defeated leaders flee from the field (*Degrevant* 335; *Erle* 110) and take refuge in their castles (*Degrevant* 373; *Erle* 111).
    (viii) Their wives, having previously attempted to make peace, assure them that there is poetic justice in defeat (*Degrevant* 377–80; *Erle* 139–44).
    (ix) Their remorse (*Degrevant* 381–4; *Erle* 145–50).
    (x) The triumphant leaders give thanks to God for victory (*Degrevant* 365–6; *Erle* 119–20).

L 243–5. **founde, stownde, ronde.** In this MS., OE. *und* is so spelt (see 249, 251), also *ound, ownd* (see above) and *ond* (see 507). As it is impossible to determine whether the vowel in this poet's dialect was short or long, the MS. forms have been retained in these and in all similar cases.

245, 246, 256. See *Sir Beues* (MS. A) 1023–5 —
    Ase he com ride be a cost
    Twei kni3tes a fond of Beues ost;
    Of his stede he gan doun li3te.
See also *Destr. Troy* 4852, 5280.

C 251. The dichotomy is imperfect. **Grounds** is the general term including the whole of the knight's lands (see OED. *s. v.* Ground 10c); by **green** is meant the grassy parts of them (*ib. s. v.* Green 12). Similarly, the distinction between *woods* and *warren* (439, 1771) is not absolute.

L 252. **heue:** perhaps a scribal error for *houe*, but more likely a form of *hue*⟨OFr. (*n.*) hu, shout, clamour, here used as a tr. vb. in the sense of 'direct or guide by shouting'. See OED. *s. v.* Hue, $v^2$. For OFr. [y]⟩ME. *eu*, see Jordan, *ME. Gr.* §230. I. In view of the difficulty of C at this point, **heue** may be the original reading.

259. **chefe cheftayne.** Cf. Henry's *Wallace* III 165; *Siege Jerusalem* 337.

265. Cf. *Ferumbras* 1750.

C 266. **chartur of pes.** Cf. *Morte Arthure* 3058.

L 267. The use of *have* in an absolute sense is uncommon, but is well substantia*ted* (see OED. *s. v.* Have *vb.* 1 b.). **som** (C) may therefore be an interpolation.

275. Cf. 'And then they advanced banners and smote together' (Malory, Book II, Chap. X).

C 279. **thare:** a scribal repetition from 277.

L 282. The form **grayede** is well established in this dialect, though scribes are sometimes reluctant to recognize it. In the *Cursor Mundi* 3533–4 there occurs the rime *sayde, grayde* (Fairfax) where Cotton has *said, graythid*; Göttingen *said, grayd*, and Trinity *seide, greiþed.* See also *ib.* 3685–6 etc.; *York Plays* xii/141 (r. w. *saide*); xii/190 (r. w. *layde*); *Sege off Melayne* 1600–1 (*graythede, displayede*).

L 289. **Iunede** r. w. **funede, soynede.** The first two are northern forms. In the *Kingis Quair*, stanza 133, *Iunyt* r. w. *fortunyt.* AN. *ui* in other ME. dialects was usually written *oi, oy* (see Wright, *EMEGr.* §207). On the phonetic value of these forms, see Luick, *Hist. Gram.* §434/2, and Note 3.

C 290. Cf. *Morte Arthure* 1897-8 —
    At the furthe in þe fyrthe with ferse men of armes
    Thare faughtte we in faythe and foynede with sperys;
also *ib.* 2163, 3689.

C 294. Cf. *Sege off Melayne* 262 —
    Riche hawberkes were all to-rent.

L 296. **gleterand**: an error (perhaps scribal) due to repetition from L 295.

C 300. **heþe heldus**: MS. **heþene heldus**. The scribe miswrote **heþne**, added an **e** above the **n**, and omitted to erase the blunder. Hence previous edd. read **heþene**, and Miss Rickert translates 'heathery hills', unnecessarily assuming the existence of an unrecorded adj.⟨OE. hǣþ. But **heldus** is a pl. vb., 'sink'.

C 301. MS. **Then foughten**: **foughten** lacks a subject, which can be supplied by supposing a scribal alteration of **they foughte then** to **then foughten**.

L 302. Cf. *Ormulum* 3446; *Wars of Alexander* 304; *Patience* 330.

307. Cf. *Morte Arthure* 4238; *Wars of Alexander* 2450.

L 308 **knyghttis** has been substituted for **ledis**.

L 320. **scheldis** is perhaps a pure scribal error for **stedis**.

L 324, continuing the rime scheme of the previous stanza, and upsetting that of stanza XXI, is also to be ruled out on metrical grounds, as the medial dip contains the unusually large number of three, perhaps four, unstressed syllables.

313. Cf. *Morte Arthure* 2159.

C 316, 320. **dede, stede** wrongly substituted for plural forms.

319. **þe bent so browne**: cf. *Rauf Coilȝear* 800; *Thomas of Erceldoune* (ed. Brandl) 306.

C 322. **Br[yt]tenes**, MS. **Brghtenes**. The MS. reading probably owes its form to **bryght** at the end of the line.

L 329. **hym** is unnecessary to the sense and impairs the metre. The phrase **houed and byhelde** occurs elsewhere (1255, 1311), and is always used of the Earl. It is implied that he is a coward, who remains as a mere spectator of all battles. Here, the object of **byheld** is 331.

L 332. Though **s[at]t vnsownde** is not meaningless, confirmation of its use in other ME. poems is lacking, and the use of *sit* is inappropriate here. For *sigh unsound* on the other hand, the OED. (*s. v.* Unsound *a.* 1 b) quotes two other examples (*Morte Arthure* 3290; *Golagros and Gawane* 638), and this, in a derivative poem like *Sir Degrevant*, is an argument for its being the right reading.

L 333. **hade** (C **ledde**): a typical example of literary dilution due to memorial carelessness.

336. **wondide** / **ywounded**. The form of the past participle with *ed* / *id* ending may have been independently substituted for the rarer monosyllabic form *wo(u)nd* (here required by the rime) by both scribes independently, or may derive from a slip in the archetype. The OED. (*s. v.* Wound *v.*) cites an example of the contracted past tense *wound* in *Young Hunting* iv (Child's Ballads II 148/1); for the pp. used adjectivally, see *Ancren Riwle* (ed. Morton) 136.

340. An error in both texts probably deriving from the common original X. Considerations of rime and sense show that the author wrote—
    To dethe þay þam denge.
In X, the pl. pron. and vb. had been made sg. and the line was transmitted in this form to C. For the common tag *ding to dethe*, L substitutes the even commoner *dight to dethe*, and recasts the following tail-rime.

L 348. The C reading, with **on**, seems to be far more in conformity with ME. idiom. Though *spring* can be used transitively in the sense of 'cause a horse to gallop', the OED. quotes no example before 1737 (*s. v.* Spring *v.*[1] 18c).

349. Cf. *Awntyrs of Arthure* 298.

L 356–360. The relative pronoun **þat** (now 360) seems to require a personal antecedent (i.e., it could scarcely be the *sides* of his foes that had wrought harm to Sir

Degrevant). Quite apart from the witness to the true text offered by C, the sense makes it clear that the lines have been interchanged, and should be restored.

C 369. **Dight** is almost always used transitively in ME., and if used reflexively, 'prepare oneself to do something', the reflexive pronoun is always expressed. C's version here is not to be relied upon.

375. **sawe / ses.** The original reading I take to be *seʒ*, saw (normalized to **sawe** by L in conformity with his usual form of the word, as in 539, 1093), which then becomes corrupted to **ses** through the intermediate form *\*seʒ*.

378. **perkes to chase / perkes and chas.** In both versions **chase** is probably to be taken as a noun, and **to** in its customary ME. sense of 'for'. The objection to regarding **chase** as a verb in L is that the word does not seem to be used, like **hunt** in C 190, to mean 'ride through (a district) in pursuit of something'.

C 383–4. As in L, the Earl's general meaning, that which agrees best with the context and with his transient mood of remorse, seems to be simply 'I won't do it any more', but to fit this to the words is another question. What he appears to say is just the opposite: that he forgoes the opportunity of righting wrongs (for another example of the phrase see *Destr. Troy* 11615-6—Bot god . . . all giltis godely beholdis, And wrangis in his wrathe writhis to ground). The L-reading gives no help and is almost certainly corrupt, partly because of the repetition of **maystries** from the previous tail-rime line (L 380), and partly because the rime is spoilt, anticipating the sequence of the following stanza. The awkwardness in C may therefore be original. Since it occurs at the end of a stanza, the author may have been desperate for a rime. The L-reading will then be an attempt at emendation, equally desperate. **Dyghte** (L 384) may be an unconscious reminiscence of 369, and **maystres** an echo of 112.

L 386. **ownn auant.** The C-reading, **auennaunt**, is undoubtedly the better, and the process of gradual corruption may have occurred in some such way as the following:—auennaunt⟩*auenn aunt⟩*awenn auant⟩*owenn auant⟩*ownn auant. The single word is misconstrued as two, and the second half is rewritten in conformity with what a later scribe feels to be the sense, though the re-writing involves the addition of a letter, and the confusion of vocalic and consonantal *u*. He may have thought that the **auant** referred to 227–232.

387. Cf. *Morte Arthure* 1811, 2140, 2259, 2451: *feraunte stedez*.

L 388, 392. Dislocation is the result of confusion between two well authenticated ME. phrases: *at right*, properly (see OED. *s. v.* Right *sb.*[1] 12b, and *Brus* X 312; Henry's *Wallace* IV 278, etc.), and *armed at rights* (*ib*. 13; *Coer de Lion* 3123; Chaucer *Knight's Tale* 2102, etc.). For the first of these, apparently only Scottish authority can be found, but it appears to have been known to a reciter of the L-tradition, who substituted it for the second.

390. The rimes **rade, hade, habade** are quite satisfactory in this dialect. Barbour's *Brus* I 481-2 has the rime *had, maid*, made; I 513-4 has *maid, haid*; both of which point to long vowels. On the phonology of **hade**, see Luick, *Hist. Gram.* §428/1.

C 391. **barnekynch.** The form of the word is exceptional (see OED. *s. v.* Barmkin), and may even be unique. The second element is possibly to be related to *kink*, a twist, or to *kinch*, of the same meaning, found only in Scottish texts, since the passage through the barbican leading to the main castle gate often had a twist in it. If there were forms in *-kink* and *-kinch*, the former might quite conceivably have been reduced to *-kin* in the northern dialect, under the influence of the diminutive suffix.

The likelihood of this suggestion is diminished owing to **lordelych** in the following line; since no parallels to **barnekynch** are found elsewhere, it may be merely a scribal error for *barnekyn*, the outcome of inadvertent assimilation.

395. **courses of were** is the usual phrase for tilting bouts. Cf. 1231–2; *Ferumbras* 473; *Rowlande and Ottuell* 812, 1298, 1363; especially *Morte Arthure*, 1681, where the number specified is three, and *Avowing of Arthur* xxiv —

Take thi schild and thi spere
And ride to him a course on werre.

398–9. The original may well have read —

Þat he wold be messynger
And gare hym have ansuere.

The rhythm, at any rate, would be much improved by adopting such a reading, and,

NOTES

on the assumption that both versions were written down from memory, it is not difficult to see how otiose words have gradually crept in. For the rimes **messynger, ansuere,** see 410-11, and *Cursor Mundi* 1889-90.

400. **he,** i.e., the porter.

412. 'To perform his errand (Cf. L 580, and see OED. *s. v.* Walk *vb.*[1] 4c).

L 415-6. 'There is no-one here ready to put to shame the deeds of this doughty fellow Sir Degrevant'. The construction is possible, *Sir Degrevant* then being an example of the northern uninflected genitive, as in L 467, C 583; but it is undoubtedly a corrupt version of the C-reading.

417. C has missed the point of the carefully thought out localization of the incident and has repeated the rime-word of the first line in the preceding stanza. Sir Degrevant and his knights remain outside the castle while the porter goes to the Earl with the message. As they are waiting, the Countess and her daughter appear on the castle *wall*, not in the *hall*. 539 makes the author's intention quite clear.

421. **Scho (She)** refers to the Countess; this is her first attempt to make peace, but she does not succeed until after her second appeal in 1757.

C 422. **sey[t]h:** MS. **seygh.** The mis-spelling is probably the result of the form **seyght** in 420.

433-5. **stroyed,** etc. The spellings of both sets of rime-words are merely scribal, apart from **drawed** (L 434), which is a memorial error. **stroyed,** should be **stryde** or **stryed:** the OED. gives *distried* (Wyclif *Serm.* Sel. Wks. I 25); *distrye* (Bradshaw *St. Werburge* II 694), etc. **anoy(e)de** should be **anyde** (*anyed* in *Ferumbras* 364). **endreyde** (apparently a ἅπαξ λεγόμενον) made dry, is a SE. form (see Luick, *op. cit.* §373 a, c.) No doubt the original reading was **endryde.**

L 433-4. **perrkes and veuers** is a legal phrase found in the sections in the *Statutes of Westminster* dealing with this very matter of trespass (see *Statutes of the Realm* I, p. 32, quoted in G. J. Turner, *Select Pleas of the Forest,* Selden Soc., Vol. 13, p. cxxi). **Veuers** is a better reading than C's.

437-40. Repeated almost verbatim in the Countess's plea for reconciliation 1769-72.

C 446-7. 'He that has slain my foresters shall pay compensation (to their kinsfolk) as soon as I can (contrive it).' The construction is awkward, and involves a most unusual interpretation of **award.** The text is probably corrupt. The L-version makes better sense, but a much easier reading is obtained by taking the lines in the order 446, 447, 445. The original may have read —
   He þat my fosters has slayne
   I sall rewarde hym agayne,
   Or I sall dy in þe payne.
The order 445, 447, 446 (with omission of **he** from 446) is also possible.

463. Cf. *Morte Arthure* 4241 —
   That euer þat doughtty sulde dy.

L 467. **Erle:** a northern uninflected genitive: cf. C 583 (Englond here); *Gawain* 25 (Bretayne Kynges).

C 471. **treweloues.** The King of Hungary's daughter bids her lover acquire a shield
   Fulfylled with ymagery
   And poudred with true loues
   (*Squyr of Lowe Degre* 209-10).
As in C 1048, 1055, the word probably means 'fleurs de lis' (possibly 'trefoils'), in accordance with heraldic practice.

L 472. Cf. 528. **frely to falde** is a variant, found apparently only in this poem, of the commoner *frely and faire* (see 569 and note).

473-4. Cf. *Erle of Toulous* 328-9 —
   Two erlys hur ladde;
   Wondur rychely sche was cladde.

L 473-4. **clede, lede,** for original *clade, lade.* That both *clade* and *clede* are known in this dialect is seen from 1806, where *clede* is certified by the rime.

C 447. **wondus:** MS. **wendus,** a scribal confusion of *o* and *e*.

491. Cf. *Ferumbras* 567, 3202.

L 502 ff. Compare *Avowing of Arthur* 25–8 —
  To þe forest þay fare
  To hunte atte buk and atte bare
  To þe herte and to þe hare
  Þat bredus in þe rise;
*Morte Arthure* 656–7 —
  Founde my forestez be frythede . . .
  That nane werreye my wylde, etc.

L 504. of omitted, on the authority of C, to improve syntax and rhythm.

C 514. te[n]ede, MS. temede. No very satisfactory sense is obtained by keeping the MS. reading here. Luick retains **temede**, and translates 'widmen', referring to OED. *s. v.* Teem, $v^1$. 7, but the examples quoted there provide no true parallel. He may have been influenced in his interpretation by the corresponding reading **sent** in L, which he may have come to regard as a weak paraphrase of C. The miswriting of **tenede** as **temede** may be the result of mishearing, or of a wrongly extended *n*-suspension, or may be simply a minute error.

L 519. **inowe.** On the relation between the *-e-* and the *-o-* forms, see Wright (*EME. Gr.* §§114/2, 115) who regards the *-e-* forms as Northumbrian. For a further example of the rime *inew, slew*, see Barbour, *Brus* I 557–8. L 1421 provides another example of the same error (MS. **y nowe** for *y newe* in an *-ewe* sequence). See L 1438 for the converse error (MS. **y newe** for *y noue*, purporting to rime with **a-boue, loue**).

C 520. 'He got them into his possession.' A far stronger line, better rhythm, and a better rime are obtained by supposing that a preposition has dropped out after **hom**, and taking **wold** as a noun. Holthausen (*Anglia* XLIV, p. 78) proposed to emend **hom** to **on**, but this would not strengthen the rhythm of the somewhat exceptional type of line (see Finsterbusch *op. cit.*, pp. 99–100).

529 ff. The feeling, imagery, and diction of this stanza recall some of the *Harley Lyrics*, especially *Annot and Johon*, printed in C. Brown (13), no. 76. Our poet's music is less elaborate, but his stanza gains in directness. Another parallel is found in *Guy of Warwick* (MS. B) 3998–4034, where Sir Guy unbosoms himself to Sir Harrawde in similar terms regarding his love for Felice, and like Sir Degrevant, receives advice from him. Line 529 combines two alliterative phrases: **lely light** (cf. C. Brown *op. cit.*, p. 138/11–12, 140/22) and **love . . . light** (cf. 1540, *Launfal* 308; *Horn Childe* 345).

C 530. Cf. C 660, 692, 700, C 1523; also L 344 (an error); *Pearl* 494; *Le Bone Florence* 800.

531. Cf. *Pearl* 110.

534–5. A traditional pair of images of which ME. poets never tired. Cf. *King Horn* 15–16 —
  so whit so eny lylye flour
  so rose red wes his colour;
also *Annot and Johon* (MS. Harley 2253), C. Brown (13), p. 137/11–12; also *ib.* 140/31–2; *Death and Liffe* 66; *Guy of Warwick* (MS. B) 4656; *Rowland and Ottuell* 619–20; *Athelston* 69–71; *Erle of Toulous* 199–200; *Awntyrs of Arthure* 161–2; *Libeaus Desconus* 1244; *Emaré* 66, 205, etc.; *Launfal* 937; *Eger and Grime* 217, 795; *Sir Gowther* 34–5. The form of the idea in C is unusual and may be corrupt:—'her complexion is run (or flushed) like the rose on the branch (i.e., with red)'. One is tempted to emend to 'Rede rone hir vys', i.e., her complexion is as red as the rowan (see OED. *s. v.* Rone, *sb.*²). Since a word preceding *hit* has been cancelled, it may be that C's copy was illegible or obscure in meaning, and that he was making what sense he could of it.

L 536. **lyre** (⟨ON. hlýr) for **lere** (⟨OE. hlēor).

C 541. **leue[re]**, MS. **leue**: the comparative, as in L, is meant. For parallel, see 841–2.

542. Miss Hibbard thinks that this allusion to the legend of the Rhine gold possibly shows acquaintance with the *Nibelungenlied*. It is surely impossible to be so specific, and just as likely that his knowledge of the story came from Scandinavian sources.

# NOTES

C 544. **myn** is almost certainly an error, whether memorial or scribal is uncertain. The cause of it is probably **myne** in 541.

545. **Iwysse** seems appropriately to belong to the quotation. The squire is asseverating his loyalty to his master, and undertaking to help him in his wooing. The emphatic word is therefore in keeping with his character and his promise. For other examples of quotations beginning in the middle of a line, see L 184, 275, 377, 422, 693, etc. A particularly close parallel is found in 205, where the same punctuation has been adopted.

547. **seke hir / syker**: a memorial error in L that may be the result of mishearing, the rest of the line being altered into conformity with it.

L 549–52. The order in C is obviously neater. The parenthesis in L 550 is awkward, and **kan** is separated from its infinitive. Owing to this displacement, L has prefixed 552 with a syntactically and metrically redundant **to**.

L 553–4. An extreme example of the general literary debilitation that usually accompanies memorial transmission. **To, an athe, sall I,** pad out the line, and are unnecessary. The scribe has also had a hand in it, substituting **discouer** for the rarer, and shorter, *discure*. **Suere** (for **ensure**) may have arisen as the result of combined memorial and scribal confusions. **Ensure** loses its prefix and becomes *sure* (*v.*), perhaps ambiguously spelt **suere**; this is then taken as a form of *swere*, and **an athe** inserted to fill out the line.

556. Cf. *King Horn* 108, and see Hall's note for parallels.

L 557. Cf. *Morte Arthure* 1735.

L 561. **he said** is inessential to the idiom of the poem and upsets the rhythm. It therefore probably does not belong to the original, of which C preserves the more exact and more rhythmical version. (A similar situation arises in L 1385.) For examples of quoted speech introduced without any such interpolation, see 483, 529, 718, 739, 781, 789, 1033, 1071, 1189, 1222, etc. Interpolation of the phrase is to be suspected in both texts in other places, e.g., 693, 753. In non-riming alliterative poetry 'quoþ he' and its synonyms are often extra-metrical, e.g., *Gawain* 398, 1395; *Piers P.* B Prol. 160; A xi 163.

L 564, 568, etc. In the original dialect ME. *ẹ̄ʒ* has been raised to *ī*, as is shown by the rimes **ly,** tell lies 1748, **drye, dy, mercy; dy** 463, **trewly, lyghtly.** One is therefore justified in regarding *ī*-forms as original.

On the textual problem of whether **tye** (as in C) or **hy** represents the original rime-word in 568, one may be guided by the principle that the less familiar word is likely to be the right one, and by the further fact that the line as it stands in L is pointless.

For parallels to the phrase in L 564, cf. L 1748; *Sir Beues* (MS. A) 2147 —
  What helpeþ hit, to make fable?
*Sir Launfal* 633 —
  What help hyt for to lye?

C 568. The expression is unusual, but see the Scottish *Buik of Alexander* (ed. Ritchie, STS., Vol. II, p. 108, l. 10):—Canadas . . . had him lukkin in lufis lace; also Chaucer, *Knight's Tale* 1817.

569. **frely and faire** is occasionally found in alliterative poems of the fourteenth and fifteenth centuries, but I have been unable to find examples in the tail-rime romances. See *Morte Arthure* 970; *Wars of Alexander* 785; *Chevalere Assigne* 266, 274; *Awntyrs of Arthure* 682; *Buke of the Howlat* 308; *Pistill of Susan* 17. Oakden (*Alliterative Poetry in Middle English* II 239) quotes examples from the *Katherine* group.

574. **hir body alle bare**: cf. *Destr. Troy* 5821, 7914, 7922; *Cursor Mundi* 869; *Guy of Warwick* (MS. B) 3967, and especially 7067–8 —
  I had leuyr the body all bare
  Of yowre doghtur wythowten mare.

L 577. See 184 and note.

C 587–8. The use of **But**, and also, and only, is exceptional in an affirmative sentence.

588. Cf. Minot I 50; *Hymns to Virgin* (EETS. 24, 1867) 65/215–6.

L 588. **ʒoure** is metrically superfluous, and is probably not original. Its appearance here is probably scribal repetition of the word in 580, 584, 586.

C 592. Cf. OE. *Riddles* xl. 4; *Gawain* 2025; *Awntyrs of Arthure* 9, 347; *Pistill of Susan* 26, 186. For the substitution of *v* for OE. *w*, in **Vlonkest**, see Jordan, *ME. Gr.* §163.

L 593–4. **Degreuant, auant.** The corrector has superscribed the *a* in the first, and the second *a* in the second word. He has mechanically done the same with **recreaunt** (in the third of the triplet rimes) which in consequence has one *a* too many. For the phrase *make avaunt*, see also C 965, 1889; *Ferumbras* 485.

L 604. **ane** is from OE. āna, āne, only, misunderstood and corrupted in C to **owun**.

616. **knyghtis of pryde.** An unusual phrase, but see L 1302 (C 1301); 98 (lorde of pryde); *Avowing of Arthur* 791 (lades of pride).

631. In *The Squyr of Lowe Degre* the hero wooed his mistress in her father's 'arber' and frequently avowed his love, leaning 'hys backe to a thorne' (see 63–67).

637. **þay herde a belle.** In *The Erle of Toulous* 289 ff. the Empress bids Sir Trylabas accompany the hero to her chapel when the bell rings for Mass.

638. The chapel is almost certainly in the garden, separate from the main castle building, since Melidor has to go through the garden to reach it. This arrangement is rare in England, but is sometimes found in France (see C. Enlart, *Manuel d'Archéol. Française*, 2 ed., Paris, 1932, Vol. II, p. 550).

641–56. This is a thorny passage, ten lines out of the sixteen presenting some kind of textual problem. It will therefore be convenient to survey it as a whole, before considering the problems separately. Neither text is wholly satisfactory, though C, as usual, provides the greater number of good readings, if the bad spellings are overlooked. In one place (the **and** in 651) both texts have gone astray in the same way, probably owing to corruption in X, the archetype. The possibility that it was difficult to read at this point may account for the extraordinarily high proportion, even for this poem, of variants to invariants, and also for the omission of four lines (652–5 in L). This passage is not a quatrain: the tail-rime precedes the triplets. The last tail-rime of the stanza is included; it is attached to a passage where it does not belong, and makes nonsense. Two lines of the corresponding passage in C are also corrupt (654–5), defying both satisfactory interpretation and emendation. This divergent error may likewise have been caused by some obscurity in X; Z making what he could of it, and Y cutting the knot by omission.

641. The OED. quotes several examples, including this one, of **Violet** (C) in the sense of 'cloth or dress of violet colour'. In the remainder, the word is used with a more general meaning than that found here; most of them conform to the type 'She was clothed in violet.' The words denoting other colours may be used similarly in ME.: 'Twenty bookes clad in blak or reed', 'purple and fine linen'; but the idiom 'a black', black dress, is not recorded. I conclude that the indef. art. in both texts is not original. This conclusion is supported by two further facts (i) the number of weak syllables (4) between the two lifts in this line is exceptionally high, (ii) the idiom 'a veluet' (L) velvet dress, is not recorded elsewhere. As it is a vaguer word, it also is probably not original.

These two variants may be accounted for by supposing that the poet wrote
        Scho come in vyolet,
which was transcribed by X in the form
        Scho come in a vyolet,
and this was imperfectly remembered by the reciter in the L-tradition.

641 ff. With this description of jewels and fine raiment cf. *Squyr of Lowe Degre* 717–22 —
        Ye ware both golde and good veluet,
        Clothe of damaske with saphyres set;
        Ye ware the pery on your head,
        With stones full oryent, whyte and read;
        Ye ware coronalles of golde,
        With diamoundes set many a foulde;
also *Parlement of Thre Ages* 117–135; *Wars of Alexander* 1529–1552.

L 643. A further example of literary dilution, weakening the sense, and impairing the alliteration and the metre. **Saphyrus**, presumably stressed on the second syllable (as *Kyng Alisaunder* 5667, Bodl. MS.), was corrupted to **faire**, and the rest of the line re-written to fit the context. For the phrase **saphyres .. isett**, see *Wars of Alexander* 4880; *Squyr of Lowe Degre* 718, 796.

NOTES 129

C 646. n[o]uche and nevyn, MS. nuche (?*miche*) and nevyn. Previous editors have read the first word as *miche*, which they have been unable to interpret. The scribe has written four almost equally spaced minims, which are almost certainly intended for *nuche*, jewel. The spelling is unusual, though the aphetic form *uche* is found in the fourteenth and fifteenth centuries (see OED. *s. v.* Ouch). I therefore adopt the commoner form *nouche*, and assume corruption, perhaps by memorial transmission, to **cowchide** (L). **Nouche** will then make a good alliterative pair with the following word.

In the OED., Nevyn is defined as 'App. some precious stone', and the only other example is taken from a Latin will of 1393: 'unum monile de auro cum tribus neuynys super illud positis et cum tribus scutis'. Better sense of the line from *Sir Degrevant* is made by taking the word to mean some sort of ornament or clasp; and the passage from the will can bear the same interpretation, the 'neuynys' fastening into the 'scuta'.

As nothing is known about the derivation, the question of whether the *v* in our text is a true *v* or a *u* (as in the will) cannot be settled. Though the L-reading (**Cowchide with newyne**) seems to favour *u*, in view of the wide divergence of the versions in the early part of the line it actually does nothing more than raise suspicions whether L knew the meaning of the word. Owing to L's habit of misunderstanding and rewriting his copy, no reliance can be placed upon this form. **Cowchide** may be a memorial anticipation of L 1487.

C 647. **anurled**: derived from the AN. variant *\*anurler* of the OFr. *\*enourler*, the existence of which is implied in the examples (*Purity* 19, *Morte Arthure* 3244) given in the OED. *s. v.* Enourle. **Anerlud**, the MS. form, I take to be a scribal error. **Furede** (L) is a weak paraphrase of this.

C 648. **ouert**: almost certainly the original reading. The cloak was thrown open to display the rich lining, as in the description of the Green Knight's array in *Gawain* 153; **couerde** is a scribal or memorial error.

649. **dure / toor**: L has undoubtedly the better reading, as **toor** makes a bad rime with **asure**, etc. C was apparently led astray by the hackneyed phrase *tor to tell*.

650. **anamelde with asure**. Cf. *Morte Arthure* 765, Oundyde of azure, enamelde full faire; *Purity* 1411, in asure and ynde enaumayld ryche; also *Morte Arthure* 3355, *Purity* 1457.

651. The **trechoure** (see OED. *s. v.* Tressure) was the gold ribbon of which was made the reticulated head-dress, or fret, which first came into fashion in the thirteenth century and which continued in use for 300 years (see J. R. Planché, *Cyclopædia of Costume*, Vol. 1, illustrations on pp. 269, 271, 272, 276). An illustration in the Gawain MS. (Cotton Nero A x, f. 125) depicts the lady of the castle wearing one. See Tolkien and Gordon's ed., frontispiece, 1738 and note. The *ch* is an AN. spelling for the OFr. *c, ss*.

Though sense can be made of C as it stands, it is improved by emending **and** to *hur*. The error is possibly derived from X, as it is found also in the text of L, who has inserted a **with**. But in view of the corruption of L's line as a whole, the error may well have arisen independently.

The OED. has used this line to illustrate Tressure in the sense 'diminutive of . . . bordure' (2). The objection to accepting this is that it is not, like the other examples given, in a heraldic context. I therefore translate: 'It would be hard to count her buttons, enamelled in sky-blue; her head-dress was set with topazes for the occasion.' This interpretation (together with the emendation of **and** to *hur*) was independently suggested by Gollancz in his ed. of *Gawain* (EETS. 1940) 1739n.

L 651. The peculiar forms of the two nouns (**terepys, tredoure**) are best accounted for as scribal blunders. I assume the original of **terepys** to have been *topyes* (as in C) or something like it; if the cross of the *t* had been misinterpreted as an *er* suspension and extended, and the *o* mistaken for an *e*, the word would assume the form *terepyes*, which is very close to the MS. form in L.

C 653-4. I am unable to give a satisfactory interpretation of these lines. Their omission in L may be due to a corruption of long standing, going back to the archetype.

657-8. Holthausen (Anglia XLIV, p. 78) in an inaccurate note on the passage, proposes to emend *on gold(e)* to *on mold(e)*, on the ground that *on gold(e)* makes nonsense. By *on gold(e)* he means **on hold(e)**, which is difficult to explain. His emendation is plausible (cf. 1055, and see OED. *s. v.* Mould, *sb.* 2 'the top or dome of the head').

L 660. A memorial confusion.

C 660. worthelych[er]e: MS. worthelyche. A smudge obliterates che wy3th. The same hand has re-written these letters below the line, but has omitted the necessary er-suspension.

L 662. chayere: an inferior reading to geyr: there is no reason why a chair should be intruded into a description of Melidor's apparel. On the other hand, the rime geyr, fair, payr is difficult to justify.

663. boses. "BOSSES. Certain projections of the head-dress of ladies of the fourteenth century". (J. R. Planché, *Cyclopædia of Costume*, Vol. 1, p. 49, illustrations *ib*. p. 270, figs. 2, 6.) The extravagances of contemporary headgear were repeatedly and ineffectually satirized by reforming writers, and this detail was singled out as the object of special attack (see *Against the Pride of Ladies* in *Political Songs* 154/1, Camden Soc. 1839; MS. Royal 8 E 17: [elles] . . . 'portent les boces com cornue bestes'; and Wyclif, *Sel. Wks.*, ed. Arnold, III, 124: 'And in þis pride synnen wymmen in makying of hor bosis').

666. Of the Oryent is evidently a phrase of special commendation. Cf. *Pearl* 1, 3, 255. *Morte Arthure* 3461 has 'perry of the Oryent' and *The Squyr of Lowe Degre* 720 has 'stones full oryent'. The phrase was originally used to describe jewels imported from the East, but in later times pearls 'are called orient, because of the clearness, which resembleth the colour of the cleere aire before the rising of the sun' (Harrison, *Description of England* III, 81, ed. New Shakspere Society). Whether Cyprus would precisely represent 'þe oryent' for our author or his audience is not determinable.

673. A commonplace in the romances (see *Erle of Toulous* 373, 1003; *Rowlande and Ottuell* 337; *Ferumbras* 47; *Sir Eglamour* 529–32.

677. For the blowing of trumpets before a meal, see *Amis and Amiloun* 1898–9; *Sir Eglamour* 1097–8; *Sir Gowther* 325.

678. Thay wesche and went to þe sete. A collocation of ideas of apparently French origin. Cf. *Durmars* (ed. E. Stengel, Stuttgart 1873) 1015 —

Quant ont lavé, seoir s'en vont.

But it is also found often enough in English poetry; e.g., *Gawain* 887 —

Þe wy3e wesche at his wylle, and went to his mete;

also *Emaré* 217; *Avowing of Arthur* 1069; *Guy of Warwick* (MS. A) 232–3; *Lybeaus Disconus* 97–9. A general account of mediæval eating habits is given in Thomas Wright, *The Homes of Other Days*, London 1871, p. 259.

681. borde / lordys. Luick, apparently following C, misreads the L-text as *lorde*. Though the first letter is not well made, and though its lower part is followed very closely by the *o*, it is undoubtedly a *b*.

A parallel to L is found in *Guy of Warwick* (MS. B) 10521–2 —

When þat þey had eton all
And þe bordys let downe falle, etc.

As bordys is undoubtedly the original reading, C has been emended.

L 681–3. drawen, layne, agayne. The Thornton scribes seem to have been reluctant to recognize the form *drayne* (<EME. dræien, OE. drǣgen) as found in C 1630 (see also L 758, L 1630). In *Sir Degrevant*, in the *Sege off Melayne* 711 ff. (*drawen'*, *mayne*, *slayne*, *agayne*), and *Sir Perceval* 849 ff. (*slayne*, *drawen'*, *agayne*) the form used goes back to OE. dragen. A possible explanation is that in the dialect into which these poems are transcribed the spelling *drawen'* was conventional, and could be used to represent the pronunciation required by the rime.

692, 700. wy3th. Well-authenticated examples of rimes on identical words with identical meanings are rare in the poem; others are found 1348, 1360 (*may*); 1389–91 (*sete*).

710. L has the alliterative, the more rhythmical, and hence the better version. The repeated to in C is awkward, and difficult to explain syntactically.

714. The vizors of Sir Degrevant and his squire prevented their recognition (see 601–2).

L 719. The omission of wele (as in C) improves the rhythm. It has been inserted by L, perhaps anticipating ill at the end of the line, perhaps for rhetorical emphasis.

722-3. Cf. *King Horn* 1455-6 and note in Hall's ed., especially *Seven Sages* 3019-20 —
> And wele he saw that by na gyn
> Allane tp hir myght he noght wyn.

L 727. [e]f: MS. Of. Scribal e/o confusion; cf. also L 767, L 1533, L 1547, C 899.

736. Cf. C 855; *Ferumbras* 1919, 1936, 2754, 2993, etc. The more usual forms of this phrase are *heyly hang, hanged on hye*, etc. See *Guy of Warwick* (MS. Caius) 304, 636; *ib*. (MS. B) 1928, 2639, etc.; *Amis and Amiloun* 636; *Squyr of Lowe Degre* 290; *Gamelyn* 879; *Morte Arthure* 464.

In *Guy of Warwick* (MS. A 629-46) there is a similar dialogue between the hero and Felice. When he makes protestations of love, she threatens him with her father's wrath and with hanging, in spite of her maid's pleadings on his behalf. But his answer, implying that there is no privilege that he would esteem more highly than to die in the cause of love, is in contrast with that of Sir Degrevant, who appeals to his lady's pity, and failing that, will rely upon his own valour.

L 739. wakyn (my) woȝhe is an unusual phrase, formed apparently on the pattern of the commoner *waken woe*: cf. *Isumbras* 227, 323, 419; *Destr. Troy* 1404, 2046, 8183; *Pistill of Susan* 297.

L 751-2. In his fondness for filling out lines, L (reciter or copyist) has omitted to observe that the addition of words has dislocated the syntax: **lyke** now lacks an appropriate subject.

C 765. [b]e ton: MS. leton, perhaps *beton*, as the two words are written as one, and the first letter is closely followed by the second. The bow of the *l* (or *b*) is not brought round to meet the upright. Similar combinations are found in 775 (**berde**) and 786 (**let**); the disputed reading resembles the second more closely than the first. Luick reads **let on**.

C 771. Cf. *Parlement of Thre Ages* 485, 496.

L 773. **stirred** for *sterde*: the rime demands the form derived from *i* lengthened and lowered: cf. *Cursor Mundi* 24101-2 —
> Mi steuen þat i was wont to stere
> Vnnethes moght i self it here;

also Luick, *Hist. Gram.* §393/1. *stere* is the usual northern form. The *i*-form is a scribe's blunder, **in hert** a reciter's interpolation.

781. 3ole-nyȝhte: apparently a translation loan fr. ON. Jólanótt, and probably meaning Christmas Eve, at least in English. Both Julius Cæsar (*BG.* VI, 18) and Tacitus (*Germ.* 11) refer to the Germanic custom of reckoning the day from nightfall to nightfall; and Bede (*De Temporum Ratione* 15), in discussing the season of Yuletide, records the observance among the ancient Angles of a *modranicht* (night of mothers) which he identifies with the Saviour's birth. See also *OE. Martyrology* ed. G. Herzfeld, EETS. 1900, p. 2.

A fourteenth-century carol from Stuttgart mentions the belief that the Saviour was born at midnight—
> Quando noctis medium
> factum est silentium,
> virginis in gremium
> misit deus filium, etc.

See F. J. Mone, *Hymni Latini*, Friburg 1853, I 41; also Mirk's *Festial* ed. T. Erbe, EETS. ES. 1905, I 21.

789-91. Both versions seem to have gone astray, though in different ways. L 789 is in oblique narration, and C 789 is in direct speech. As L is less dramatic than C, and as the following lines are in direct speech in both texts, C is to be preferred in this regard.

In 790-1 the order is reversed, and the meaning of **let(t)** is in question. **Lett** (L) means 'hinder'; **let** (C) means 'allow' (OE. *lettan, lētan*, which may have the same form in ME.). Here L seems to preserve the better reading, which I take to mean 'If only you don't disturb me, you may do what the devil you please.' This more completely expresses the impatience that seems to be implied, than the three parallel main clauses in C, the effect of which is comparatively tame. On the other hand the order in L, which makes the *if*-clause into a parenthesis, is awkward. The original may therefore have read something like this —

> 'Damesel, (?go) do þi best,
> ' So þou ne let me of my rest;
> 'Go glad the with þi gest
> 'In twentty deuyll way.'

L 798. **euermore**: the -*more* produces a halting line. It is probably not original.

C 808. Cf. 1160; *Octavian* 414.

C 811-2. are repeated 1427-8. Cf. also *Triamour* 1694. The same or similar alliteration is also found in *Gawain* 979; *Morte Arthure* 162, 235.

C 815-6. Cf. *Perceval* 1325 —

> Scho made hym semblande so gude
> Als þay felle to þaire fude,
> The mayden mengede his mode
> With myrthe at þe mete.

C 838. Cf. L 1749; *Perceval* 44.

C 840. The last twelve lines of this stanza return to the lyrical feeling of stanza XXXIV (see 529n). The phrase *wonges wete* is more characteristic of the ME. lyric than of the romance. See C. Brown (13) 9/19, 108/14, 141/1, 26; C. Brown (14) 4/13, 34/88, 42/66; *Cursor Mundi* 18308, 25552; *Destr. Troy* 1521; *Joseph of Arimathie* 647; *York Plays* X 275.

C 848. Cf. 1288, C 1416 'I assure you that it is so'. One of the numerous ME. phrases asserting the truth of what is said, **hand** being used symbolically for the taking of a pledge. *Sir Degrevant* has **(do yow) with outen (owt of) drede** (441, C 873); **sertaynly** (605, L 1913); **withouten nay** (213); **in hert es nott to hyde** (196, 1104, 1340); **(es) noght to layne** (682, 1629).

C 861. 'The Duke has sent to say that he wants a tournament to be held for her, and my lord has agreed to hold it here.'

**Gerle** is probably a fictitious name. Chevalier (*Sources Historiques du Moyen Age, Topobibliographie*, Vol. I) notes that *Gelre* is a form of *Gueldres*; but in *Sir Degrevant* it is implied that Gerle is in France (1183).

C 865. This use of *of* to indicate the relation between the Duke and his accompanying retinue is exceptional. The more usual idiom in ME. as in ModE. is *with* (see OED. *s. v.* With 22).

C 885. Luick's *igyf I* is based on a misreading of the MS. The **I** preceding **gyf** is the normal capital; after **gyf** is a single stroke (resembling *l*) which I ignore. An *i* representing OE. ge- is improbable in the present tense at this date.

891. On the question whether a knight by virtue of his rank alone had legal authority to confer knighthood on another, the views of historians are conflicting. Since this authority was sometimes expressly given to a man of exalted rank (e.g., a commander of the royal army), the natural inference is that it did not belong by right to others. (see G. G. Coulton, *Knighthood and Chivalry*, Encycl. Brit. 11th ed., Vol. XV, pp. 857-8, and the authorities there quoted.) The implication of the following lines is at variance with what we find in *Sir Degrevant* —

> To be called a kniȝte is faire . for men shal knele to hym;
> To be called a kynge is fairer . for he may knyȝtes make.
> *Piers Plowman*, B. xix, 28-9.

C 893. The absolute use of *recommand* is rare in ME. The more frequent formula is 'I recommand me to your Lordship', particularly common in fifteenth-century letters; cf. also 896, and the list of epistolary formulas collected in H.C. Wyld, *History of Mod. Colloquial English*, p. 379. The *me* has possibly fallen out of the text.

C 894. The original may have read

> To þy lady and myne,

thus avoiding the rime on the identical word in the following line.

C 899-900. As it stands, the text is impossible to interpret, since Sir Degrevant had no cause to *thank* his lady for being poor, whatever meaning is given to *poor*. I therefore emend **þonke** to **þenke**, and translate:—'lest she rashly make up her mind that I am a worthless creature'.

NOTES 133

C 904. The reciter has forgotten the true reading, now irrecoverable, and has filled in with a tag, anticipating the sense of the following line.

C 913. **I take on hand**, etc. A similar sentiment occurs in *Sir Beues* (MS. A) 82 —
    Dame, boute ich do þe nede
    Ich graunte, þow me for-bede
    þe londe þourȝ out.

C 923. **watur-wal**: in spite of the definition given in the OED. ('wall which rises by the side of water'), Miss Rickert's translation 'moat' has much to commend it. The passage as a whole seems to imply a distinction between the **wall** and the **watur-wal** (the OED. apparently assumes that they are identical). If so, the poet may well have in mind some sort of channel or arm of the sea, furnishing protection against attack from that quarter, capable of being waded at low tide, and overlooked by the skirting-wall of the castle, which was pierced at one point by a secret gate ('a place in þe wall'). It could not have been a moat in the ordinary sense, as we are given to understand that Sir Degrevant was being introduced to something that he did not previously know of; he would have had to cross a moat at some point in order to enter the castle at all. Such a channel could well have been forty feet wide, but a stone wall of such thickness is unlikely.

C 932, C 936, C 940, C 944. An odd collocation of textual errors in the tail-rimes: **byfore, cornes, morow, hawþrone**. The original must have had *byforne, corne, morne, hawporne*.

C 941. Cf. 1579, 1690; *Morte Arthure* 3718; *Wars of Alexander* 3844.

C 946. **reten[ue]**: MS. **reten**. An instance of purely scribal corruption due to misreading of *u* as *n* in the successive stages *retenue, retenne, reten*.

C 949–50. The method of transition known by the rhetorician's name of *occupatio* (see 1425–6; Geoffroi de Vinsauf, *Poetria Nova* 1159; Chaucer, *Squire's Tale* 652, etc.)

C 986. A *ne* may have dropped out before *emperour*.

C 991. Gifts of rings are common in the romances, but usually they have some supernatural significance. Cf. *Ywain and Gawain* 737, 1527. In *Perceval* 425, 474, the original virtue of the rings has been ignored in the English version.

C 1007–8. 'And if my chamber were prepared, nothing would go amiss.' This is almost certainly what is meant, though it involves taking **for-ȝood** in an unusual sense. Elsewhere in ME. it is nearly always transitive.

L 1014. **tonage**: *n* not clear, and is possibly *u*. Tonage, however, can be taken to mean 'wine allowance', parallel to *bouche of court*, 'food allowance'. This makes better sense than C's **and waȝe**, which can be accounted for by supposing an intermediate version *touage*. For a contrary opinion, see the Glossary of Luick, who takes *touage* as a scribal error for *to wage*.

L 1021–4. A quatrain has been displaced: these lines correspond to C 1025–8 in stanza LXV. This dislocation may be a memorial error, followed by deliberate editing. The line corresponding to C 1028 has to be adapted to its new position in stanza LXIV, and is re-written on the pattern of L 1200, which makes poor sense here. But the editorial process is not completed: L 1028 continues the rime-scheme of stanza LXIV, and has nothing to do with that of LXV. Whether the L-text was substantially as it is now before it was committed to paper cannot be determined, but the resulting untidiness, obvious enough in a modern edition, would not be nearly so apparent in a text written straightforwardly in columns, with no break between one stanza and the next.

The transposition has had the effect of slightly improving continuity, in the sense that the words of the interview between Duke and Earl are contained in one stanza, and not divided between two, with a descriptive passage intervening. The corresponding lines in C provide poor sense, which would be improved by adopting the line-order of the displaced passage in L, and reading —
    þe ryche Duke, when he hym mete
    With mayd Mildore þe swet,
    þe Eorl hertely hym hete
    To haue hyr for ay.
But no emendation can remove the awkward syntax of both versions: **Duke** is taken to be the subject of the main verb until the introduction of **Erle** and the unskilful juggling with pronouns in L 1027 (C 1022).

L 1022 (C 1023). For **swete** as applied to the heroine, see also 1296.

C 1028. Cf. *Coer de Lion* (ed. Weber) 4921; *Siege of Jerusalem* 355; *King Edward and the Shepherd* 787; *Rowlande and Ottuell* 118.
The usual meaning in ME. of *make it tough* is 'make difficulties about doing something, show reluctance' (see OED. *s. v.* Tough, 8). Here the expression is being used in some extended sense: 'be persistent'. The Earl's knights were prepared to hold the Duke's chivalry in esteem, since he proclaimed his devotion to women, and persisted in his courtship of Melidor.

C 1030. **armes he hadde [t]onn**: MS **conn. armes** for *harmes* is either a memorial error or a dialectal omission of *h*. The same substitution has occurred in the other MS. (see below, L 1117). *Conn* for *tonn* is a scribal *c/t* confusion.

1045–55. A difficult passage, partly owing to the author's amateurish heraldry, partly to textual divergence. It is actually impossible to blazon the whole achievement from the details given.
Certain facts, however, are clear enough. The achievement contains a double tressure and a saltire engrailed. The double tressure is part of the Royal Arms of Scotland, and was granted only to Scotsmen related to the Royal House. It is usually borne flory counterflory, a heraldic term translated (in C only) as 'With . . . **trewellouus bytwene**'. The saltire is also Scottish; the engrailing is a mark of cadency distinguishing the second son, i.e. Gawain apparently being the elder. As a matter of history, the two together do not seem to have been granted to any of the Scottish noble houses. Hence Sir Degrevant's coat of arms must be regarded as a poetic fancy, and Miss Rickert's suggested identification of him with James, Second Earl of Douglas, cannot stand. (A writer attempting such a portrait, and expecting it to be recognized, would almost certainly include in the blazon a crowned heart, or three estoiles, or both). The typically Scottish arms are given to the hero to emphasize his descent from Lot, King of Lothian and Orkney.
The relative disposition of saltire and tressure is a question not so much of heraldry as of textual interpretation. L implies that they covered the whole field; C that the saltire was borne in chief. The difficulty involved in the first interpretation is textual: if **schelde** be original, how came it to be displaced by a rarer word employed in a highly technical sense? That involved in the second is heraldic; if the double tressure be the main charge, the result is a very empty-looking achievement; the double tressure enclosing, apparently, nothing at all.
The next difficulty is the meaning of **bagges**. There is a heraldic device, borne by the Earls of Moray, that in old blazons much resembles a bag (see W. Fraser, *The House of Douglas*, Edinburgh 1885, Vol. 1, facing p. 450). It is known heraldically as a *cushion*, and is the conventional representation of a wool-pack. Cushions are usually employed in threes, and possibly this number might be used to fill the space left in the centre of the double tressure. The objection to this course is that they never seem to have been called *bags*.
A better though not wholly satisfactory explanation is that **bagges** means 'badges', and refer to the lion and the oak-tree in the following lines. But in strict heraldry the badge was never included in the blazon; it was a retainers' emblem not worn by the owner, hence the description in the poem would not help the Duke to recognize Sir Degrevant (see A. C. Fox-Davies *Complete Guide to Heraldry*, London 1909, pp. 452–3). To take **bagges** in a non-technical sense, signifying the main charge on the field, is to raise the question of why it is plural.
In observance of the rule that metal shall never be placed on metal, nor colour on colour, **blake** must mean either 'white' or 'yellow', and both senses are possible (see OED. *s. vv.* Blake, Bloke, OE. blāc); then **gold** (C) must stand in preference to **gowlys**, gules. The badge was therefore a white (or yellow) lion tied to an oak-tree with green leaves and gold (i.e. yellow) acorns; i.e., 'an oak-tree proper fructed or'.
The crest consisted of a dolphin (colour not mentioned) with a fleur-de-lis on its head.

L 1046. **sawtour**: MS. **sayntourr**. An obvious error: a *sayntour*, or *seynture* (OFr. ceinture) is a girdle, but no such device was known to contemporary English heraldry.

1056. Cf. 1492.

1057. The divergence in reading is possibly due to scribal confusion of *l* and *b* (for an earlier instance, see 681 and note). C has the better reading here, but not in the following line; it is doubtful if C 1058 makes sense at all.

1062. Cf. L 1130. St. Martin is frequently invoked in the romances, perhaps because the best known legend about him tells how he divided his cloak with a beggar, and gifts of clothes (see 86–7 and note) were welcome to minstrels. The actual name of Martin was also useful as a riming word, and in the following poems is employed as such: *Octouian* 705; *Sir Beues* 1049, 2903, 3504, 4302; *Guy of Warwick* (MS. A) 2903; *ib.* (MS. B) 6468; *Gamelyn* 53, 225; *King Edward and the Shepherd* 804. In none of these examples is he called 'Saint Martin of Tours'.

1063–4. The Earl is alluding to the prevailing notion (see also 1129–30, 1305–7) that the faithful lover makes the best knight-at-arms, and also to the hero's reputation for lack of interest in women (see 60–64). The idea is made specific in a passage irrelevantly introduced into *The Sowdane of Babylone* 963–78.

C 1077. **sonne**: a *c* inserted above the line, between the *s* and the *o*, and the word cancelled, owing probably to confusion with the following word. The present MS. reading may be regarded as a modified haplography: the scribe wrote **sonne**, then his eye picked up the following word **scho*n*ne** in his copy, and he assumed he had made a mistake in the word already written. So he inserted the *c*, saw there was no room for the *h*, cancelled the word without referring to his copy, and went on with **scho*n*ne**, thinking he was repeating the word already cancelled.

**en clere**: apparently a Fr. idiom, though the only example quoted in Tobler-Lommatzsch (*Afr. Wörterbuch*) refers to sound, not to light (*Li covenans Vivien* 1473, ed. Jonckbloet, 1854). As an adj., *cler* is constantly used of the sun in OFr. (li soleilz fut cler, *Chanson de Roland* 157). L preserves the more normal ME. expression, but it is not necessarily original.

1080. Cf. 1628.

1088. Cf. *Gawain* 151; *Golagros* 603.

1089–90. Cf. Barbour's *Brus* V 111–2 —
off þaim was nane sa hardy
Þat euir ischyt fourth to þe cry;
*Perceval* 1618–20 —
To þe castell gan he cry
If any were so hardy
[For] the maistry to fyghte;
also *Avowing of Arthur* 39, 103.

1095. **thank** with *of* is the usual construction in ME. (see OED. *s. v.* Thank (*vb.*), 3c.

1103. **frouschen** (C), more vivid and expressive than **pressed**. As it contributes to the alliteration, it is probably original.

C 1107. 'Knights were scattered in the street'. The slight obscurity produced by the ellipsis of the auxiliary (see 1823) may have led L astray, for the corresponding line in that MS. contains a finite verb. **Strewed** may have passed into **tombled** possibly by way of *stombled*.

1110–2. A more satisfactory order than that in the text would be —
With swerdis swyftly (smartely?) þay smite,
Þare was ne lengare lyte,
Þay teme sadils full tyte
Thies worthy in wedys.,
This re-arrangement avoids the awkward parenthesis of 1111, with 1112 being left without syntactical relation to the rest of the sentence. Another possibility would be to re-punctuate, putting a full stop after **lyte** and deleting that after **wedys**, but this course is applicable only to L. C has an inferior version: **delyte** for **lyte**, and **sadely** for **sadels**. For parallels to the phrase **þay teme sadils**, see *Morte Arthure* 1801; *Sir Gowther* 431.

L 1111. **langare lyte**: a rare phrase, and probably original. Cf. *Cursor Mundi* 15574; (MS. Cott.) 5790.

L 1113–6. In the MS., 1114 comes after 1115. We invert this order in the text on the authority of C, which avoids the awkwardness of separating **schuldirs** from **beryns** by a complete line. The MS. order is scribal, the result of the turn over after 1112. The scribe wrote 1113 at the head of the new column, referred to his copy, picked up the wrong line (1115), and then added 1114 without drawing attention to the blunder.

But 1116 is now open to suspicion, for three reasons —
   (i) C has a different reading, unimpeachable on syntactical grounds at least. (*Bleed*, used intransitively, emit blood, the more usual sense at this or any period.)
   (ii) L 1114 and 1116 if read contiguously make inferior sense, as *bleed* is not usually employed transitively except to mean 'draw blood from'.
   (iii) The lines (1115, and 1116 in its unemended form) —
       Bryȝhte crounes and brent
       And brathly bledis
are not satisfactory. 1116 has therefore been re-cast by removing **And** (cf. C).

The substitution of **crounes** for the **browus** of C is a memorial error. The author may have had in mind a line from the *Destruction of Troy* (3030) —
   With browes full brent, brightist of hewe.

**Brent** is a northerly word (see OED. *s. v.* Brent *a.*, 2, where the examples invariably alliterate with *brow*), apparently unfamiliar to C, who substitutes **bent**. (For further ME. examples of the phrase *browes bent*, see *Ferumbras* 1074, 1954; *Romaunt Rose* 542, 861, 1217.)

1122. Cf. 1279; *Morte Arthure* 1545.

1123. Cf. *Morte Arthure* 2954: Cheses to sir Cheldrike, a cheftayne noble.

L 1125. **doȝhety**: apparently a memorial dilution, which has the effect of leaving the sentence without a verb.

1126. Cf. C 1330.

1128. The horse of the vanquished knight passes into the victor's possession. Cf. 1135, and *Ferumbras* 476.

1131–2. We are usually told specifically that the knight's mistress actually sees him fight from the castle (see *Bone Florence* 394, 478, 808; *Triamour* 721; *King of Tars* (A) 526; *Launfal* 646; *Ywain and Gawain* 1892; *Perceval* 59, 1399, 1400, *Degaré* 799; *Ipomedon* B 1897–8.

1139–40. 'All the glory of the tournament came to that noble knight.'

1154. Cf. *Ferumbras* 3093.

1155. Neither version is wholly satisfactory. L repeats **Duke,** and the metre of C stumbles. A smoother line would be —
       With þe Erle and a trayn.

1161. Parallels can be found in romance literature to this use of an alternative form of a character's name where rime or alliteration requires it. Cf. *Guy of Warwick* (MS. Caius) 2071–2: *Guyoun* (usually *Guy. Gij*, etc.), *lyoun*; 2411–2 (*Guyoun, reesoun*); *Guy of Warwick* (MS. B) 3745–6 (*Swevon, Gyowne*); *Thrush and Nightingale* 88, quoted in C. Brown (13) 104 (*witnesse, Wawain*) *Gawain* 559 (*worthe, Wawan, wende*), 1010, 1477, etc.; *Sir Beues* (MS. Chetham) 861–2 (*Bevoun, down*).

C 1162. Since **repurueaunce** is apparently a ἅπ. λεγ., and has the authority of only one MS., the re- may be merely a scribal error, caught from the line below.

1165–7. An example of divergent error. In 1165, L's **of** is to be preferred to C's **at,** but as C makes sense of a sort, I have let it remain. Again, C 1167 is difficult to interpret as it stands, though L 1166 provides the clue to the original reading. C's **Whyle . . . lefte** are almost certainly scribal errors for **Where . . . lef**, and I emend accordingly. On the other hand, C's order is easier than L's.

1168. Cf. 1440; *Avowing of Arthur* 772, 1080.

1170. It is doubtful what sense can be made of the line as it stands in C; the noun and the verb have been confused. The text is emended by adopting the verb from L. The original reading may have been 'þat tournayde þat daye out', *out* having the sense of 'to the end' (see OED. *s. v.* Out, *adv.* 7, 7c). Without is apparently not found with this meaning.

1173–5. Cf. *Erle of Toulous* 271–2 —
       And c pownde y have to mede
       And armour for a nobull stede;
*Morte Arthure* 2628–9 —
       He . . . . . . . gafe me gret gyftes
       And c. pounde and a horse and harnayse full ryche.

L 1177 (C 1178). Cf. *Sir Gowther* 39.

C 1187. **to[w]**: MS. **tolly**, which Luick retains in his text, suggesting emendation to *jolly* in the Glossary. (In the Notes, he claims that the *t* might be a *c*, but this is not so.) Though *jolly*, gallant, makes sense of a kind, **tow** is a much easier reading in the context. Sir Degrevant would be accompanied by a small number of knights on such an expedition, and it is reasonable to suppose that the number would be mentioned. Palæographically, the emendation to **tow** has much to commend it, since a badly made *w* could be misread as *lli* and transcribed as *lly*. The reading **tolly** for original *iolly* presupposes an original *i* mistranscribed as *t*, and this is less likely. The L-reading ( . . . **a knyghte**) lends additional support to **tow**.

1188. **proudest** / **pryuest**. The author probably wrote **preuest**, most valiant (ME. preu⟨OFr. preu, brave), which was independently corrupted to **proudest** (memorial dilution?) and **pryuest** (doubtful spelling for *pryuyest*, most secret). C's error, involving confusion of *u*-vowel and *v*-consonant, is at least partly scribal.

1189–92. Four lines are missing in L. There has been an attempt to fill the gap by adopting the first four lines of stanza LXXVI into LXXV, and by re-casting the tail-rime 1204.

1190. The OED. does not record *damsel* in the sense of 'young man', but this must be the meaning here, since there is no thought of Sir Degrevant's knights disguising themselves as girls. The word is common enough in OFr. in the form dameisel (ModFr. demoiseau). For examples, see *Couronnement de Louis* 217; *Aucassin et Nicolete* 2, 10; 5, 15.

C 1198. **topteler**, which the OED. regards as of uncertain etymology and meaning, is probably a compound of French origin. The general meaning required by the context is obviously some item in a horse's harness.

The first element I derive from OFr. top, toup, a Germanic borrowing (cf. L.G. \**topp*- OFris. *topp*, etc.) meaning 'tuft of hair'. One of the special senses of the diminutive *toupet*, both in French and English is 'forelock of a horse'. *Toppet* (OFr. topet) has the more general meaning 'top, tip'.

The rest of the word is to be connected with OFr. telerie, Mod. Fr. toilerie used in the general sense of 'cloth goods'. **Topteler** will then mean some kind of decorative headpiece made of cloth.

L has omitted the first element and re-duplicated the suffix.

L 1201. **hilled.** The scribe has confused ME. *hele* < OE. helian with ME. *hyl(e)* < OE. \*hyllan or ON. hylja. See OED. *s. v.* Hele (*vb*¹), etymological note.

C 1210. The MS. reading **in his rest** is suspicious on account of the identity of the rime-sound. *Rest* can mean 'holder for a spear', but not 'holder for a helmet'. L has the better reading.

1216. Cf. 1304.

L 1217 (C 1218). The knight (or the messenger) rides up to the dais soon after the assembled company have sat down to table, and especially while the first course is being served. Cf. *Gawain* 135; *Perceval* 486, 953, 1341; *Horn Childe* 544; *Lay le Freine* 43; *Torrent of Portyngale* 1143; and especially *King of Tars* 85–7 —

> As þe soudan sat at his des,
> Yserued of þe first mes,
> Þai com in to þe halle.

C 1227. **sweme**: the scribe has confused (1) ME. *swyme*, OE. swīma; (2) ME. *sweme*, derived either from OE. -swǣman, or, in view of the sense, more probably from ON. svimi, svimr (with lowering and lengthening of the stem vowel), giddiness. See OED. *s. vv.* Swime (*sb.*) and Sweam (*sb.*) and etymological note.

The phrase *swowne in swyme* is uncommon, but cf. *Destr. Troy* 8046, 10365. *Morte Arthure* has it in more extended form —

> he swounnes on þe swarthe *a*nd one swym fallis.

The scribe has also omitted the *n*-suspension from **in**; the line as it stands in the MS. looks as though he had taken **sweme** to be a verb.

The use of **other**, the one or the other (of us), appears to be archaic at this period: OED., *s. v.* Other *absol.*, B. 1, quotes several examples from OE. and EME., but none later than the fourteenth century. Yet it probably belongs to the original poem, and the iambic line in L is a modernized version.

## NOTES

**1239. Reson:** the motto. Cf. *Squyr of Lowe Degre* 213–4 —
>Above the head wrytten shall be
>A reason for the love of me.

**1247. Bryght** is the author's favourite epithet for the heroine: cf. 1359, 1471, L 1611, C 1775, C 1777.

**1256.** Cf. *Sege off Melayne* 948, 969, 1236; *Rowlande and Ottuell* 166, 802, 1396; *Ferumbras* 545; *Isumbras* 170.

**L 1268, 1272.** Another example of division of the stanza into two parts resulting from corruption of tail-times.

**L 1271. awen** upsets the rhythm and is unnecessary to the sense. It is probably not original.

**C 1272.** An easier line is made by reading 'Tak what hap ledis'.

**C 1282.** Sense of a kind can be made by taking **iusset** with its etymological meaning of 'approached'. OFr. juster < late pop. Lat. juxtāre. OFr. joster, juster, is frequently used in this sense. But **iusset or** is almost certainly a scribal misreading of *in ffe(u)tor*, as in L.

**1292.** Cf. 1424, 1719; Halliwell's note in his ed. of the poem, p. 301; *Morte Arthure* 204 —
>Vernage of Venyce vertuouse and Crete.

**Crete:** not found in the OED. A further example in *Extracts from the Account Rolls of the Abbey of Durham* (ed. Surtees Soc. 1899) Vol. II, p. 563: *Empcio Vini.* In 1 lag. et 1 pynte de Crete empt. in villa per Capellanum, 4s. 6d. (the date is c 1360).

**C 1294.** [ġ]o, MS. so: a scribal error. Confusion is easy between certain forms of *s* and *g*, e.g., those used by Hand B in this MS.

**1295. sett all on seuen,** 'fight with all my strength'. Cf. *Morte Arthure* 2131; *Golagros and Gawain* 668, taken from OED. *s. v.* Seven, B. *sb.* 3*b*.

**L 1305. knyght[e]**, MS. **knyghtis**. Emendation is necessary in order to avoid the change of number in 1307. This seems to be an example of purely scribal corruption, due to confusion of the contractions for *sir* and *es/is*. *Sir Aunterous* is the fanciful name for Sir Degrevant (cf. 1385 and also 422).

**1313.** Miss Rickert's suggestion that **damesele** refers to the waiting-maid appears to be without foundation. To lead her knight a fresh steed in the midst of the tournament is a fearless and spontaneous act that is far more characteristic of Melidor. Sir Degrevant has shown himself to be worthy of her, and she chooses this method of recognising him as her lover, quite prepared to flout the convention that young ladies should remain outside the lists (1131–2) during the tourney. The tone of her remarks to the Duke in the following lines is equally decisive.

**L 1313.** MS. **The ta damesele:** so also Luick's text. His Glossary has the following note: "in der Verbindung *the ta* vielleicht 'der eine' . . . . ; wahrscheinlich aber Schreibfehler und zu tilgen". According to the OED. *s. v.* To (*a*.), the word is always used in pointing contrasts. Since there is nothing of the sort here, and since the word is not found in C, the first part of Luick's suggestion is less acceptable than the second.

**1318. On this stede will I ryde,** etc. Cf. *Sir Beues* (MS. A) 1511–2 —
>he wolde in to his cite ride
>Vpon Arondel be fore is bride.

**1323.** Cf. 1622.

**L 1327. byddand:** 'offering battle, challenging'. See OED. *s. v.* Bid, $v^1$. 2.

**L 1335. for sothe** is metrically unnecessary, and has been inserted apparently for rhetorical emphasis.

**C 1343.** MS. **y haþe nat y my lyff**. The error is probably scribal. Confusion between *þ* and *Þ*, and also between *may* and *my* have combined to bring it about. Parallel to this is the form *Þy* for *Þay* in C 1282.

**1360.** Cf. *Destr. Troy* 471.

**1382. In his armes,** etc. Parallels are abundant. See *The Squyr of Lowe Degre* 281, 1090, and especially 1067–8 —
  The squyr her hente in armes two
  And kyssed her an hundreth tymes and mo;
also *King Horn* 430; *Havelok* 2162; *Degaré* 671–3; *Eger and Grime* 1163–4; *Guy of Warwick* (MS B) 1347, 3821, 10460; *Ywain and Gawain* 4006–7; Chaucer, *Troilus* V 191. *Nun's Priest's Tale* 4367 parodies the cliché.

  L 1382. **hent**: on the development of *e* > *i* 'vor gedecktem Nasal, namentlich im Norden und angrenzenden Teilen des Mittellandes' see Luick, *Hist. Gram.* §379c. The scribe has substituted the more common and unraised form.

  L 1385. See note on 561.

  1389. **fett** (probably) / **isete**. An example of the common confusion of *f* and long *s*, but which is the original reading is not clear. The first letter of the word in L is indistinct, owing to the scribal habit of elongating the preliminary stroke of the *e*. Luick's text has *sett*, and 'vielleicht *fett*' in a footnote.

  1397. **yuore** (C) < OFr. yvoire is original, as it fits the rime. L has **yvorye** < N.Fr. ivurie. The details in this passage—the ivory table-top, the trestles to support it, and the table cloth—may be paralleled in French and German romances. See A. Schultz, *Das höfische Leben zur Zeit der Minnesinger* I 66 and notes.

  1401. **Alsame, Eylyssham**, is modern Aylsham (Norfolk). It lies about fourteen miles north of Norwich, in the hundred of South Erpingham. "This Town in the Time of *Edward* the 2d and 3d was the chief Town in the *County*, for the *Linnen Manufacture*; In old Records, nothing more common than the *Ailesham Webbs*, the *Fine Cloth* of AILESHAM, the *Ailesham Linnens*, &c. but about the Time of Henry VIII. I find it much decreased, and the Woollen Manufacture had got the upper hand." (F. Blomefield, *History of Norfolk*, London 1769, Vol. III, p. 558.)

  The towels in *Sir Degrevant* were probably of linen. The following will show the contemporary importance of the industry, and the widespread fame of the product —
  1. *In Orig' de anno regni D'ni E[dwardi III] Regis Angl' & Franc' videl't Angl' decimo nono Franc' sexto.*
  R. concessit Jo𝔥i de Heythe de Oulton custodiam assaie tela*rum* de Aylesham & panni linei de Betele & flammiolo*rum* de fili lineo que vocant' coverchiefs de Salle hend' q*u*amdiu, &c., *per*cipiendo de qualibet pecia de Aylesham & de quolibet panno de Betele & de qualibet duodena flammiolo*rum* fact*is* in com' Norff' *pro* labore suo & *pro* consignacio*n*e eo*run*dem un*um* quadrantem salvis R. forisfacturis, &c. (*Rotulorum Originalium Abbreviatio* II. 173; see also *Calendar of Close Rolls*, 1345, p. 596).
  2. *Calendar of Patent Rolls*, 1301, p. 603. Grant to the mayor, bailiffs, and good men of the town of Oxford of murage for five years. The customs include, on every 100 of linen cloth of Aylesham . . 1d.
  3. *Calendar of Charter Rolls*, 1462, p. 159. Grant of franchises and liberties to the burgesses of Ludlowe who may take the following tolls and customs on the following . . . from every hundred and fifty four of web of Aylesham . . . 1d.

  1406. **basyn and ewere**: cf. *Octouian* 1299–1300 —
  Lauor and basyn they gon calle
  To wassche and aryse;
*Floris and Blauncheflour* 845–6 —
  With water and clooth and basyn
  For to wesshe his hondes ynne.

  L 1407–8. The reading is impossible: the basin and the ewer cannot be 'of' the river. **Þe ryuere** (L) is the result of memorial contamination with C 810 (not in the present text of L, owing to a leaf having been torn from the MS.), itself prompted, perhaps, by a vague memory of the original **Watyr** (C) after the rare word **euerrose** has been forgotten.

  Rose water was used in the mediæval toilet, and is sometimes alluded to in the romances (see A. Schultz, *op. cit.* Index, *Rosenwasser*).

  1409. Allusions to feasting and accounts of feasts with or without details of the food consumed are common in English romances. Most of the feasts described there are elaborate public meals presided over by the King or some other important person.

The situation in *Sir Degrevant*, wherein the meal is served in the lady's bower or in some other private place, is comparatively rare. Cf., however, *Gawain* 875 ff.; *Degaré* 817 ff.; *Eger and Grime* 843–6; *King Edward and the Shepherd* 303–7, 395–400; and especially *Sir Beues* (MS. Chetham) 860–4, where the lady receives the hero after battle and gives him food and drink —
> A borde was sett, a cloth was spred.
> Whan she had on-armed Bevoun,
> At the Bord they set ham down
> And made them well at ease and ffyne
> With riche metes and nobull wyne.

L 1412, 1416. These lines provide one more example of how a stanza is halved by the re-writing of tail-rimes. 1416 is particularly open to suspicion in this context as it virtually repeats 1411. The tail-lines came to assume their present form owing probably to the fact that they are both colourless expressions and hence interchangeable, and partly perhaps because the form **hete** (OE. hēt, contr. past tense of hātan, used as an infinitive) was unknown to L. Neither scribe, apparently, knew the ME. form *wete* < OE. witan.

C 1414. Tolkien and Gordon quote the following from *The Master of Game* (*Gawain* 1456n) — 'þei (boars) haue herd skynne and stronge flessh, and specially vpon þe shoulder, þat is called þe shelde'.

**Scheld** is a better reading than **schuldir** (L 1415). Cf. *Avowing of Arthur* 166.

L 1421. See L 519 and note.

1425. See C 949–50 and note.

1430. Cf. *Launfal* 344; *Sir Beues* (MS. A) 2303; and especially *Morte Arthure* 203 —
> Rynisch wyne and Rochell, richere was neuer.

L 1438. See L 519 and note.

C 1439. **Þe chaumbur of loue**: the bower, appropriate for love-making.

1441 ff. A similarly elaborate description of the inside of a room is found in *Wars of Alexander* 3664–3703. For a general study of mediæval bedroom furniture, etc., see Thomas Wright, *The Homes of Other Days*, London 1871, pp. 123 ff., 258 ff., 408 ff.

L 1442. **aboffe**: probably a repetition of **aboue** in 1437, or an anticipation of 1443.

1444. **beşantes full bryghte** Cf.1499; *Morte Arthure* 3256; *Winner and Waster* 61.

1446. C offers a better text than L, though good sense cannot be made of it without emendation. The MS. form **oger** I take to be a scribal error for **ogee**, the diagonal rib of a vault, which then makes a good pair with **parpon**, binding stone (see OED. *s. v.* Parpent, of which **parpon** might be a variant form). Both these were new words at the time of *Sir Degrevant* (indeed, if **ogee** is an acceptable emendation it will slightly antedate any example in the OED.). **Ogee** then becomes **Egir** in the L-tradition through confusion of *o* and *e* through some such stages as *ogee* (*oȝe*, *eȝe*), *egir*. **Egir** is then taken to be the hero of the English romance of *Egir and Grime*, and Urban is given him as a partner.

L cannot be seriously considered as preserving the original reading. To do so will raise the question why Egir and Urban should be put up in the ceiling, and indeed why they should be mentioned together at all.

By **Vrbane**, L probably means Urban of the Black Thorn, a minor figure in the so-called Didot *Perceval*. While guarding a ford at the request of his lady, he challenges Perceval and is overthrown. His lady helps him with her maidens transformed into birds. Perceval kills one of the birds; it becomes a woman again and is carried off by the others to Avalon. Urban is not mentioned in the English Romance of *Sir Perceval* or in Chrétien's poem.

C 1451. 'fifty, each after the same design'.

The L reading is inferior, and **on þe molde** is scarcely more than a tag. The most satisfactory text is produced by conflating readings from both MSS. —
> Þer men myght, whoso wolde,
> Se archangells of golde,
> Fefty made of a (?ane) molde,
> Lowand full light.

L's **gleterand** replaces the relatively uncommon **lowand**.

## NOTES 141

The author is probably referring to stone corbels carved in the form of archangels and then gilded. In a church of the period the corbels might be set at the end of vertical shafts dividing the spandrels of the arches, and helping to support the roof. The fifty gilded archangels all alike clearly suggest the frozen glories of the Perpendicular style.

**1455, C 1466, 1467.** Compare *A Song of Mortality* (School of Richard Rolle) in C. Brown (14) 96/13–14 —
>War þou als wyse praysed in pryce als was salomon,
>Fayrer fode of bone and blode þen was absalon . . . etc.

The author, unlike our poet (whose aim is glorification), goes on to expatiate upon the vanity, *sub specie æternitatis*, of the mental and physical qualities that these two characters typify—wisdom and bodily beauty. A similar thought is found *ib.* 238/13–15, in a list which also includes *aristotil þe filosofre*.

The parables of Solomon are *The Book of Proverbs*. To decorate a room in such a fashion is most unusual in romances. A possible parallel is found in *Aye d'Avignon*, p. 78 (ed. F. Guessard and P. Meyer, Paris 1861, quoted in A. Schultz, *op. cit.* I, 60, note 8) —
>Ens une chambre painte de l'evre Salemon.

The significance of *evre* is vague: it might refer, as in *Sir Degrevant*, to Solomon's writings, or to scenes from his life, or even to his seal, the pentangle.

**1465–8.** Both MSS. are wrong. The starting point of the error is probably the reading **lyked** for **layked** in both: *þat layked ful ylle* 'who behaved very badly.' This identity in error goes back to X, but the rest of the quatrain is apparently reproduced with accuracy in C. During the period of memorial transmission in L, the order of 1466-7 was inverted, and the remaining variants may be regarded as due to reciter's forgetfulness and a desperate attempt to repair the damage from a recollection of Absalom's story. **purtred** becomes **paynted** (L substitutes **paynted** for **paued** in 1485, **fylesoferus** becomes **fele feris** (Absalom's confederates, presumably), **ylle** becomes **wele**, impairing both sense and rime. I have attempted to restore the original in both texts.

**L1470. curse** (Luick *ourse*) / **ours**. Though the MS. character is badly made, it is almost certainly a *c*. The original reading, however, may well be *ours*; L, who substitutes *c* for *o*, and Luick, who substitutes *o* for *c*, have been led astray by the same type of illegibility.

**1473. Corven wyndows**, etc. Glazed windows were still, even in the late fourteenth century, the occasion for comment when used in houses. Cf. the description of Priam's palace in the *Destr. Troy* 1648 ff. —
>The windowes, worthely wroght in a mesure,
>Shapyn full shene all of shyre stones,
>Caruen in Cristall by crafte of Entaile,
>Pight into pilers prudly to shewe
>The bases & bourdurs all of bright perle;

and that of the room of the princess in the *Squyr of Lowe Degre* 93–5 —
>In her oryall there she was
>Closed well with royall glas;
>Fulfylled it was with ymagery;

*King Alisaunder* 7666–8 —
>Theo bemes ther weore of bras,
>Theo wyndowes weoren of riche glas.

**1479. Kyngges** (C) is a better designation of the three Christian Worthies than **Knyghtes**.

**1481.** The Nine Worthies were classified into three sets of three: 'three Paynims, three Jews, and three Christian men'. Only the Christians are here portrayed. For quotations from texts illustrating the Nine Worthies (see Gollancz, Appendix to *The Parlement of the Thre Ages*, especially his quotation from *Les Vœux du Paon*, and note on 1519–20 below).

**1482-3. de** / **þe**: a common confusion; cf. OED. *s. v.* The *dem. adj.* 10 c. The rimes show that the original probably read—
>(Syre?) Godfray de boyloune
>And (*or* Sir) Arthur þe Bretoune,

i.e., the Briton, as Bretayne (L) makes a bad rime. L has assimilated both readings to **de**, C to **þe**, or its equivalent.

**1485–6.** Parallels exist for both versions —
>All wyndowes and all the wallis
>With cristall was peyntid
>>(*Sir Beues*, MS. Chetham 1131–2)
>—but not the floor;
>With a flore þat was fret all of fyne stones,
>Pauyt prudly all with proude colours.
>>(*Destr. Troy* 1660–1).

One is also reminded of how Pandarus found his niece and her friends reading 'withinne a paved parlour' (Chaucer, *Troilus* II, 82). The second and third of these conclusively establish *paued* as the right reading for C, as against Luick's *paned*. The original, too, probably read **paued**, replaced by **paynted** owing to the relative frequency of the word in the passage (see 1456, 1465, 1507). The notion of having a room paved with crystal may be of ultimately French origin (see Benoit de Sainte-More, *Le Roman de Troie* [ed. A. Joly, Paris 1870] 11626–7) —
>. . . une chanbre à or ovrée
>Et de cristal pavimentée;

*Roman D'Alexandre* (ed. Armstrong, Princeton and Paris 1937), Vol. II, Branch III, 3682 —
>li pavemens est a cristal assis.

L 1487. **ouer-cowchid**: MS. **ouer chowchid**. A scribal error due possibly to the *ch* in the latter part of the word. No parallel examples can be given, though **cowchide** in the sense of 'set (with jewels)' is found in L 646. Cf. also OED. *s. v.* Couch *v.* 4, and Over- *pref.* 8.

**1494.** Amadace and Edoyne are frequently mentioned in Middle English poetry along with Tristram and Iseult as the heroes and heroines of romances of ideal love (see *Luue Ron* 67, in *Old English Miscellany* 95; *Cursor Mundi* 20; *Emaré* 121–6; *Parlement of Thre Ages* 614; Gower, *Conf. Am.* VI, 879), though no English romance survives telling the story. The English poem taking Amadace as its hero (see Robson's *Three Metrical Romances*, Camden Soc. 1842) omits all mention of Edoyne, though there is an Old French poem on the subject of the lovers (see G. Paris, *Sur Amadas et Idoine*, in *An English Miscellany presented to Dr. Furnivall*, Oxford 1901).

**1495–6.** Cf. *Squyr of Lowe Degre* 798 —
>With popiniayes pyght with pery read;

*ib.* 837–8 —
>Your tester pery at your heed
>Curtaines with popiniayes white and reed.

Popinjays and 'trulofeȝ' are brought together in the description of the embroidered covering of the hero's helmet in *Gawain* 611–2.

**1497. stowt dedis / scochenus.** The latter is the original reading, and **stowt dedis** a diluted version.

C 1500. **trewelouus** is a better reading than **tressours**. As in C 471, C 1048, it is probably being used in the sense of 'fleurs-de-lis'.

**1505–10.** Cf. *Sir Beues* (MS. Chetham) 3769–70 —
>And an hunderid beddus of sylke
>Also white as any mylke;

*Generides* A. 285–6 —
>Panes of gold, coueringes of silk
>Shetes of lawn, white as mylk;

and especially the *Wars of Alexander* 4916–7 —
>With curtyns all of clene silke. & coddis of þe same,
>With comly knottis & with koyntis. & knopis of perle.

**1508. tasselde / touseled.** The OED. quotes the line from C to illustrate Tousle, *v.* in the sense of 'pull about roughly, . . . disorder', etc. This interpretation is open to doubt, on the grounds of sense alone: implying that the bed was unmade, it is utterly out of keeping with the rest of the passage, since everything else in the chamber is such a splendid array. Thus the reading in L is to be preferred to the interpretation of the OED.

The EDD. records Tossell, Tossle, as variant dialect forms of Touzle, quoting examples from Northumberland; and Tossel is still a widespread provincial form of Tassel. The two ideas 'tassel' and 'disorder' have now a common spelling *tossel*; it it can be supposed that this spelling was equally possible in the northern dialects of the fifteenth century, there will be no difficulty in also supposing that C confused them. Out of some such spelling as *tosselde* (actually found, perhaps, in the MS. that C was copying), which was ambiguous, came the form **touseled**, which as it stands could have only one meaning, and that an inappropriate one. It seems certain that C intended the other meaning, but the form has been left as it is, because it is not the ordinary type of scribal error.

There are several illustrations of mediæval bedrooms in MSS., and tassels are often seen attached to the pillows (see T. H. Turner, *Domestic Architecture in the Middle Ages*, Oxford 1851 ff., Vol. 2, p. 96; Thomas Wright, *Homes of Other Days*, pp. 124, 413; P. Lacroix, *Les Arts au Moyen Age*, Paris 1869, pp. 20–1), but never to the sheets, as in C—another reason for rejecting C here. On the other hand, the repeated **coddis** in L is suspicious, the first being probably a reporter's anticipation of the second (see Introduction, p. xxvi). Again, **Chalked whyte** is obviously an error, perhaps scribal, for the more familiar *chalk whyte*. The most satisfactory way out of the tangle is to conflate the readings. Originally the poem may have read something like this —

  Faire schetis of silke
  Chalk-whyte als the mylke,
  Coddis poyned of þat ilke
  Tasseldē þay ware.

1511. **Westwale / Westfal.** The original probably read *Westuale* (Westphalia) which later took on the forms with *w* and *f*, of which the latter is the less ambiguous. All three forms are found in *Morte Arthure* 2656 (*u*), 2826 (*f*), and 621 (*w*).

C's statement that the product of Westphalia was **knoppus of crystal** can be substantiated up to a point. *Knop* is of Low German origin, and the manufacture of crystal gems and other objects was carried on in Germany from Carolingian times until the sixteenth century at least (see Brit. Mus. *Guide to Mediæval Antiquities*, 1924, pp. 56, 68, 102).

According to L, it is (apparently) the silk pillows that were made in Westphalia. The statement, in an inferior text, need not be taken seriously.

1513–6. Cf. *Gawain* 854, 857 —
  . . . cortynes of clene sylk . . .
  Rudeleȝ rennande on ropeȝ, rede golde ryngeȝ.

1518–20. As in 131, there is confusion of proper names in both versions, though C preserves the sounder text. The author is apparently alluding to the Duke Betis of Jacques de Longuyon's fourteenth-century romance *Les Vœux du Paon* (see *Les Vœux du Paon* ed. in parallel columns with Barbour's *Buik of Alexander* by R. L. G. Ritchie, STS. Vol. II, l. 162).

Betis's lady is Ydorus (see Ritchie, *op. cit.* 1648–1795) whom he marries. Her name has been corrupted to **Edoyne** in L, owing to the mention of Edoyne (from quite a different story) in 1494; and to **Medyore** in C, owing probably to the name of Melidor as the heroine of *Sir Degrevant*, and to the influence of the neighbouring alliteration.

Since the incident alluded to in our poem is not found in the French, it must be supposed that the author was merely invoking famous names in order to show how wonderful the 'cordes' were. *Les Vœux du Paon* in particular quite markedly avoids the supernatural altogether; there is no mention of mermaids. On the other hand, it is at least possible that there once were other, and no longer extant, versions of the story that would explain our poet's allusion.

In the fourteenth and fifteenth centuries, *Les Vœux du Paon* came to be widely known in England. Indeed, our author's allusion to the Nine Worthies (1481–4) is probably derived, perhaps directly, from his knowledge of a famous passage in the poem (7484–7579). Besides the Scottish translation referred to above, a fragment of another has been preserved; it is found in the same Cambridge MS. as *Sir Degrevant* (see K. Rosskopf, *Editio Princeps des me. Cassamus*, Erlangen 1911). The poem is also alluded to in Lydgate's *A Praise of Peace* 159 (H. N. MacCracken, *Minor Poems of John Lydgate*, EETS. II, 790).

In the romances, mention is sometimes made of hair being used for decorative purposes. Thus, in *Escoufle* 1146, there is a description of embroidered flowers surrounded by an inscription, the letters of which are stitched with the golden hair of the embroideress; *Les Vœux du Paon* itself tells us (7459–51) how King Arthur killed a giant who made himself a garment with the beards of Kings (the same incident as in *Morte Arthure* 998–1004).

1530–6. Cf. *Sir Beues* (MS. A) 3163–8 —
Nouȝt, þeȝ i scholde lese me lif,
Boute ich were þe weddede wif;
ȝif eni man me scholde wedde,
Þanne mot ich go wiþ him to bedde.

1557–60. The widely distributed folk-custom of courtship in bed without sexual contact is here alluded to. The following is quoted in the *Edinburgh Review* (Vol. X, p. 109) from Charles William Janson's *The Stranger in America* (London, 1807):—
"I have frequently heard of an *amusement* in New England, and particularly in the State of Connecticut, called *bundling*. It is described as being resorted to by lovers. The young couple retire to bed, and there the lover tells his soft tale. One author says that 'bundling has not its origin in New England, as supposed. It has been practised time immemorial in Wales, and is also in general practice in the Isle of Portland. I was informed that servant-girls in Connecticut . . . receive their gallants in the night in bed, with their petticoats tied to their ancles. In Holland, too, this is practised among the peasants, who call it queesting'."

See also Craigie and Hulbert, *Dictionary of American English*, s. vv. Bundle v., Bundler, Bundling; M. Kowalewsky, *Marriage among the Early Slavs*, *Folk Lore*, Vol. I, p. 469; C. Masson, *Narrative of Various Journeys in Balochistan*, etc., Vol. III, p. 287–8; and C. S. Wake, *Evolution of Morality*, Vol. I, p. 401. In the last of these, reference is made to the existence of the practice in Ireland. The custom is too widely spread to help the localisation of *Sir Degrevant*.

1565–6. These lines refer to the squire (now made knight) and the waiting maid. By a memorial error anticipating 1898, she is made into a Countess by L. For a further example of the phrase **countase so clere** (by no means common), see *Athelston* 117.

1573. **knyghte / knyghtus.** C keeps to the same grammatical number throughout and avoids the ambiguity of L, where **knyghte** does not refer to the same person as **knyghte** in 1571.

1575. **foster**: the work of the mediæval forester was to watch for and arrest trespassers, and to preserve the game. He was paid no salary, but he himself paid the forest warden for the privilege of his office, and lived by various acts of extortion from the dwellers in the forest. Popular feeling against foresters was strong, and with good reason. The author is exploiting this feeling by making the forester betray the lovers to the steward (i.e., probably the forest warden, see note on 121), though technically the man was doing his duty in reporting what amounted to an act of trespass on the part of Sir Degrevant.

L 1580, 1584. The tail-rimes of the latter part of the stanza have been re-written. They still form a pair, but the rime does not conform with that of the former part. Each of the lines is exceptionally feeble.

1581. Cf. *Perceval* 1214 — The wayte appon þe walle lay; *Sir Gowther* 325; and *Ipomadon* A. 3087–93.

C 1584. **mende**: see OED. s. v. Mean vb.[1] and examples cited from Wyclif (*Sel. Wks.* ed. Arnold II, 6) and *William of Palerne* 1925.

L 1585. **pesse**: scribally substituted for the more regular *pays(e)*. The rime with sayse, curtayse, is thus satisfactory.

C 1585. **pypere**: probably a player on the bagpipes. This instrument was in use throughout Europe during the Middle Ages (see Gustave Reese, *Music in the Middle Ages*, London 1941, pp. 383, 409).

C 1588. 'And (it is) reasonable that they should be'.

1593. The steward is the conventional figure of evil in the romances, and as here is often made to impede the progress of true love by telling tales. In *Amis and Amiloun* 769 ff. a steward reports of Belisaunt to her father, and the action is disapproved of by the author (probably a minstrel), even though the steward was fulfilling his duty. In *Guy of Warwick* (MS. A) 3161, a jealous steward wrongfully accuses the hero of dishonouring the Princess Clarice, daughter of the Emperor. In *The Squyr of Lowe Degre* a steward overhears the lovers' conversation, and betrays it to the King (283–300; 339–354), grossly exaggerating the facts. Like the steward in *Sir Degrevant*, he ambushes the hero, who cuts his head off (648).

# NOTES

*Sir Beues* (MS. A 837 ff.) contains a steward who envies the hero's prowess in slaying the boar, and plots against his life, but is himself slain. A steward tries to prevent the entry of Sir Cleges into the King's presence (*Sir Cleges* 325 ff.), and is beaten. In *Guy of Warwick* (MS. B 8881 ff.) the Emperor's ambitious and powerful steward Barrade does his best to ruin Tyrry, who is cast into prison. There is a jealous steward in *Generides*, and false stewards in *Sir Triamour*, and *Roswall and Lilian*.

But the steward is not always evil. Sir Degrevant's own steward, though he comes in for only casual mention in the story (121) is obviously a faithful servant doing his best for his master against the Earl's depredations. Guy of Warwick's father is a steward, and a good man. In *Roswall and Lilian* there are two stewards, one true, one false. In *King Horn* there is a faithful steward, and the part of talebearer is given to someone else. There is also a good steward in *Sir Orfeo*.

L 1594. **gracyous**, in view of the steward's behaviour and of the lack of confirmatory evidence from the other MS., must be regarded merely as a stop gap. The mistake may have arisen owing to a misapprehension of the meaning of **cheualrous**, which is here employed in the neutral sense of 'bold', with no intention of paying a compliment.

Here and in 1649 the steward is called *Sir Aymere* (or *Eymur*); in L 1729 he is *Sir Gaymere*, probably owing to memorial error.

C 1594. **kayous** may mean either —
  (i) Resembling Sir Kay, hence 'uncourtly'.
  (ii) 'Left-handed' derived from ODan. *kei*, left, and a French suffix. Even this may be intended in the sense of 'gauche'.

The balance of probability inclines, perhaps, to (i), as Sir Eymere, like Sir Kay, was a steward. ME. *kay*, left, is a rare word (it is found in *Gawain* 422) and so far as the recorded evidence goes, appears to be confined to Lancashire and Cheshire.

Another possibility is that the MS. form is a scribal error for *kaytyuous*, having the quality of a caitiff, hence villainous. The word is not recorded elsewhere, though the OED. lists several other related compounds in ME.

1601. See 1070 and note.

1608. **paire / hor**: i.e., Sir Degrevant's and her own.

1613–6. The Deity is often invoked by the author speaking in his own person, on behalf of a character, especially when in peril. See *King Horn* 156–8; *Sir Beues* (MS. A) 1262, 1332, 2784, 3619; *Sege off Melayne* 348; *Song of Roland* 253; *Ferumbras* 252, 1508, 2612, 2719, etc.; *Guy of Warwick* 2538, 9466; *Havelok* 331, etc.

L 1617–20. A travesty of the correct version reproduced in C, and a clear example of memorial paraphrase. C gives specific information: **at euenely3th, Two gownes of grene**. L makes a tag of the first of these, and upsets the rime-scheme with the second. He has then to re-cast 1624 to rime with the new sound.

C 1619. **for sy3th**: as a precaution against being seen (see OED. *s. v.* For, 23d).

C 1620. Cf. *Avowing of Arthur* 610.

L 1623. [**þay bere**]: MS. **of were**. The error, caught from the previous line, is merely scribal.

1625. Cf. the account of the ambush in *The Erle of Toulous* 421–456; the similar account of how the hero walks unsuspectingly into a trap set by a steward in *The Squyr of Lowe Degre* (501 ff.) is almost certainly later than, and may possibly be derived from, *Sir Degrevant*.

C 1627. Owing to the hole in the MS., only the last three letters (*ute, nte*) of the first word are visible. **Stoute** is suggested as a possible restoration, partly because the hole is big enough for no more than three letters, and partly because of the alliteration.

1632. Cf. 1668; *Morte Arthure* 1760; Minot XI, 2.

L 1646. **s[ch]rade**: MS. **strade**. The original form, which we restore to the text, was clearly **schrade**, i.e., the past tense of *schrẹde* (OE. scrēadian), cut to pieces (cf. C 309). C has **scharde**, the metathesized form.

C 1654. 'It was inconvenient for the corpse.' A similar type of humour occurs in 1732. Cf. *Avowing of Arthur* 49–50 —

  He is ha3er þenne a hors
  That vncumly corse.

1655. **force / fosse.** Force, ON. fors, waterfall, is probably the original reading. Being a north country word (it is a formative element in the place-names of Yorkshire and Lancashire), it was replaced in C by **fosse**, Fr. fosse, ditch. The rime **fosse, hors, cors,** would be possible only if the *r* had become assimilated to the following *s* (see Jordan, *Mittelenglische Grammatik*, §166; and Wyld, *Colloquial English,* pp. 298–300). This seems the simplest explanation of what has occurred, in view of the L-reading and of other substitutions of the same sort found in C (for a representative list, see the Introduction, Section III). But it is conceivable that **fosse** may represent the assimilated form of *force*, the other rime-words retaining their traditional spelling. The form *fosse* occurs in *Fossedale,* 1280, 1283 (see A. H. Smith, *Place Names of the North Riding of Yorkshire*, Cambridge 1928, p. 259). This assimilation may be older than the ME. period; it is found already in OWScand (see Noreen, *Altisländische Grammatik*, 4th ed., §272.3).

C 1656. **astray:** Dr. C. T. Onions in *The Fate of French -é in English* (SPE. Tract LXI, p. 14) notes two characteristics of this word relevant here: (i) its frequent application to horses in ME; (ii) the tendency to analyse it as though it were a formation parallel to *away* (L **on straye**).

L 1657. **faride**⟨ME. faren substituted for the less familiar **ferde**⟨OE. fēran.

C 1658. **erþe** for **erde:** a similar substitution, also scribal.

L 1664. A memorial reconstruction, influenced by the rime-word in 1652.

C 1670. 'In any way they see.' It is just possible to make sense of this as it stands, though in view of L, the original may have read —
For þe sy3t þat þay sees.
The alliteration of this restored line is very obvious, but not more so than in the poem as a whole.

1680. **feftene** is frequently used in ME. romance to indicate a substantial number, especially of companions: cf. 1832; *King Horn* 37 (and Hall's note); *Tristrem* 817 (and Kölbing's note). The usage is found also in OE. (see *Beowulf* 1583; *Genesis* A, 780).

L 1683. **passede awaye,** 'escaped', not 'died'. For a similar contrast between those who 'passed away' and those who were killed, see *Guy of Warwick* (MS. B) 4932–4 —
All the Lorens at the laste
Were woundyd and slone that day;
Vnnethe xxx[ti] passyd away.
See also *Middle English Sermons* (EETS. 209) 180/11.

1688. **to:** 'if I were to' (see OED. *s. v.* To, B 10b).

L 1700. **swerdis** for **spere:** the error may be merely scribal.

L 1702. **ryuen** is suspect, not only because it makes an imperfect rime, but also because it repeats an idea already expressed in 1698 (and again in 1710).

L 1705–6. These lines, probably containing an awkward repetition of **sayd(e),** are probably corrupt. But C here has the curious phrase **sat semely,** the meaning of which is doubtful.

L 1706. For examples of **þat semly** as a noun, see *Purity* 870; *Gawain* 672; *Destr. Troy* 390, 442, 455, 461, 503, 3004, etc.

1716. Wine was frequently taken spiced in mediæval times, especially at the conclusion of the feast (see *Squyr of Lowe Degre* 825–6; Mead, *English Mediæval Feast,* pp. 127, 128, and list of authorities quoted on p. 244).

L 1735. **haulle:** an early spelling of the developed pronunciation of ME. a+l; whether it indicates the sound [au] or [ɔː] is uncertain (see Wyld, *Colloquial English,* p. 201).

L 1736. **ty3andis,** from ON. tíþ(endi) with the usual ON. -and- ending and an English plural suffix, owes its peculiar form to the fifteenth-century confusion of the spirants *þ, 3, y* (see 1796 and OED. *s.* Th-).

1755–6. For very similar sentiments, see 1786, *Havelok* 317; *Erle of Toulous* 137; *Guy of Warwick* (MS. B) 3695–6, 5121–2, 9687; *Triamour* 103–4; *Sege off Melayne* 1192, and especially *Athelstan* 170–1 —
Meete ne drynk schal do me goode
Tyl þat he be dede.

# NOTES

L 1758 (C 1759). Cf. *Perceval* 2043; *Eglamour* 25–6; *Sir Gowther* 388.

L 1759–60. That these lines are not original is proved by the omission of the link (**cryid**) with the next stanza—a link that C preserves.

C 1772. ȝe made hem all tame apparently is, or conceals, a technical expression, which L dilutes to a form of the commonplace **wild and tame**.

1785. To decide between these variants is a matter of some delicacy, since both make good sense. **Hald it so ġrete** (L) means 'regard it as so important', and hence 'make so much difficulty about it'. The rime sequence on ẹ̄ is perfect. There would be no trouble in accepting this line as original were it not that the corresponding line in C offers a reading that is quite as good or better from the point of view of meaning. **Holde vs a ġret** means 'keep us in (a state of) sorrow', a being the weakened form of *on*. But to regard it as original is to raise the question of rime, since **ġret** has a tense *ẹ̄*. Normally, the poet avoids riming tense and slack *ē* together, even before dentals (see Luick, *Hist. Gram.* 361, note 2, p. 343). Since, however, there is at least one example of such a sequence (565–7), the possibility of there being another cannot be ruled out.

The interpretation offered by the OED. can be rejected. The editor reads **a ġret** as *a-gret*, and quotes the line to illustrate Agreed in the sense of 'brought into harmony, united in feeling or sentiment'. This would be acceptable (apart from the question of rime) only if the conjunction **And ġiff** could be taken to mean 'unless'; i.e., 'unless you bring about a reconciliation between us (the Earl and Melidor), I shall, etc.'. But there is no evidence that it can ever have such a meaning; to assume identity of error in both texts and to emend to *But giff* is here a dubious procedure. The OED. interpretation was perhaps influenced by a reading in *Pearl* 560, where *a gret* was erroneously derived from OFr. à gret, according to mutual agreement (see *Pearl* ed. Gollancz, London 1891, the etymology and interpretation being rejected in the 1921 ed.).

L 1797. [**come**]: MS. **full**, repeated from previous line. The emendation, with C to support it, is simple and obvious.

L 1799–1800. The redundancy in these lines indicates corruption.

L 1805. **h[ym]**: MS. **hir. hym drede** had fear for himself (see OED. *s. v.* Dread *vb.* 4).

C 1805–6. **drade, clade:** (see note on L 473–4).

L 1809–10. The inversion of lines in L is awkward and is unlikely to be original.

1816. L has the neater and more metrical, and perhaps therefore the original version; C reads like a memorial paraphrase.

1819. The original form of this line may well be —
>Þe Erle hym hade kyssed.

1821–3. Cf. *Awntyrs of Arthure* (MS. Douce) 660–1 —
>Withe outene more lettynge,
>Diȝte was here saȝtlynge;
*Ywain and Gawain* 2643–4 —
>Þus he helpid þe maiden ȝing,
>And seþin he made þe saghtelyng.

1823. **ȝynġe.** The OED. regards OE. ġing as Northumbrian, though examples are found also in Mercian texts (see Bülbring, *Altenglisches Elementarbuch*, §307c). In ME. interesting parallel rimes occur in a number of dialects, with the north and east midlands predominating on the whole: see *Cursor Mundi* 3223–4 (*fostring, ying*), 3589–90 (*thing, ying*); *Squyr of Lowe Degre* (W) 358 (*ying, benynge*), 1101 (*yonge* [for *yinge*], *weddyng*); *Guy of Warwick* (MS. A) 1061–2 (*ȝing, tiding*); 1307–8 (*bring, ȝing*); Bokenham, *Legendys of Hooly Wummen* 2445, 2711, 4102, 7285, 8585, 8610 (*brynge, yinge*, etc.). It is a backformation from OE. ġingra.

1824. **to hys lyues ende.** Cf. 1844. A formula not infrequent in descriptions of weddings: see *Sir Beues* (Pynson) 3217–8 —
>to Beuys hyr wedded blyue
>Unto the endynge of hyr lyue;
also *Isumbras* 303; *William of Palerne* 4741.

L 1825. **slyke**: MS. **slylke** is probably a scribal blend of ME. *swylke* and *slyke* (< ON. slíkr).

1843. Cf. *Havelok* 1216.

C 1846. **Reuestyd**: Halliwell and Luick read *Revescyd*, and, I think, erroneously. The scribal forms of the ligatures *sc* and *st* are very similar in construction and appearance. The long *s* is made with the upstroke; the pen is brought round and the vertical part of the *c* (*t*) is made with the downstroke. The flat top of the *c* or the cross of the *t* is made separately, the only difference being that the cross of the *t* extends on both sides of the downstroke, while the top of the *c* meets the downstroke without crossing it. (Typical forms in this part of the MS. are **schamely** 1702, **schylde** 1758, **schene** 1828, **scrye** 1875, **castel** 1807, **sterne**, **stoute** 1810, **wyste** 1817.) Though it is faint on the left-hand side, the horizontal stroke extends on both sides of the downstroke in the word under consideration. I therefore read **Reuestyd**. The point is of some importance, as *Revescyd* has found its way into the OED. *s. v.* Revesh.

L 1847. **dyd**. Though the most frequent verbs signifying 'celebrate' (a mass) in ME. are *sing, say*, and occasionally *bede* (offer), there is authority for the use of *do*. See OE. Bede, ed. Miller, p. 328 (2 examples); *Vices and Virtues* 65; *Bury Wills* (Camden Soc.) 28; *Havelok* 1176; *St. Editha* 305; Lovelich, *Merlin* 25807.

L 1851 (C 1850). Cf. Chaucer, *General Prologue* 460; *Wife of Bath's Prologue* 6; and the authorities cited in Skeat's note on the first passage.

1866. Cf. *Morte Arthure* 200–1 —
>Þane clarett and Creette clergyally rennen
>With condethes full curious, etc.

1869–72. Almost certainly a masque or 'disguising' is being described, similar in kind to the 'daunces disgisi' associated with 'alle maner menstracie' which the Emperor of Rome provides in *William of Palerne* 1620. Such entertainments were usually given at Christmas (see E. K. Chambers, *Mediæval Stage*, Chap. 17). I have not found allusion to any other having the douzepers of France as its subject.

1881. Þ**at fourtnyghte.** With this passage, compare *Eglamour* 1331–4 (near the conclusion) —
>To holde brydale they hente
>Hyt lastyd a fourtenyght.
>When the brydale was alle y-done,
>Eche oon toke ther leve to gone;

*Guy of Warwick* (MS. B) 7099–7102, 7107–8 —
>A ryche brydale was ordeyned thare;
>Hyt stode fowrtene nyghtys and mare.
>There were mynstrels on all manere:
>Moche yoye there men myght here.
>. . . . .
>They partyd on the fyftenyth day:
>Every man wente hys owne waye;

*Squyr of Lowe Degre* 1123–4 (at the end of the wedding feast)—
>And sithen they revelled all that day,
>And toke theyr leve, and went theyr way.

C 1882. **seryd** might mean 'crowded together' but the vb. *serr* is not recorded in OED. before 1562.

L 1884, 1888. The last two tail-rime lines of this stanza have been corrupted, and their rime no longer corresponds with the first two. A lapse of memory, followed by a desperate attempt to make it good, is the probable cause.

L 1885. Cf. *Amis and Amiloun* 106–7 —
>Opon þe fiften day ful ȝare
>Þai token her leue forto fare.

The divergent reading of C is due to an omitted *n*-suspension.

1893–6. Cf. the account of the gifts sent by the King of Macedon to the Sultan (*Sege off Melayne* 847–54) —
>Sexty Fawconns faire of flyghte,
>And Sexti stedis noble and wyghte,
>. . . . .
>Sexty grewhondes vn to þe gamen
>And Sexti Raches rynnande in samen.

In *Eglamour* 1324-6, the distribution of gold to the populace at the wedding feast is expressed in language similar to that in *Sir Degrevant* —
>There was throwyn golde in that stounde
>The mowntans of a thousand pounde,
>Gete hyt who so myght.

1905-7. Cf. the *Erle of Toulous* 1214-6 —
>Wyth yoye and myrthe þey ladde þer lyfe
>Twenty yere and three.
>Betwene þem had þey chyldyr **xv**.

C 1910. Cf. *Havelok* 2931.

1911-3. *Sir Perceval* ends in the same way—
>Sythen he went into þe holy londe,
>Wanne many cites full stronge,
>And there was he slayne, I undirstonde.
>(*Perceval* 2281-3).

1917-20. Assuming that the device of beginning and ending the poem with the same thought is deliberate, one may reasonably conclude that that version (C) in which the words most exactly correspond is nearer to the original. With L, however, cf. *Cursor Mundi* 18813-4 —
>He send us ai þat ilk grace
>Þar to se his blisful face.

*Guy of Warwick* (MS. B 11973-6) ends similarly.

# GLOSSARY

All words falling into the following classes have been included, at least in intention:—
(i) those that have become obsolete or unusual in Mod. Standard English, (ii) those employed in unusual or unexpected senses, and which might therefore give difficulty to the reader, (iii) unusual spellings, likely to be of philological interest, (iv) northern word-forms. No attempt has been made to include all words in what may be called common form in ME., or words that survive into Mod E. with virtually unchanged meanings, or to give a complete list of references to common words of whatever form. Such references are marked 'etc'. Nouns and verbs are glossed in the form in which they occur in the texts, but the inflected forms of nouns and weak verbs have usually been omitted if the uninflected form is found. Lists of references to inflected forms are not necessarily complete. Nouns have been entered under the singular where it exists in the text. Similarly, verbs are entered under the form of the infinitive; if this is not found, under that of the present tense; failing this, under that of the past tense or one of the participles. If no attention has been specifically drawn to the form of the verb, that of the infinitive or that of the present tense may be inferred.

Where more than one form of the same word is given, those occurring in L, the more consistently spelt MS., are given first, as far as possible. Synonyms have not been given if the word has remained in use with substantially unaltered meaning. Etymologies have been included only exceptionally. Verbs whose tenses are formed from different stems should be looked for under the initial letter of each stem.

Reference numbers without prefix are used to designate words found in the same line in both texts. The prefix L (or C) before a line-number implies that the other text has a different reading. If, owing to the displacement of the text, the same line has not the same number in both MSS., that of L is given first, and that of C immediately follows in brackets, e.g., L 39 (C 38). An asterisk* preceding a reference number means that the word has been recovered as the result of emendation or restoration. An n suffixed to a line-number is a reference to the Notes.

The alphabetical arrangement is similar to that adopted in Tolkien and Gordon's ed. of *Sir Gawain and the Green Knight* and in Tolkien's Vocabulary to Sisam's *Fourteenth Century Verse and Prose*. Mere spelling variation between 3, Gh; þ, Th; I, Y (vowel); I, Ȝ (=[dȝ]); U, V has been disregarded: words involving these letters have been classified according to sound, irrespective of spelling, 3 (initial or medial), Gh (medial) following H; þ, Th following T. Verb-forms with i-, y-prefixes are glossed under i, unless the verb is found without prefix elsewhere in the text.

## A

**a** *indef. art.* 9, 15, C 30, 37, 587, etc.; **an(e)** 63, C 69, 97, C 158, 245, C 908, etc.
**a** *prep.* on, in C 1197, C 1636, C 1785.
**abad** *n.* delay C 129, C 1213.
**abay, abey** *n.* (at) bay, surrounded by dogs 254.
**abey, abye** *see* **haby**.
**abyde, abad(e)** *see* **habyd**.
**aboue, aboffe** *prep.* upon C 744; *adv.* in addition 1437.
**abowte, about, abouȝt** *adv.* 107; *prep.* L 170, 1521.
**ac(c)ord(e)** *n.* reconciliation 1801.
**ac(c)ord(e)** *v.* agree 486.
**ac(c)orde** *adj.* reconciled 1783.
**acheue** *v.* terminate, result C 480.
**adayes** *adv.* at present C 822.
**aferre** *v.* terrify 771; *pp.* L 775, C 830, C 834.
**afore** *adv.* before C 489.
**ageynsay** *v.* deny C 720.
**agreue** *adv.* unkindly C 483.

**ayen** *adv.* again C 145, C 361; **aȝeyn** C 683, C 849; **aȝe**, C 1352; **eyan** C 447; **ayenese** *prep.* against, in opposition to C 560.
**ayere, ey(e)r** *n.* heir 570, 1901, 1910.
**ayere, eyre** *n.* brood 46.
**aywhare** *adv.* everywhere L 80.
**ake** *n.* oak 1051.
**alaund** *adv.* in the land, in the place 508.
**almo(u)s-dede** *n. pl.* acts of charity 81n.
**amorous(e)** *adj.* enamoured L 1032 (C 1027); **amerus** C 671; *quasi-n.* C 671.
**an** *prep. see* **on**.
**anamel(e)de** *pp.* enamelled 650.
**and** *conj.* if C 221, C 223, 232, L 582, etc.; so long as C 1747.
**an(e), on** *adj.* one 363, 767, L 1227, etc.; **at ane** reconciled 451.
**ane** *adv.* only L 604.
**anȝre, angur** *n.* sorrow 1787.
**anyede, anoyde** *pp.* troubled 435.

## GLOSSARY

any3thus *adv.* by night C 1591.
ankyre, anker *n.* anchorite 63n.
anon(-ry3thes) *see* onane, onon-ry3t.
anurled *pp.* bordered *C 647n.
apace *adv.* quickly C 931.
apay *v.* please 590.
ap(p)on *prep.* on, upon L 178, L 252, C 276; *see* opon.
arbere, erbere *n.* flower-garden 711.
archede *pp. adj.* separated (from the chief) by means of an arch L 1048.
are *adv.* before, previously L 360, 1236, 1252, etc.; *conj.* L 1383, L 1789; ar C 267, L 1133, C 1383, etc.; *see* er, or.
arey *n.* troop of men C 492, C 865.
areþede *n.* people of long ago 8.
armes *n. pl.* injuries *see* harmes.
ase(y)th *n.* reparation, amends 490.
assayle, asayl *v.* make trial of, challenge 1034, 1090.
as(s)ent *n.* will, consent C 863, C 1118.
astered *pp.* excited, disturbed C 773.
astray, on straye *adv.* 1656n.
at *prep.* by, from 246, L 1351; in the presence of C 1827; according to C 847, 1271.
at *conj.* that C 1226.
atent *n.* intention L 1795.
athe, owth *n.* oath 210, L 553.
atwo *adv.* in two C 346.
au3th *n.* possession C 842.
au3th *adv. see* oght(e).
aunter(o)us *adj.* daring, valiant L 442, L 1081, L 1305; *quasi-n.* C 421, C 1305, 1385.
auaunt *n.* declaration L 386; make avaunt assert 594, C 965; praise L 1889 (*C 1889).
auant, avaunt *adv. used as int.* forward, advance 275.
auena(u)nt *adj.* agreeable L 730; pleasant C 967; handsome, well-favoured 1325, 1891; at his auennaunt *quasi-n.* at his pleasure C 386, C 730, C 813.
aueres *n. pl.* draught-horses L 150 (Anglo-Lat. aver(i)us ⟨OE. eafor(?).)
avyse *n.* opinion C 184, C 577.
awen *adj.* own L 148, L 1162; awn L 570; *see* owun.

### B

bacenett, bassonett, basenet, basnett *n.* steel headpiece, light helmet 1635; *pl.* 322, L 341 (C 342).
bachelere, bachylere *n.* young knight 1098, 1565.
bagges *n. pl.* badges L 471, 1047.
bake, bac *n.* back 351 C 1627.

bald(e) *adj.* bold L 407, L 516, L 563, etc.; *quasi-n.* L 359, L 468, L 1178.
baldly *adv.* boldly L 1027.
band *n.*[1] deed of gift C 887, C 973.
bandis *n.*[2] *pl.* ornamental strips L 1475.
bane, bonus *n.* (*pl.*) bone(s) 1754.
baneret *n.* knight banneret 1033, C 1098; *pl.* 474.
bar(e) *n.* boar L 42 (C 43), 1256, 1713, *pl.* L 71.
bare *pt. sg.* bore off C 40; *pl.* thrust 1637, displayed 1240.
barga(y)n *n.* affair, business 454.
barnekynch barbican C 391n.
barresse outer fortification L 391.
bate *n.* boat C 935.
batell(e) *n.* battle array, battalion C 282, C 289; *pl.* L 289.
bathe *adv.* both L 234, L 370, etc.
bawndonly *adv.* boldly, daringly 392.
be, by *prep.* by means of C 272, 1361; according to 151, L 152; to the number of 111; be þat *adv.* thereupon 637; *conj.* (at the time) when 673, 1681.
bey, bye *n.* ring 572.
belayn *pp.* lain with C 1744. *see* forlayne.
ben *inf.* be C 398, C 1099; by C 927; bes *pr.* 2 *sg.* C 855; ben *pl.* C 1588; be *pr. subj.* 198, 457, etc.; bene *pp.* 627, L 796, 1703; be C 796; byn C 830.
bent(e) *n.* heath, pasture land 55, 215; battlefield 293, 319, 1113.
berd *n.* beard C 835.
bere *n.* bier L 1731 (C 1729).
beryel(u)s *n. pl.* funeral rites 1899.
beryns, burnes, bernus, barnus *n. pl.* warriors, knights, men L 7, 317, 516, 563, L 1113, 1860.
besantes, besauntus *n. pl.* gold discs, diaper-work 1444, 1499.
besene *pp.* seen, having an appearance (*defined by adv.*) C 1702.
best *n.* beast 503.
by *conj.* when C 978.
by *v.* & *prep. see* be, ben.
byddand *pr. part.* offering battle L 1327.
bydene *adv.* utterly 191; together 1861; unanimously 1145.
bydyght, bedy3th *pp.* arrayed 664, C 1900; (ill-)used 144.
by(e) *inf.* pay the penalty L 187, 753; make amends for 771.
bylefte *pp.* left behind C 1901.
bird(e), burde, berde *n.* lady 607, 624, 668, 701, 705, C 775, 785, C 825, C 950, 1529, etc.; *pl.* 1149.
bysett *pt.* blocked, obstructed C 1767.
bytwen(e), bytwyne *prep.* 922, etc.; *adv.* at intervals 471, 1048, 1500.

## GLOSSARY

**bytwix** *prep.* 604, L 1802.
**blak(e)** *adj.* white, yellow 1049 (?1128, L 1627). (OE. blāc).
**blan(e)** *pt. sg.* ceased 511, 1133.
**blyue** *adv.* quickly C 785, C 803; **bylyue** C 1793; **bleue** C 369.
**body** *n.* trunk 1653.
**boghe, bow** *n.* bough 738.
**borde, bourd** *n.* table L 681, 1397; *pl.* \*C 681.
**bord(o)ure** *n.* heraldic border 1491.
**borly, borlich** *adj.* stately 775; *quasi-n.* 468.
**borowes** *n. pl.* castles L 100 (*see* OED. *s.v.* Borough).
**bosys, boses** *n. pl.* 663n.
**bost(e)** *n.* pomp, display 247.
**bot(e)** *n.* use, profit 564, 1748.
**boteler(e)** *n.* butler 1665.
**botouns, botenus** *n. pl.* buttons 649.
**bouche** *n.* food allowance granted by a noble to his retainers when away from home 1014.
**boure** *n.* bower 1149; *pl.* L 1131.
**bowe** *inf.* go, take one's way C 55.
**bown** *pp. adj.* prepared 1057.
**bownteuous, bountyveus** *adj.* valiant 327.
**brad(e)** *adj.* broad, ample L 99, L 100, L 216, C 1215, etc.
**brade** *adv.* wide, widely L 1215.
**brag(e)** *n.* ostentation, display 247.
**brandes, brondus** *n. pl.* swords 1484.
**brathly, brodelyche** *adv.* profusely 1116.
**brede** *n.* breadth C 924.
**breke** *inf.* enter by force 191; **brak(e), brac** *pt. sg.* broke into 107; burst forth 1626.
**brent** *adj.* lofty, broad L 1115 (\*C 1115).
**brest, brist** *v.* break asunder L 341, L 1525; **brast(e), bryssed** 1638, L 1636; **brasten** *pp.* C 1636.
**bright(e), bry3t(h)** *adj.* beautiful 607, C 950, 1149, 1247, etc.; *quasi-n.* 1223.
**bryme, brem** *adj.* fierce 1256.
**brittyns** *pr.* cuts to pieces L 322 (\*C 322).
**broche** *n.* brooch 572.
**brount** *n.* stress, impact L 172.
**buk** *n.* buck L 42 (C 43); *pl.* **bokes** 511.
**buschement** *n.* ambush C 1597, 1626.
**busk** *v.* get ready 386, C 804, C 948, L 1572 (\*C 1572); array, adorn L 167, 1443; go L 55, L 614, L 1244; come 640; betake oneself C 130, L 614, C 1244.

### C

**caysere** *n.* emperor C 1544.
**calde, cold** *adj.* dispiriting, sad 524.
**can** *v. pt.* did C 348, C 402, etc.

**carp** *v. see* **karppe.**
**case** *n.* circumstances, condition 526; deed L 1674.
**celly** (=selly) *n.* something unusual L 1707.
**celure, seloure** *n.* canopy 1490.
**certis** *adv.* assuredly L 61, L 1533; **certus** C 61; **sertys** L 589; **sertes** C 1533.
**cesse** *see* **ses(s)e.**
**cetoyle** *n.* pear-shaped musical instrument with four wire strings and ribs L 35.
**chalanges, chalangys, chalangeth** *pr.* accuses 432; lays claim to 1220.
**chalk-why3th, chalke-whyte** *adj.* white like chalk C 1507 (\*L 1507).
**chalk-whyte** *adj.* white like chalk C 1507 (\*L 1507).
**champed** *pp. adj.* having an ornamental design L 1510.
**charter, chartur** *n.* deed of gift C 975, C 978; contract C 266.
**chasande** *see* **schased.**
**chas(e)** *n.* unenclosed hunting-ground 378, 525; pursuit C 1675.
**cheef** *n.* upper third of the escutcheon C 1045.
**chekir** *n. used attrib.*, having a chequered pattern L 1490.
**chere** *n.* entertainment C 881.
**ches(e)** *pt. sg.* took his way 1123, 1219.
**cheualry(e), chyualre, chyualry** *n.* retinue, men-at-arms, knights C 826, L 1030 (C 1031), 1158, 1183, 1798.
**cheualrous(e), chyualrous, chyualerus, cheualerouse** *adj.* valorous, bold 326, C 422, 1593, L 1674 (C 1675); *quasi-n.* L 421.
**cheue** *v.* come to pass 481.
**childe, chyl** *n.* child L 1758 (C 1759); **childir, chyldur** *pl.* 1907.
**cyprus** *n.* cloth (?) of gold from Cyprus C 1498.
**clede, y-clade** *pp.* clad 473, L 1806; **clade** C 1806.
**clen(e)** *adv.* properly, completely 469, 1080, L 1672, etc.; finely 1056, 1492.
**cler(e)** *adj.* beautiful 1566, 1898.
**clere** *adv.* L 1077; **en clere** brightly C 1077n.
**closed** *pt.* enclosed, put a fence round 145.
**clothes, clopus** *n. pl.* bedclothes 1558; **clathes, clopus** cloths 1399.
**coddis, coddys** *n. pl.* pillows L 1505, L 1507, C 1509.
**coler(e)** *n.* armour protecting the neck 1651.
**come(s)** *n.* coming 1336.
**com(m)andment** *n.* behest 1794.
**commely** *quasi-n.* fair lady C 844.
**comowne, comoun** *adj.* open, unenclosed L 143, \*C 143n.

## GLOSSARY 153

**conand, conant, couenand, couenaunt** *n.* agreement 1259, 1326.
**condyt** *n.* fountain C 1866, *pl.* **condyths** L 1865.
**conn** *v.* know C 807.
**contenans, countenauns, countynaunce** *n.* conduct, comportment 1182; show, display C 1871.
**coronal** *n.* circlet C 658.
**corven** *see* **kerues.**
**costage** *n.* expense 1013.
**cost(e)** *n.*¹ direction, quarter 246.
**costes** *n.*² *pl.* qualities, characteristics, behaviour C 380.
**courchefs, kercheuus** *n.* head-gear 669.
**cours(e), curse, cors** *n.* course L 1470; tilting bout 395, C 1232, 1306.
**coursurs** *n. pl.* battle chargers L 609 (*C 609).
**coup(e)** *pt. sg.* could C 1063, C 1874 (L 1875).
**couer** *v.* cover 1399, 1672; *pp.* ? *scribal error for* **ouert** *q.v.* L 648n.
**cowchide** *pp. adj.* set, as of jewels L 646.
**cownt, counte** *v.* esteem 207, L 1712 (*C 1712).
**cres(se)** *n.* something of little value L 206 (C 207).
**crete** *n.* wine from Crete 1292, 1424, 1719.
**cry** *n.* appeal for justice 77; proclamation 1034, 1090.
**cumpaste, compasyd** *pp.* contrived 1056, 1492.
**cunyngs, conyngus** *n. pl.* rabbits 1421.
**curious, curyus** *adj.* finely wrought 669.
**curtayse, corteys, cortays** *adj.* gracious L 693 (*C 693), 745; versed in the etiquette of courtly love 1587; *quasi-n.* C 909.

## D

**dayntese, dentepus** *n. pl.* dainties, luxuries C 811, 1427.
**damesel(le), damesele, dammisel, damessel, damysele** *n.* damsel 639, L 718, L 789, C 873, C 881, etc;. young man C 1190n.; **damysel** *gen.* C 1190.
**dar** *v.* dare C 48, C 581, etc.; **durst(e)** *pt.* 776, C 845, etc.
**dawed, dewe** *pt.* dawned C 613, C 1681, 1808.
**de** *prep.* of (in titles) L 1482, L 1483 (*C 1482).
**dede, derne** *n.* death L 340, 567, 750, C 896, 1751.
**dedus** *memorial error for* **bledis** C 312.
**de(e)re** *n. pl.* deer 60, 264, 339, 507.

**degrade** *v.* humiliate, bring to dishonour L 104.
**delyte** *n.* delay C 1111 (*see OED. s.v.* Delite).
**delyuer** *v.* grant, engage (in) 394; hand over 1223.
**dell** *n.* amount C 68.
**demaynus** *n. pl.* possession C 69n.
**den** *n.* dwelling-place 339.
**denges** *pr. t.* beats, strikes C 340.
**departed** *pt.* divided C 346.
**dere** *n.* injury, harm L 356 (C 360).
**der(e)** *adj.*¹ precious 544; expensive C 811, 1427.
**der(e)** *adj.*² bold 25, L 1518.
**dere** *adv.* dearly 1372.
**dere** *v.* harm L 710, 1708; shame C 958; **y-deryd** *pp.* C 829.
**derely** *adv.* expensively 664.
**derewrope** *adj.* precious C 1447.
**derne** *n.* concealment 623.
**desdeyne** *n.* dislike L 101.
**des(e)** *n.* dais, raised platform L 1218 (C 1217).
**dewe** *see* **dawed.**
**dyghte, dyȝth** *v.* L 384, C 684; **dyȝthus** *pr.pl.* **dight(e), dyȝt** *pt.* 233, L 684, C 809, etc.; **dyght(e), dyȝt, i-dyȝt, i-dyȝth** *pp.* 153, C 927, C 1007, C 1335, etc.; treated, handled 1349; composed 153; *refl.* prepared (oneself), made (oneself) ready 233, 1073, 1251, L 1321; *trans.* prepared, made ready C 809, 1189, 1335; adorned 1498; set (of jewels) 1448; make one's way, go 369, C 684.
**dynt, dent** *n.* stroke 356, 1286; *pl.* 1700.
**discouer, descur** *v.* reveal 554.
**disonowre** *n.* indignity C 859.
**do** *v.* cause C 1001, 1370, etc.; **doys** causes C 839; **do me** throw myself 747; *pt.* **dud(e)** C 360, C 1252, etc.; **duden** C 679; **dede** C 442; *pp.* **don** C 202, C 488.
**doctours, doctorus** *n. pl.* Doctors of the Church 1463.
**doghty** *adj.* doughty, valiant L 12, L 305; **doghety** L 1091, etc.; **doghtty** L 1147; **douȝty** C 1091, etc.; **dowghty** C 12, etc.; **dowȝty** C 999; *quasi-n.* 104, 310, 415, etc.; *pl.* **douȝthy** C 1273, etc.
**dole, dool, doel** *n.* pain C 576, 1752.
**donryght** *adv.* utterly, completely C 140.
**dotered** *pt.* fell unsteadily, tottered C 1125 (*L 1125).
**down(e), doun(e)** *adv.* C 177, 256, etc.; overthrown L 141.
**dowte** *n.* fear, uncertainty 171.
**drade** *adj.* afraid L 597.
**draye** *n.* violence L 492; disturbance, noise L 1200.

P

## GLOSSARY

**drawed, drawen, drawin** *see* **drowe**.
**dred(e)** *n*. fear 627, C 832, etc.; **do out of drede** assure 441.
**drey, drye** *v*. endure 576, 1752.
**dresse** *adj*. equipped C 1233.
**dressed, dressyd** *pt*. arrayed C 1321.
**drowe** *pt*. approached C 1097, etc.; **drowhe** pulled (along a net), C 113, etc.; *pp*. **drawed** L 434; **drawen, drawin** 681, etc.; **y-drayn** C 1630.
**Dugepers, Doseperes** *n. pl.* paladins of Charlemagne, illustrious knights 1870.
**dure** *adj*. hard L 649.
**dured** *pt*. continued C 1567.

### E

**ef** *conj. see* **ġyf**.
**eftyr** *prep*. according to L 1794.
**eyan** *see* **ayen**.
**eyer, eyr, eyre** *see* **ayere**.
**elde, ȝelde** *n*. old age 1066.
**enbuschement** *n*. ambush L 1597.
**endentid, endent** *pp*. inlaid 665, 1448.
**endreyde** *pp*. made dry C 434.
**endur(e)** *v*. continue to be 555.
**engrelyd(e)** *pp. adj.* scalloped, with the points directed away from the centre 1046.
**enleue** *adj*. eleven C 358.
**ennioined** *pt*. joined together, engaged C 289.
**enpayre** *v*. injure L 1903; *see* **peyr** *v*.
**ensent** *n*. assent, will C 869 (*apparently scribal error for* **entent** intention).
**ensoynd** *pp*. excused C 291.
**ensur** *v*. promise, pledge one's word C 553.
**entent, entaunt** *n*. purpose, intention 54.
**envyous** *adj*. malicious L 423.
**er** 3 *pl.* are C 578.
**er** *conj*. before C 765; *see* **are, or**.
**erbere** *see* **arbere**.
**ert(e)** *pr*. 2 *sg*. art 715, L 1613.
**erþe** *n*. C 1126, C 1330; *scribal error for* **erde** C 1658.
**es** 3 *sg*. is L 31, L 123, L 159, etc.
**ethe, eyth** *adv*. easily 489.
**eþer** *see* **aythir**.
**euerrose** *n*. rose-water C 1407 (OFr. ewe rose).
**euen(e)** *adv*. straight, directly L 175, 1205, 1294.
**euen(e)-lyȝth** *n*. twilight L 1185, C 1617; **euyn-lythus** C 1185.
**euerychon** *adj*. every one 1454, C 1466.

### F

**faa** *n*. foe L 460, L 596; **foo** C 460, C 596; *pl.* **face** L 426, C 1674; **fase** L 1675; **faas** L 1762; **foas** C 1762; **foos** C 426.

**fay** *adj*. doomed 771, L 1106.
**faye, fey** *n*. faith; **in f** C 110, 120, L 448 (C 444), 512, 716.
**fayn(e)** *adj*. glad, happy L 146, L 362, 759, 1290, etc.; **fyen** C 146, C 362.
**faire, fay(i)r** *adv*. courteously L 691, C 1012, 1694; quietly, without haste C 941, C 1690.
**fayrly** *adv*. quietly, without haste, L 1690.
**faythly** *adv*. faithfully C 557.
**falde, folde** *v*. enfold, embrace L 472 (C 476), 528, L 1864.
**falde** *pp*. made to fall, felled C 1067.
**fame** *n*. foam L 562, C 1402.
**fande, fond** *v*. undertake, perform 118.
**fare** *n*. demeanour 1260.
**fare** *pr. pl.* prosper 1564; **fayr** L 331; *pt*. **farede, faride** L 331, L 1657; go, make one's way 502, 1156, etc.
**fast(e)** *adv*. violently C 1658; earnestly L 1012.
**fausoned** *pp*. wrought C 543.
**fee** *n*. property, goods 88.
**fele, felle** *adj*. many C 45, L 341, C 1106, etc.
**fel(le)** *n*. hill 1165.
**fel(le)** *pt. sg.* befell C 1216, 1304; fell 1380.
**feraunt, ferraunt, ferawnt, ferauns** *adj*. iron-grey 387; *quasi-n.* iron-grey steed 1094, 1262.
**ferde** *pt*. went, happened C 1657 (OE. fēran, go, journey).
**fere** *n*. company; **in fere, y-fer(e)** together 5, C 260, L 1078 (C 1079), 1103, 1667, 1899, L 1905.
**fere** *adv*. far C 538.
**feris** *n. pl.* companions 323, L 1467n.
**ferly** *adv*. extraordinarily L 691.
**fersted** *see* **thirsted**.
**fett** *v*. fetch L 763, L 1389, 1396, L 1410.
**fewtyr** *n*. support for lance or spear attached to a knight's saddle 1282.
**fyn(e)** *adj*. delicately wrought 645, 1199.
**fley** *pt. sg.* fled C 347.
**flemyd** *pp*. put to flight, banished C 915.
**flyght, flyȝt,** *n.* **of flyght, flyȝthes** on the wing 1555; for the pursuit of game 1896.
**flode** *n*. water, sea C 941, 1579, 1690.
**floreyne, floren** *n*. florin 543.
**fol(l)y** *n*. act of foolishness 585, C 997.
**foo(s), foas** *see* **faa**.
**for** *prep*. as 19, 24, etc.; in spite of, notwithstanding 189, 208, 772, 1092, 1260; against 767; as precaution against L 1620; **for to** in order to, to 2, L 82, etc.
**forby** *adv*. by L 78.
**force** *n*. waterfall L 1655n.

## GLOSSARY

**for3elde** *v.* requite C 876.
**for3ood** *pp.* neglected *C 1008.
**foriustyd** *pp. adj.* overcome in jousting C 1914.
**forlayne** *pp.* lain with L 1744, see **belayn**.
**formast** *adv.* first C 1631.
**forþermast** *adv.* foremost L 1631.
**forthi, forþy** *conj.* for this reason 29, C 153, 1549.
**fosse** *n.* ditch C 1655n.
**foster, forster** *n.* forester 1575, 1589, 1598; *pl.* 114, 446, C 1769.
**fouchesaff** *v.* grant, bestow C 959.
**fouled** *pp.* trampled, trodden down 1106. (*see OED. s.v.* Foul, *v.*²).
**founde** *v.* set out L 57; *pt.* C 57.
**fowly** *adv.* shamefully L 144.
**fra, fro** *conj.* from the time that L 1866 (C 1865); since, if 725.
**fray(e)** *v.* attack, raid 253, 500.
**frayn** *v.* ask for 1736.
**fre(e)** *adj.* noble, gentle 33, 693, 1011, 1573, etc.; liberal, generous 84; gratis L 1867; *quasi-n.* 429, 761, C 939, C 959, 1140, etc.
**free** *adv.* splendidly 1233.
**frek** *n.* man L 1381.
**frek** *adv.* quickly, eagerly C 1381.
**frekly** *adv.* readily, lustily L 301.
**frely** *adj.* beautiful L 472 (C 476), 528, 569, 661, L 1864.
**frenchepys** *n. pl.* friends C 1290.
**freschely** *adv.* fiercely L 288, L 290, 323.
**frythe, freth** *n.* wood 313, C 502; *pl.* frythis, fryþþus 1732.
**frount** *n.* front C 131n.
**frountell** *n.* band worn on the forehead L 665.
**frouschen** *pr. pl.* rush C 1103.
**ful(l)** *adv.* very 26, 180, 345, 470, etc.
**funde, found(e)** *inf.* go, hasten L 57, C 1191; *pt.* C 57, 241, 505.
**fune** *adj.* little L 195.
**funede, foynede** *pt.* lunged 290.

### G

**ga(a), goo** *inf.* go 456, 1184; **gase** *imper.* L 763; *pp.* **gane** L 630, etc.; **go** C 630; **gon** C 1915.
**gabelettes, gablettus** *n. pl.* small gables 1478.
**gaffe** see **gyf(f)**.
**gay(e)** *adj.* merry 36; attractive, pleasant L 476, 639, L 670, etc.; sportive L 1023 (C 1027); finely arrayed C 106, 1196; brightly coloured 1478; **geyest** *superl.* happiest C 766.
**gayly** *adv.* splendidly 1900; lightly L 1705.

**gayn(e)** *adj.* straight, convenient 1692.
**gaynesay** *v.* deny L 720.
**galentyn, galantyne** *n.* sauce L 1414 (C 1415).
**gambassowne, gambisoun** *n.* cloth or leather tunic worn by soldiers to protect trunk and thighs 318.
**gamen** *n.* mirth 3, 1919; (course of) action C 222, L 270; *pl.* sports 41; chase 509; birds and beasts of the chase 56.
**gan** *pt.* did 183, L 323, C 820, etc.; **ganne** C 47; **gon** C 1157, C 1314; **gun** L 47, L 162.
**gare** *v.* cause, bring about L 399; *pt.* **gart** 343; **grat** C 355; **gert** C 359.
**gate, 3at(t), 3ate** *n.*¹ gate C 629, C 933, C 1215; *pl.* L 629, C 831, C 833, L 1215.
**gatis** *n.*² *pl.* paths, ways L 1578, 1600, 1692.
**geddis** *n. pl.* pike L 519.
**geldene** *adj.* made of gold C 296.
**gentill** *adj.* of gentle birth, noble L 319; **gentyl** C 949, C 1147; **jentell** C 419; excellent, fine C 814, C 875.
**gentryse, gentriese** *n.* clemency, mercy 497, 747.
**gere, geyr** *n.* array, harness C 662, 1195, 1321.
**germentes, garnementus** *n. pl.* garments 1880.
**gest** *n.* guest L 790 (C 791), 1366; *pl.* 4, 85, C 1920; men, fellows L 766, 1211.
**gestened** *pt.* were entertained C 951.
**gete, geete** *n.*¹ black marble 1477.
**get(e)** *n.*² style 1197 (OFr. jet).
**geterne** *n.* gittern, kind of guitar with wire strings C 36.
**gyde** *n.* dress, gown 656.
**gyf** *conj.* if C 767; **yef(f)** C 201, C 393, etc.; **3if** L 555; **ef** *L 727, *L 767.
**gyf(f)** *v.* give L 229, 1066; **yeff** C 229; *pt.* **gaf(e)** L 34, L 51, C 1210, etc.; **gaff** C 891; **gaffe** L 139; **yaf(f)** C 34, C 51, C 139, etc.; *pp.* **gyf** C 973; **gyff, 3if** *subj.* 1764; **yeff** *imper.* C 2.
**gyle** *n.* trickery C 832.
**gylte, gyld** *pp. adj.* gilded 1405.
**gyn(ne)** *n.* stratagem, trick 722, C 917, 1361.
**gyrdis, gerd** *pr. pl.* strike 1298.
**gytternyng** *vbl. n.* playing on the gittern L 36.
**glad(e)** *v. imper.* make glad L 790 (C 791).
**glayues, gleues** *n. pl.* swords 295.
**gle(e), glew** *n.* mirth 3, C 1919; music 34; sport 60.
**glemerand** *pr. part.* glittering L 656.

glemyd *pt.* (*causative*) made to gleam, gave a sheen to C 656.
glent *pt.* glanced, struck obliquely 295.
gleterand, gleteryng, glyteryng *pr. part.* glittering 295, L 296, L 1452, 1855.
gnede *adj.* niggardly 1175.
godlyche *adv.* courteously C 691.
gomes *n. pl.* warriors 318.
gospellers, gospellorus *n. pl.* evangelists 1457.
gowlys *adj.* gules, red 1052.
grace *n.* favour (of God) 366, 425, 797, etc.; (of a lady) L 698 (C 699).
gracyous, gracious *adj.* pleasing, 670; (epithet of courtesy) L 1594.
grade *v.* degrade, humiliate *C 104.
graythe, greyþ *v. imper.* make ready, harness 1195; *pp.* arrayed 1088; grayede drawn up L 282.
grame *n.* sorrow, injury, ill-will 727, 1388.
gramercy *int.* 801.
grane, gron *v.* groan 766, 1298.
grauntid *pt.* consented L 1551.
gre(e) *n.* prize for victory C 96, 1148.
grene *adj.* L 190, 1600; *as n.* green colour 1052, 1088, etc.; grass-lands C 190, C 252.
grese *n.*¹ hertes of grese fat harts 265.
grese, *n.*² stairway, 1375.
gret, *n.* sorrow C 1785.
gret(e) *v.* greet 1388; *pt.* 691; *imper.* 485.
greue, greff *n.* offence, displeasure 483, 1341.
grewhund(es), grehundis, grehondes *n.* (*pl.*) greyhound(s) 42, L 251, L 1895.
gromys *n. pl.* men L 251.
gro(u)nd(e), grownd *n.* earth 59, 507, etc.; *pl.* lands, parks C 251.
gud(e), god(e), goode *adj.* good 54, 240, C 321, etc.; *as n.* good deeds, good fortune C 7, C 1004, 1755.

ȝ

ȝare *adj.* ready L 279.
ȝar(e) *adv.* quickly 640, 804, C 948, 1244, etc.
ȝe *adv.* yea C 98.
ȝeddyngus *n. pl.* songs C 1437.
ȝede *pt.* went L 1347, ȝode 1691; ȝoode C 127; ȝoud C 942.
ȝelde *n.* see elde.
ȝerd *n.* court(yard) C 676.
ȝer(e) *n.* year 1567, 1897, L 1906.
ȝerne *adv.* quickly 621.
ȝif *conj.* see gyf.
ȝyng(e) *adj.* young 1823n.
ȝyte *adv.* yet C 1002.
ȝole-nyȝte, ȝowlus-nyȝth *n.* Christmas Eve 781n.

ȝonde *adj.* yonder C 783.
ȝondir, ȝondur, ȝonder *adv.* yonder 1327, 1334, 1728; *adj.* C 744.
ȝone *adj.* yon L 744, L 783.
ȝoode *see* ȝede.
ȝorle *n.* Earl C 1753, C 1809, etc.

H

habyd, abyde *inf.* remain, delay L 161; await 624, 1336; *pt.* habade, abad(e) L 161, 391, L 1178 (C 1179).
haby(e), abye, abey *v. trans.* suffer for, repent 454; *intr.* pay the penalty C 187, 1071.
habirgeon, haberiown *n.* coat of mail or scale armour without sleeves 1638.
haf(e) *v.* have, possess L 267, L 303, L 1295, etc.; *pr.* 2 *sg.* has(e) L 195, L 202, L 757, etc.; 3 *sg.* L 122, L 488, etc.; *pl.* hafe L 91, etc.; ha C 1297; han C 202; *imper.* ha C 1189.
haylsede *pt.* greeted, hailed L 178, L 1812.
haynes, haynus *n. pl.* parks 70.
hald(e) *v.* C 597, 623, etc.; keep to 1259, 1326; esteemed 1026, 1091; *pp.* haldyn L 326, L 459; holden C 459; y-halden C 326; upheld, honoured C 91; *imper.* hald(e) 1549.
halfendele, halvendel *adj.* half L 358, C 828, C 908.
haly, holy *adj.* holy 117, 1911.
hal(l)e *adj.* whole 1880.
hally *adv.* wholly L 1539, C 1838.
halowed *pp.* honoured C 91.
halowede *pt.* shouted C 252.
ham(e), hem, hom(e), whom *n.* home L 90; *adv.* 90, 217, 373, C 945, etc.
hamward(es), hammard *adv.* homewards 1249, L 1347.
hand(e), hond *n.* 15, C 977, 1288, etc.; possession 65; with his hand by means of a charter 1910; take on hand undertake C 913; *used symbolically, giving validity to an assurance* C 848n., C 1416 (=L 1412).
hap(pe) *n.* fortune, chance 1216, C 1272, 1304.
hard(e) *adv.* severely 1647.
hardyly *adv.* without fear of contradiction L 1765.
hare *n.*¹ hare L 43 (C 42).
hare *n.*² hair *see* here *n.*²
harmes, harmus, armes *n. pl.* injuries L 1031 (C 1030), 1117.
hasteletes, hastelettus *n. pl.* pigs' entrails L 1414 (C 1415).
hauraud, heroud *n.* herald 1157.
hawberkes *n. pl.* coats of mail, tunics C 294.
he *pron.* she C 1758; *see* scho.
heghte *adj.* lofty L 406.

## GLOSSARY

**heyle, heyly** *adv.* loudly C 1070, C 1601.
**heldus** *v. pl.* sink C 300n.
**hele** *n.* welfare, well-being C 1782.
**hem, hom(e)** *pron.* 3 *pl. acc. and dat.* C 2, C 7, C 324, C 1417, etc.; *refl.* C 233, C 684, etc.; **her(e)** *adj.* their C 240, C 610; **hore** C 1695.
**hend(e)** *adj.* expert (in arms), valiant L 405, C 1580, L 1617; *quasi-n.* valiant knight C 11, 1812; gracious lady C 909, 1848; ladies and gentlemen 1459.
**hent(e)** *v.* seize, take C 223, 609, 779; **hent(e), hynt** *pp.* 122, 1382, 1795; received C 1117.
**here** *n.*[1] host, people 583.
**her(e), hare** *n.*[2] hair 657, 1520 (OE. hēr; ON. hár).
**here** *v.* hear 6, L 27, etc.; **y-her** C 27; *pt.* hard C 1695; **herd(e)** 77, L 637; **hurde** C 637; *imper.* **heris, herus** 1459.
**here byfore** *adv.* hitherto L 489.
**heryede, y-hery3ed** *pp.* pillaged 140.
**hert, herd(e)** *n.*[1] heart 196, 372, 1104, etc.
**hert(e)** *n.*[2] hart L 43 (C 42); *pl.* 254, L 510, etc.; **herdus** C 71.
**hete** *pr.* 1 *sg.* C 848, 1288; 3 *sg.* **hightis** L 400; **hytus** C 400; *pt.* **highte** L 166, L 478, etc.; **hyeght** C 478; **hy3th** C 782; *pp.* **hight** L 225; **i-hy3t** C 1005; **y-hi3th** *C 1609. Promise, assure 400, C 848, 1288, etc.; called, prayed L 225; was called L 10 (C 11), L 166, etc.
**heþe** *n.* heath C 300n.
**hethyn, heþene** *adj.* heathen 119.
**heue** *pr. pl.* direct by shouting L 252n.
**heuede, hed(e)** *n.* head L 1603 (*C 1603), 1651.
**hy(e)** *n.* haste 237, 413, 453, etc.
**hy(e)** *v.* hasten 621.
**hye** *adv.* aloud C 1760.
**hight(e)** *v. see* **hete**.
**highte** *n. in phr.* **vpon (on, an) hy3th** etc., aloft C 226, L 406, 736, 1469, etc.; aloud C 961, 1333, etc.
**hy3thtyd** *pp.* adorned C 657 (*see OED. s.v.* Hight *v.*[3]).
**hill, hull** *n.* 618, 744, 1209.
**hillyd, held** *pp.* covered L 657; saddled L 1201 (OE. helian).
**hymself(e)** 735; *pron. absol.* L 1592.
**hynde** *n.* hind, female deer L 43.
**hyne** *n.* (*pl.*) servant, 'fellow' 1728.
**hynge** *v.* hang L 736, 1514; **hanged, honged** *pp.* C 736, L 758, C 853.
**hir** *see* **scho**.
**hit, hyt** *pron. see* **it**.
**ho, hoe** *pron.*[1] she, *see* **scho**.
**ho** *pron.*[2] who, *see* **wha**.
**holtus** *n. pl.* woods 1699.

**honour(e), honor, honowre** *n.* nobility C 912; high rank C 299, 1151, 1377, 1546; mark of favour L 1850 (C 1851).
**hoo** *see* **scho**.
**hope** *v.* expect L 1343 (*C 1343).
**hors(e)** *n.* L 176, etc.; *pl.* **hors(e)** C 150, C 1017, 1195, C 1201; **horses** L 1201.
**Hospitall** *n.* headquarters of the Order of Knights Hospitallers 1833.
**houre** *n.* C 908; **ours** *pl.* C 1470.
**houe** *v.* tarry, remain, be present 329, 465, 1255, 1311.
**howsomeuer** *adv.* in whatever way L 481.
**hur** *see* **scho**.
**hurtelyng** *vbl. n.* collision, conflict L 1699.
**husbandes, husbondus** *n. pl.* manorial tenants, villeins 139, 146.

## I

**y-clade** *see* **clede**.
**y-drayn** *see* **drowe**.
**y-her** *see* **here** *v.*
**y-lau3th** *pp.* embraced C 843.
**i-ly3th** *pp.* kindled C 890.
**ilk(e)** *adj.* each, every L 52, C 354, etc.; **ylke** L 89, etc.; *pron.* same 1507.
**ylkone, ilkane** *pron.* each one L 1454, L 1467.
**ill, yl(l)e** *adv.* wrongfully 202, 719; with offence 458, etc.; with aversion 752, 1532, etc.; severely 1339.
**in** *prep.* among 8; at C 1378; upon 1379, C 1855.
**inewe, ynoghe, ynowe, inow** *adj.* many, in plenty 519n, 1040, L 1421, L 1438.
**innes** *n. pl.* dwellings L 142.
**intill** *prep.* to L 1212.
**inwyth** *prep.* within, inside C 70, C 314.
**iryn, yren** *n.* iron 602.
**is** *adj.* his C 386.
**i-sete** *see* **sitt**.
**y-slayn** *see* **sla(a)**.
**y-speryd** *pp.* shut C 831, C 833.
**y-stade** *see* **stade**.
**it, hit, hyt** *pron.* L 31, L 182, 201, 458, etc.; *indef.* 729, C 1304, etc.
**y-venkessyd** *see* **vencust(e)**.
**yvorye, yuore** *n.* ivory 1397.
**i-wysse, y-wys(e)** *adv.* in truth, certainly 114, 205, L 509, 545.

## J

**japon, jepun** *n.* padded tunic 307.
**jentell** *see* **gentill**.
**jessera(u)nt, jesseraund** *n.* coat of armour made of small plates of metal rivetted to each other 307, C 814.
**jolly** *adj.* magnificent L 1474.
**junede** *pp.* met in conflict L 289.

## 158 GLOSSARY

**just** *n.* joust; *pl.* C 95, C 409.
**iuste** *v.* joust C 865, C 878, 1267;
**iusset** approached C 1282.
**justyng** *vbl. n.* jousting L 409, C 1882, L 1914.

### K
**kayous** *adj.* C 1594n.
**kant** *adj.* bold L 248.
**karppe, carp** *v.* tell 9, C 952; speak C 1370.
**kende** *pp.* known, acknowledged L 1588.
**kene** *adj.* valiant 19, C 314, 1076, 1596, etc.
**kepe** *v.* keep, watch over 629.
**kercheuus** *see* **courchefs.**
**kerues** *pr.* cuts C 1652; **corven** *pp.* L 1473.
**keste** *pp.* kissed C 1819.
**kynde** *adj.* noble, well-born L 315.
**kyngh** C 13n, **kynyght** C 179, **kynghus** C 314, **knytht** C 129, **knygh** C 343, **knygt** C 405, *scribal forms of* knight.
**kyn(n)** *n.* lineage 1363.
**kyrk-dure, kyrke-dor** *n.* church door L 1851n. (C 1850).
**kyth(e)** *n.* own country L 315 (C 314).
**kythe** *v.* display 380.
**knaue** *n.* manservant 794.
**knell** *v.* kneel C 343.
**knyfe, knyef** *n.* 556.
**knylle** *v.* ring 1472.
**knoppus** *n. pl.* knobs, ornamental buttons C 1510.

### L
**lay(e), lay** *n.* law 1843.
**laiked** *pt.* behaved *1468n.
**layn(e), leyn** *v.* conceal 682, L 1368 (*C 1368), 1629.
**lare** *n.* learning, *used vaguely for* skill 1512.
**lathe, lothe** *adj.* unwilling, *hence* regretful 211n.
**laund(e), land** *n.* glade, clearing in forest 255, 261, etc.; open place 1257; *used attrib.* C 612.
**ledes** *n.* men, warriors C 308.
**lef** *adj.* agreeable *C 1167n.
**leff** *v. imper.* believe C 1537.
**ley** *n.* lake, pool C 255.
**lelely, leliche** *adv.* faithfully, truly 529.
**lem(m)an(e), lemon** *n.* lover 62, 1319, 1542.
**lendid, lent(e), lende** *pt.* remained, halted 244, 611, 1576.
**lene** *v.* grant 1615; **lent** *pt.* gave 147, L 150; *pp.* granted C 425; bestowed, *hence* in the possession of L 698.
**lenges** *pr.* lingers, tarries 1356.
**lepe** *v.* run 631, 770.
**lere** *n.* cheek C 536.
**les(e)** *n.* falsehood 1121, 1229.

**let, lett(e)** *n.* hindrance L 690 (C 689), 1537.
**lett(e)** *v.* hinder, obstruct L 173, L 791, 1599; restrain oneself 497, 786, C 837, C 916, 1612.
**leue** *adj.* dear L 1563, L 1703 (*C 1703); **leuer** *compar.* rather 541, 841; **leueste** *superl.* most agreeable C 1436.
**leue, lyff** *v.* live L 1343 (*C 1343); **lyued**(e), **lyffed, leuede** *pt.* 8, 64, L 1905 (C 1906); **lyuand** *pr. part.* C 654.
**lewtyng** *vbl. n.* lute-playing C 38.
**ly, ley** *v.* tell lies 564, L 1748 (*C 1748).
**lyard(e)** *adj.* spotted with white or silvery grey 76.
**ly(e)ghtly, ly3thely** *adv.* readily, easily 462, C 899.
**light(e)** *v.* alight, settle, dismount 177, C 676; *pt.* **lyght(e)** 256, 392, L 1641; **lyghted** L 1574; **ly3th** C 1574; *pp.* **y-lyeght** C 529; **ly3th** C 1540.
**lyght(e), ly3t** *adj.*[1] happy L 676, 1554.
**lyghte, ly3th** *adv.*[1] actively, nimbly 770.
**ly3th** *adj.*[2] light, bright 613.
**ly3th** *adv.*[2] brightly C 1452.
**lykyng** *vbl. n.* liking, heart's desire C 847.
**lynd** *n.* tree C 611.
**lyng(e)** *n.* heather 352.
**lyre** *n.* cheek L 536.
**lyste** *v. impers.* pleases 521.
**lyte** *n.* delay L 1111.
**lyuere** *n.* allowance of food 1019.
**loggede** *pt.* lodged, camped 244.
**lordelych** *adv.* in a lordly manner, with dignity C 392.
**lorkus** *pr. pl.* lurk C 1671; **lurkede** *pt.* L 1671.
**lorn** *pp.* lost C 955.
**loplych** *adv.* dreadfully, shamefully C 144.
**lou3hwes** *pr.* laughs C 961; **loghe, lou3h** *pt.* 737, C 954, 1069.
**lowynge** *pr. part.* glowing, C 1452.
**lowtte, loute** *v.* bow 1241, 1811.
**luces** *n. pl.* pike C 519.
**lufly** *adj. quasi-n.* lovely lady L 536.

### M
**ma(a), mo(o)** *quasi-n.* more 452, 1172, 1316; *adj.* 463, 1680, 1832.
**made** *adj.* mad C 597.
**may** *n.* maid 523, 591, L 789, 1722; waiting-maid 685, L 1361.
**maylis, maylus** *n. pl.* coats of mail L 294, 311.
**maynes** *n. pl.* demesne lands L 69.
**maystry** *n.* victory, L 303; *pl.* **maystris** (feats of) skill 112, L 380n, L 384.
**mak(e)** *n.* mate, wife, equal C 838, 1064, 1132, L 1749 (*C 1749).

GLOSSARY 159

maluesyn(e) *n.* malmsey wine 1431.
maner(e) *n.* manor 137.
manhede *n.* human kindness 83.
many *n. see* menȝe.
mantelete, mauntolet *n.* horse-blanket 1198.
**mappamonde, mappemound** *n.* world 31n.
marchal *n.* master of ceremonies 1678.
mas(e) *pr. pl.* (*sg.*) make(s), cause(s) 1763.
maugre, mawgre *n.* bitterness, ill-will 431, 588.
maungery(e) *n.* repast, banquet 1159, C 1178; mangery C 1865; mawngery L 1177; L 1866.
ma(w)gre *prep.* in spite of 491.
mede *n.* reward 443, 588, 1174, etc.
mekill *adj.* L 72, L 92, etc.; michel C 772; mychel C 807, C 923, etc.; mechell C 98, C 208; muchel(l) C 431, C 1613, etc.
mende *v.* make amends for L 207; *pr. subj.* L 203.
mendis *n. pl.* amends L 220.
menȝe *n.* retinue L 134, L 763, etc.; many C 763; mene C 1739; meyne C 1010; meney C 134; meynye C 872.
menske *n.* humaneness, courtesy 83.
merymaydyns, meremaydenus *n. pl.* mermaids 1520n.
meruelle *adj.* wonderful L 1513.
mescheue, myscheff *n.* evil plight 1342.
mes(e) *n.* course, meal L 1217 (C 1218).
mynt, ment *v. pt. and pp.* aimed a blow 1285.
mirthis, murþus *n. pl.* pleasures, joys 1438.
mysse, mese *n.* fault, misdeed L 207 (C 206).
myssede *pt.* were unsuccessful C 1303.
moynelus *n. pl.* mullions C 1475.
mold(e) *n.*¹ earth 659, L 1284, L 1451.
mold(e) *n.*² top of the head *657n, 1055.
molde *n.*³ mould, design C 1451.
mon *v.* must L 606.
mot(e) *v.* may 456, C 964, C 981, 1184.
moue *v.* make, excite C 1438.
muchel(l) *see* mekill.

N

na, no *adj.* 62, L 152, 266, L 722, etc.
na, no *adv.* 501, 762.
na *conj.* nor L 1176.
nay *n.* denial 213.
naker *n.* kettle-drum C 1101.
nakerere *n.* drummer L 1101.
nan(e), non *pron.* 302, 414, C 988, L 1050, 1180, etc.; *adj.* 61, C 129, L 458, C 625, C 722, etc.
nat *see* noght(e).

naþeles *adv.* nevertheless C 702.
nathyng, nothyng *sb.* 571, C 1008; no-one L 1607; *adv.* in no wise 283.
naume *n.* name C 561.
ne *adv.* not, L 79, 186, etc.; *conj.* or, nor 14, 62, 364, 1545, etc.
ned(e) *n.* need, emergency 240, 354, C 1284; *pl.* business 412, C 580, C 1191.
neghede, neyȝed *pt.* approached 540.
ney *adv.* nigh, near C 1681.
nel *v.* will not C 1002; nolde *pt.* C 161.
neuen(e) *subj.* mention, speak of 1530.
newyne, nevyn *n.* ornamental clasp (?) 646n.
nobulle *n.* display C 92.
noght(e) *adv.* not, L 161, L 177, etc.; nat C 177, C 194, etc.; note C 1723; nott L 196; nouȝth C 1368.
nom(e) *pt. sg.* took 126.
no(o)ke *n.* corner 181.
norloge *see* orrelegge.
not(e) *n.* song, melody L 38 (C 39); *pl.* 1434.
noþer *adj.* no noþer none other, no other L 152, L 590, L 722, L 1604.
nouche *n.* jewel *646n.
nowþer, noþur *pron.* 1621.

O

o *adj.* one C 985, C 1451.
of(f), (o C 907) *prep.* of, for L 39 (C 38), C 101, 366, etc.; in, as regards C 12, 742, 1151, etc.; (consisting, made) of 645, 1390, etc.; belonging to 30, 1062, etc.; during C 907 *expressing gen. of description* L 113; upon L 1760; off ·779.
offerand, offorand *vbl. n.* offering 1838.
ogee *n.* diagonal rib of vault *1446n.
oght(e), auȝth *adv.* at all, anywhere L 90, 1708.
on (an C 252, etc.) *prep.* (up)on; in(to) L 47, 709, 1267, etc.; a- C 982, L 1591, etc.; (of time), in, by 111, C 237, etc.
onane, on(n)one, anon(e) *adv.* straightway L 219, C 233, C 241, 400, C 505, 684, L 744, 1757, etc.
onon-ryght(e), anon-ryȝth(es) *adv.* straightway 688, 728, C 1589.
opon *prep.* on C 178; opo C 154; *see* ap(p)on.
or *prep.* before 49, 53, 496; *conj.* L 267, 452, L 487, etc.; *see* are, er.
ordayned, ordeyned *pp.* devised 1398.
ordyr *n.* rank C 891.
orrelegge (L norloge) *n.* clock 1469.
ost(e) *n.* body of men 245, L 282.
other *conj.* or C 198.
oþerwhile *adv.* now and again 1435.
o[u]þer *pron. absol.* one or other (of us) *C 1227.

## 160 GLOSSARY

**oueral(l)e** *adv.* all over, everywhere 1485, 1733.
**ouercowchid** *pp.* overlaid, carpeted L 1487.
**ouerfret** *pp.* covered, embroidered 642.
**ouerkeueryd** *pp.* covered over C 1487.
**ouert** *adj.* open C 648.
**ouertrasyd** *pp.* set with tracery C 652.
**ours** *n. pl. see* **houre**.
**owere, ewer** *n.* ewer 1406.
**owun** *adj.* own C 1502; *see* **awen**.
**owt-drawen** *pp.* drawn L 1630.
**owttake** *v.* exclude, except C 988.

### P

**pace** *n.* pass, predicament 799.
**pay, pey** *v.* please 590, C 963, *pp.* 281, 702; *impers.* C 884.
**pay(e)** *n.* liking C 796; payment, punishment 1660.
**payn(e)** *n.* trouble, effort, risk L 445, 548, 1688.
**payn(e)demayne, paynmayn** *n.* fine white bread 1291, 1409.
**paynted, payntyd** *pp. adj.* depicted 1456, L 1465; decked L 1507; adorned L 1485.
**payr** *see* **pere**.
**pays** *see* **pes(e)**.
**pak(ke)** *n.* company, gang 350.
**pall(e)** *n.* rich cloth 87, 537, 1487, L 1878 (C 1879).
**palle-werke, pall-work** *n.* work in rich cloth 645.
**pantelere, panter** *n.* pantler 1665.
**papeiayes, papageyes** *n. pl.* parrots 1496.
**Parabylls, Parabolus** *n. pl.* Proverbs 1455.
**par amour(s), paramoure** *adv.* as a courtly lover, passionately C 857, 1063, C 1130, 1150, 1307.
**parpon** *n.* binding stone extending through a wall from one side to the other C 1446.
**pavilyons, pauelouns** *n. pl.* tents 243.
**peyr** *v.* outshine, put at a disadvantage C 1903. *See* **enpayre**.
**pelers, pyllorus** *n. pl.* pillars 1458.
**pere, payr** *n.* pear, thing of no consequence 364, 1712.
**perys, peres** *n. pl.* nobles, magnates 1903.
**perry, perreye** *n.* jewellery 1495.
**per(r)ke, parke** *n.* enclosed land 47; *pl.* C 70, 107, 143, 145, 191, 378, 433, etc.
**pertede** *pt.* divided L 346.
**peruenke** *n.* paragon C 746.
**pes(e)** *n.* peace 266, 1194, etc.; **pess(e)** 1231, etc.; **pays** C 1585.
**pyght** *pt.* pitched C 243.
**Pyne** *n.* Passion C 893.
**pypere** *n.* minstrel 1585n.
**Pistils, Pystolus** *n. pl.* Epistles 1454.

**place, plas(e)** *n.* place of battle 365; manor, estate 138, 427.
**play(e), pley** *n.* activity 1682; exercise, tourney C 867; sport 51, 109, 521; jest 1727.
**play(e)** *v.* 37; disport oneself L 614 (C 615), 686, 712, L 1766.
**playtede** *pt.* bent C 342.
**plighte** *n.* state or condition (of destruction) L 48, L 140.
**plyght(e), ply3th(e)** *v.* pledge 424, 696, 1038, 1222, 1371, etc.; *pp.* C 889.
**ploughes, plows** *n. pl.* measures of land 69.
**plouerrs, plouerys** *n. pl.* plovers 1418.
**poyned** *pp.* embroidered C 1507.
**pontyfycalle, pontifical** *adj.* belonging to a bishop L 1846; *n.* episcopal vestment C 1846.
**porter(e)** *n.* gate-keeper 397, 401, 627.
**powdird, poudryd** *pp.* seasoned 1418.
**pres(e)** *n.* throng 1122, 1279.
**pryce, prys(e)** *n.* value 192, 746, L 1874 (C 1875); glory 1139; pre-eminence 40.
**pryd(e)** *n.* magnificence, splendour, wealth 98, L 163, 648, 1092; high estate 616, 1302; self-esteem 208, 772; elation 1317.
**prykkus, prikes** *pr. sg.* rides C 1122, C 1279; **prekid, prikked(e), prycked** *pt.* L 1122, 1154, 1203, L 1279.
**pryme** *n.* first hour, sunrise 1225.
**proferrys** *pr. pl.* C 857, make offers; **profird, proford** *pt.* proffered 1291.
**prout** *adj.* proud C 1575.
**prow(e)** *n.* advantage L 230 (C 231).
**pruest** *adj. superl.* most valiant *C 1188n.
**purtred** *pp.* depicted C 1465.
**purueance, puruyaunce** *n.* provision L 1162, 1825; supply L 1871.

### Q

**qwykke** *adj.* living L 518.
**qwyssyns, quyschonus** *n. pl.* cushions 1390.
**qwyte, quite** *v.* requite 443.

### R

**rachis** *n. pl.* hounds L 250, C 510.
**rad** *see* **rede**, *v.*
**rade** *adj.* afraid 598.
**rade** *pt. sg.* rode L 106, 130, etc.
**rase** *pt. pl.* rose, left the table L 682; **rysen** *pr.* C 682.
**raughte, ra3ht, rau3th** *pt.* reached, handed 774, 1322; dealt 1124.
**rebuke** *n.* rebuff C 879.
**rebundys** *pr. pl.* leap about 251.
**receuyd** *pp.* received (?) C 653n.
**recumaund(e)** *v.* commend C 893, C 897.

GLOSSARY 161

**rede** *n.* advice 566, C 875; judgement L 751; course of action C 751.
**rede** *v.* advise 203, 451, 621, 1773; give advice 232, C 928; interpret, expound 1239; **rad** *pp.* read C 978.
**redrischt, redressyde** *pp.* righted 1818.
**rehersyng** *vbl. n.* talk 1821.
**reyally** *adv.* splendidly C 510.
**reyde** *pp.* drawn up, arrayed C 282.
**reyn, ryne** *n.* Rhenish wine 1430.
**ren(c)kes** *n. pl.* warriors 1105; spectators L 1301 (C 1302), 1314.
**repayre, repeyr** *v.* resort 47.
**repurueaunce** *n.* provision, purveyance C 1162n.
**reso(u)n** *n.* motto 1239; sense 1270, etc.
**reste, riste** *pt.* ceased 513; **risted** rested L 634.
**retenans, retenaunce,** *n.* retinue, 1163.
**retenue** *n.* *C 946n.
**reueryse** *n.* robbery L 498.
**reuestyd** *pp.* vested, robed C 1846n.
**rew(e), row(e)** *v.* rue, regret L 231 (*C 230), 751, 1531; *impers.* 382.
**rewelle-bane, ruel-bon** *n.* ivory 1445.
**riddels, rydalus** *n. pl.* curtains 1514.
**ryght(e)** *n.* 155, 227, etc.; **at ryghtus** *pl.* at all points C 388, C 1186.
**ryght(e)** *adv.* 32, 87, etc.; **ry3th** C 1249; straight 1249; exactly, suitably, quite, just 187, 232, etc.
**rynnes** *pr. t.* runs L 1735; **ran(e)** *pt. pl.* 510, 1517; *sg.* L 1865 (C 1866).
**ryse, ris** *n.* twig, branch L 534 (C 535).
**rysen** *see* rase.
**risted** *see* reste.
**ryvaye, revey, revay** *v.* "hunt or hawk along the banks of rivers" (OED.), 50, 522, C 823; **revayde, i-reuayd** 675.
**ryuen** *pp.* torn to pieces L 1702.
**roberyse** *n.* robbery C 498.
**roche** *n.* sweet French wine 1430.
**rod(e)** *n.*[1] complexion 534n.
**Rode** *n.*[2] Cross C 1000.
**ronne** (obscure) *see* C 534n.
**rosere** *n.* rose-tree 634.
**rot(t)e** *n.* lyre-shaped instrument 37.
**rowte, rout(e)** *n.* company 106, 1171.

**S**

**sa, so(o), swa** *adv.* C 94, 273, 464, etc.
**sadils, sadelus** *n. pl.* saddles L 1110 (*C 1110).
**saghtelyng, sau3thlyng** *n.* reconciliation 1822.
**sayne, sent, seynt** *n.* saint 713, C 877, 1062, L 1130, etc.
**sale** *n.* hall L 1857, 1876; hall-dwellers, retainers C 1857.
**saler(e)** *n.* salt-cellar 1405.

**sall** *v.* shall L 229, L 230, L 1223, etc.; **shullen** (*pl.*) C 603; *pt.* **solde** L 6, L 187, etc.; **sold** L 479; **suld** L 1801; must go C 603; (obligation) 629; was to 1132.
**same** *adv.* together C 1412.
**sanappis, sanappus** *n. pl.* tablecloths 1403.
**sant** *n.* (*corrupt*); perhaps **sand** something sent, *i.e.*, God's help *was* intended L 1095.
**sar(e), sore** *adv.* 382, C 819, 1264, etc.
**sau3th** *adj.* reconciled C 841.
**sau3thle** *v.* become reconciled C 1773.
**sauely, saffly** *adv.* without risk of error 581, C 845, C 1765.
**sawtour, satur** *n.* saltire, diagonal cross C 1046 (*L 1046).
**sawtree, sautre** *n.* psaltery 35.
**schak** *v.* shake C 835.
**schalmous, scalmuse** *n.* shawm, reed instrument like an oboe 1102.
**schamely, shamly** *adv.* dreadfully C 1114, C 1702.
**schamesly** *adv.* shamefully, pitiably L 1114, L 1702.
**schane, schon(n)e** *pt. sg.* shone 1077, 1570.
**schar(e)** *pt. sg.* cut C 816, C 817.
**schased** *pt.* pursued 357; **chasande** *pr. pple.* L 361.
**schaw(e)** *n.* small wood 1632, 1668.
**schede** *pp.* cloven L 309 (see OED. *s. v.* Shed *v.*[1]).
**scheld** *n.* tough skin and flesh at shoulders C 1414n.
**schen(e)** *adj.* beautiful, shining 470 1632, 1668, 1828, 1863.
**schen(n)t, y-schent** *pt. and pp.* killed, destroyed 94, C 224, 778, C 871; harmed 1114; desolate, waste 138.
**schetus** *n. pl.* sheets C 1505.
**schygynge** *pr. part.* trotting C 361.
**schylde** *pr. subj.* forbid C 1758.
**schyr** *adj.* bright C 309.
**scho** L 377, etc.; **sche** C 419, etc.; **she** C 377, etc.; **he** C 1758; **ho** C 1793; **hoe** C 779; **hoo** C 702; *pron.* she; *pron. acc.*; **hir** L 552, etc.; **hyr** C 1382; *adj.* 418, 474.
**schore** *n.* threat, menace 152.
**schott, shote** *v.* shoot 280.
**schrede** *v.* cut to pieces C 309; **schrade** *pt.* *1646.
**scochenus** *n. pl.* escutcheons 1497.
**scrye** *v.* describe C 1875.
**seche** *adj.* such C 499; **syche** C 799; **suche** C 990, etc.; **swych** C 1286; *see* swylk(e).
**se(e)** *v.* 2, 606, 735, etc.; **i-se** C 1228; **ses(e)** *pr.* 3 *sg.* C 375, 1342; **sees** *pr. pl.* 1670; **saw(e)** *pt.* L 375, L 1093; **say** C 539; **se(e)** C 1093, L 1152; **seye** C 1400; **y-sen** *pp.* C 1592.

see-fame, seys-fame *n.* sea-foam C 562, L 1402.
seet, sete *see* sitt.
sege *n.* warrior, man C 291.
seyȝne *see* syne.
seyt *adj.* sweet C 39.
seke, sekes *v.* seek out, visit L 755; *imper.* 427.
sekirly *adv.* assuredly L 1543.
seloure *see* celure.
semblaunt *n.* appearance C 815; **mad hym s.** gave him friendly entertainment.
semble *n.* gathering L 1084.
sembled, semelede *pt.* assembled 1857.
semes *v. impers.* L 423; *pt.* suited 662.
sendal(e) *n.* thin silk 1509.
sen(e), seyn *prep.* since C 1664; *conj.* 501, L 762, C 906, 1749; *adv.* then C 1909.
sent *n.* assent L 1118.
sentus *pr.* 3 *sg.* assents C 1551.
sere *adj.* various L 1480 (*C 1480).
seryd *pp. adj.* pressed close together, serried C 1882n.
sertys *see* certis.
seruant, seruaunt *n.* lover 695, 731.
seruyce, seruise *n.* food L 1875 (C 1874).
seruitourus *n. pl.* servants C 1081.
ses(s)e, cesse *v.* cease 267, 1230.
sessid, sesyd, seysed *pt. and pp.* settled 65; endowed 1910.
set(t)e *n.* seat 678, 1479.
sett on seuen *see* seuen 1295; settand *pr. part.* appropriate C 67.
sethens *adv.* after that *C 179.
seþþe *adv.* thereupon C 55, C 1417; *conj.* since C 762, C 826.
seuen *n. in phr.* sett on seuen perform feats of prowess 1295.
sex *adj.* six L 1906.
sexten *adj.* C 257.
sexty *adj.* L 257, etc.; **sexti** C 511; **syxty** C 1135, etc.; *n.* 111, C 1161; **sexxty** C 48.
shaunce *see* chaunce.
shullen *see* sall.
syd(e), side *n.* edge, outskirts 612; slope 1165; point, place 644; party (in a battle) L 291, 1096.
syȝth(e) *pr.* sighs C 819, C 1264, C 1788; syghed(e), syght *pt.* C 225, C 332, L 376, L 1264, L 1788.
syker *v.* assure C 547.
syle *v.* fall, sink down 359.
symplust *adj. superl.* lowest in rank C 795.
syne, syen *adv.* then, afterwards C 1205; **seyȝne** C 1724.

sitt *v.* withstand L 15; **seet** *pt.* sat C 1412; **sett** L 1433; **sete** C 1433; **sittand(e)** *pr. part.* sitting L 1479; appropriate, proper L 67; **i-sete** *pp.* C 1391.
sythes *n. pl.* times 1383.
sythyn, sythen *adv.* afterwards, then L 55, L 179, L 1205, L 1724, etc.
skill, schkyll *n.* reason 1270, 1338, C 1588, L 1904; **to (with) skill** in accordance with what is reasonable 203.
sla(a) *v.* L 1168, L 1324; **sle** C 1168; **sleye** C 1440; **slo** C 1324; **slew(e)** *pt.* L 114, L 1678; **slogh** C 114; **slow(e)** C 518, C 1678; **slay** *pp.* C 1667; **slayn(e)** L 257, C 363, etc.; **slawe** C 349; **slane** L 450, etc.; **slon** C 1031; **y-slayn** C 257, etc.
slak(e), slac *n.* small valley 349, 1625.
slyk(e) *adj.* such L 1216, *L 1825.
slowes *n. pl.* marshes C 1672.
smale, small(e) *adj.* 419; lowly 679, 1242, etc.
smartely *adv.* forcibly 1109.
socour *n.* encouragement C 911.
soynede *pp.* excused, absolved L 291.
solas *n.* entertainment C 1084.
sold(e) *see* sall.
solemply, solempnely *adv.* with proper ceremony 1845.
sommdele *adv.* somewhat L 68.
son(e) *adv.* soon C 448, etc.; straightway L 126, L 785; **as sone** thereupon C 219.
so(o)re *adj.* reddish brown 76.
sort *n.* fate, doom C 1670.
soth(e) *n.* truth L 116, L 436, 504, C 892, C 904, 1138, etc.; **south** C 436.
soþely *adv.* truly C 708, C 788, L 1839.
soufft *adv.* in a low voice, quietly 1727.
soup(p)e *v.* sup C 1006, 1159.
sowdane, soudon *n.* Saracen ruler 1914.
sowe *v.* sow C 149; **sew** *pt.* scattered L 1853 (*C 1853).
space *n.* opportunity 697.
spanne *n. (obscure)* C 653n.
spare *v.* refrain from killing 503; show forbearance 1780; be used sparingly 812, 1428.
spede *v.* (cause to) prosper 228, C 920, L 1272, etc.; go quickly C 1347, 1807.
speris, sper(u)s *n. pl.* spearmen 335, 1634.
spyll *v.* betray to death 748; **spylt(e)** *pp.* poured out 742; killed 1789.
spyt *n.* rancour C 101.
spred(e) *pp.* spread 1558; *perhaps corrupt,* fully armed or accoutred? C 1058.
stabillede *pp. adj.* stabled L 75.
stade, y-stade *pp.* beset, pressed 1647

# GLOSSARY

**stak(e)** *n.* post, boundary-mark C 1060, 1136.
**stand** *see* **stond.**
**stane, ston** *n.* anchorite's cell 63 (*cf.* ON. steinn).
**stede** *n.* place 566, 749.
**stelyd** *pp.* steeled, protected 1059.
**stent** *v.* stop C 222; **stynt** *pt.* 1383.
**steraps, styroppus** *n. pl.* stirrups 1287.
**sterff** *pt. sg.* died C 320.
**steryn, sterne** *adj.* brave in battle 105, L 169, 1169, L 1809 (C 1810); *superl.* 1211.
**styff, styfe** *adj.* stalwart L 16, L 1280.
**styken** *pr. pl.* stab C 296; *pp.* L 320.
**styll(e)** *adj.* silent 617; under control 1549.
**stilly** *adv.* silently L 242.
**styrres** *pr. pl.* C 1281; **stirred** *pt.* L 1281; **stirred, sterid** *pp.* moved, excited L 773, L 1658.
**styrte, sterte** *pt.* sprang up 1221; leaped C 1655.
**stype** *adj.* valiant, mighty C 16.
**stonayde, stony(ȝ)ed** *pp.* bewildered, stupefied, dazed 1108, C 1331.
**stond** *v.* stand C 1488; resist 1060; **stont** *pr. pl.* halt L 242; **standand** *pr. part.* L 1458.
**store** *n.* live stock, cattle 72, L 148; reserve supply C 148.
**stotede** *pt.* halted C 242.
**stotyede** *pt.* faltered L 1331.
**stour(e)** *n.* conflict C 297, C 1061, C 1129; **stowres** *pl.* L 1061, L 1129.
**stownde, stound(e)** *n.* time, while 29, 242, 328, etc.; þat **stownd,** then C 1331.
**stowte, stout(e)** *adj.* valiant 105, L 169, 773, 1169, L 1497, etc.; *superl.* 1211.
**strak(e), strok** *n.* stroke L 15, L 1060, 1124.
**stroyed** *pp.* destroyed 433.
**stryfe, stryeff** *v.* strive L 560 (*C 560).
**strykys, strykus** *pr.* 3 *s.* C 1309; **strykys** astray gets out of its right path C 1656; **strak(e)** *pt. sg.* L 1309; turned aside L 1655.
**suld** *see* **sall.**
**swa** *see* **sa.**
**swer(e)** *v.* 581, 797, etc.; *pr.* 3 *sg.* **suerres** L 1293; *pt.* **sware** L 210; **swor** C 210, C 778, etc.; **swore** L 778, C 1293, etc.; *pp.* **sworne** L 1070, L 1601; **swornne** C 1601; **i-sworun** *C 1070.
**swylk(e)** *adj.* such L 112, L 380, L 384, etc.; **suylke** L 1286; *see* **seche.**
**swyme, sweme** *n.* faintness, swoon 1227.
**swyth(e)** *adv.* quickly 279, 1389; grievously 376.

## T

**take(n)** *v.* 383, C 860, etc.; **tak** C 887; *pt.* **to** L 1019; **tuk(e)** L 182, L 213; **toke** C 182, C 213, etc.; *pp.* **tane** L 765, L 1297; **ton** C 765, C 1297; *imper.* takes L 458, C 483; **tak(e)** L 483, L 1315.
**tame** *adj.* 72, C 1772, *used absol. as n.* domesticated animals, store cattle L 1772.
**tane** *pron.* one L 231.
**tasselde** *pp. adj.* adorned with tassels L 1508.
**teche** *v.* show C 917; point the way C 930; **tauȝth** *pt.* C 1043.
**tell(e)** *v.* L 9, 156, 461, etc.; count, describe 649, 1425; declare to C 716, etc.; **tald(e), told(e)** *pt.* 526, 1589, etc.; **I tell the for** I count thee as C 224.
**telerer** *doubtful form of* **topteler** (*q.v.*) L 1198n.
**teme(s)** *v.* empty 1110.
**tenandrye, tenantrie** *n.* tenants' holdings, houses, etc. 141.
**tene** *n.* anger 189.
**tenede** *pt.* angered C 514n.
**tent** *adj.* tenth C 1016.
**ter(e)** *adj.* difficult 1425.
**testere, testur** *n.* canopy C 1490, *C 1501.
**tethe, tyeth** *n. pl.* teeth 491.
**tye** *n.* bond, net C 568.
**tyde** *n.* time; þat **tyde** then 620, 652, etc.
**tyȝandes, tyȝandis, tythyngus** *n. pl.* tidings 1736, 1796.
**tyll** *prep.* to C 47, C 125, C 137, C 502, 619, 777, 1524, etc.; *conj.* until C 487, L 613, 635, L 1550.
**tynt** *pt.* lost L 1117, 1287.
**tyte** *adv.* quickly, soon 1110.
**to** *prep. before infin.* 1688n; until C 896; for C 52, C 334, L 378, 552, C 809, etc.; *conj.* until L 1298.
**to** *adv.* to so (?) ever so C 999.
**to-brest** *v.* burst asunder C 1525; **to-brast(e)** *pt.* 1283.
**toghe, tow** *adj.* tough, tenacious C 1028n.
**to-morne** *adv.* to-morrow L 496, L 1071, etc.
**tonage** *n.* tonnage, allowance for wine L 1014n.
**toor** *adj.* tedious C 649.
**topy(e)s** *n.* topaz C 651n (*L 651).
**topteler** *n.* ornamental covering for horse's head C 1198n.
**to-torn** *pp.* torn to pieces C 1710.
**toþer** *adj.* þe t., the other L 1096.
**tournay(e), tornay** *v.* C 866, 1039, 1100, L 1170 (*C 1170).
**touseled** *pp.* tasselled C 1508n.
**towne toun** *n.* village 142.

## GLOSSARY

**trayne, treyn** *n.* trickery 1740.
**trapped** *pp.* accoutered 1198.
**trauelus** *v.* trouble (yourself) C 850.
**tre(e)** *n.* Cross 734, 1741.
**tressour(e), trechour(e)** *n.* heraldic ornament C 651n (*L 651); tressure, narrow band (usually double) surrounding a shield 1047, L 1500.
**trewelufe** *n.* fleur-de-lis L 1055; *pl.* **treweloues, troweloues** C 471, C 1048, C 1055, C 1500.
**tristis** *n. pl.* trestles L 1398. *See* OED. *s.v.* Trest *sb.*²
**tromped** *pt.* sounded the trumpet 677.
**trompers** *n. pl.* trumpeters C 677.
**trouþe-ply3th** *pp. adj.* betrothed C 971.
**trow** *v.* believe, think 599, L 1799, L 1800.
**twa** *adj.* two L 346, L 1300, etc.; **two** C 604, C 1300; **to** C 474, C 1277, etc.; **tow** C 609, *C 1187n, etc.
**twa-hand, two-honde** two-handed 1659.
**twey** *adj.* two C 1623.

## Þ, TH

**þaire, þeir** *pron. absol.* theirs 571.
**the** *v.* prosper C 964.
**þe** *pron.* they C 1110, C 1298; **þy** C 1282.
**thyng** *pl.* C 487.
**thynk** *v. impers.* seem L 265, 707, etc.; **þenke** *C 899; **thow3th** *pt.* C 1871.
**thir** *dem. adj. pl.* these L 1273, L 1276, etc.; *dem. pron. pl.* L 1463, L 1728, etc.
**thirsted, fersted** *v. impers.* thirsted 1714.
**þis** *adv.* thus C 1349.
**þo** *demon. adj.* that C 904, C 961, C 1561.
**þo** *adv.* then 1757.
**þonked(e)** *pt. and pp.* thanked C 1095, C 1673.
**þor** *adv. indef.* there C 923.
**thorow(e), thorgh, þorw** *prep.* across C 1154, L 1202; according to C 1794.
**thorn(e), þornne, þorun** *n.* thorn-tree *C 1602, 1709.
**þow, þo** *conj.* even if C 999, C 1533.
**thra, þro** *adj.* angry 345, 1308.
**þus** *adj.* this C 403, C 580, C 1916.
**thritty, þrytty** *adj.* C 1383, L 1906 (C 1905).

## U

**vncomely** *adj.* unseemly, inconvenient C 1654.
**vndron, vndurne, vnderun** *n.* midmorning 636, 1225.
**vnfayn(e)** *adj.* unhappy 1732.
**vnright(e)** *adv.* unjustly 432.
**vnschene** *adj.* muddy C 1762.
**vnsownde, vnsound** *adv.* grievously 332.
**vntalde** *adj.* uncounted, *hence* enormous 520.
**vnwynly** *adv.* unpleasantly, sorrowfully L 495, C 839.
**vp** *prep.* upon C 1094, C 1262.
**vpbare** *pt. sg.* bore up 1516.
**vschen** (=ischen) *pr. pl.* enter C 1078.
**vschere** *n.* door-keeper L 1678.
**vseþ** *v.* is accustomed to do C 822.

## V

**velany, vylony, vilany, vylany(e)** *n.* evil deed 455, 755, 1035; ill-usage 587.
**veluete** *n.* velvet dress L 641, L 1199, L 1390.
**vencust(e)** *pp.* conquered L 426, L 1675; **venkest** C 1674; **vencoust** C 426; **y-venkessyd** C 1142.
**vernage** *n.* sweet white wine from Italy 1292, 1424, 1719.
**veuers** *n. pl.* fish-ponds L 113, L 434.
**vyolet** *n.* violet-coloured dress C 641, C 1199, C 1390.
**vytayled** *pt.* stocked with supplies C 935.
**vlonkest** (=wlonkest) *adj. superl.* richest C 592.
**vow(e)** *n.* 229.

## W

**wa(a), wo** *n.* woe L 314 (C 315), 608, 1176, 1648, *adj.* miserable, sorrowful 347, 1312.
**wad** *v.* wade C 938.
**wage** *n.* payment C 1014.
**wayn** *n.* wagon C 147.
**walde** *pt.* would L 49, L 268; *see* **wol(l), wull.**
**wale** *n.* choice *C 1888.
**walk(e)** *v.* 711; be spread, be rife 204; busy oneself 412, 580.
**wan(e)** *n.* place; **wyese in wane** wise in this life 449.
**wapyn, wepon, wepen** *n.* weapon 287, 1323, C 1622, C 1663; *pl.* L 1622, L 1663.
**waryson** *n.* reward 782.
**warrayne, warreyn, waryn(e)** *n.* land enclosed for hunting 439, 1771.
**war(r)e** *adj.* prudent 533.
**wase** *see* **were.**
**wat(e)** *see* **wit** *v.*¹
**watur-3ate** *n.* gate opening on to the water C 934.
**watur-wal** *n.* wall abutting on the water C 923.
**wathely** *adv.* grievously L 336.
**wathes, wothes** *n. pl.* dangers 204.
**wed(d)e** *n.* pledge, hostage 334.
**wede** *n.* armour 236, C 408, 1238; clothing 592, 1908; *pl.* L 316, L 408, etc.

# GLOSSARY

**weyt** *n.* watchman, trumpeter C 1581; **waytis** *pl.* L 1581.
**weld(e)** *v.* wield 287, 304, L 1663 (*C 1663); hold sway over 1065.
**wele** *n.* weal, good 608, 1176, 1648.
**wel(l)** *adv.* very C 450, C 1166.
**wene** *v.* suppose, think 17, C 996, 1044, 1607.
**were** *pt.* 2 *s.* C 754; **weren** *pl.* C 1284; **wase** C 257; **wore** L 1399.
**werid, wared, werred** *pt.* warred C 437, L 1769 (C 1770).
**wer(r)e, wer** *n.* war 395, 409, 582, etc.; **on wer(r)e** prepared for fighting 709.
**werreyde** *pt.* made war L 437.
**werse, worse** *adv.* worse 364.
**wesche(n)** *pt. pl.* washed 678, 1408.
**weste, wete** *v. see* **wit** *v.*
**wexe, wax, wexen** *pt.* 209, 311, C 524, 635, 1263. 1753.
**wha, who** *pron.* 303, 1068, 1449; **ho** C 1868.
**whatkyns** *adj.* whatever L 1751.
**whylk** *rel. pron.* C 1170.
**whyls** *conj.* until L 618, 1316.
**whom** *n. see* **ham(e)**.
**whone** *n.* few C 195.
**wyd(e)** *adv.* L 204; **wyde opyn (opon)** at full length 351, 1310.
**wy(e)** *n.* man 579.
**wyghte** *n.* creature, being, man L 235, 479, 700, 1523, etc.
**wyght(e), wyȝth** *adj.* brave, strong L 11 (C 10), 24, 102, C 150, 407, 1075, etc.
**wyȝhtly** *adv.* valiantly C 287.
**wyld(e)** *adj.* 503, 1367, 1415; *as n.* wild animals, beasts for hunting 440.
**will** *n.* good will, consent 1550.
**wyndus** *pr. t.* goes, runs C 1735.
**wynly** *adv.* pleasantly C 495.
**wyn(ne)** *v.* win 552; come, go, escape 723, C 918, L 1664; **wan(e), whan** *pt.* L 40, C 96, 1128, 1135, 1518; **wonnen** *pp.* L 1142, L 1148.
**wyntur** *n.* winter(s), year(s) C 1905.
**wyrchip** *n.* dignity L 1850 (*C 1851), L 1888.
**wys(e), wysse** *adj.* expert, skilled (especially in courtly ways) L 236, 408, 1873, etc.
**wysse** *imper.* show 1527.
**wyt** *n.* mind C 1697.
**wit** *v.* know, learn C 399; **wiet(e)** L 546, L 1266; **wyte** C 546, C 1001; **wytt** C 1266; **wat(e)** 1743; *pt.* **wist(e)** L 115, L 302, etc.; **wyste** C 115, L 1246; **weste** C 302; *pp.* **wyste** L 1608; **wyten** C 1608; *imper.* **wete** L 1299, L 1537; **wytt(e)** C 1299, C 1559.

**wite, wytt** *v.* blame, accuse 430, C 739, 1738.
**witterly** *adv.* clearly, without doubt L 302.
**wit(h), weth** *prep.* with, (having), among 248, 466, etc.; to 17, C 18, accompanied by 58, etc.; (away) from, of C 1351; against 764, C 878; by (means of) 119, 722, 1512; in (one's) case C 129; like 23; (indicating quality of main v.) 247.
**withall(e), withal** *adv.* as well, in addition 418, 1679, L 1879 (C 1878).
**withsett** *pt.* beset L 1767.
**withskapid** *pt.* avoided, escaped L 1180.
**wod-boȝhe, wod-bowe** *n.* leafy glade 1032.
**wode** *adj.* out of one's mind C 996; violently angry 1753.
**wodelech** *adv.* grievously C 336.
**wode-rys(se)** *n.* branch of a tree (suitable for gallows) 188.
**woȝhe, wouȝth** *n.* injury 1036; **with wouȝh** wrongfully C 739.
**wold** *n.* possession C 520.
**wol(l)** *v.* will C 206, C 222.
**wondid** *pt.* wounded L 477; *pp.* **wondid(e)** L 336, L 374; **wonded** C 374; **y-wounded** C 336.
**wondir, wonder, wondur** *adv.* exceedingly C 1570, 1811.
**wongus** *n. pl.* cheeks C 840.
**wonnes** *pr.* dwells 1033; *pt.* 97, L 164.
**word** *n.* speech 1317; *pl.* 180, 274, 1044.
**wore** *see* **were**.
**worth(e)ly** *adj.* noble, gracious C 530, C 1888, C 1908; **worþelych** C 692; **worthelychere** *comp.* *C 660; **worthliest** *superl.* L 592.
**worthy** *adj.* L 287, L 660, L 1112, L 1919; having worth, costly 1447.
**worthily, worþilych** *adj.* brave L 235, L 1276; honourable L 692, 700.
**wote** *v.* know L 39 (C 38).
**wowe** *v.* woo 565.
**wrang, worng, wrong** *n.* wrong 558; *pl.* C 384, 1818.
**wrathe, wroth** *adj.* angry L 209 (*C 209).
**wrekes** *pr. sg.* C 314; **wreke** *pl.* L 315.
**wryth(e)** *n.* anger L 314 (C 315).
**wrythe** *v.* C 384n.
**wull** *v.* will C 189.

## Y

**yeff** *v. see* **gyf(f)**.
**yeff** *conj. see* **gyf**.

# INDEX OF PROPER NAMES

## A

Absolon(e) L 1466 (C 1467).
Almayne Germany L 1849.
Alsame L 1401; Eylyssham C 1401n, Aylsham.
Amadas(e) 1494.
Ambrose C 1462; Ambrosius L 1462.
Arrtor C 17; Arthur(e) L 17, 1483.
Austyn St. Augustine 1461.
Aymere L 1594, L 1649; Eymer(e) C 1649, C 1730; Eymur C 1594; Gaymere L 1729.

## B

Betyse C 1518n.
Boloyne Bouillon L 1482; Boyloune C 1482.
Bretayne Britain L 22, L 1483; Bryttayne C 22.
Bretoune Briton C 1483.

## C

Charles 1481.
Criste L 694.
Cypirs L 166; Cyprese L 667; Sypirs L 1498; Syprus C 667.

## D

Degreeuant C 513.
Degreuance L 1827.
Degreuans L 1161, L 1181.
Degreuant(e) L 10, L 225, L 263, L273, L305, L321, L337, and *passim*.
Degreuaunt C 11, C 321, C 416.
Degreuuaund C 262.
Degreuua(u)nt C 225, C 273, *C 353, *C 385, C 405.
Degrevaunt C 305.
Degriuaunce C 1161.
Degriua(u)ns C 1093, C 1181.
Degriuaunt C 593, C 617, C 625, C 671, C 687, C 689, C 737, C 1127, C 1133, and *passim*.
Degriuuance *C 1827.
Degriuuant C 337, C 1738, C 1805, C 1890.
Degryuaunt C 729.

## E

Edoyne L 1494, L 1519; Ydoyne C 1494.
Egir L 1446.
Egriuaunt C 1085, C 1185.
Englond C 14, C 583, C 1826; Yngland(es) L 583, L 1826.
Eylyssham *see* Alsame.
Eymere, Eymur *see* Aymere.

## F

Flaundres L 131.
Florence 1624.
France L 14, L 22, L 1183, L 1826, L 1870; Fraunce C 14, C 22, C 1826, C 1870; Frauns C 1183.

## G

Garnad Granada C 131n.
Gawayne 23.
Gaymere *see* Aymere.
Gaynore L 18; Gwennor C 18.
Gerle C 861n, C 1005.
Godfray(e) 1482.
Granade, Granada *L 131
Gregorius L 1461; Gregory C 1461.

## H

Haythynnes, Heþenesse Mohammedan countries 21.

## J

Jame 713, L 1759.
Jerome 1462.
Jhesu L 1, 227, 694, L 1917.
John L 1453; Jon C 1453.

## L

Luke C 877.

## M

Martyn 1062, L 1130.
Mary L 228; Mare C 228.
Medyore C 1519n.
Melidor C 523.
Melydor C 561.

# INDEX

**Mildor** L 591, L 1296, L 1433, L 1605, L 1611, L 1722, L 1823; **Mildore** C 685, L 1026, L 1219, L 1247, L 1471, L 1687, L 1828.
**Mylder** C 591.
**Myldor** L 523, L 561, C 1219, C 1247, C 1296, L 1359, etc.; **Myldore** L 685, C 1023, C 1359, C 1433, C 1471, etc.

## P
**Paulis** L 1454; **Powlus** C 1454.
**Perceuelle** L 23; **Persevall** C 23.
**Petur** C 1746.
**Pokalypps, Pocalyps** n. Apocalypse 1453.
**Port Gaff**, Jaffa C 1913.
**Portyngale** L 1835; **Portyngall** C 1835.
**Powles** see **Paulis**.

## R
**Reyn** the river Rhine C 542, C 1720; **Ryn(e)** L 542, L 1720 (see *Glossary*).

## S
**Salamon** C 1455; **Salomone** L 1455.
**Scotlande** L 14.
**Sere** L 166.
**Spayn(e)** 21, L 437, L 1769 (C 1770); **Spyan** C 437.
**Sypirs, Syprus** see **Cypirs**.

## T
**Toure** Tours C 1062; **Towres** L 1062, L 1130.

## U
**Vrbane** L 1446.

## W
**Westfal** Westphalia C 1511.
**Westwale** L 1511.

## Y
**Ydoyne** see **Edoyne**.
**Yngland** see **Englond**.